S. F. Hallgarten was born in 1902 in Winkel, Rheingau, an important centre of German viticulture since Roman times. Son of a wine broker and merchant, he was both involved and interested in the whole process of wine production from his school days. His subsequent career in the law was interrupted by the advent of Hitler, when he emigrated to London and soon established himself as an importer of wines from the Continent. After forty years he sold his interest in the company he had founded, and returned to legal practice in Wiesbaden, although he still considers London his real home.

German Wines

Faber Books on Wine (*edited by Julian Jeffs*)

SHERRY Julian Jeffs
THE WINES OF EUROPE Julian Jeffs
MOSELLE O. W. Loeb & Terrence Prittie
THE WINES OF SPAIN AND PORTUGAL Jan Read
ITALIAN WINES Philip Dallas

---

other books by the author:

Alsace and its Winegarden
The Great Wines of Germany
(together with André Simon)
German Wine Law 1969
Rhineland Wineland

GERMAN WINES

S. F. HALLGARTEN

FABER AND FABER
3 Queen Square
London

First published in 1976
by Faber and Faber Limited
3 Queen Square London WC1
Printed in Great Britain by
Western Printing Services Ltd
Bristol

ISBN 0 571 10149 6

Dedicated to my many friends
in the K.C. students' fraternity
with whom I have shared many
a good bottle

Contents

Author's Note on German spelling 12
Acknowledgements 13
Introduction 15

BOOK I German Viniculture and Viticulture

Chapter 1 History of German viticulture 19
2 German viticulture within the E.E.C. 30
3 German wine legislation 35
4 The German vinelands 42
5 The new Vineyard Register 49
6 German wines and vines 59
7 The wine grower's work 79
8 The harvest 87
9 From vine to bottle 90
10 Categories of wine 100
11 Grading and vinification 112
12 Further treatment of the wines 123
13 Examination of quality wines 134
14 Further development of bottled wine 139
15 Naming of the wines 145
16 Recent vintages 169
17 Schaumweine, Sekt and Prädikatssekt 179

BOOK II Wine Journey

18 Wine roads and wine museums 189
19 Rheinland-Pfalz 192
Palatinate 194
Rheinhessen 209
Nahe 230
Mittelrhein (including Nordrhein-Westfalen) 241
Mosel-Saar-Ruwer (including Saarland) 244
20 Hessen 285
Rheingau 285
Hessische Bergstrasse 301

21 South Germany 303
Baden-Württemberg 303
Württemberg 304
Baden 312
22 Bavaria 323
Franken 323
23 Red hocks 333

Maps 339
Glossary 355
Appendices 357
Bibliography 381
Index 385

Maps and Plans

1	Ihringen before and after the reorganization of vineyards	340
2	World wine distribution	342
3	a. The viticultural zones of the E.E.C. b. Zones A and B of Germany, Luxemburg and part of France	342
4	The German wine regions a. Table wine b. Quality wine	343
5	Palatinate, showing *Grosslagen*	344
6	Rheingau and Rheinhessen, showing *Grosslagen* (Maps 5 and 6 by kind permission of Deutscher Weinwirtsschaftverlag, Diemer Co. Meinger KG)	346
7	Nahe, showing *Grosslagen*	348
8	Mittelrhein and Ahr	349
9	Mosel-Saar-Ruwer, showing *Grosslagen*	350
10	Baden, Württemberg, Franconia and Hessische Bergstrasse	352
11	The Nierstein sites	354

Author's Note on German spelling

The German umlaut ä, ö, ü can be spelled ae, oe, ue; likewise the letters C and K are interchangeable in many place names, for example Berncastel – Bernkastel, Cues – Kues, Cochem – Kochem. Both ways of spelling are still used in Germany and one may therefore find both variants used in this book.

Doktor and *Doctor*. When I refer to the vineyard of this name in Berncastel, Doctor is the correct name as entered in the new Vineyard Register, otherwise the correct spelling is Doktor, under which other Doktor vineyards have been registered.

Acknowledgements

The author and his publishers wish to express their thanks to the following:

Herr Dr. Knapp (Weinbauamt Eltville).
Prof. Dr. Wilhelm Gärtel of *Weinberg und Keller* for permission to reprint Prof. Alleweld's graphs in his article: 'Die Qualitaets – und Ertragsbildung von Rebenneuzüchtungen Hessische Lehr & Forschungsaustalt'.
Herr Heinrich Strieth (Hess-Lehr – Forschungstalt für Wein-Obst Gartenbau – college for vinicultural research) for permission to use graphs published in the *Deutsche Weinfachzeitung* of 8 January 1971.
Herr Prof. Karlinke of Geisenheim, whose research and statistics published in the *Deutsche Weinfachzeitung* were of great help in rounding off the picture of the development of German viticulture.
Prof. Jacob of the Viticultural College, Neustadt.
The mayors of all those wine-growing towns and villages who supplied statistical material and other information, including viticultural maps of their communities, such as Nierstein.

And I am also grateful to:

The editor of this series of books on wine, Julian Jeffs, and the publishers, Faber and Faber.
My son Peter for his help in checking the chapter on the treatment of wine.
My wife, not only for her patience and assistance, but also for reading the manuscript, the proofs and preparing the index.
Weinwerbungen (Public Relations Offices) of all the districts.
Stabilisierungfonds for permitting me to use certain of their published material, including maps (Ihringen).
The respective Ministers of Agriculture of the Federal States of Western Germany, Rheinland-Pfalz, Hessen, Bavaria, Baden-Württemberg.

Introduction

In the preface to the fourth edition of *Rhineland Wineland* André Simon wrote:

'Poems, plays, novels and all works of imagination are reprinted for one generation after another without a single word of their text being left out or altered. Not so, however, books on wine: they have to be brought up to date from time to time. The wine student – and all who love wine are lifelong wine students – demands and expects to find in a wine book, information that is truly reliable, hence not obsolete. Every year, all the great vineyards of Germany bring forth a fresh crop of grapes from which wines will be made, possessing the outstanding features that belong to all wines born on their soil, but there will be from year to year differences that may be slight, yet of very real importance to the wine lover: such differences are inevitable, since the hours of sunshine and the inches of rain are never quite the same from year to year.'

This was never more true than now. The year 1970 saw great changes in the laws affecting German viticulture, since Germany's membership of the E.E.C. imposed adoption of the European wine laws. In fact in 1969 Germany had enacted a new wine law, but as the European law now overrides national law, this has been superseded by the wine law of 1971. As I shall explain in later chapters, many important changes have recently occurred in the treatment, blending and, last but not least, the naming of German wines.

Great progress has been made in viniculture and viticulture after many experiments with new crossings. These have proved successful and these new vine crossings in some districts have superseded vines which had covered the various sites for centuries – a new taste in German wines has developed.

Therefore this book is not just an enlarged edition of *Rhineland Wineland*: it is a new book on German wines. I have worked for many years to prepare it. As far as the statistics are concerned, it has been impossible to bring them all up to the date of 1976. I must therefore apologize to my readers if, despite the long time for research, some tables are not complete. In cases where detailed information on areas in in hectares for vineyards is not available, figures have been omitted.

Before putting down my pen I should like to say that I have done my utmost to give my readers an up-to-date picture of German viticulture and viniculture. I have checked and rechecked most carefully. Should you discover a mistake, be it an unimportant printing mistake or a really big blunder, please inform me.

I could – as an excuse – quote the Under Secretary of State of the Ministry of Viticulture of Rheinland-Pfalz, as reported in July 1973:

'The wine law is at present a jungle of regulations, partly of national, partly of E.E.C. origin, so that it is difficult for anyone to disentangle it, especially as the German wine law is not fully in compliance with the Community law with its over 100 amendments, and even judges and lawyers have trouble in recognizing right from wrong.'

BOOK I

German Viniculture and Viticulture

1

History of German viticulture

The culture of the vine can be found in all countries of the world, wherever there is a mild climate. The oldest and most important wine districts were situated in the Middle East and the countries round the Mediterranean, whence viticulture has expanded all over the world:

6000 B.C.	Israel and neighbouring countries, Caucasia – round the Caspian Sea
4000 B.C.	Mesopotamia
3000 B.C.	Phoenicia
2800 B.C.	Egypt
1600 B.C.	Greece, Crete
1000 B.C.	Sicily, Italy, North Africa
600 B.C.	Persia
500 B.C.	France, Spain, Portugal
140 B.C.	China
100 B.C.	North India
A.D. 100	Other Balkan countries, north of France, *Germany*, England
A.D. 1520	Mexico, Japan
A.D. 1560	Argentine, Chile
A.D. 1580	Peru
A.D. 1655	South Africa
A.D. 1770	U.S.A., California
A.D. 1813	Australia, New Zealand

The grapes in these countries are not all grown for wine making only, but often for producing table grapes and raisins.

In some countries like France, Italy, Spain, Portugal, Greece and Algeria, viticulture is a very important part of the life of the community and of its agriculture. It is of special importance in hot countries and those which have very little rainfall, because the vine can grow on steep and dry hills where other plants of agricultural use cannot survive.

We do not know how the knowledge of making wine from grapes was acquired. The Bible tells us that Noah was the first to plant a vineyard, and further, that he drank some of the wine and became drunk. The story goes on 'and Noah lived three hundred and fifty years.' Perhaps wine was the reason?

Less well known is a Persian story about the discovery of wine. The person concerned in this discovery was Jemshed, first king of Persia and, according to legend, a grandson of Noah. He liked to have the juice of grapes pressed by his servant, as he was already old and had lost his teeth and could not chew the skin and the pips. As he wanted to enjoy the juice of the grapes in winter also, he ordered a stock of it to be put down and kept in great containers. After a few days, however, he noticed that the juice had changed its appearance and tasted bitter. He was very sad about it and thought the juice had gone bad, and poisonous. He therefore ordered it to be brought into a cellar and the doors to be locked. On the cellar door he had a skull painted with the inscription 'Poison'.

Soon afterwards, his favourite slave suffered so much from a terrible headache that she wanted to die. She did not know of any way to commit suicide, but remembered the cellar and opened the chamber in which the 'poison' was kept. After she drank a little she felt gay, she did not feel the pain any more, and she thought how lovely it was to die in such a way. She drank more and more of the 'poison' and, with each drop she drank, the juice tasted better and better. Soon she dropped down and fell asleep in the middle of the cellar. Servants found her and brought her to her master but could not awaken her. She who had not been able to sleep for a long time, lay for two days and nights in a very deep sleep. And when the king – worried about this – hurried to her side, she awoke in his presence and smiled because she felt so happy and healthy. The king was overjoyed, and he tasted the 'poison' himself. The juice, which had become wine, made him gay and young, so he gave it the name 'Medicine for Kings'.

Whereas the Persians celebrate King Jemshed as founder of viticulture, the Chinese celebrate Kokhi (3000 B.C.), the Egyptians Osiris, and other countries have their own candidates.

From the beginning, wine enjoyed preferential protection. We know that the great law-givers of Greece, Drakon and Solon, considered damage done to vineyards equal to murder or burglary of a temple. *Lex Salica*, the sixth-century law book of the Franks, stated that a wine grower's life was so important that the damages paid for murdering him had to be double those laid down for murder of an ordinary agricultural worker. In the German law of the Middle Ages, a person who destroyed a vine received the same punishment as one guilty of manslaughter – loss of the right hand.

The special esteem which the vine enjoyed in the *Old Testament* is shown in the decree that he who planted a vineyard might stay at home and be free of army service, so that he should not die in war before the vineyard had borne its first fruit. So we see that wine growing was the first 'officially reserved occupation'.

Looking back at the historical table at the beginning of this chapter, we see that German viticulture started relatively late, but even this date is only approximate.

Throughout history there are incidents which seem so insignificant at the time they happen that contemporary historians do not notice them or think them worth recording. Then after a generation has passed, questions are asked: 'How did it happen?' 'Where did it start?' And then it is very often too late for a correct answer. This is the case with German viticulture. Were there vineyards on the Rhine before the arrival of the Romans? If we answer this question in the affirmative, we must then ask: 'From which country, in what districts did the vineyards appear first?' 'Did the Romans bring the vines with them?' 'Where from?' 'When?' Tradition says that the first vineyards *were* planted by the Romans, but it is still possible that Greek colonists brought vines to Germany from the south of France before Caesar's legions arrived in about 50 B.C. We certainly know that at least 500 to 600 years before that date, Greeks from Asia founded the colony Marsilia (Marseille) at the mouth of the Rhône and planted vines brought from their homeland. The Roman Trogus Pompeius tells us that these Greeks taught the inhabitants of Marsilia not only a civilized life, but also agriculture and viticulture.

It is generally assumed that the vine moved to Germany from Marsilia, up the Rhône. This assumption overlooks one important fact, namely that the wild vine, the *vitis silvestris*, has been found in certain districts, especially between Rastatt and Mannheim, near Germersheim. It is known that this wild vine existed from the time of the last ice age and, judging from seeds which have been found, it must have been in existence in Germany more than 4,000 years ago. The pips of the vine which were found indicate that the population of these districts ate the bluish and greenish wild grapes as part of their diet. It can also be assumed that, long before the Romans entered Germany, German tribes must have produced some alcoholic beverage from the wild grapes. Whether or not they also tried to cultivate the vine cannot be confirmed, but some believe this to be so.

The many containers of Roman origin which have been found show that the German tribes had a great love of wine. Long before the Roman occupation, at the beginning of the first century B.C., the Roman writer Posidanius (135–51 B.C.) wrote that the Germans drank a lot of undiluted wine. About the same time, we hear from Diodor that Italian merchants brought wine into the interior of Gallia in order to exchange one amphora of the beverage against a slave. From

Caesar we learn that the Suebs and the Nervi between the Meuse and the Somme prohibited the importation of wine in order to prevent their people from becoming soft.

Caesar visited the Rhineland twice, in 55 and 53 B.C., and he does not mention anything about viticulture. It is almost certain that he who was so observant would have mentioned the fact that there was viticulture, if only to draw the attention of Roman wine exporters to the danger of competition! We have, therefore, to assume that viticulture was unknown in the Mosel and Rhine regions at that time.

It is clear, however, that the German tribes living on the right bank of the Rhine must have known wine at the latest in the first century A.D. Tacitus reports in his *Germania* (written 150 years later) that they bought wine from the left bank of the Rhine, but that the usual drink was a beverage produced from barley and wheat, similar to beer. He did not know anything of Rhenish viticulture, but mentioned that the German tribes living near the Roman frontier bought wine which was unknown to them. Although Tacitus never visited Germany, he was well informed on everything about which he wrote. He must have had a very fine intelligence service! He would not have overlooked viticulture in the Rhineland if it had existed.

We know from Cicero (106–43 B.C.) that a decree of the Roman Senate prohibited viticulture in the provinces of the Empire in favour of a Roman wine monopoly, and it was Cicero who ironically remarked: 'We, the most just people, do not allow people outside our frontiers to plant the olive tree and the vine for one reason – so that our own olive trees and vineyards have a higher value. We are clever, but we are not just.'

A second decree prohibiting viticulture was made by the Emperor Domitian in A.D. 91. This was changed in the second century when the Emperor Probus denounced Rome's monopoly in viticulture and the wine trade and did all he could to further viticulture in the occupied countries.

This new development arose not only from economic but also military reasons. The new wine districts became settlements for reservists, reliable reservists whose task was to police the districts and keep down any of the German tribes who might start rebelling against the occupation army. They were the defenders of the hinterland behind the '*Limes*' – an enormous range of fortifications, the limits of the occupation zone.

In times of peace, the Roman settlers did not work in the vineyards. This work was done by prisoners of war and serfs. The Roman was the merchant who would go beyond the '*Limes*' and visit the free tribes to do barter – and, of course, wine was part of his coinage. In addition to this he acted as spy for the occupation army, and it is said that the prohibition of some tribes from importing wines was made in order to prevent spies from entering their territory.

In any case, from the first centuries A.D., the Romans produced wines in many German districts. Beside the great military roads along the Rhine via Speyer and Worms as far as Mainz; along the foot of the hills via Neustadt, Deidesheim, Gruenstadt and Alzey to Bingen. In proof of this, numerous Roman tools and utensils for wine cultivation have been found, as well as inscriptions, sculptures and so on. Many German technical expressions, too, are of Latin origin, for example: the word wine itself (German *Wein*) from *vinum*; the German *Most* (must) from *mustum*; *Keller* (cellar) from *cellare*; *Kufe* (coop) from *cupa*; *Kelter* (wine press) from *calcatorium*; *Schemel* (stool) from *scamellum*, to give only a few examples.

The documentary proofs of viticulture in Germany become more numerous after this early period. In the fourth century the Roman poet Ausonius sang the praises of the Mosel wines, and before him other Roman authors had done so in simpler language.

In the Palatinate, seventy villages are known to have had vines planted since Carolingian times. Certainly the vineyards of the Rheingau were not planted until the reign of Charlemagne. The story goes that one day, while standing in his palace in Ingelheim, he saw how on the other side of the Rhine the snow melted first on the hills of Johannisberg and, on account of that, he gave the order to plant vineyards there. These were very soon extended to other sites in the Rheingau – in particular, the Steinberg, which was planted in the eleventh and twelfth centuries by monks.

Speaking of Carolingian times, I should emphasize that after the death of Charlemagne, when his country was divided up between his three sons, the middle part of this vast domain was allotted to Louis the German, 'in order that he might have wine in his kingdom'.

In Franconia, it is said that St. Kilian introduced viticulture, and in the tenth and eleventh centuries this was extended to Thuringia and Saxonia so that nearly all districts of Germany showed some wine cultivation here and there, even in Silesia and Pomerania. A small remnant of these still exists in Silesia.

During subsequent centuries German viticulture was widely extended – even to Northern Germany and the Baltic provinces – mainly through the monasteries, which produced their own wines for celebrating Mass. It was, of course, easier for the monks to produce their Mass wine at the place where they lived; it was also safer and cheaper than importing wine from the south. For liturgical purposes, the Church preferred the wine to be red, so it followed that the planted red vines were those that grew round the Mediterranean. This explains why the production of red wine was much larger than that of white wine even on the Mosel, where today no red wine at all is to be found.

Later, the volume of the monks' production went beyond their own needs, and they started to trade in wine. It is interesting to note that many of the monks were peasants' sons who could read Greek and Latin works on agriculture and viticulture, and whilst working in the monastery vineyards made good use of their studies.

Others besides monks began to perceive the value of possessing and enlarging vineyard property, not only abbots and ecclesiastical princes, but also hard-drinking knights and secular authorities. Thus, in the early Middle Ages the area devoted to the culture of wine increased considerably, reaching a maximum in the early fifteenth century which has never since been equalled.

The wine grower of early times was a serf. The vineyards belonged to a monastery or a feudal lord. The vintner could not decide for himself when and how he should pick the grapes. He had to wait for the decision of his lord and to deliver to him a *Zehnt-wein*, i.e. a tenth of his harvest of grapes or the must from them, also paying other charges. This was one of the reasons why quantity was all that mattered to the grower, and why nobody thought of cultivating quality wines.

Giant casks and drinking vessels bear testimony to the immense consumption of wine at the drinking-bouts and festivals customary at the time. The best known of the giant casks is at Heidelberg. These casks are not only a proof of how much wine was drunk during this period, but one has to take into consideration the places where they were found, mostly in fortresses where they served to store as much wine as possible, as provision in times of war.

After the end of the sixteenth century viticulture decreased to a large extent. Climatic conditions in north Germany were really not good enough for viticulture, but the land could be and was used for other forms of agriculture. This explains the disappearance of more and more vineyards, leaving only those planted on hillsides.

A second peak of prosperity for the vintner occurred in the eighteenth century. Better transport created better sales for the produce of good wine areas, but competition proved too formidable for the less favourably situated villages. Simultaneously, the increase in population led to a rise in the importance of agriculture which, in many districts in the plains, began to displace viticulture. Gradually the restriction in cultivation led to an improvement in the quality of the products, brought about by the planting of superior vine species.

The aftermath of the French Revolution helped to consolidate this trend of improving quality. The feudal lords disappeared, the tithe, the *Zehnt*, of grapes disappeared with them, and the grower was free on his own ground for the first time. The enforced sales of secularized vineyards by feudal lords and the Church changed leasehold into freehold. The result was that the freed wine grower looked forward to growing quality vines and harvesting quality wines.

Soon after the formation of the Customs Union in Germany in 1834 no room remained for mass-produced wines. As soon as the wines from the important wine-growing districts, the Palatinate, Rhinehessia, the Rheingau, etc. could be transported all over Germany, without paying duty from one principality to the next, the price of the very ordinary, mass-produced wines fell considerably. Actually in 1850 they fell from 250 thalers to 10–20 thalers per 1,000 litres.

In the last 2,000 years the extent of the German wine area has varied considerably. From the eleventh to the thirteenth centuries it reached its greatest range, extending as far as the northern and north-eastern provinces. According to the statistics of May 1972 the viticultural area of Western Germany covers approximately 83,379 hectares of which 72,000 ha are under cultivation.

1971: 80,923 ha
1970: 77,737 ha
1969: 75,575 ha

The wine-growing areas of France cover thirty times as much, Italy thirty-four times as much, Spain twenty-seven times as much, Portugal seven and Greece three times as much. The viticultural area of the whole of Europe amounts to more than 6 million ha of which Western Germany only has 0·8 per cent.

German viticulture and methods of vinification have never in their long history seen so many changes as they have over the last few years. Let us not forget that vine growing had decreased over many decades owing to the many enemies and diseases of the vine, which the vine grower had not the means of preventing or fighting. Furthermore, a great change has taken place in the structure of the population on account of industrialization, better transport and tourism. Many workers in the wine industry saw the possibility of earning a better living in other industries and therefore left viticulture, not only the ordinary labourer, but even the sons of wine growers who decided rather to seek their fortune in the towns than to stay in the country.

Two World Wars and immense economic changes between the wars brought great damage to viticulture. This is best illustrated by the following facts. In 1878 the whole viticultural area cultivated and producing grapes for wine making was 88,747 ha, but at the end of the Second World War the area did not reach 50,000 ha. The cultivated areas were partly planted with vines which had grown too old or which had been attacked by phylloxera and needed renewing.

Over the last few years we have seen the development of various institutions to help and educate the suffering wine growers. These include the viticultural colleges, and we can find at least one college in each region.

Owing to the application of the various wine laws, including the regulations of the E.E.C., viticulture has been rationalized and this has led to better methods of production.

One cannot consider viticulture without mentioning phylloxera which brought so much damage to all wine districts and which made it necessary to plant vines on phylloxera-resisting root stock. It was first discovered in Germany in 1874 on the Annaberg near Bonn. The influence of the arch enemy of the vine on the history of viticulture is so great that I intend to deal with it here in all aspects and not in Chapter 7 where I discuss enemies of the vine.

These are the facts about these dangerous insects. In the summer, the winged females of the species, carried by the wind over wide stretches of territory, lay their ova on the stems of the vines. The ova develop into wingless 'grape-lice', which penetrate through the soil to the vine roots and there suck out the vitality of the plant for their own subsistence and that of the countless generations which they produce with incredible rapidity. In one year a single phylloxera grub may have anything up to twenty-four million 'offspring'. Where the vine roots have been attacked, they become knotted and deformed, the surest sign that they are victims of the phylloxera. Again with unimaginable fertility the phylloxera spreads underground from root to root, from vine to vine, and in a very few years the sick vines, from which the sap has been sucked away, wither and die.

The pest spread quickly and was soon found in all German wine regions. No individual wine grower was able to tackle phylloxera single-handed, and the State had very soon to intervene.

The very first German 'phylloxera law' of 6 March 1875 allowed 'investigations'. The Prussian *Reblausgesetz* of 27 February 1878 already contained procedures for destroying vineyards, based on the recommendations of the French Academy of Sciences. This law was extended on 23 March 1885, and an international convention agreed on 3 November 1888. It was finally adopted for the whole of Germany on 6 July 1904.

The German method of fighting phylloxera was to destroy the vineyard attacked by the pest and special laws were passed to enforce this.

To combat the scourge, the earth is saturated with petroleum, carbon bisulphide, and other poisons, so that it seems inconceivable that grape-lice or any other vermin could survive. For six years no vines may be planted on soil that has been so treated.

The destruction of vineyards to fight phylloxera was not always a method acceptable to the growers. I was assistant to the Public Prosecutor in Wiesbaden and personally engaged in an investigation against wine growers who used force against the officers who intended to destroy their vineyards. At the time the growers received compensation of between 70 to 90 pfennig per vine which was equal to approximately two years' income. This money bore no proportion to the actual damage, because generally speaking it takes seven years before vineyards can be replaced and bear fruit.

When the officers appeared at Hallgarten in March 1927, the growers were prepared to give them a warm reception. The ringing of the bells of the ancient church was a signal, and in a very short time about 500 inhabitants of the village had assembled to prevent a policeman and 25 workmen from destroying the vineyards. Not one shot was fired, no real assault made. But that was not the end of the affair. A few of the leaders were arraigned and sent to prison. As a result, however, the compensation of the growers was reconsidered. Although nearly 25 ha of the Hallgarten vineyards were destroyed over the following two years, the vineyards were reconstructed, replanted and Hallgarten remained as before, the most vinous village in the whole of Germany.

Perhaps in the not too distant future we shall have the means of preventing or killing phylloxera without destroying the vineyards. We already have reports that treatment of the soil with a chemical solution can be successful over some period as a protection of the vine against phylloxera. So far, attempts to free vines that have been suffering from phylloxera for some time have not been successful, but experiments are being continued.

Usually the phylloxera has been carrying on its subterraneous devastation for years before it is found. Long before remedies are applied, the warmth of summer days will have attracted it to the surface, a puff of wind will have carried the tiny thing possibly miles away. And if where it is finally dropped, it happens to land in a vineyard, then the procreative process begins anew, a fresh phylloxera focus is established and the deadly work goes on in the new locality. Again it may be years before the first signs of withering – caused by the constant deprivation of vital sap – appear on the vines, and are discovered by the Phylloxera Commission on its regular visit of inspection.

It has been observed that certain American species of vine are either never attacked by phylloxera or are not noticeably affected by its depredations. On the other hand, these vines do not yield drinkable wines. Therefore one has to graft some of the best German vines – Riesling, Silvaner, etc. – on to American vine stock. The grafting of the vines is carried out by the English method (tongue grafting). Experiments were long and tedious, and many failures were recorded.

But today, in the affected areas, many a vineyard contains vines with American roots proof against phylloxera. Since 1926 vine-grafting nurseries have been kept at work in all wine regions. Climatic conditions in Germany do not allow grafting to be done on the spot, in the vineyard. Growers in infested regions establish 'Vine Rehabilitation Associations' and the State grants maximum aid.

Germany has now started a systematic rebuilding of her vineyards on phylloxera-proof foundations. The rapidity with which the pest spreads, thus affecting vast areas, has made this project a vital necessity. It has been estimated that badly infected areas must be completely reconstructed within 15 years, less badly infected within 30 years. Consequently there is a tremendous demand for root stocks. In 1940 the demand reached the figure of 35 million, but has now risen to 40 million, so that something like 32 million must be imported annually, the main producer countries being Italy and France.

The Phylloxera Commissioners have been appointed to keep German vineyards under constant observation and to take the necessary steps against phylloxera wherever it appears. This service is maintained the whole year round, and all vineyards are systematically examined at regular intervals. Nevertheless it has not yet been found possible to prevent the spread of these insects altogether.

During the war years it was not possible to carry on the fight against phylloxera with the desirable intensity. In the Palatinate alone, a comparison of the year 1948 with the years 1895–1940 showed an increase of infected vines of not less than 150 per cent. In the Palatinate only 3,000 ha remain free of phylloxera; in Rhinehessia only thirteen villages have not been infected. Many of those affected had to be completely destroyed. In Baden the phylloxera pest has brought productivity down to 60 per cent as compared with 1937. And in the whole of Western Germany, no less than 35,000 ha of vineyards are infected by phylloxera.

For a long time the Mosel regions were spared this plague. It is true that before the First World War the Upper Mosel near the Luxembourg border had suffered considerably, but for some time the trouble was confined to this district. Curiously enough, the Middle Mosel region, the part that produces the best quality wines, was at first not affected. It was in 1947 that phylloxera was discovered for the first time in vineyards between Trier and Koblenz, and in 1972 at Wehlen.

In 1969 only one-fifth of the German viticultural area had root stock, whereas nearly two-thirds of the viticultural area had been attacked by this insect. All new planting now has to be with grafted vines. One of the major means of overcoming this difficulty is the *Flurbereinigung* (Reorganization of German vineyards).

Great progress has already been made. The cultivated area has increased to 83,379 ha. The danger of phylloxera has passed. Old vineyards have been replanted and partly with new vines, new crossings. Last but not least, not only have working techniques been modernized, but average production has increased tremendously. Whereas in the decade 1950–60 52 hectolitres per ha were produced, in 1961–70 it increased to an average of 83·6 hectolitres per ha. In addition, there has been progress in the methods of harvesting and vinification (see Chapters 8–11).

Wine production in Western Germany in the years 1965–71 was divided between the wine growers (55·2 to 61·8 per cent) the co-operatives (26·4 to 31·2 per cent) and the wine merchants (10·7 to 13·8 per cent).

There are 39,000 estates which press their own grapes and produce wine. 30,000 estates sell their wine in whole or part to the wine trade or to grocers, whilst 11,000 growers bottle their wine and sell it in part or as a whole to the consumer direct. In 1972 1·2 million hectolitres were sold direct to the consumer, and that represents approximately 20 per cent of the whole of Germany's production. Wine products in the hands of the wine merchants are handled by 850 wholesale and 270 retail enterprises. Here it must be noted that the wine trade and other groups situated in wine-producing regions buy either grapes on the vines, or the must (pressed grape juice) and treat it – in other words they are what the French call '*Négociants éleveurs*'.

2

German viticulture within the E.E.C.

There is a certain amount of viticulture in Eastern Germany, namely in Thuringia, Saxony and Silesia, but these districts will not be included in the following survey.

The acreage of German vineyards may still increase though a limit has been set, to some extent, by the law 'Gesetz über Massnahmen auf dem Gebiete der Weinwirtschaft' (law and regulations governing German viticulture). It contains regulations about the setting up of new plantations. The aim of these directions is to preserve and improve the quality of German wine, and to safeguard its ability to compete in the European economy. For that reason the relevant federal state's special permission is necessary for the plantation of wine grapes, including replantation, and no permission is to be granted if the land is unsuitable for production of wine.

The permit can carry special conditions, either by dictating the species to be planted or stating those species which must not be planted in particular districts.

A commission of specialists has to investigate and to verify the suitability of a site, and the department of agricultural meteorology in the German weather service must confirm the climatic suitability of the site. Its evaluation is based on the average quality over 10 years, the decisive factor being the minimum sugar content of the grapes for the wine district and for the vine replanted.

Of first importance is the altitude at which the vineyard is situated. Second in importance is the aspect and steepness of the site, because the angle at which the sun's rays meet the soil and the vine is important for ripening.

If a vineyard is situated in a valley there is a strong possibility that though it is facing south, very early in the day the shadow of the opposite hillside will cover the vineyard, shortening the hours of sunshine and bringing about a later ripening of the grapes. Of importance also is the degree of exposure to the wind, and even more, the incidence of frost in the area. We know that in the vineyards of the northernmost wine-producing countries in particular, early frost in autumn and late frost in spring are very dangerous. If frost falls on grapes which are not ripe and damages them, then the resultant must and wine get a special 'frosty' taste. It also endangers the brightness of the wine. If a frost occurs late in spring, then the new buds are damaged and the production of grapes may fail altogether, although today German growers have special ways of minimizing damage if given plenty of warning that frost is expected. But frost may be so widespread that it becomes impossible for the grower to protect the whole area of his vineyards.

Last but not least is the effect of water. One knows only too well what great influence the Rhine has on the vineyards of the Rheingau. Experience of the last few years shows how much an area of water influences the vineyards (see p. 44 for more details).

LAW AND REGULATIONS GOVERNING GERMAN VITICULTURE (*WEINWIRTSCHAFTSGESETZ*)

The law illustrates how earnestly German growers are working to maintain the high quality of their vineyards and of their wines, hence the restriction upon the extension of existing vineyards.

A very large part of the *Weinwirtschaftsgesetz* is the formation of a 'Stabilization Fund' (*Fond*). Its purpose is:

1. To increase the quality of wine, and improve publicity about it.
2. To assist wine growers, co-operatives, and wine merchants financially, to keep stock of wine.
3. To store and to take over wine of average quality if this appears necessary in the interests of the market, in order to guarantee to the grower a sound return for his labour and his investment.

All this takes into consideration the higher costs of production of German wines in comparison with costs in other countries. Higher costs can only be offset by higher quality, therefore the principal aim is to help improve quality.

It goes without saying that however high in quality the wine may be, publicity is absolutely necessary. It is therefore a constant preoccupation to advertise German wine and its quality, and to make sure that no difficulties arise when some vintages produce exceptional quantities (as in 1960). The *Fond* has been called upon, and actually successfully intervened before and during the harvests of 1964 and, in particular, 1970.

A special vineyard 'Land Register' (*Weinbaukataster*) was established in 1961 to ensure more and better control of viticulture.

Wine is subject to control by wine legislation from the planting of the vines up to the time it is ready for consumption. If we look back we find rules and regulations already in biblical times and all through the ages. German wine legislation covers all aspects from grape to glass, and not only the naming of a wine.

The aim, all over the world, is the protection of the consumer against misleading and unfair treatment and against deception, because of the differing interests of the producer and the buyer of the goods. Competition is fierce; producers want to sell their goods and are always fighting to gain as many customers as possible, and they want to push their goods forward by their quality, price, trade marks, packaging and so on, and thereby distinguish them from the goods of competitors. The consumer should be fully informed from whom the goods originate and is to be protected against abuse and deception.

It is only a short while since the British Parliament passed a law protecting the consumer against deception, the Trade Descriptions Act. Such deceptions are known as *Unlauterer Wettbewerb* in Germany, as *Réclame trompeuse* in France and *Misleidende reklame* in Holland.

German viticulture is in a difficult position in the E.E.C. France and Italy have very much more favourable climates, and are the biggest wine-growing countries. It is generally much less hard work to produce wine in these countries, and production is also cheaper. The wines from the more southern countries are generally higher than German wines in alcoholic strength, but in Germany it is the bouquet, the fruity acidity, the elegance and the many and varied characteristics of the wines that decide their value.

In order to remain competitive, German viticulturists have to take special steps to keep the price of wine within the limits which people can afford. To increase competitiveness it is necessary to bring about a reduction in the labour used, to ease the work of the vineyard labourer, to increase the quality of the wine, and also, if possible, the quantity per hectare. In order to achieve this Germany has tried to reorganize her vineyards over a long period, and in recent years great progress has been made in this direction.

Those engaged in viticulture, as in every form of industrial activity, have been at great pains to find more economic ways of working, simplifying and rationalizing their methods. Vine pests are combated by the most modern scientific devices, only such fertilizers are employed as have been thoroughly tested, cellars are equipped as far as possible with the latest improvements.

In many communities a network of paths has been built through the vineyards, in others plans have been drafted for a system of paths to improve access. There are also plans for regulating the water supply and particularly for collecting water from springs, draining pools, constructing basins for the collection of rain water in case of heavy rainfall to avoid whole vineyards being swamped away, as this has happened quite frequently in the past – in other words building a system of water control.

It was a tradition that on the death of a vineyard proprietor the vineyards were divided amongst his children, each child receiving his share of every vineyard, since all were interested in getting part of the best vineyards. On the Mosel, for instance, many vineyards existed which had been divided and subdivided as the result of inheritance, often into more than 100 plots under separate ownership. Some of these plots were awkwardly placed and so inaccessible that they could only be reached by the most sure-footed after an arduous climb. One could always see the result of such subdivisions. One effect was that new paths had to be trodden, and so other people's property had to be invaded. I remember well one case where the owner of many very small vineyards, situated in many different parts of a village, spent more time in reaching the sites of his vineyards than he actually spent working in them!

This has been changed through reorganization of the vineyards (*Flurbereinigung*). Now, with Government financial aid, some entire vineyards have already been reshaped and some hills have even been given different orientations, in order to improve the vineyards' exposure to the sun. Vineyards are interconnected with new roads and tracks, and each grower has been re-allocated his share in a sensibly-shaped rectangular plot, easily accessible from the top or bottom, so that the most highly efficient viticultural machinery available today may be used.

On the Mosel this rationalization is going ahead so successfully that one expects some two-thirds of the vineyards to have been improved by the late seventies.

In some villages the regions were subdivided into various phases for reconstruction. So in one village one finds some vineyards of the ancient style, some already reorganized.

In Geisenheim, the vineyards were reorganized in such a way that the lines go from north to south, and in the north and south are roads, and so the question of water supply has been solved in an ideal way. The principal roads are equal to any B roads, and even the smaller paths are strong enough to carry machinery and cars.

Many growers who were anxious about the result of rationalization find that they can now reach their vineyards comfortably, and so do their work in less time. They also benefit by arrangements made to collect an abnormal rainfall, so that it does not reach the vineyards and wash the soil away on to the road. Thus there will no longer be erosion after heavy thunderstorms, and there will be a great saving of time in the future.

Mention must also be made about the result of the Vineyard Register. Until 1951 the Geisenheim Land Register showed no less than forty-one different site names. In 1951 reconstruction took place and all vineyards which produced wine of similar quality and character were put under one new name. By 1971 only eight site names remained, but the Geisenheim folk do not want to forget the old site names and so have decided that the roads and fields should keep their old names.

The plans of vineyards in Ihringen, Baden (Map 1), before and after reorganization show a great difference. An enormous amount of work was involved. Much land was bulldozed away and rocks were dynamited so that now machines can be used, ploughs can enter the vineyards and cultivation costs less time and money.

State of vineyards reorganization beginning 1972

Weinanbaugebiete in	Total area	Area in production	Area which needs no reorganization	Already reorganized	Still to be reorganized
Nordrhein-Westfalen	35	16	—	—	35
Hessen	3,877	3,338	334	1,602	1,941
Rheinland-Pfalz	61,881	52,854	1,800	21,786	38,295
Baden-Württemberg	22,629	16,548	2,600	8,624	11,405
Bayern	3,500	2,725	500	1,395	1,605
Saarland	90	33	—	90	—
Total	92,012	75,514	5,234	33,497	53,281

3

German wine legislation

I have just mentioned that the planting of the vineyard is subject to permission by the federal state of the area. In the case of grapes intended for wine making, they are also subject to a special wine law and supervision from the vine to the consumer. The new German wine law came into force on 19 July 1971.

For fifteen years the 'new wine law' was discussed in Germany, and when I published the fourth edition of *Rhineland Wineland* I stated that I had expected to include a chapter about it. It had been anticipated that the new law would be dealt with during the parliamentary sessions of 1965. But discussions went on and on; the first bill put before Parliament was rejected and sent back to be redrafted.

Then something happened: the European Economic Community published, in 1968, a supra-national wine law directing viticulture and vinification for the member states. This was a wine law created for the needs of the French wine trade and French wine growers which, if ever adopted for the whole European Community, would have carried a death warrant for German viticulture. Forty per cent of the German wine harvest could not have been used as table wine at all. A large part of the German wine crop would have had to be condemned for use in distillation or for the making of vinegar, or for the producer's own consumption, and it would no longer have been eligible for sale. As one of the German wine trade papers remarked – there would always be too much wine from outside Germany unless one wanted to kill oneself by drinking, and German wine would be too expensive for the fate designed for it, namely vinegar or spirit.

This was the moment when Germans had to forget their fights amongst themselves – wine grower against wine trade, co-operative against single grower and wine trade – and this was the moment (1969) when the new German wine law was actually born. The pregnancy had lasted far too long! But even so this law was stillborn. The 1971 law is now in force, the E.E.C. having accepted many of the objections raised by Germany.

Before we examine the present wine law, it is essential to take a glance at the history of wine legislation through the centuries. The first thing we come to realize here is that what we consider 'falsification of wine' today may not have been considered such centuries ago. Many things have changed, and what was permitted or even desirable in the past is perhaps condemned today. Similarly, some treatment given to wine which we consider essential today, was a punishable offence centuries ago.

Of course, as long as a farmer grew wine only for his own and his family's consumption, he made enough for his own use and treated it to his own liking. But when the question of barter and sale arose, the idea of increasing the volume of the wine and thereby making more money came about through human greed.

As we know from the history of only the last few decades, when goods are in great demand but in short supply, there is the temptation to replace highly acceptable goods wholly or partly with substitutes. This happened with wine.

Needless to say, often those who committed such offences were not citizens of the wine districts. Wine brewers had their businesses outside the wine-growing areas, and as we can see from literature, Hamburg, Bremen, and Stettin were three of these centres. In a book published in 1835 attention is drawn to the 'fabrication' of wine in London. The story comes to mind of the grower who, when he was on his death-bed, called his children together in order to give them a trade secret – and told them: 'It is also possible to make wine from grapes.'

This was not just a joke. It is a fact that artificial wine has been manufactured in all eras; sometimes without even the assistance of the fruit of the vine. As today, fruit wines were then made from figs, dates and so on, mixed with all kinds of spices. In his time Pliny could say that he was not surprised that centuries previously many kinds of artificial wine had been invented, and he himself provided a list of several artificial wines in which the grape had played no part at all.

When prices for German wines were very low (and chemistry undeveloped) and imported wines difficult to obtain, chemical treatment of wines was known in Germany, but only to a very small extent. Because the price of wine was so low, it did not pay to 'manufacture' an unnatural product.

But when the wine-growing districts shrank and prices increased, the fabrication of artificial wine came about on a large scale. As a result people who loved their wine and were connoisseurs complained, and these complaints led to the first laws for the protection of wine. It is interesting to note that long ago in ancient Rome offenders received corporal punishment at the Forum and their wine containers were broken up and destroyed in public.

In the ninth century Charlemagne prohibited the blending of wines from various vintages. The *Capitulare de Villis* contains instructions about care and cleanliness in production methods of wine.

Various laws were promulgated in the tenth to fifteenth centuries. In Zürich, for example, the addition of water to wine was prohibited; a fine of £5 had to be paid for each cask thus adulterated. Edward III of England decreed in 1327 that much imported wine had to be poured away. Again and again we hear of decrees ordering that wine had to be left exactly as it was and that additions were prohibited.

This was the start of wine laws by various German cities. For instance: 'It is prohibited to add water and various chemicals, including sulphur,' whereas the addition of herbs and spices was permitted. In 1475 growers were told to leave the wine 'as God had created it'. However, by the end of the fifteenth century sulphurous acid was recognized as a preservative.

Moving on to the eighteenth century, in 1706 a cooper was hanged for watering wine. A true pioneer wine law is contained in a decree of Karl Friedrich von Baden, issued in 1752, where heavy punishment was stipulated for anybody acting against the regulations laid down by him. Any addition of sugar, raisins or anything which might be harmful to the human body, was prohibited. Isinglass and other finings, even finings which can be used today, were prohibited in those days.

Wine is in the first instance a food, and Germany's Food Act of May 1879 included it when prohibiting the production and sale of falsified, imitated or otherwise spoiled food for marketing under a description which could deceive the buyer. The first actual wine law in Germany was published in 1892 and the next one in 1901, this for the first time giving a definition of wine. It introduced control by food inspectors, and prohibited the manufacture and distribution of artificial wine. It laid down the exact amount of sugar solution which might be used and also when and where it could be used. What the law had in mind was the prohibition of the sale of sweetened, chaptalized (sugared) wine as natural wine. Long discussions had preceded these wine laws, and some of the interested parties wanted the fact that a wine had been sweetened stated on the label, the others did not; and the result was a law which prohibited the sale of sweetened wine as natural wine.

This was again followed by a new wine law in 1909, and finally succeeded by the wine law of 1930.

The wine law of 1909 brought new ideas into the thinking of wine producers and growers because, for the first time, strict regulations were laid down and definitions given for actions which were ignored before. We already find in the wine law of 1909 a full list of treatments which were allowed, rules which were laid down for the improvement of wine, not only so far as locality was concerned, but also as to the time when sweetening should take place. This was, for the first time, subject to registration with the authorities. The use of geographical denominations and the denominations of blends were all laid down in order to enable the authorities to control production, treatment and distribution of wines, and also of beverages of a vinous character, sparkling wines and brandy. This third German wine law permitted *blending of red and white* and *the blending of German and foreign wines* to the extent of 51 : 49 per cent, which endangered the financial situation of growers and honest merchants.

Over the last four decades we have got accustomed to think of the wine law of 1930 as the basis of all jurisdiction about German wine. The 1930 law left many questions open, however, which were partly settled by an amending act of 1932, and other amendments in 1935, 1936, 1951, 1954 and 1958. Even then, not all these questions had been settled, and the courts tried to fill the gap by interpreting the wording of the law as they saw it. The result was not always a happy one.

The 1930 law created a careful distinction between natural and sweetened wines. At one time the German drinker preferred a small, empty, but natural wine to any good glass of *verbessert* (improved, i.e. sweetened) wine. The wine law of 1930 laid down special rules about treatment, denomination, etc. and book keeping for the wine from the vine to the glass.

It also included two most important regulations: the prohibition of blends of white and red wine, and of German and foreign wines; and the prohibition of growing and selling wines produced from hybrids (crossings between American and European wines). German vineyards containing these hybrids had to be destroyed and replanted with grafted vines.

As we know, modern technology has invented many new ways of treatment and bottling. Very often theory was much quicker than practice, and many possibilities of treatment which were adopted by one country were never adopted in others. In Germany it was always the case that one could say 'what is not specifically permitted by the wine law is prohibited.'

The new wine law of 1971 brought German legislation about viticulture into line with the international law planned by the countries belonging to the European Economic Community. For many years discussions had taken place in Brussels about this international wine law, discussions dominated by the larger wine-producing countries: France and Italy. Some years after they had signed the Treaty of Rome, German officials discovered that they had not known what they were doing at the time. The 1971 E.E.C. wine law has at last given full recognition to the special needs and conditions of German viticulture.

It is of some interest to compare the wine laws of various countries and to see what importance they attribute to the question of natural or non-natural wine. Whereas Germany thought this worth codifying, France declined to do anything of the kind. In France, nobody ever asked whether a wine had been sweetened or not, so long as the wine had been treated in the right way and tasted all right. Only Austria, and to a smaller extent Switzerland, imitated the German law. In Luxembourg the old German wine law of 1909 was actually still valid until it was superseded by the supra-national law of the E.E.C.!

The European laws Nos. 816 and 817 cancelled many regulations of the German wine law of 1969, and made another law necessary, which came into force in July 1971, and brought great and basic changes to the vinification of German wines. Actually the whole German wine law of 1971 is based on the directions contained in the E.E.C. wine law. For instance, quite new for Germany is a regulation governing the minimum content of sugar of any grapes to be used for the making of wine. Furthermore, the classification of wine into Tafelweine and Qualitaetsweine is new (see Chapter 10, Categories of wine).

It must be emphasized that for many years a great number of commercial and growers' associations had been asking for new legislation. Many changes have been taking place in viticulture technology dealing with the treatment and bottling of wine, production and, last but not least, the distribution of wine. New wine drinkers have found their way to wine, and this has made a different approach to all these questions desirable and opportune. The essence of the new wine law is that it should apply to everything from production to distribution, not only in Germany, but in the whole European and world wine market.

The German Parliament had to bear in mind that wine is not of the same composition in all parts of the world, that differences exist between production methods and the quality of wine of the Mosel, Saar, Ruwer and Rhine and those of other countries from which wines might be imported into Germany. Everything made from fermented grapes is called wine, but of course there are many – and a great variety of – approaches to wine.

The German wine grower had to be protected because production in Germany, the most northern wine-producing country in the world, is more difficult and more expensive than elsewhere. Nevertheless he has to compete with wines from other countries. But a major consideration in the debates on the wine law was the protection of the health of the consumer, to protect him so far as quality was concerned, and also to shield him from any misleading statements which could induce him to buy a wine which he would not want.

The new wine law deals with table wine and dessert wine, sparkling wine, beverages similar to wine, and brandy. It is, however, important to bear in mind that the law still shows some gaps, which will have to be filled by amendments.

THE FEDERAL STATES

Viticulture is not found in all the federal states of Germany. The wine-producing federal states have been empowered to issue certain by-laws about wine, with which I shall deal later (pp. 376–7). Here I only want to indicate that these in particular govern the minimum sugar content of the grapes for producing quality wines and quality wines with predicate.

This power was given to the federal states, because they are fully acquainted with regional specialities and peculiarities and can therefore make reasonable decisions. Furthermore, each federal state had to decide if it wanted to allow the blending of a wine from one German region with that from another, and it acted on economic or political motives, or just because it was concerned with the quality of the wines. This power, however, ended on 30 August 1973. Blends can be made to improve the quality, or to decrease the price of the wines, but it is the duty of the Government to give the consumer the best deal and therefore it will examine the question only from this point of view.

Another decision left to the federal states is the fixing of the proportion of unfermented sugar to actual alcohol. Here again it is supposed that the federal state government knows all the qualities and the defects of the wines of the district, and that it will know best what proportion of unfermented sugar can be left in the finished wine in order to make it rounder, more balanced, more harmonious and more saleable.

For those who wish to study the laws and by-laws in detail I would refer to *Verordnung ueber Wein Likoerwein und weinhaltige Getraenke* (Weinverordnung 15 Juli 1971):* *Verordnung zur Ueberwachung des Verkehrs mit Wein, Likoerwein, Schaumwein, weinhaltige, Getraenke, Branntwein aus Wein* (Wein-Ueberwachungsverordnung 15 Juli 1971).†

H.M. Stationery Office has published *European Communities Secondary Legislation*. The English text, Part 41, deals with wine as at 10 November 1971 (357 pages). It is expected that authentic English texts will be published in due course in an English-language edition of the official journal of the European Communities. Excerpts from the text of the two most important decrees, 816 and 817, can be found in Appendix 1.

The new wine law is divided into eight parts, with ninety-seven clauses. The following subjects are dealt with:

* Decree concerning wine, dessert wine and other beverages with a wine basis.

† Decree concerning the control of traffic in wine, sparkling wine, other beverages with a wine basis and brandy produced from wine.

1. German wines:	Clauses	1–17
2. Foreign wines:	,,	18–24
3. Sparkling wines:	,,	25–28
4. Beverages containing wine, and spirits produced from wine:	,,	29–51
5. Supervision and wine control:	,,	57–62
6. Regulations for transitional period:	,,	63–66
7. Criminal Code with the wine law:	,,	67–70
8. General regulations regarding the authority of the federal states:	,,	71–75
9. Additional regulations:	,,	79–82

The law remains flexible, especially with regard to new viticultural developments in the various federal states, and also in vinification. There are clearly things which cannot be known at the time of publication of the law, as nobody can foresee any new means of vinification. Furthermore, if any difficulties arise in interpreting the new law, in order to avoid expensive law cases, the wine-producing federal states can establish the correct interpretation by by-law.

The following summary of the new wine law attempts to set out its purposes:

1. To improve the quality of wine, and to facilitate its selection and distribution.
2. To conserve the special characteristics of German wine.
3. To accept any progressive procedure in vinification which leads to the improvement of quality.
4. To avoid misleading labelling, and allow only labelling which is clear and true. ('Wahrheit' and 'Klarheit' as main principles in naming the wine. See p. 146.)
5. And last, and perhaps the most important: to protect the consumer, especially so far as his health, but also so far as his purse is concerned.

The last is perhaps the most striking point in the new law. By commanding that the labelling of a wine be true and correct, and also easily comprehensible, the man in the street is enabled to understand the nature and value of the wine on offer, and this must strengthen his confidence in the quality of the wine. Another important step was that the new Vineyard Register (*Weinbergsordnung*) was to be started (see Chapter 4 and Part II).

There cannot be any doubt that with the E.E.C. draft law regulating the planting of new vineyards and the production of quality wine, and the new German wine law, a chapter of German viticultural history has ended and a new chapter begun. This leads us to a review of the present state of German viti- and viniculture.

4

The German vinelands

Let me begin with some statistics giving the political distribution of viticulture in federal states of the Federal Republic of Western Germany in 1973:

I. Rheinland-Pfalz		55,517 ha
1. Rheinpfalz-Palatinate	19,823 ha	
2. Rheinhessen	19,027 ha	
3. Mosel-Saar-Ruwer	11,176 ha	
4. Mittelrhein	901 ha	
5. Nahe	4,106 ha	
6. Ahr	484 ha	
II. Nordrhein-Westfalen (Mittelrhein)		14 ha
III. Saarland (Mosel)		82 ha
IV. Hessen		3,250 ha
7. Rheingau	2,943 ha	
8. Hessische Bergstrasse	307 ha	
V. Baden-Württemberg		18,776 ha
9. Württemberg	7,194 ha	
10. Baden	11,582 ha	
VI. Bavaria (Bayern)		2,983 ha
11. Franconia	2,964 ha	
12. other	19 ha	
		80,622 ha

Germany is the most northern wine-growing country. Travelling through it one finds vineyards to a much smaller extent than in southern countries. Not every piece of land is apt for viticulture. Only if various factors such as climate, soil and situation are favourable can a vineyard be planted. Here are some outlines of these factors.

SOIL, CLIMATE, WIND

SOIL: The planting of a vineyard is dependent upon the climate. If the climatic conditions are suitable, then the vine can grow on nearly any soil. If the climatic conditions are not favourable, it will be necessary to plant the vines in heat-retaining soil, and/or hill sites which face south, south-east or south-west.

Actually the vine does not ask much of the soil. It must in the first instance not contain too much water, and, if possible, it must be warm. If the soil is too fertile, then very often the wines produced on it are of low or mediocre quality.

It has always been the rule: the greater the yield, the worse the wine. The more the vine has to work to get its food from the soil, the better the wine when the grapes come to full ripeness. Differences in the wine are very often due to differences in the soil. The greater the variations in soil in a district, the more varieties of wine, as is seen in Germany and the Côte d'Or.

CLIMATE: The main factors are humidity and the amount of sunshine hours, both of which are very important. The most satisfactory climate is found in the warm, moderate zones of the world, between the 35th and 45th latitude North and between the 20th and 40th latitude South (see Map 2). The deciding factor which makes viticulture possible further north or south than the 45th latitude is when the climate of the district is favourably influenced by near-by river valleys or lakes, as we see in some German regions, (the Mosel and Ahr valleys which actually extend to the 51st latitude). The vineyard furthest north in Germany is in Boeddiger, an *Ortsteil* of Felsberg on the river Fulda near Kassel (see under Rheingau, p. 286).

It is important to remember that the white wines which are grown in the most northern part of the viticultural areas are specially renowned for their very fine bouquet, but on the other hand they contain more acidity and less alcohol than wines which come from further south.

The average temperature required in wine-growing districts lies between 9°C and 21°C. The finest wines are produced at an average annual temperature of from 10°C to 12°C, which means a mild autumn and a mild winter. The average summer temperature in the German vinelands is approximately 20°C, the winter temperature around 0°C, i.e. freezing point.

Too much warmth is not good for the vine, therefore we do not find any vines grown nearer the equator than approximately 20th North or South latitude. The seasons must be suitable, that is to say spring must not be too late, summer should be long and warm, and there should not be too many frosts, either in spring or in autumn. The temperature in winter should not drop below −20°C. The vegetation period of the vine is, of course, dependent upon the average temperature of the district. Whereas in the south of France this period (the time from the beginning of the formation of the leaves and the budding of the vines, until they fall off) is 244 days, in Germany it is between 175 and 190 days.

Ampelographies divide vines into three classes: early-, middle- and late-maturing.

Temperature is very important for viticulture. During the time of flowering, if the temperature falls below 15°C fertilization and therefore productivity is poor. The average temperature of a district also decides the maximum altitude at which the vine can be planted – in Germany usually 300 metres (900 feet) above sea level, with the exception of the Lake of Constance, where vines grow up to 400 metres.

Warmth is of great influence, but of equal importance are humidity and the amount of rain. The vine does not need much soil humidity and can, therefore, flourish on dry hillsides, and very often better there than any other agricultural products. In Germany rainfall in the wine districts is mostly 500–600 mm per annum, but for instance, near the Black Forest, on its western hills it is 800–1,000 mm, and quite good wines are made there. Of course, if there is much rainfall, there is a great danger of diseases of the vine, moreover an early gathering of the grapes may become essential. Generally speaking, one can say that dry sites produce better quality wines in dry years whereas the sites which are damp produce much larger quantities.

The air humidity is of great importance, as is specially shown in the valleys of the rivers Rhine, Main, Neckar, Mosel and Nahe, and the Lake of Constance, where the evaporation of the water in the river or lake in summer or autumn is the cause of a very good temperature balance. The formation of fog, too, acts in preventing frosts in spring and autumn. It has also been proved that during the time of flowering, warm rain is much more favourable for fertilization than dry, warm weather.

The wine grower wants a warm autumn, which means the month of September without rain and with much sunshine. It is a combination of warmth and humidity which decides the growth of the vine and the quality of the wine. For instance, if from time to time 20 mm of rain falls on one day, with a few hours of sunshine daily during the whole week, that can be of great benefit to the growth of the vine; but if 20 mm altogether falls during a week (some 3 mm a day) and there is some sunshine in between, then you have a warm humidity similar to that of a greenhouse, which very often causes the harmful fungus *peronospora* to develop.

Taken all in all, the vine needs 400–500 mm of rain, if there is no artificial rain; a maximum after harvesting, but a minimum from July to September. When growing red wine grapes, one never wants a high humidity with warmth on account of the danger of *peronospora* as mentioned before, which in autumn can cause rot; certain white grapes, on the other hand, require humidity and warmth at the right time in order to produce noble rot (see p. 97). The best example of this was the 1959 vintage, where humidity was missing, not many grapes were attacked by *botrytis*, and only a few Rhine Trockenbeerenauslesen were made.

The amount of sunshine is important, because the assimilation of CO_2 and water by the leaves is very dependent on the warmth of the soil: it is said that a wine district should have annually at least 100 days and 1,300 hours of sunshine. The more sunshine there is in summer and autumn, the better the quality of the vintage. If the summer months are wet and cold, and there is a lack of sunshine, then there is little chance of the grapes ripening, though a mild autumn with many sunshine hours can still lead to a good vintage. Of course the longer the more vertical rays of the sun are able to strike the soil, the greater the warmth of the soil. It follows that in Germany, sites which slope to the south, where the sun's rays and warmth of soil are more favourable, are best for viticulture and produce first-class results. So far as sunshine is concerned, its intensity alone is not decisive; but a certain amount of sun has to penetrate the grape to assimilate its water content and produce sugar.

Frequent changes of climate from cool to warm days and vice versa cause the grapes to ripen very slowly and sugar, acidity, bouquet and taste develop in harmony. It is just this harmony of bouquet and aesthetic finesse with its fruity acidity and its low alcoholic content which make the German grapes and German wine so different from wine produced in other countries.

Here are some more detailed statistics relating to the main areas:

	Average Temperature °C		*Average Rainfall*	
	Year	May–Sept	Annual	May–Sept
Palatinate	9·4–9·9	16·0–16·9	584	268
Rheinhessen	9·0–9·7	15·5–16·2	500/50	230/70
Franconia	8·8–9·4	15·4–16·4	550/90	270/300
Baden	9·3–9·9	15·6–16·6	600/750	330/520
Mosel	8·8–9·7	15·0–15·8	550/700	270/330
Rheingau	9·3–10·0	15·8–16·5	550/630	250/320

	Sunshine Hours
Rheinhessen	1,500
Mosel	1,375
Franconia	1,660
Palatinate	1,870

For a comparison of weather conditions in 1967 and a 60–year average see Appendix 2.

WIND: Wind also is of importance. Strong and cold winds from the north and north-east are most unsuitable for viticulture, whilst very often even the warm winds from the south-west are not of very great benefit. The vines should be planted on sites which are protected against all kinds of winds. We therefore very often find that walls and other fences have been erected in order to protect special sites against northern winds. In the Rhine valley the surrounding mountains act as a wind barrier. On the other hand the wind has its own role to play, as it makes a particular contribution towards the racy character and spiciness of German wines.

The quality of German wines is greatly influenced by the climate of the sites (*Lagen*), and for many years research has been going on in Hessen and Franconia to examine soil and the vines which suit it. In Hessen (Rheingau and Hessische Bergstrasse) the result is set out in the *Standortkartierung der hessischen Weinbaugebiete-Atlas* published by the Hessisches Landesamt für Bodenforschung, Wiesbaden, 1967. This new system of evaluation should lay the foundation for plans for the planting and choice of vine according to locality. It also deals with areas not yet covered or planted with vines, but it is primarily concerned with finding the right sites for the principal vines.

Knowledge of this data was very important when the new Vineyard Register was drawn up, and especially the *Grosslagen*. To fulfil the conditions for creation of the *Grosslagen* one can combine only such neighbouring single sites the soil of which will produce wine of equal value. This is discussed in detail in Chapter 5.

In Germany important studies of the micro-climate have been made, especially in Hessen and Franconia. Soil, the affinity and adaptability of the various vines to the soil, and also the climate for each site, have been published in many maps. These findings only confirm what one knows, what my grandfather and my father knew and what I had heard in my early childhood, that the best Rheingau vineyards are: Ruedesheim, Schloss Johannisberg, Schloss Vollrads, Steinberg, some vineyards in Kiedrich and Rauenthal and the Marcobrunn; in other words, the scientists only confirmed the correctness of the winetasters' judgement.

DIFFERENCES OF VITICULTURE BETWEEN GERMANY AND SURROUNDING COUNTRIES

The basic differences result from the difference in climate. We find first of all that the countries round the Mediterranean produce primarily red wine, and only a small part is devoted to the cultivation of white wine. Germany suffers in many years from a lack of the necessary summer heat, but very rarely does it suffer from lack of humidity or rain. In many of the other wine-growing countries, it is just the other way round: they have a surplus of heat, but not enough rain or humidity. These countries are in a position to produce heavy wines, rich in alcohol. If there is a lack of humidity, the vine is working faster and full ripeness is achieved earlier. But we must not forget that fruit which has been grown under glass tastes quite different from fruit grown in the open. In a temperate climate with sufficient humidity the grapes grow more slowly, but they have time to develop all the fine bouquets. This is the reason why the German wines are distinguished by their freshness, fruitiness, elegance and particularly by their special '*Bekömmlichkeit*'.

I have given above the sunshine hours for the principal German districts (1,500–1,870). By comparison in the south of France there are 2,700 hours of sunshine, in northern Italy 1,700–2,000 and in southern Italy 2,400 hours. It is instructive, too, to compare vegetation periods. These are: in Germany, 162 days; in Alsace, 175 days; in Bordeaux and the Loire districts, 200 days.

The viticulturist's studies include the structure of all outer parts of the vine; the study of cells, plasm, chromosomes; the study of the wood, the root, leaves and other parts of the vine; all functions of the organs of the vine – breathing, nourishment, evaporation, fertilization and genetics of the vine; detailed analysis of the content of wine – its treatment, fining, filtering and diseases; the weather and the climate surrounding the wine-districts; diseases and enemies of the vine and also study of the affinity of the vine to soil and climate. Finally, there is study of the developments of the vine which is observed all the year round and recorded in statistical form.

Every village has its own official observer and everything he observes is entered in special maps, from which, after some years, it is possible to discover some sort of regular pattern of events. The following are examples of data which an experienced grower can ascertain from these maps of many former vintages: when the first buds appear in the vineyards; at what stage the leaves begin to grow; the start and approximate duration of the blossoming period; when the grapes ripen into maturity; at what period the 'noble rot' stage is attained; and finally, when the leaves take on their autumn colouring and first begin to fall. Data which cannot be entered on the maps but which are, nevertheless, necessary to complete the picture, are the sugar and acid content of the grape juice. Correlation of the above by a viticulturist or an expert enables certain near-positive conclusions to be reached, on which he will base his advice to the wine grower. These charts are also valuable pointers in determining the desirability of a site for viticulture.

No vintage passes without the grower and expert adding something to their knowledge, and science assists them in integrating this knowledge into a unique analysis: all of which goes to show that wine-growing requires immense skill and expertise. During the winter months, for instance, the grower will go through his vineyards after every frost, observing and marking those vines which have suffered and will not produce grapes.

All these factors have been considered and taken into account in the laws of the European Economic Community, which stipulate the European Viticultural Zones. This division into zones is based on the different climates of the zones. Although a minimum alcoholic content has been fixed for each since higher alcohol is produced in warmer districts, one must not make the mistake of thinking that alcoholic content has anything to do with quality. I shall return to this question later.

The E.E.C. has divided the viticultural districts in '*partes tres*', namely three zones A, B and C. Zone C is again subdivided into three parts, C1, C2, C3 (see Map 3a) with different laws and regulations governing treatments.

The German vineyards are situated in Zone A, with the exception of Baden which belongs to Zone B. The only district in Zone A which is not German are the vineyards of Luxembourg.

To Zone B belong also the following French wine areas: Alsace, Lorraine, Champagne, Jura, Savoy and the Loire valley wines.

Zone C1: Important regions which are not Zone B, i.e. Bordeaux, Rhône and Burgundy belong to this zone.

Zone C2: The south of France (but see under C3), Italy (but see under C3).

Zone C3: The rest of France: Corsica, part of Pyrénées Orientales, Dept. of Var. In Italy all vineyards situated south of Rome, and those on islands.

5

The new Vineyard Register

German vinelands are now divided into five *Weinbaugebiete* (areas of wine cultivation):

1. Rhein
2. Mosel
3. Main
4. Neckar
5. Oberrhein (subregions Roemertor for South Baden, Burgengau for North Baden)

The *Weinbaugebiete* are divided into '*bestimmte*' *Anbaugebiete* (b.A.) (Special areas of cultivation).

This is best illustrated by two maps covering the same area (Maps 4a and b).

The Rhine *Weinbaugebiet* contains the following *Anbaugebiete*:

	Official No.
Ahr	1
Hessische Bergstrasse	2
Mittelrhein	3
Nahe	5
Rheingau	6
Rheinhessen	7
Rheinpfalz (Palatinate)	8

The Mosel *Weinbaugebiet* contains the following *Anbaugebiet*: Mosel – Saar – Ruwer 4

The Main *Weinbaugebiet*:	*Anbaugebiet* Franconia	9
The Neckar *Weinbaugebiet*:	*Anbaugebiet* Württemberg	10
The Oberrhein *Weinbaugebiet*:	*Anbaugebiet* Baden	11

The specific regions are subdivided into subregions, *Bereiche* (districts), villages and parts of villages, and their *Lagen* (sites). The

Bereiche occupy a midway position between the regions and the villages and their *Lagen* (*Einzel-* and *Grosslagen*).

A *Bereich* is a district within a region covering sites situated in villages in close proximity in the region of production, where usually wines of *similar* taste are produced.

The Ahr region has	1 *Bereich*
Rheingau region has	1 *Bereich*
Palatinate region has	2 *Bereiche*
Rheinhessen region has	3 *Bereiche*
Franconia region has	3 *Bereiche*
Mosel-Saar-Ruwer region has	4 *Bereiche*
Baden region has	7 *Bereiche*

Each *Bereich* includes a number of villages; each village is divided into one or more single vineyard sites – *Einzellage*. Where the name of a *Bereich* appears on a label it must always be preceded by the word 'Bereich'. I consider this word a most unfortunate introduction into the law. There exist plenty of internationally known expressions which could have been used by the new law. Such expressions as 'district' or 'region' would have been understood by most people speaking English or a language derived from Latin.

A *Lage* or *Einzellage* (site or single site) is an exactly defined 'area' of a vineyard and is the smallest unit: the vineyards of a village are divided into several *Lagen* with names to distinguish one from the other, e.g. in Ruedesheim: Roseneck, Rottland, or in Bernkastel: Lay, Graben, Doctor, etc. A *Grosslage* (greater site) consists of a number of sites, also exactly defined; the wines produced in one *Lage* or one *Grosslage* are supposed to be of equal value and equal taste. A *Grosslage* may cover part or the whole of the vineyards of one community or a lot of communities. A *Lage* may be part of the vineyard of a village or several villages or a region.

The following are examples of *Einzellagen* covering parts of two or more villages:

Fuchsmantel:	*one* site, partly situated in Bad Dürkheim and partly in Wachenheim (a former generic name)
Bischofsgarten:	situated in Forst, Friedelsheim, and Wachenheim
Michelsberg:	situated in Bad Dürkheim and Ungstein.

These are some of the Palatinate sites; there are a great number of such *Einzellagen* in all regions.

As another example the single sites of the former village of Mittelheim in the Rheingau and now part of the town of Oestrich-Winkel, form part of three *Grosslagen*! The Grosslage Burgweg covers all vineyards producing white wines of Lorch, Lorchhausen, Assmannshausen, Aulhausen, Rüdesheim and part of Geisenheim. The Grosslage Erntebringer covers all vineyards of Johannisberg, part of Geisenheim, Winkel and Mittelheim. In Baden *all* former districts known as '*Ortenau*' have become *Bereiche*, the whole Ahr region is congruent with the *Bereich*!

In the Land Register of the German States there were thousands of site names – perhaps 25,000 altogether – of which perhaps only half were used by the growers and perhaps only for the local trade, where everyone knew the site and the wine and that was the end of the site name.

It must be mentioned that not all *Einzellagen* belong to *Grosslagen*. There are quite a number of villages which are free of *Grosslagen* (*grosslagenfrei*). Bavaria always liked to go its own way, and a great number of her villages have preferred to remain *grosslagenfrei* to have single sites, not belonging to any *Grosslage*.

An investigation into the meanings and origins (with appropriate classification) of the site names yields an astonishing fund of discoveries and unsuspected connections:

1. There are names embodying historical events: Kosackenberg (Geisenheim), Blüchertal (Kaub).

2. There are names with an ecclesiastical flavour that carry allusions to churches, church dignitaries, ecclesiastical institutions, monasteries: Altar (Uerzig), Domprobst (Graach), Probstberg (Longuich), Kirchenpfad (Zeltingen), Pfaffenberg (Berncastel), Praelat (Erden), Klosterberg (often!), Nonnenberg (Martinsthal, Filzen, Wehlen), Nonnengarten (Puenderich, Briedel).

3. Or there are names that recall theological conceptions, picturing for example various aspects of heaven and hell: Himmelreich (Graach, Zeltingen), Paradies (Kroev), Hoelle (Johannisberg), Gottesfuss (Wiltingen-Saar), Engelsberg (Zeltingen), Engelgrube (Neumagen).

4. At times a name has been inspired by the particular colour of some vine-bearing rock or mountainside: Rothenberg (Rauenthal, Nackenheim), Rotley (Zeltingen).

5. And – naturally enough – vineyards specially favoured by the sun's rays are frequently the bearers of names indicating either the sun itself or the effects of its light and warmth: Sonnenschein (Schweich), Sonnseit (Wintrich), Sonnenberg (Eltville, Canzem), Sonnenuhr (Wehlen, Zeltingen), Sonnteil (Trittenheim).

6. Other sites have been given the names of birds or animals: Vogelsberg (Longuich), Kuckucksberg (Hatzenport), Taubengarten (Piesport), Hahnenberg (Waldrach), Hahnenboehl (Forst), Schwanen (Berncastel), Bienengarten (Winkel, Senheim), Hasensprung (Winkel),

Hasenlaeufer (Brauneberg), Wildsau (Martinsthal), Wolfsberg (Canzem).

7. Then again we find vineyards with poetical, humorous or grotesque appellations: Amorpfad (Berncastel), Goldtroepfchen (Piesport), Vogelsang (Serrig, Laubenheim (Nahe)), Wuerzgarten (Uerzig), Badstube, Bratenhoefchen (Berncastel), Herzchen (Briedel), Nacktarsch (Kroev), Lump (Escherndorf).

I have listed some site names giving their meanings and their location, even if these names have disappeared.

The wine trade, however, had to look for better and larger supplies and very often used a generic site name. This was a site name which covered a radius of approximately 15 km round the registered 'generic' site.

One aim of the new wine law was to do away with all these superfluous names, and to introduce a *Weinberg Rolle* (Vineyard Register) with *Lagen* and *Grosslagen* to satisfy those who like to have their wine from an individual single site available in small quantity and therefore at a premium price or from a *Grosslage* with larger quantities available at more economical prices.

Already under the 1930 law any wine grown in the borough of Rüdesheim could be called 'Rüdesheimer', but it could only be called 'Rüdesheimer Roseneck' if it had been grown in that part of the borough of Rüdesheim which is known as 'Roseneck'. A site is a piece of land; where one ends the next starts, and the sites keep their distinctive names even where they overlap the local community boundary. In other words, the names of the sites within a wine district are like the names of municipal districts within a city. Like all names, they are used to distinguish their owners' wines and make them easier to recognize.

Now some site names have disappeared. A very good example of the restriction of site names is Nierstein. Until 1971 nine leading site names were used comprising dozens of other site names, all of which could still be used by the grower. In other words, the grower could sell the wine under the old name entered in the Land Register or he could use the newer site name (see list on pp. 54–5).

The modern development of viticulture and distribution has created the demand for large quantities of identical wine and the demand for continuity of supply has influenced the old wine tradition so that names are now restricted still further.

The way the system works, and the nature of the changes effected, can be understood by considering the example of Nierstein.

A *Lage* should not be smaller than 5 ha, but exceptions are admissible, and in my opinion too many exceptions have been granted to permit some owners of small vineyards to hold on to a monopoly of a name.

Let me quote an example from the new Vineyard Register. In Hessen there are two *Anbaugebiete.* One of them, the Rheingau, has 11 *Grosslagen* and 112 *Einzellagen.* The other *Anbaugebiet* in Hessen is the Bergstrasse, with 20 single sites, 3 *Grosslagen*, 2 *Bereiche.* We have to compare this with the state of affairs before the new law came into force: there were no fewer than 1,000 single sites in Hessen, now reduced to 132, and instead of the 30 generic sites, there are now only 13 *Grosslagen.* This certainly means progress, though I consider there are still too many *Grosslagen*!

The original purpose in merging sites into greater sites was to help the consumer, so that in fact '*Wahrheit und Klarheit*', i.e. verity and clarity, would be the basic principle of the new wine law. Looking at the actual results, considering everything which has been written, and everything which has been done, I doubt that the slogan 'Verity and Clarity' can any longer be announced as the ruling principle. The *Lagen* have been enlarged, the *Grosslagen* have been created. Whereas under the old regulations the generic name covered only other nearby vineyards, today a *Grosslage* can cover large districts including many villages, and if a wine originates in such a *Grosslage*, the name of any of the villages within the *Grosslage* can be given as the place of origin. For example, the Grosslage Bischofskreuz, the largest *Grosslage* of the Palatinate, covers all the vineyards in nine villages, with an area of 1,547 ha. A wine which originates from any of the nine villages can be given the name of any of the nine villages. There is one condition: once a name has been chosen, the choice is once and for all, no second thoughts are possible. Likewise any wine produced for example in 'The Grosslage Gutes Domtal' can be sold with any one of the names of the villages according to the grower's or merchant's choice:

Niersteiner Gutes Domtal
Dexheimer Gutes Domtal
Dalheimer Gutes Domtal.

What does this mean for the wine drinker? He may have taken a fancy to a wine of a special vineyard and would like to continue to drink the wine from the same vineyard. The same vineyard name does not guarantee him a wine from the identical place. The smaller site may have been enlarged, and incorporated into a larger site. Here is an opportunity to start afresh the study of German wines, to forget the ones one has enjoyed and go for something new. This also applies to new grapes (see next chapter).

The Ministries of Agriculture, Viticulture and Forestry of the

NIERSTEIN'S VINEYARDS *Names before 1971*	*NEW VINEYARD REGISTER*	Area ha
Spiegelberg: Bettzüge, Böllengewann, Diebsweg, Domtal,* Findling, Flossgewann, Geisenberg, Grasweg, Hessbaum, Kindswiese, Klauer, Klostergewann, Loch, Lörzweilerweg, Mittelgewann, Mommenheimer Weg, Nackenheimer Loch, Nassgewann, Ohrenberg, Ohrenbrunnen, Ohrenfloss, Pulver, Hoher Rechen, Uber der Rehbacher Steig, Vorderer Rolländer, Hinterer Rolländer, Steinrutsch, Warte, Hintere Schmitt, Leimen Schmitt.	Grosslage Spiegelberg	516·1773
	Einzellagen:	
	(a) Paterberg	147·7570
	(b) Bildstock	92·9692
	(c) Hölle	5·7437
	(d) Brückchen	19·1619
	(e) Ebersberg	40·0000
	(f) Rosenberg	60·3531
	(g) Klostergarten	74·6987
	(h) Findling	79·3807
	(i) Kirchplatte	111·0029
	(j) Hohenrechen	5·1101
	(k) Engelsberg (Gde. Nackenheim)	60·0000
	(l) Rothenberg (Gde. Nackenheim)	20·0000
GUTES DOMTAL Trademark for all Niersteiner wines	Grosslage Gutes Domtal	*c.* 1200·0000
	Einzellagen:	
	(a) Pfaffenkappe 35·0000 ha	
	(b) Gemeinden Dexheim, Dalheim, Friesenheim, Weinolsheim, Undenheim, Köngernheim, Selzen, Hahnheim, Zornheim, Mommenheim, Lörzweiler, Nackenheim, Sörgenloch, Nieder-Olm	
Paterberg: Brückchen, Burgrechen, Burgweg, Darheimer Brunnen, Ober dem Dalheimer Brunnen, Dauzkhlauer, Essigkaut, Fahrt, Galgenberg, Galgenhol, Gemarkrech, Haasenwörth, Heuwiese, Hölle, Hummertal, Ober dem Hummertal, Hummertaler Hohl, Kanal, Ketzenrechen, Monzenberg,* Die 13 Morgen, Auf den 16 Morgen, Oppenheimer Strasse, Ottenberger Gewann, Ober dem Langen Rech, Scheinbügel, Taubhaus, Wiesengewann Die Glöck, Brudersberg, Das Taubennest, Die zehn Morgen Fockenberg: Stumpfenloch, Brudersberg, Fritzenhölle,* Vorderer Rosenberg, Hinterer Rosenberg, Schmitt,	Grosslage Auflangen	156·7177
	Einzellagen:	
	(a) Schloss Schwabsburg	42·5833
	(b) Orbel	18·8109
	(c) Heiligenbaum	16·4264
	(d) Ölberg	60·7017
	(e) Kranzberg	16·0880
	(f) Glöck	2·1074

NIERSTEIN'S VINEYARDS *Names before 1971*	*NEW VINEYARD REGISTER*	
Kleiner Schmitt, Fockenberg, Schnappenberg,* Weisenberg, Ober die Fläschenhahl. Hipping: Eselspfad, Fläschenhahl, Fuchsloch, Unterer Hipping, Oberer Hipping, Hinterer Hipping, Kehr, Pfütze, Sommerbirnbaum, Tal. St. Kiliansberg: Bergkirche, Dorf, Kiliansweg, Kiliansäcker, Unterer Granzberg, Oberer Granzberg, Kreuz, Langgewann, Mockenberg, Reisenberg. Auflangen: Unterer Auflangen, Oberer Auflangen, Hinter den Häuser, Pfuhlweg, Löhgasse, Rohr, Hinter Saal, Ober der grossen Steig. Olberg: Olberg, Oberer Oelberg, Schiessmauer, Schlangenberg, Steig, Streng, Warte. Heiligenbaum: Bruch, Entenpfuhl, Heiligenbaum, Kelterbaum, Orbel, Schwabsburger Weg, Stall, Riedmühle. Bildstock: Bildstock, Brückchen Bleiche, Fäulingsbrunnen, Hörsterweg, Läusbrunnen, Mittel, Muhl, Die Neunmorgen, Oberdorf, Ostergärten, Ried, Riedmühle, Rossberg, Säuloch, Daubhaus, Riedmühle, Heugasse.		
Rehbach: Floss, Pettental, Untere Rehbach, Obere Rehbach, Rehbacher Steig, Sommerseite, Hinkelstein.	Grosslage Rehbach	85·3919
	Einzellagen:	
	(a) Hipping	31·1106
	(b) Pettenthal	32·3827
	(c) Goldene Luft	0·5686
	(d) Brudersberg	1·3300

* Denote the former generic site names (*Gattungslagen*).

federal states have done a great deal of work to sort out the question of site names. They acted throughout in consultation with the representatives of the wine growers and the wine trade. Site names were chosen and districts established in collaboration with all interested parties. In other words, solutions were found which suited all parties, so that instead of the thousand different site names and dozens of site names in each village, there are now larger sites which will give the grower and the trade the possibility of greater continuity of a wine, even if the variety has decreased.

We shall of course not find some old familiar site names any more, and on the other hand we meet some new ones in the Vineyard Register. We have to remember that some villages have been incorporated in larger neighbouring towns, others have been merged or are planning to do so. In many cases the enlarged village becomes an *Ortsteil* (suburb) and can as such still appear on the label, but this is not obligatory. As an illustration I take Neustadt/Weinstrasse (see p. 201). Other examples are the famous Johannisberg (Rheingau) with Schloss Johannisberg, which will be incorporated in Geisenheim; Lorch and Lorchhausen will become one town; Oestrich, Mittelheim and Winkel have merged and are now Oestrich-Winkel. In the long run some of the famous labels will disappear, some have already gone.

The Vineyard Register has done much to clear the way for the future marketing of wines. The register is the basis for the labelling of all wines, especially the quality wines. By-laws of the various governments of the federal states were issued laying down procedure for registration of new names, but no government has copied any other goverment's legislation.

Let me summarize. As a statement of the origin of wine, *only those names can be used which are entered in the Vineyard Register*. This applies to site names, *Bereiche* and names of villages, suburbs (*Ortsteile*), the names of defined areas, viticultural areas (*Weinbaugebiete*) and viticultural sub-areas (*Untergebiete*). Let us remember that the old Land Register contained names for many reasons. Some names had been created through popular usage (*Volksmundlagen*) and these were of great importance. I need only remind my readers of such names as Kroever Nacktarsch and Zeller Schwarze Katz. In the case of Forster Jesuitengarten, adjoining vineyards were also named Jesuitengarten, a fact which had been recognized by the highest German court.

So far as the new names were concerned, the basic aim was to preserve the tradition and if a registered name was not used, the new name should at least resemble the old registered names. Local feeling insisted that names based on culture history and the countryside had to be retained.

In drawing up the register of site names, obscene, misleading, confusing and ridiculous names cannot be registered. If in spite of this regulation anybody should apply for such a name, the Committee of Experts will decide after the hearing of applicants. This clause in the law of sites was caused by the enormous *réclame* connected with 'Kroever Nacktarsch' (nude bottom). This wine had such a success in Germany and abroad that many villages tried to compete with Kroev to find a name for their sites as vulgar or more vulgar and, they hoped, as popular as Nacktarsch. This clause therefore prevented those who were unsuccessful in registering obscene trade marks from having obscene site names registered.

Incidentally there exist some viticultural areas which do not have a registered site name. Their geographical denomination is the *Bereich* in which they are situated. The creation of a *Bereich* is important in connection with the naming of a Qualitätswein* mit Prädikat. From 1975 onwards the birthplace of such a wine must be one Bereich. A blend of Qualitaetsweine originating from two *Bereiche* loses the right to a Praedikat whatever the actual quality after the blending may be.

The final decision about site names lies with the Chamber of Agriculture. Strict regulations were issued to enforce these decisions. First, if a site name existed in the old Land Register the proprietors and leaseholders could suggest the registration of a single site. The application had to be made to the local council and could be considered only if the applicant gave 'wine grower' as his principal profession and not as a side line, and if he could prove that he had used this site name regularly, and that the retention of this site name was of paramount importance to his business interests.

I have mentioned that there are exceptions to the rule that a site should not be less than 5 ha. The Nierstein sites include three sites under the normal size of 5 ha as concessions to growers who had introduced their wines under these names:

Goldene Luft	0.5686 ha
Brudersberg	1·3300 ha
Gloeck	2·1074 ha.

Another exception to this rule is for villages whose vineyards cover less than 5 ha altogether and who want to sell their wines under the village and vineyard name and not under the name of the *Grosslage* covering the area. As an example I quote only a few names from the north Palatinate district.

In the Grosslage Zeller Schnepfenflug vom Zellertal, we have the following villages:

Bolanden Schlossgarten	2 ha
Ruessingen Breinsberg	2·53 ha
Rittersheim am hohen Stein	3 ha
Kerzenheim Esper	2·30 ha.

On account of the small size of the vineyard these wines are rarities by name, but not by quality – frankly speaking one can do without

* For an explanation of this term and others referred to, see pp. 107–8.

them. There is nothing to distinguish the Goldene Luft or the Brudersberg from the Pettenthal or Hipping, but the grower who has created some goodwill for his monopoly site, is allowed to continue using it.

I should, however, mention that these decisions are not final. There will be opportunities to apply for registration or alteration in the sizes of the sites, for instance, or their names. These alterations may be based on a change in the area of vineyards, or viticulture, or on account of changes in distribution, or in order to improve the sales of wines of different regions.

All the problems raised above should have been settled before 16 July 1971, when the new wine law came into force, but a few are still not solved (October 1975).

One awaited with interest the development of sites like Berncasteler Doctor of 1·32 ha, the demand for which grew so enormously that only by blending with nearby sites could it be even partly satisfied. Doktor und Graben, Doktor und Badstube, Doktor und Bratenhöfchen were used as site names. In future, such combinations of two site names are prohibited: a blend must contain 75 per cent of the *one* name-giving site – I shall return to this subject when writing of the specific districts. An exception is the Trockenbeerenauslese where 50·1 per cent are sufficient for a name giving site.

Summary of Vineyard Register

Specific region	Villages or suburbs	Sites	Greater sites	District
Rheinpfalz	247	362	27	2
Rheinhessen	136	422	24	3
Mosel-Saar-Ruwer	177	505	19	4
Baden	323	296	16	7
Württemberg	250	204	16	3
Nahe	64	324	7	2
Rheingau	30	112	10	1
Franken	89	148	16	3
Mittelrhein	60	114	8	2
Ahr	12	43	1	1
Hessische Bergstrasse	10	20	3	2
Together	1,398	2,543	147	31

6

German wines and vines

What is *wine?* The German wine law of 1930 gave this precise definition: 'Wine is the product of fermented grape juice, made from freshly gathered grapes.' This places very definite restrictions on the meaning of the word 'wine' and excludes its use to designate concoctions made from raisins, currants, or other fruits worked up into alcoholic liquids.

The new wine law of 1971 interprets the meaning of 'fresh grapes' and adds further conditions: 'Wine grapes are considered fresh as long as the juice pressed from them in the traditional manner can start to ferment by itself–without any additions or assistance.' If the must is prepared from *eingeschrumpften* or *edelfaulen* grapes (shrunk or attacked by noble rot) it may be fermented by the addition of cultured yeast.

Wine, then, is the beverage produced by alcoholic fermentation from the juice of fresh grapes which contains at least 55g actual alcohol per litre and in which the carbonic acid pressure at 20°C does not exceed 2·5 atmospheres. Beerenauslesen and Trockenbeerenauslesen, however, need only contain – as an exception to the basic rule – 45g actual alcohol per litre. The fermentation can have been proceeding on grape mash and even after the addition of sugar and grape must concentrate.

The inclusion of these additional definitions for wine show the difference between Stillwein and Perlwein.

Having defined what wine is, before discussing the technicalities further, it will be necessary to understand some of the other terms commonly used in the art of making wine.

Perlwein can be any wine if, when ready to drink, it contains effervescence caused by carbonic acid, and at a temperature of 20°C this carbonic acid pressure is not more than 2·5 atmospheres. (If the pressure is higher, then the wine becomes a sparkling wine.)

Traubenmost is the name for the juice of fresh grapes, so long as it has not become 'wine'.

Ungegorener Traubenmost (unfermented must) is the name when it contains less than 5g alcohol per litre.

Traubenmost-Konzentrat (grape must concentrate) is the dehydrated juice of Traubenmaische or Traubenmost.

Traubenmaische (unfermented grape mash) is a grape mash containing less than 5g alcohol.
Traubensaft (grape juice) is unfermented, unsweetened grape juice which has been prevented from fermenting and is 'conserved' and destined to be drunk unchanged or after mixing with food – this is not subject to the wine law as it cannot become wine.

KINDS OF VINE

Even the most poetical titles are not worth very much. . . . A vineyard name, though it may truly reflect and symbolize an ideal, carries no guarantee that the quality of the wine from that site will always remain the same – vintages in Germany vary far too much from year to year for any such expectation. A good pointer to the quality of a wine is to be found on its label in the designation of *the species of grape* from which it is produced *in conjunction with* that of the place of origin.

German wine growers are aware that they can only justify the immense costs of their vocation and indeed their own right to exist if they produce high-grade wines. The authorities supervise the establishment of any new vineyard and have enacted general rules limiting the kinds of grape that may be planted. Some species of grape may be planted anywhere, others only in certain districts, while others again may only be planted under a special licence from the authorities.

The European wine law has decreed a classification of the vines which are allowed to be planted in the community, and these are divided into 'Recommended Vines', 'Admitted Vines' and 'Temporarily Admitted Vines' (see tables below). In future replacement and new planting must consist of the 'Recommended' and 'Admitted' vines only. The wine produced from vines not in the list cannot be sold as 'Tafelwein' (table wine).

The list of these vines is based on the administrative political units, in most cases the counties (*Regierungsbezirke*), not on viticultural regions. This results from decisions of the E.E.C. Commission and needs some explanation.

Köln (Cologne) refers to the State Rhineland-Westphalia = northern part of Middle Rhine
Trier Mosel, Saar, Ruwer
Koblenz } Lower Mosel
Montabaur } Middle Rhine (includes Lahn valley)
Saarland: 4 villages on the Upper Mosel (see Bereich Obermosel)
Darmstadt: Hessen, Rheingau and Hessische Bergstrasse
Rheinhessen-Pfalz includes the Nahe region.

All other names are the names of the specific regions.

In the following lists we find colours preceding the name of the vines, as *blau* blue, *rot* red and *weiss* white. The 'blue grapes' produce in all cases red wine. Red as part of the name of the grape does not indicate that it produces red wine. As a rule they produce white wine, as in the case of 'rote' Traminer, 'rote' Gutedel, and 'rote' Elbling.

The colour as part of the official name of the grape does not otherwise appear and especially not on labels.

VINES FOR THE PRODUCTION OF WHITE WINES

RIESLING (No. 20 of the official list) When the first edition of *Rhineland Wineland* was reviewed by the press, the *Sunday Times* of 2 September 1951 published a review by H. Warner Allen with the headline: 'Sad news of Hock'. He wrote: '*Rhineland Wineland* administers some rude shocks to the lover of German wines who has been hoping that they will soon return to their pre-war standard. It is clear that phylloxera which 20 years ago was almost unknown on the Moselle and only sporadic on the Rhine, has definitely established itself. Possibly the Rheingau will have to abandon its cultivation of the Riesling grape and adopt other kinds. Surely Mr. Hallgarten might have broken more gently the news of such a disastrous prospect. Is the noblest German vine, the only vine that can bear comparison with the Pinot of Champagne and Burgundy and the Sauvignon and Sémillon of Sauternes, to disappear even from the grafted stock in its own home? For many years the scientists have been trying to breed an improved Riesling without success. To look elsewhere for a Rheingau grape would spell ruin.' The last two decades have, however, shown that Mr. Warner Allen's fears were not justified.

The white Riesling still produces Germany's most distinguished wines with a rich bouquet, and its Trockenbeerenauslesen are the greatest of all German wines.

The Riesling vine is the noblest that anyone in Germany has up till now succeeded in cultivating for the production of white wines. It is distributed over all German wine regions, and on the Middle Mosel, the Saar and the Ruwer it was, until a few years ago, the only type of vine cultivated in the district.

It produces small healthy berries that ripen to a brilliant brown-yellow colour; they grow more slowly and ripen later than other varieties of grape. Once the grape has attained its full, sweet maturity, it develops to highest perfection the delicate elements of its exquisite bouquet – the incomparable aroma, the entrancing taste, which are somehow reminiscent of all the best in other kinds of fruit. Peach,

Recommended Vines

Vines	Cologne County*	Mosel-Saar-Ruwer-County Trier	Koblenz-Montabaur**	Rheinhessen Pfalz
1 Auxerrois	×	×	×	×
2 Faber	×	×	×	×
3 Früher Malingre			×	×
4 Grüner Silvaner			×	×
5 Huxelrebe			×	×
6 Kanzler	×	×	×	×
7 Morio-Muskat	×		×	×
8 Muskateller gelb			×	×
9 Muskateller rot				
10 Muskat-Ottonel			×	×
11 Müller-Thurgau	×	×	×	×
12 Perle	×		×	×
13 Roter Gutedel			×	×
14 Rieslaner	×	×	×	×
15 Ruländer (gr. Burgunder)	×	×	×	×
16 Scheurebe	×	×	×	×
17 Siegerrebe	×	×	×	×
18 Gewürztraminer			×	×
19 Weisser Burgunder	×	×	×	×
20 Weisser Riesling	×	×	×	×
21 Roter Traminer				
22 Roter Elbling	×	×*	×*	
23 Weisser Elbling	×	×*	×*	
24 Veltliner			×	
25 St. Laurent				
26 Freisamer				
27 Weisser Gutedel			×	×
28 Blauer Frühburgunder			×	×
29 Blauer Spätburgunder	×		×	×
30 Blauer Portugieser	×		×	×
31 Heroldrebe				×
32 Helfensteiner				
33 Blauer Limberger				
34 Blauer Trollinger				
35 Müllerrebe (Schwarzriesl.)				
36 Samtrot				

* Mittelrhein (Nordrhein-Westfalen)
** Mittelrhein (Rheinland-Pfalz including Bereich Lahn)

	Saarland	Darmstadt	North Baden	South Baden	North Württem-berg	South-Württem-berg Hohen-zollern	Franken
1	×	×	×	×			×
2	×						×
3							
4		×	×	×	×	×	×
5							
6	×						×
7							×
8				×	×		×
9				×	×		×
10		×	×	×	×		×
11	×	×	×	×	×	×	×
12							×
13				×			×
14							×
15	×	×	×	×	×	×	×
16	×	×	×				×
17	×						×
18			×	×	×	×	
19	×		×	×	×		×
20	×	×	×	×	×		×
21		×	×	×	×	×	×
22	×*						
23	×*						
24							
25			×		×		×
26			×	×			×
27			×	×	×		×
28			×	×	×		×
29		×	×	×	×	×	×
30			×	×	×	×	×
31					×	×	×
32			×		×	×	×
33			×		×	×	
34					×		
35			×	×	×	×	
36			×	×	×	×	

Admitted Vines

Vines / Counties	Cologne	Trier	Koblenz-Montabaur	Rheinhessen-Pfalz
1 Freisamer	×	×	×	×
2 Früherroter Malvasier	×	×	×	×
3 Veltliner (rot und grün)		×		×
4 Weisser Elbling		×	×	×
5 Roter Elbling		×	×	×
6 Grüner Silvaner		×		
7 Huxelrebe		×		
8 Morio-Muskat		×		
9 Muskateller		×		
10 Muskat-Ottonel		×		
11 Perle		×		
12 Roter Gutedel		×		
13 Weisser Gutedel		×		
14 Siegerrebe				
15 Früher Malingre		×		
16 Blauer Trollinger			×	×
17 Blauer Limberger			×	×
18 Helfensteiner			×	×
19 Müllerrebe (Schwarzriesl.)			×	×
20 Samtrot			×	×
21 St. Laurent			×	×
22 Heroldrebe			×	×
23 Blauer Portugieser				
24 Färbertraube			×	×

walnut, pineapple, blackberries, blackcurrants – the Riesling fragrance seems compounded of them all. Pleasantly sweet, not too strong in alcoholic content, stimulating and refreshing through their acidity, the Riesling wines at their best have earned a world-wide reputation.

In good vintages the wine is full of body and character with a distinguished fruity acidity, and even in average vintages the wines are fresh and light, dry and thirst-quenching.

We drink much better wines than our forefathers did, and these include wines made from varieties other then Riesling. I have tasted wines produced from the Scheurebe and from the Rieslaner which have shown the finesse, elegance and the fruitiness of the Riesling grape.

Riesling will stay, however, on the best sites in Germany which will produce ripe Riesling grapes every year and every vintage or at least in eight vintages out of ten; on sites where there is more sunshine than in others and where the vineyards are inclined to the south so that the first rays of sun touch them in the morning and the last in the evening. Of course, where soil and climate are such that there is no place for the Riesling we have to consider which vine will succeed here, perhaps the Müller-Thurgau vine or perhaps one of the new crossings. Observations

	Saarland	Darmstadt	North Baden	South Baden	North-Württemberg	Südw.-Hohenzollern	Franken
1	×						
2	×						
3	×				×		
4	×						
5	×						
6	×						
7	×						
8	×	×					
9	×	×					
10	×						
11	×						
12	×		×		×		
13	×	×					
14		×					
15	×						
16							
17							×
18							×
19							
20							×
21							
22							
23							×
24		×					

are contained in tables which take the following factors into consideration: the altitude of the site above sea level, quality of budding, date when in full blossom, strength of the individual vines, harvesting results in 1965 and 1966, quantity of grapes, acidity, tartaric acid and malic acid.

Unfortunately the name 'Riesling' is misused in many countries. Many wines labelled 'Riesling' are not produced from the real Riesling grape. A Welschriesling is not a Riesling. Furthermore, the Riesling produced in other countries, under different climatic conditions and in different soil, gives wines which are far removed in character from the German Riesling.

TRAMINER (No. 21) and GEWÜRZTRAMINER (No. 18)
This is one of the oldest known white vines of Germany, supposedly grown here for more than 1,500 years. It was named after Tramin, a wine-growing village in South Tyrol. It is a rather late variety. As the blooms are liable to be destroyed by bad weather, the yield is not assured. Nevertheless big estates grow it because the soft mellow wine has a strong rose-vanilla-violet bouquet.

Nowadays the main cultivation areas for the Traminer proper is in

Temporarily admitted vines

Vines	Counties	Cologne	Trier	Koblenz-Monta-baur	Rhein-hessen-Pfalz
1 Bukettriesling			×	×	×
2 Neuburger			×	×	×
3 Räuschling			×	×	×
4 Wannerrebe			×	×	×
5 Früher roter Veltliner					
6 Früher roter Malvasier					
7 Auxerrois					
8 Roter Urban				×	×
9 Schwarzer Urban				×	×
10 Tauberschwarz				×	×
11 Blauer Silvaner					×
12 Färbertraube					
13 Affenthaler					
14 Samtrot					

Baden where it is extensively grown, particularly in the neighbourhood of Durbach, producing good, rich wines. It is now found as well in most other German wine regions.

The Gewürztraminer (spiced or aromatic Traminer), said to have been developed from the Traminer proper and superficially very like it, used to be widely cultivated in Rhinehessia and the Palatinate, contributing greatly to the fame of many districts and many sites. Excellent Gewürztraminer wines were, for example, formerly produced in Deidesheim, Wachenheim, Ruppertsberg and in Gau-Algesheim (near Nierstein and Worms). The famous Zeller Schwarzer Herrgott owes its great reputation to the Gewürztraminer vine. Except for fragmentary remains, all these cultivation centres have disappeared. Those which are still produced are rarities in great demand and deservedly so.

Attempts are now being made to cultivate it again in these and other districts. I have come across it in Guntersblum, in Bingen-Büdesheim (Hessian Domain, Binger Schlarlachberg) and even in Hallgarten in the Rheingau. In these districts, however, the wine is often not marketed as a pure Traminer, but blended with Riesling.

Traminer is rich in alcohol, soft and velvety with a fine aroma, perfumed and flowery and full of character. The Gewürztraminer has a truly magnificent bouquet, which may even become rather too overwhelming, but which makes it eminently suitable for mixing with other wines with less natural bouquet. The result, even with small quantities of the stronger wine, is a delicate aroma; such blends are very popular in Germany. The Gewürztraminer is all the more sought after because it is so sparsely cultivated and therefore comparatively

	Saarland	Darmstadt	North Baden	South Baden	North Württem-berg	Sudw.-Hohen-zollern	Franken
1							
2							×
3							×
4							
5					×		
6					×		×
7				×	×		
8					×		
9					×		
10			×		×		
11					×		×
12							×
13					×		×
14							×

Notes to tables: Adjectives as part of name of vines

blau	blue	rot	red	spät	late
früh	early	schwarz	black	weiss	white
grün	green				

Tables are reproduced here by kind permission of the publishers of *Der Deutsche Weinbau* (1970, p. 1229).

rare. Even in small and average vintages the Traminer is elegant and mellow.

SILVANER (No. 4) (the official spelling, though one sometimes encounters the spelling Sylvaner). The Silvaner is said to have originated in Austria, and in some districts it is known as 'Oesterreicher' (Austrian), but actually its origin cannot be reliably ascertained. It is the main strain used in many German viticultural districts such as Rhinehessia, the Palatinate and Franconia. It is also cultivated in Baden, Württemberg, the Rheingau and on the Middle Rhine. It may be safely assumed that in Germany it is still more widely planted than any other species of vine.

It is also one of the most valuable kinds, as it is very fertile and ripens comparatively easily. It is known to mature on sites and in regions where the Riesling never attains full maturity; in such places it yields fuller and mellower wines. Its light table wines are mild and agreeable; often full-bodied, fine flavoured, and in good years and on good sites the grape produces wines of rich sweetness with exquisite bouquet, including the great Auslese wines of the Palatinate and Franconia. The 1959 Würzburger Stein Silvaner Trockenbeerenauslese (Estate Bottling State Domain) is a giant, still alive and fresh in 1975.

In average and small vintages the wine has a more neutral bouquet, an agreeable and still acceptable roundness and body. In spite of this the Silvaner is less and less used in new plantations and more and more replaced by Müller-Thurgau and other grapes, mostly new crossings.

THE MÜLLER-THURGAU (No. 11) This grape has become popular in many parts of Germany, particularly in Rhinehessia, Franconia, Baden and Württemberg, and lately on the Mosel. Attempts to cultivate it are being made in all German wine-growing districts.

It is known that the Swiss authorities oppose the name Müller-Thurgau. The name for the wine originates from the breeder, Herr Müller who was born in Thurgau, and the Swiss have drawn attention to the German-Swiss agreement about the protection of names of origin. 'Thurgau', i.e. the Canton Thurgau in Switzerland, is a denomination reserved solely for wines produced in that canton, and the Swiss assert that this was the reason that not only in Switzerland, but also in Baden-Württemberg in Germany, the name Thurgau had been used for years. However, the name Müller-Thurgau has never been used as a statement of origin of the grape and everybody has always understood this perfectly well.

Müller-Thurgau is the official name of the grape. It will be explained in a later chapter that no other but the official name of a grape must be used for the denomination and labelling.

For many years it had been assumed that the wine known as 'Müller-Thurgau' was a crossing between Riesling and Silvaner, and actually the whole wine trade adopted this as correct, many wines originating from the Müller-Thurgau grape being sold as 'Riesling × Silvaner'. The denomination 'Riesling-Silvaner' could lead to a misunderstanding that the wine was a blend made from Riesling and Silvaner grapes, or that the wine originated from a grape which had been propagated by the crossing of Riesling and Silvaner.

Based on the examinations and experiments by experts, the vine Müller-Thurgau is not the product of a crossing between Riesling and Silvaner – that is the reason why in all legal decrees and other official statements the wine is called Müller-Thurgau and nothing else. This is also the name which has been entered into the list of admitted vines.

I am sure that this denomination will have to be adopted. Luxembourg has tried to find another way, by naming the Müller-Thurgau grape 'Rivaner'. Unfortunately this, too, can lead to misunderstandings as the former Mainriesling has been accepted by the Baden-Württemberg government as 'Rieslaner'.

The wine produced from the Müller-Thurgau grape is mild, aromatic and pleasant with a slight Muscatel flavour; grown on suitable sites its quality, particularly in a generally poor season, exceeds that of

Silvaner and even of Riesling wines. At auctions in Rhinehessia and on the open market it attains good prices and can be recommended if intended for consumption not more than two years after pressing. It is certainly not a wine that improves in the bottle. But that is not to say that even in this particular field some Müller-Thurgau wines cannot compete with Riesling or Silvaner wines. Possibly their quality will one day surprise the connoisseurs when the vines are older and can infuse a greater strength into the ripening grapes.

Over the last few vintages Müller-Thurgau wines have been produced in the Auslese, Beerenauslese and Trockenbeerenauslese class, but one must remember that a Müller-Thurgau Spätlese has not the staying power of the Riesling. It should be enjoyed when still comparatively young, a Spätlese when three to five, an Auslese when four to seven years old. With less acidity it matures quicker and can be, and usually is, exceptional.

THE RULÄNDER (No. 15) This strain comes from France, and was formerly more widely cultivated in Germany than is the case today. The Ruländer is a genuine Burgundy vine, sometimes called Grey Burgundy (Pinot Gris) and is to be found mainly in Baden (especially at the Kaiserstuhl) and Franconia.

The grape has a recognizable white Burgundy taste – delicate, noble, aromatic. The wine is heavy, strong, round and mellow, with a delicate bouquet; its appeal is to a refined palate and its acid content is usually low.

Owing to modern German vinification methods the Burgundy character is often overshadowed by some remnant sweetness, and therefore I have not found any German Ruländer to my own liking.

I can, however, imagine that these wines, treated in good vintages in white Burgundy fashion could become attractive.

THE RIESLANER (No. 14) This is a crossing of Rhine-Riesling and Franconian Silvaner. It ripens a fortnight before the Riesling grape and produces on good and even average sites a really fine wine with all the characteristics of the original Riesling. Its former name 'Mainriesling' has been discontinued, as it is not a pure Riesling and the name was considered misleading. For the time being the wine is known as the 'Rieslaner'. I personally think it should be baptized 'Breiderrebe' to honour a scientist, Professor Dr. Breider, who has done so much for the improvement of viticulture in Germany and other countries.

This wine is on a par with Riesling, yielding good to best wines on average to good sites. Rieslaner wine shows a fruity bouquet reminiscent of peaches, mirabelles and apricots; it is full-bodied, strong and rich in character. In small vintages it often shows a harsh dryness, in great vintages it gives grand wines, full-bodied. There is a great demand for the small quantity produced at present, for these wines are a great success in Germany, despite the fact – or perhaps because – they are expensive.

THE WÜRZBURGER PERLE (No. 12) (Gewürztraminer × Müller-Thurgau) Franconia suffers from the Continental climate, and frost and cold winters cause enormous damage, especially to vineyards lying in the hollows. Frost protection, which is only partially effective, costs £60–£80 per ha. Professor Dr. Breider's new vine is a frost-resistant variety, 'Perle', that can stand −35°C in winter and −6°C in spring, whereas the Silvaner and Riesling freeze at −2°C. It ripens in late mid-season, with modest requirements as regards climate and soil. Perle is the result of cross-pollinating Gewürztraminer and Müller-Thurgau.

Perle wines must not be confused with Perlwein (Pearlwine) which is a slightly sparkling wine (crackling). Perle wines are still wines, with a fine rose-muscat bouquet, mellow in character, even in small and average vintages.

THE SCHEUREBE (No. 16) The best-known new variety after the Müller-Thurgau is the Saemling 88 (S 88) or Scheurebe, so called after the late Mr. Scheu, who has done an enormous amount of work to improve German viticulture, especially by creating new vines. Scheu himself says about this wine: 'The ordinary Scheurebewein is in some districts strong and not to everybody's liking. The Spätlese and Auslese wines show a more balanced bouquet of a natural fruit cup.'

In small vintages these wines are often used for blends. They are characterized by a strong peach-rose bouquet, sometimes mixed with a taste reminding one of blackcurrants which is not always to their advantage, especially in wines of average and small vintages. Their body, however, is elegant, their flowery bouquet unique. Scheurebewein is a speciality, and even more is the Auslese. The Beeren- or Trockenbeerenauslese are quite unique on the palate and made me a lover of Scheurebe as well as many of my friends. The area growing Scheurebe is small, producing grand wines.

THE MORIO-MUSKAT (No. 7) This cross between Silvaner and Pinot Blanc produces large crops with low sugar content and average acidity. A light wine, full of aroma. The bouquet is so strong that very rarely is the wine sold unblended. It is used to assist in blends with little or no bouquet.

KANZLER (Müller-Thurgau × Silvaner) (No. 6) This produces a small crop with high sugar content and average acidity. Full-bodied, fruity wine.

HUXELREBE (Gutedel × Courtillier musque) (No. 5) This gives a light, fruity, flavoury wine.

FABER (Weissburgunder [Pinot Chardonnais] × Müller-Thurgau) (No. 2) Gives an average crop with high sugar content and average acidity. A full-bodied pleasing flowery wine.

FREISAMER (Silvaner × Ruländer) This grape produces a satisfying crop with average sugar content and high acidity. It makes some light wine and some fuller wine with a very neutral bouquet, pleasing.

KERNER (Trollinger × Riesling [white]) This grape has a high sugar content and average acidity. It is pleasing, full-bodied and fruity.

WEISSER BURGUNDER (No. 19) This grape produces light, mild, neutral wine.

AUXERROIS (No. 1) This gives a pleasing neutral wine.

I should like to remind the reader again that with German vinification the latter two wines are seldom fully fermented (dry), and therefore do not show a 'white Burgundy' character. If fully fermented the wine list will state '*durchgegoren*' or '*Diabetikerwein*' (for diabetics).

SIEGERREBE (Madeleine Angevine × Gewürztraminer) (No. 17) Average size crop, high sugar content, average acidity, fruity with much grape bouquet, seldom left unblended. Some unblended ripe wines make very attractive after-dinner wines.

EHRENFELSER (Riesling × Silvaner) Average crop with high sugar content and average acidity. A racy, strong and fruity wine.

MUSKAT-OTTONEL (No. 10) Produces a small crop; sugar and acidity are average; wines have a pleasing bouquet.

ELBLING (Nos 22, 23) This is the German grape which in the Middle Ages produced the '*huntsche Wein*' which was planted in mixed vineyards. Elbing is a grape which grows on any soil, anywhere, produces light wines without much character and those in quantities. It is also known as Albling, Alben, Grober, Grobriesling, Kleinelbling, Kleinpereich and Kleinberger.

GUTEDEL (Nos. 13, 27) This is a vine known in many countries under many names, such as Chasselas in France, Fendant in Switzerland. It is the predominant vine in the Markgrafschaft in Baden. It was introduced from the Lake of Geneva in about 1780. It is very much dependent upon soil and climate, and produces a very mild wine with agreeable bouquet. It ripens early with low acidity. Gutedel can be white or red, but both produce white wines of identical character.

VINES FOR THE PRODUCTION OF RED WINES

THE FRÜHBURGUNDER (No. 28) This is an early red wine variety which the Germans praise as being velvety and full-bodied, but in my opinion it is only a substitute for real Burgundy. Still, it is worth trying when in Germany.

HELFENSTEINER (Frühburgunder × Limberger) (No. 32) This produces an average crop with high sugar content and average acidity. A pleasing neutral wine.

MÜLLERREBE (No. 35) The crop is average, also sugar and acidity content. A pleasing natural wine.

PORTUGIESER (No. 30) Large crop, low sugar content and acidity. The wine is light in colour and taste, mild and neutral.

BLAUER SPÄTBURGUNDER (Pinot Noir) (No. 29) Average in crop, sugar and acidity. A wine of the Burgundy type when fully fermented, otherwise sweetish, reminiscent of Tarragona.

BLAUER TROLLINGER (No. 34) A large crop, low sugar content and average acidity. Produces a light, neutral racy wine.

HEROLDREBE (Portugieser × Limberger) (No. 22) As Blauer Trollinger.

THE DEVELOPMENT OF VARIOUS VINES IN GERMAN WINE-GROWING REGIONS

The Federal Statistical Office of West Germany keeps detailed records of all plantings of grape varieties. From these it can be seen (table

p. 25) that the area for the production of grapes has increased in 1969–72 from 75,166 ha to 83,379 ha, in other words by 11 per cent. In Baden-Württemberg the area increased by 20 per cent, in Bavaria 19 per cent, Saarland 16 per cent, Rheinland-Pfalz 11 per cent, Hessen 6 per cent and only the smallest of the wine-producing federal states, namely Nordrhein-Westfalen, shows a reduction in wine-producing areas from 26 to 21 ha.

The Silvaner was formerly the predominant grape but it has now been overtaken by the Müller-Thurgau. There is no doubt that, as the table shows, the newer vine finds much favour with the growers. The reason for this has already been stated.

This change, and others shown in the table, have quite obvious causes. Everywhere growers are looking for early-ripening grapes, especially those with a really fine bouquet such as, for instance, the Müller-Thurgau. In 1950 only 6 per cent of the German viticultural area had been planted with it, and today, just over twenty years later, its extent is 26 per cent. Only in the Rheingau is there a reduction in coverage; in all other areas Müller-Thurgau takes first place among all new plantings. Some new crossings have arrived in competition with Müller-Thurgau, such as the Bacchus and Kerner vines, which have an early or at least a medium-early ripening date. Quite important too are the Ruländer, Spätburgunder, Morio-Muskat and Scheurebe.

The vines which have decreased in acreage are the Silvaner and the Portugieser. The underlying motive of the growers is that they want to have some assurance of an average harvest every year, which means 12,000 kg per ha. They want a sugar content which, even in the unfavourable weather conditions of secondary vintages, is that of ripe grapes. They are not so anxious to have Auslese wines every year, but they like to have wines which they can keep natural, in other words, under the new wine law, wines of Kabinett quality (see p. 103).

The next important factor in the selection of the vines is the acidity, because sharp acidity will never find friends. The grower is therefore looking for vines which produce grapes with a good balance between sugar and acidity, which means in a proportion of 10:1.

The list of vines contains quite a number of names which I am sure my readers have never before heard of. These are new varieties. German viticulturists have tried for the last fifty years to find new strains of grapes with characteristics necessary to produce quality wines in this northern climate. Germany needs vines suitable for the soil of each district, which are endangered neither by phylloxera nor by other pests, nor susceptible to damage through cold winters.

Leading these experiments until a short while ago was Professor Dr. Hans Breider of Würzburg. He reported in July 1971 (*Weinberg und Kellar*) about new crossings: those already known such as Ortega, Mariensteiner, Albalonga, and those in an experimental stage such as the Fontanara, Montagna, Osiris, Canfaro Sisi, Muscatona and Augusta/Luise.

In his experiments the product of the first crossing of original grapes is used for a second crossing:

(Riesling × Riesling) × (Madeleine Angevine × Gewürztraminer)
= Ortega
Silvaner × Siegerrebe = Sisi
Silvaner (Mother) × Rieslaner (Father) = Mariensteiner
Rieslaner × Müller-Thurgau = Fontanara
S. 2765 × Müller-Thurgau = Cantaro
Rieslaner × Müller-Thurgau = Montagna

In order to understand the nature and purpose of these experiments one must know how seedlings are cultivated and how the grower proceeds with the cultivation of these new crossings. When the scientist has selected the varieties of grapes he intends to cross, he selects a few good vines of one kind and inseminates them with the pollen of the crossing variety. For this purpose the 'mother' vines are castrated before they have blossomed, to prevent self-insemination. Before blossoming time the individual blooms are opened by lifting off the little lid, and the male parts, the stamens, are removed. The blooms are then wrapped in paper bags to prevent their insemination from outside by other vines. During blossoming time these castrated single blooms are inseminated with the pollen of the variety whose properties are required to link with those of the inseminated variety. Generally the late varieties are used as the mother, because it has been observed that the late varieties yield more and better germinating seedlings than the early varieties. From the resultant grapes the pips are removed in autumn and used for sowing.

It would be erroneous to think that all, or even part of the seedlings produced possess the properties which would make them 'highly noble and early ripening'. The vast majority of the seedlings are thoroughly inferior. This is due to the fact that, after all, one does not know all the hereditary properties of the vine varieties. With all these hybrids there is a tendency to revert to the inferior much more often than to a better variety. Thus, the problem is not quite as easy as one might be led to think. Still, once in a while, a vine turns up that seems worthwhile. That vine is then propagated and planted in vineyard conditions. But again, on examination, most of the seedlings drop out for one reason or another and only a few of them survive the examination as 'promising'. The main purpose of this hybridization is to obtain a variety which has qualities surpassing those of the older varieties.

Great efforts are made to find new crossings with a first-class character. Research goes on for many decades before a decision can be made whether a new crossing is suitable for general planting. Below are some crossings which are at present considered to have a chance (they are generally known by numbers only). Time will show if they will make their way to the vineyards. As is the case with other cultivated plants, the breeding of grape vines will be successful only after a certain number of generations has been observed and selected from. Continuing efforts are being made to secure appropriate crossings for use in every vineyard in Germany. A wide number of new varieties is under trial; we have to wait for the results. Here are some examples:

Albalonga	Rieslaner × Silvaner	B 51-2-1
	Silvaner × Rieslaner	B 51-7-3
	Müller-Th. × Siegerrebe	B 48-21-4
Septimer	Gew.-Tram. × Müller-Th.	AZ 3952
Nobling	Silvaner × Gutedel	Fr 128-40
Optima	(Silva. × Rieslg.) × Müller-Th.	Gf 33-13-113
Findling	Mutation of Müller-Th.	KP 1
Rotberger	Trollinger × Riesling	Gm 3/37
Deckrot	Ruländer × Färbertraube	Fr 71/119/39

It might be of interest to mention here the quantities produced and the proportions of the various kinds of grapes. Out of 80,622 hectares of vineyards, 69,628 hectares planted with white grapes, the balance with red grapes, 3,993,000 hectolitres of wine were produced in 1962 and 10,696,780 in 1973 (for production figures in 1950–70 see Appendix 3).

It is generally assumed that the Riesling grape represents the greatest proportion of the white grapes but this assumption is not correct.

The change in the various vines planted in various areas is shown in the following tables which show the development of the German cultivated viticultural area in hectares and the development of various vines.

Vines (hectares)	1968	1969	1970	1971	1972
Müller-Thurgau	17,571	18,276	19,416	20,930	21,808
Riesling	17,931	18,055	18,292	18,627	18,841
Silvaner	18,161	17,846	17,623	17,223	16,739
Ruländer	2,067	2,218	2,406	2,702	2,929
Morio-Muskat	1,455	1,570	1,825	2,211	2,381
Scheurebe	813	990	1,165	1,392	1,722
Elbling	1,275	1,293	1,288	1,279	1,265
Gutedel	1,162	1,165	1,169	1,189	1,210
Kerner	—	0	60	375	780
Weisser Burgunder	597	615	659	711	748
Gewürztraminer	335	360	384	410	439
Huxelrebe	86	99	166	299	393
Faber	20	47	93	186	342
Roter Traminer	295	294	304	334	331
Bacchus	34	66	103	169	257
Other whites	954	1,024	1,051	1,215	1,494
White vines	*62,756*	*63,918*	*66,004*	*69,252*	*71,679*
Portugieser	5,450	5,321	5,178	4,939	4,738
Blauer Spätburgunder	2,639	2,727	2,770	2,879	2,944
Trollinger	1,771	1,760	1,768	1,812	1,881
Schwarzriesling	473	588	693	765	827
Limberger	401	394	384	399	406
Other reds	441	458	556	525	552
Red vines	*11,175*	*11,248*	*11,349*	*11,319*	*11,348*
Total	*73,934*	*75,166*	*77,353*	*80,571*	*83,027*

BEGINNING OF RIPENING

When approximately 50 per cent of the berries are getting soft, and if they are of the blue or red colour and have taken that colour, that is considered the beginning of the ripening process. According to the average beginning of ripening they have been graded as:

early to middle ripening (September)
medium early to late ripening (to mid-October)
late to very late ripening (mid-October to November)

(Based on *Beschreibende Sortenliste fuer Reben 1971*, Hannover 1971).

Grapes grouped according to skin colour and time of ripening

	green to yellow grape and skin	grey to red	red	early to middle ripening	middle to late ripening	late to very late (xx) ripening
WHITE WINE GRAPES						
Kanzler	×			×		
Huxelrebe	×			×		
Faber	×			×		
Müller-Thurgau	×			×		
Freisamer	×			×		
Kerner	×				×	
Scheurebe	×				×	
White Burgundy	×				×	
White Gutedel	×				×	
Auxerrois	×				×	
Ehrenfelser					×	
Grüner Silvaner	×					×
Rieslaner	×					×
Riesling	×					×
Gelber Muskateller	×					×
Muskat-Ottonel	×					× ×
Elbling	×					×
Ruländer		×			×	
Siegerrebe	×			×		
Traminer			×		×	
Perle			×		×	
Gutedel			×		×	
Elbling			×			× ×
RED WINE GRAPES						
Helfensteiner			×	×		
Müllerrebe			×		×	
St. Laurent			×		×	
Blue Limberger			×			
Blue Portugieser			×		×	
Blue Spätburgunder			×		×	
Blue Trollinger			×			×
Heroldrebe			×			×

COMMENTARY TO THE TABLE
THE RIPENING TIME OF NEW CROSSINGS

One of the most interesting characteristics of the new crossings is the ripening time of the grapes. As the table shows, ripening time spans the period end-August (very early) to end-October (very late). Among the very early ripeners are the Siegerrebe and Ortega, and among the late Optima, Ehrenfelser, Rieslaner and Freisamer. In between these we find all kinds. Even a glance at the table shows that the 'middle to late' group is very important, and this is actually the type Germany is seeking as best suited to her climate.

The ripening time of new crossings

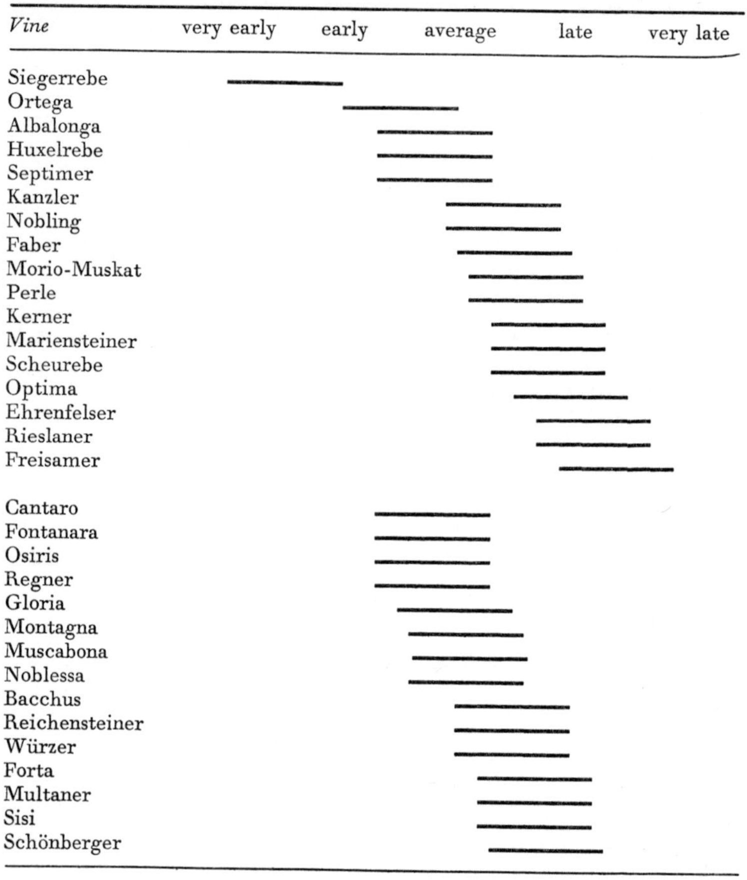

Vine
very early
early
average
late
very late
Siegerrebe
Ortega
Albalonga
Huxelrebe
Septimer
Kanzler
Nobling
Faber
Morio-Muskat
Perle
Kerner
Mariensteiner
Scheurebe
Optima
Ehrenfelser
Rieslaner
Freisamer
Cantaro
Fontanara
Osiris
Regner
Gloria
Montagna
Muscabona
Noblessa
Bacchus
Reichensteiner
Würzer
Forta
Multaner
Sisi
Schönberger

From *Weinberg und Keller* with acknowledgements and thanks to Professor Gärtel.

7

The wine grower's work

The wine grower is devoted to his work. Throughout the year he has to plan ahead, and continue his steady toil. There is no really quiet season for him. In Germany there are many vineyards on steep hills where one cannot use any machines. Work in these vineyards means manual work. In the less steep hills and the vineyards near the plain, machinery is being used and experiments are going on to make the grower's work easier (see Appendix 4). For time and costs of vineyard work see Appendix 5.

In the spring there is digging and setting up of props, and immediately afterwards the old wood must be pruned away. The soil must always be kept loose so that, like the pores in a human skin, it may be penetrated by light, warmth and moisture. This means that it must be dug over again in the summer, to avoid the formation of clumps of grass roots and weeds. And in summer too, superfluous wood must be cut away, fresh wood this time, so that the vines do not dissipate their strength in developing a number of rank, unfruitful branches.

The vine is a child of the south and as such is very susceptible to damage through severe winter cold. In some wine districts spring frosts often destroy all the young shoots. In two nights, 9 and 11 May 1947, a whole year's work was destroyed in many places. The loss due to the frost was computed at 400,000 hectolitres. Hailstorms – fortunately – are usually confined to certain regions, but they cause more harm among vines than among other crops, because they not only destroy whatever grapes may have been on the vines, but also weaken their growth for years to come; not only the new shoots suffer, but also the vine as a whole.

Apart, however, from vagaries of the weather, the wine grower has to be on his guard against pests and against vine diseases. Often he has a hard fight on his hands. Viticulture is no easy matter at its best, and the incessant struggle against difficulties and disasters can bring the grower almost to the point of despair.

Every year the authorities publish a list of officially sanctioned remedies against the pests and diseases that attack vines. To give some idea of the many remedies, I recommend study of the official list of recommended chemicals (*Deutsches Wein-Jahrbuch 1972*) – the list fills nine pages! – with quite a number of proprietary brands to fight diseases. Amongst the recommended chemical substances is one (marketed under the brand name of Lindan) against the winter eggs laid by the phylloxera.

It is evident that the danger from pests and diseases means constant inspection of the vines all the year round, over and above the normal hard work connected with cultivation. Enemies of the vine, such as various species of caterpillar, weevils, beetles, maggots, mites, larvae of various kinds and fungoids such as oidium, are apt to appear at any time and must then be attacked immediately by chemicals. The phylloxera has been dealt with in Chapter 1 (History of German Viticulture).

The fight against the diseases has led to great improvements. The mildew, the oidium, and so many other diseases of the vine have been fought. Even methods to fight frost have been found. There is no means yet against hail and there is still the green rottenness, the early rottening of the grapes in some years with bad weather. There are some virus diseases but these are being studied and one hopes that we are near to finding the means to control all those diseases.

The quality of the wines produced from grafted vines has been the subject of much controversy and expert opinions vary. So far as French wines are concerned, it must be remembered that the famous Champagne and Bordeaux wines have long been products of grafted vines. For the rest, my own experience of other wines is too small for me to give a personal opinion, particularly as I had no acquaintance with them before they were attacked by the phylloxera and cannot therefore judge whether their quality has been affected by the grafting process.

On the other hand, I have nearly sixty years' experience of tasting German wines and have followed their development closely. As regards these, therefore, I feel qualified to form an opinion on the basis of my own unbiased observation. In particular, I have tasted many thousands of wines of the years 1943 to 1973, among them a large number produced from old European vines, as well as many others obtained from grafted stock. I have also carried out specific tests comparing the two kinds with each other, in particular when both have been products of the same vineyard. One quarter of the Schloss Böckelheimer Kupfergrube from the State Domain, for example, is still derived from exclusively European vines.

It has thus been possible to come to certain conclusions. The wines derived from grafted vines are milder than the others, and therefore – having regard to present trends of taste – on the whole more popular both inside and outside Germany. On the other hand, *some* of these wines have entirely lost the characteristics – at least as far as their bouquet goes – of German products, showing that in these cases the

American stock was stronger than the German and decisive for the nature of the wine. Such wines age more rapidly and have a shorter life than those from European vines, which often have an outstanding durability. In the years 1947 to 1949, for instance, I bought old Rhine wines, including 1921 and 1937 Niersteiner Pettenthal Riesling Allerfeinste Goldbeerenauslese, and 1934 and 1937 Rheingau wines, including Rauenthaler Langenstück Riesling Auslese, all of which were outstandingly fresh and fruity, while much younger 'American-based' wines had become undrinkable. I feel quite certain that the American vines are incapable of producing wines with any such expectation of life as those from pure European stock. They must be handled quickly and should, I am convinced, be bottled before they are a year old if they are to have even an average life. Over and over again I have found when visiting growers and co-operatives that their wines which have been stored in casks for less than two years and have certainly received the best care and attention, show signs of ageing while still in the cask. They already have that special flavour peculiar to old, well-seasoned wines that even the lesser European wines do not attain before they have been stored for five or six years.

The above judgement was confirmed again and again when, in preparation of our book *The Great Wines of Germany*, my co-author André Simon and I had tastings of old wines. Some of these tastings are described in the book, to which I must refer the reader. One especially deserves to be mentioned again. In spring 1963, Hermann Schmitt, the proprietor of Franz Karl Schmitt, opened a bottle of 1893 Niersteiner Flaschenhahl Trockenbeerenauslese, a bottle of the best vintage of the nineteenth century of old European Riesling vines. It will live for ever!

To launch *The Great Wines of Germany*, my old firm took the opportunity to invite wine writers and journalists and showed the following wines from our museum:

1946 Niersteiner Auflangen Riesling Spätlese.
Estate Bottled Senfter.
1949 Berncasteler Doctor und Bratenhoefchen Spätlese.
Estate Bottled Lauerburg.
1952 Schloss Eltz Kiedricher Sandgrub Spätlese.
Estate Bottled Graf Eltz.
1953 Rauenthaler Stein Riesling Auslese.
Estate Bottled Winzerverein Rauenthal.
1945 Niersteiner Pettenthal Allerfeinste Goldbeerenauslese.
Estate Bottled Franz Karl Schmitt.
1953 Rauenthaler Langenstueck Beerenauslese.
Estate Bottled J. Wagner.

1937 Kreuznacher Brueckes Riesling Trockenbeerenauslese.
Estate Bottled August Anheuser.
1921 Winzenheimer Berg Riesling Trockenbeerenauslese.
Estate Bottled August Anheuser.

Each one of these – with the exception of the 1937 and 1945 – had never shown so well as they did on this occasion. They were all drunk before their time. The 1946 had just reached its peak; the 1952 was best in 1964; the 1953s are glorious youngsters; the 1945 has assembled a few grey hairs, its golden colour, its noble aristocratic bouquet show what the 1945 vintage might have given us had there been people to collect the grapes in this first vintage after the Second World War. The 1921 – not a youngster any more, just enjoying good middle age – might see the year 2000 in a good and healthy state if stored in the right place at the right temperature. In this range of wines it is the 'giant'.

Great hopes of preventing premature ageing in casks are attached to the new method of storing the wine in hermetically sealed vessels, where the wine is prevented from breathing and actually kept as if bottled. And it must be remembered that vineyards producing wines from American root stock are still relatively young, and it may well be that in a few years their products will be richer.

Another reason for the inferior quality of these wines as compared with those of European stock is likely to be the quantity in which they are produced. In some cases – in the year 1949 – grafted vines produced almost three times as much as the former yield from European vines, and even more in 1950. The Schloss Johannisberg vineyard produces three to five times the average quantity compared with the average quantity before 1925! It is therefore not surprising that the quality cannot compare with wines from the same vineyards of twenty and thirty years ago. I wrote in 1951: 'I am very much of the opinion that the Rheingau, in particular, has not yet found the ideal vine for its viticulture. Its wines from the grafted plants are far more reminiscent of Nahe wines than of Rheingau wines as they used to be.' Vine selection to sort out only the strongest vines for planting, etc. has restored to a large extent former quality especially of the Rheingau Riesling.

With all the destruction that phylloxera has brought about nobody would have thought anybody would ever praise it, but this has been done. Monuments have been erected and this supposed disaster has been praised and commemorated. Ordish in *The Great Wine Blight* shows two monuments erected to the conquest of the phylloxera, one in Germany (Schweigen), one at the viticultural college in Montpellier. But a third memorial can be found in the cellars of Schloss Johannisberg in the shape of a sculptured cask in thankfulness that only because of the incidence of phylloxera and the destruction of the old vineyard did they consider a replant and as a result harvest more than three times the quantity on the same ground from the same number of vines.

The German vineyards are still planted to a large extent with the old European grape. Only half are planted on American roots, but unfortunately this figure is increasing with every new planting.

The greater part of the Palatinate vineyards is of pure European stock, whereas only 14 per cent European stock remains in the Bingen vineyards.

Knowledge of these facts and of individual vineyards in all districts has helped me over the last forty years to find wines in the great vintages which wine lovers who had drunk the famous 1893 and 1921 and 1934 called the 'Best ever tasted'.

As a rule young vineyards yield quantitatively large crops in the first ten years of their existence, but, qualitatively speaking, these are inferior to the products of older vines on the same sites. This is in conformity with the general rule, already stated, that greater quantity means lesser quality. The American vines have brought forth far greater quantities than the growers ever dared to hope (1960 and 1964 producing the largest crops).

These remarks refer only to those vines where the American root has proved to be *stronger* than the European graft. Where the European vine proved to be the stronger partner, I am of the opinion that wines from grafted vines are of similar quality and do not differ much in character from those obtained from the original European vines, though their staying power is smaller.

Incidentally, the grafted vines themselves do not live nearly as long as the pure European plants; while the expectation of life of the former is estimated at twenty-five to thirty years at the most, the others are known to flourish at least twice as long.

A vine may live 100 years or more. Vines over a century old are to be found in the Rheingau today, and the mayor of Rhodt in the Palatinate assured me in November 1949 that his district could still show Traminer vines which are 200 years old and the same vines are still to be seen in 1975! The nature of the soil plays a major part in determining the duration of the vine's life. The average age is said to be fifty years. In Rauenthal and on other sites in the Rheingau, vines a century old still bear grapes of exceptionally high quality.

When the decayed vines have been removed, the land is given over to agriculture for a few years, and then – after about five years – replanted with young vines. For this purpose the soil is completely turned over to a depth of about one metre (3·37 feet); the top humus is thus brought to a low level in order that it may strengthen the development of the delicate roots of the vine cuttings (previously cultivated for two years in a 'vine plantation').

Experiments are being continued, and it is hoped that success will crown the efforts to find 'thoroughbreds' suitable for cultivation and wine production in Germany.

The importance of this for West Germany may incidentally be deduced from the establishment in August 1950 of a Federal Committee for Viticultural Research. The above observations may serve to show that complicated processes are necessary for producing wines. It is a work requiring scientific training which must include a certain amount of geology and of course chemistry. German viticulture and the German wine industry could not have attained their present eminence without scientifically trained wine growers. All German wine regions have their training colleges of viticulture. There is one in Geisenheim (Rheingau), others in Trier and Bernkastel (Mosel), in Neustadt (Palatinate), Weinsberg (Württemberg), Veitshoechheim (Franconia), Oppenheim (Rhinehessia) and Freiburg (Baden).

The purpose of these colleges is to train young people who wish to become wine growers in all subjects relating to viticulture and the treatment of wines. In addition, there are refresher courses for older people – practitioners with some knowledge and experience – in which new methods and discoveries in various fields are explained and discussed.

Then there is the experiment and research branch of viticultural science, which is of inestimable value. New apparatus and new machines must be tested, fertilizers and pest destroyers investigated; there are samples of soil, of wines, of musts to be checked, and so forth. The usefulness of this kind of work was strikingly demonstrated when difficulties were encountered by wine growers with the 1947 vintage.

In the teeth of long experience and despite the application of all the known fining methods, the 1947 vintage remained cloudy, or if it cleared at all, became cloudy again after a short period. When scientists took over, they found that the cloudiness was due to an excess of albumen. The albumen had so thoroughly disintegrated in the wine that it was barely discernible even under the finest microscope. Extremely unstable, the particles of albumen were precipitated as soon as they were disturbed from within or without. The scientific workers soon discovered the right remedy for such persistent cloudiness. It was bentonite, a substance found in a small corner of the state of Wyoming, U.S.A.

The training colleges also act in an advisory capacity to any wine grower with a problem. They tell him what fining media to use, and later test his products to make sure that the fining has been correctly undertaken.

The viticultural colleges own important vineyards which are separate from the State Domain.

Anyone interested in wines could not do better than pay a visit to the training college in Geisenheim, Rheingau, which is a model for all the other institutes. I myself took every possible opportunity of consulting the late Professor Hennig there and am indebted to him for much valuable advice.

In spite of what I said in the previous chapter, the work of the wine grower in Germany, though it has been made easier over the last years, still remains extremely hard. In most of the sites he is still compelled to use manual labour. He uses, of course, machines wherever possible. Expenses have increased, and one of the biggest increases are the wages he has to pay. The vineyard workers can easily get jobs in industry, which are better paid and have shorter hours and lighter work. It is an old story that the grower has to attend to each vine approximately twelve times a year, and in spite of all the innovations and all the help, the amount of work has not been much reduced.

The agricultural college in Geisenheim has worked out that over the period 1962–9 working hours in the vineyard have been reduced by 100 hours per hectare, and it is interesting to note the difference in working hours required in the various wine-growing districts. It varies according to the site of each vineyard, and whether it can be reached easily or whether it is situated on a steep hill. It also varies with the way a vineyard is planted, and the vines trained, whether for instance there is normal width between the lines of vines or if there is a wider space as in most Mosel country vineyards, and whether the vines are trained on wires or on sticks.

Further influencing factors are the size of the estate, the size of the individual vineyards, the distance of the vineyard from the estate, whether the work is mechanized or not, the soil (heavy or light), the weather, and last but not least the age of the workers available and the way their work is organized by the manager.

In Appendix 5 the table shows the working time per hectare expressed in actual hours of work and in percentages in the year 1969, as published by Prof. Dr. H. Karlinke and Ing.grad. S. Willner. They also give the following examples of increases in cost. In Rhinehessia the cost per hectare on flat sites rose from DM 6,700 to DM 7,400, and in the Palatinate from DM 7,000 to DM 8,100 over the one year 1969, whereas expenses on steep hills with vines trained on sticks (Lower Mosel) increased from DM 12,000 to DM 17,000 per hectare.

This I hope, gives some explanation of the high cost of German wines, and especially of the difference in the price of wines from different regions. To produce a fine Mosel wine on steep hills takes three times the man hours needed in the Palatinate.

VINES UNDER FOIL ('FOLIEN-WEINE')

The State Domain at Assmannshausen made tests with foil covering, starting at the beginning of October 1969, on vineyards in Rüdesheim with Riesling grapes, and on an even larger scale in Assmannshausen with red grapes.

Selected parts of the vineyards were covered with foil to form a roof and sheltered at the sides to protect them from rain and cold winds. The aim of the experiment was to increase the sugar content of the musts and through protection from rain prevent further rot, so that the grapes could be gathered later than usual.

An astonishing result was obtained from grapes under foil which were harvested on 12 November 1969 for an Auslese wine. The must reached 200° Oechsle. Unfortunately grapes harvested later reached only 100°, so that the result did not differ from that reached with grapes harvested in the usual way.

Tests were made to find out how much short-wave sunlight can penetrate through foil. One definite conclusion was that the risk involved in leaving grapes in the vineyard in order to produce a Spätlese is greatly lessened when foil is used to protect them.

Further experiments will show whether it might be possible to obtain an earlier start of budding in spring by covering the vineyards with transparent foil and if so the grapes should also start ripening earlier.

Another positive result was that the grapes reserved for Eiswein (ice wine) remained relatively healthy. As soon as frost comes, these particular grapes are exposed to it by removing the foil, and one can therefore *plan* to produce ice wine thus obtaining wine of higher quality and price.

Problems still remain, especially how to fix the foil to the sticks in such a way that high winds and blizzards do not tear or blow it away. Its durability has still to be established.

In any case the tests on foil have proved that it is beneficial, and faults shown initially will be eliminated in due course.

8

The harvest

In feudal times it was the seigneurs who set the date and kept a strict eye on the peasants to see that no one entered the vineyard without special permission, particularly when the grapes were nearly ripe. This was not only to guard against pilfering but also to ensure delivery of a flawless harvest of fruit and grape juice (must), for no berry was allowed to come off the vine before it was fully ripe. Incidentally, even when the grape harvest was in full swing the vineyard might only be entered at specified times, in order to prevent any grower from trespassing on his neighbour's ground and taking his fruit.

The same ancient rules are still in force, though for different reasons. Harvesting dates are set by the commissions which exist in every grape-growing community and are composed of the leading growers. Their main object is to secure the best possible vintage in every respect by choosing the most favourable date. The riper the grapes, the more juicy they are and the richer the wine, not only in sugar content, but also in the complex substances on which its bouquet and flavour depend. Even when the grape gathering has officially started, the growers are not allowed to harvest their fruit when they please. Wine must never be watery, so the commission, concerned to prevent the gathering of grapes which may be wet with dew or raindrops, takes careful meteorological observations and in accordance with these and other conditions orders the daily ringing of local church bells to denote the beginning and ending of picking time. At the sound of the early bell, whole families – men, women and children – stream forth to the vineyards, their vine cutters in their hands. There is work for all and to spare.

The new wine law establishes new regulations with the most severe consequences for those who disobey them. Grapes which have been gathered against the rules are not allowed to be used for the production of grape must and wine.

The basic rule is that grapes can only be harvested after reaching the best state of ripeness or 'near-ripeness' – in order to get the best out of the soil and climate and the fruit of the vine. Strict controls have been laid down in the 'Harvesting Orders' (*Herbstordnung*) of the federal states.

For many years there has been a controversy between leading 'experts' about the question, 'When are grapes really ripe?' After all, this was always the decisive point if late-gathered grapes could be called Spätlese. The governments of the wine-producing cities have introduced a special inspection to find out if the grapes are ripe, fully ripe, noble rotten or whatever stage they have reached. Germany produces various categories of wines – details of which follow in a later chapter. Here it should be mentioned that wine which may be sold as a quality wine with predicate must be produced from grapes in a special state: Spätlese fully ripe but with a possibility of high acidity, Auslese fully ripe without any exception, Beerenauslese noble rotten or over-ripe berries, and Trockenbeerenauslese shrunk noble rotten or over-ripe berries (dehydrated).

The control of quality wine with predicate starts before harvesting of the grapes. If the grower intends to produce such a wine he has to notify the local authorities. If he gathers his grapes without having first given this information, the resulting wine cannot be a predicate wine, whatever the quality. The federal state can decree the same control for quality wines. Nordheim-Westfalen has done so.

A grower who does not follow the general rules laid down in the harvesting decree will not produce a saleable wine, and not even a product which could form the basis for sparkling wine or brandy. He can use it as a family drink or pour it down the drain into the Rhine, Mosel, Saar, Ruwer, Nahe, Main, Lahn, Neckar and their tributaries.

He can do the same with wine originating from vineyards planted without the necessary permission, because wine from such a vineyard is not considered to be wine at all according to the 1971 wine law.

Harvesting is the process which entails the biggest demand on labour. To harvest 1 ha, no fewer than 250 to 350 working hours are necessary, but this figure becomes still higher when the principal picking is preceded by a Vorlese, when only damaged grapes are picked, and succeeded by a Spätlese or Auslese, when the working time can reach 420 hours of working time; and the steeper the hill, the harder and longer the working hours.

In wine-growing districts where there is also some industry – even if only nearby – there is heavy competition for labour, and as viticulture cannot afford high wages it is in most cases the loser.

In *Alsace and its Wine Gardens* (1957) I described a new kind of press which had at this time made its appearance. It works on the principle of an accordion. The press rotates horizontally, the ends slowly moving inwards. The ends of the press are interconnected by several chains, which become interwoven with grape cake on pressing. Whereas with older types the grape cake had to be taken out and cut into smaller pieces for the second and third pressings, the cake is now fractured by the chains, as the press ends are restored to their normal position when the piston is withdrawn. This new process decreases the working time needed by no less than 80 per cent. Experiments and analyses have shown that the tannin content of the must coming from the press is not greater than from any other type, and that there is no danger of oxidization of the must, as it is exposed to the air for such a short time.

This press has since been greatly improved. The result is a press which crushes the grapes as smoothly as human feet used to do before the invention of the first presses. The new version contains a rubber tube inside, along its whole length. When the press has been filled with grape mash and closed, the rubber tube is pumped full of air with an electrical air pump and this presses the grape mash against the inside walls of the press; the resultant must flows through the slits of the press into receptacles. There is no danger of the pips being crushed and bringing more tannin into the must.

The amount of must obtained by pressing 100 kg of grapes varies – according to the kind of grapes, the year and the degree of ripeness of the fruit – from 65 to 80 litres.

The must is then pumped from the receptacles into its appointed vats in the fermentation cellar. Vats in Germany are usually made in two sizes, holding respectively 1,200 and 600 litres (as in Rheingau and Rhinehessia, where the full size is called a '*Stück*' and the half-size '*Halbstück*', or else (as in the Mosel district and the Palatinate) holding respectively 1,000 (220 gallons) and 500 (110 gallons) litres and known as '*Fuder*' and '*Halbfuder*'.

9

From vine to bottle

G. Troost in *The Technology of Wine* sets out the aims and purpose of a good cellar technique:

'The purpose of cellar technique is to obtain must from the berries, with the aim of making wine out of it; to process the wine and to develop it into a stable wine. The natural quality should be maintained or improved, and the varietal character, the vintage, and area should be differentiated. All this should take place, so as to obtain a rational technique, which has to comply with the working requirements of cellars of various types and size and has to synchronize with the needs of the market.'

Rational working conditions can, however, only be relative, because they are automatically governed by location.

Production can only be increased by the use of equipment of a type which will ensure that the needs of the microbiological, chemical and physical characteristics of the wines are fully met.

This has forced many cellar managers to buy new machines and equipment. They had to study their requirements carefully in order to justify the purchase of expensive cellar equipment.

Coopers play a very important and responsible part in the treatment and care of wines. This is especially so in the case of the small wine grower who may be too busy with the rest of his agricultural work to give proper attention to his cellars. In such cases it is the cooper who steps in with advice and help.

It follows that the cooper is not just a man who makes casks – he has to be thoroughly well acquainted with the nature and treatment of the liquid with which his casks are destined to be filled. He is an indispensable link in the chain of those who keep watch over the nurseries and schoolrooms of infant and developing wines.

Having deposited the must in its vats to await fermentation and the rest of its gradual transformation into bottled wine, it is time to consider more closely some particular aspects of wine making.

What, for example, is must (grape juice)? Clearly must is an aqueous solution of various substances, the most important quantitatively being sugar and acids. The average sugar content is from 14 to 22 per cent. A seasonal crop of unripe berries can bring this down to 6 or 7 per cent while a crop of sleepy grapes will yield a sugar content of 35 per cent or more. Selected 1921 vintages showed as much as 52 per cent and those of 1949, 43 per cent.

The sugar content is not uniform, but is composed on the one hand of grape sugar (dextrose, glucose) and on the other of fruit sugar (levulose, fructose). Fully matured grapes contain about equal quantities of the two kinds of sugar; unripe grapes have a preponderance of grape sugar, while over-ripe and sleepy fruit has more fructose.

The more noteworthy acids found in must – some free, others combined with mineral substances such as potassium and calcium – are tartaric acid, malic acid and tannic acid. Tartaric acid, absent in almost all other fruits, is characteristic of the grape. Its quantity increases till the fruit begins to ripen and then remains practically static till full maturity is reached. At first much of this acid is free, but it has an increasing tendency during the ripening process to combine with potassium to form potassium bitartrate (cream of tartar) and also with lesser quantities of various bases.

Malic acid, a very frequent phenomenon in nature, plays the major role among wine acids. It is almost always present in free state, and increases rapidly in quantity up to the moment when the fruit begins to ripen. At that point there is far more malic acid than tartaric acid to be found in the grape. During the ripening process, however, the malic acid content decreases through exhalation, until in a good year it may drop below that of the tartaric acid; even in the ripe grape it does not disappear entirely.

The amount of tannic acid in must depends on the way the mash is treated. In any event, only traces of it are found in the fruit pulp, while the skin, pips and stalks contain respectively 1·5 per cent, 4 per cent and 2·5 per cent. The longer the mash is allowed to stand, therefore, the more tannic acid is present in the must and in the wine itself. Where the mash has been put through the wine presses immediately, the resultant wine (white) is poor in tannic acid, where the mash is allowed to stand and ferment (red wine), there is a high tannic acid content.

Besides sugars and acids, grape juice contains traces of numerous other substances, all of which have their part to play in determining the development and the quality of the wine. Among these are the nitrogenous compounds: albumen, peptones, amides, ammonium salts, nitrates – which provide the ferment with its nitrogen; and the mineral components from which the ferment derives the bases needed for its development, namely potassium, phosphoric acid, calcium.

Of inestimable value to the wine are the substances which give it its bouquet or special aromatic odour. In the must the only recognizable aroma is that of the primitive grape bouquets, the chemical origin of which is still unknown. Their nature is important in setting the style of the wine, and in certain kinds of grapes, such as Muscats, Gewürztraminer and Riesling, the primitive bouquet is particularly strong and characteristic. The original grape aroma increases with the maturing of the fruit.

Finally, the must contains colouring matter. White and red must invariably absorb decomposition particles from the chlorophyll in the grapeskin and stalks, and these latter give hock its yellow look. White wines derived from mash which has been put through the wine presses immediately, are always lighter in colour than those from mash which has been allowed to stand, because in the latter case more of the decomposition matter from the chlorophyll has been absorbed.

EVALUATION OF THE MUST

Eternal change is the play of nature. No year is the same as another, and no vintage is identical to its predecessor or successor. Often when we look at a wine and taste a wine, we see its youth, its full life before us; we can even see its past, can judge from the state of the wine the conditions during vegetation time, its growth and its ripening. If we actually want to understand the different vintages, we must know the conditions of growth of the vine. To produce a good vintage we need thirteen months of the right weather at the right time: frost, snow, rain, sunshine, everything at the right time and also in the right quantity.

All of this is in relation to the cycle of events through which the grape has to go to ripen. As a rule the vine blossoms in June, and the grape grows and ripens in July, August, and September and sometimes late in October and November. Every day from the blossoming to the harvesting of the grape the vine gives to the grape and therefore to the wine the character of the vintage. And from the progress of the vegetation of the year we can already judge to some extent what the wine will be like. There are some rules which show us how to evaluate the young must. I would put the basic rules as follows:

1. If there is a good ratio of dampness to warmth we find round, harmonious wines – wines without any corners and edges.

2. *Wet* years with *normal warmth* produce wines with a good bouquet.

3. If the weather is *too damp*, and if there is *not enough warmth*, the result is wines with quite a good bouquet, but thin and without great body. These vintages produce real thirst-quenchers; very light table wines which will not do any harm to anybody.

4. If there is *too much warmth* and *not enough dampness and rain*,

the wines do not show a good bouquet, as they appear firm and harsh and need a long time in bottle to ripen and mature. Such years are quite good for red wines, but not for white ones.

5. If there is *not enough warmth* and *not enough dampness*, the whole stature of the wine suffers: the wines are little wines.

6. In years with *normal dampness* and *a great deal of warmth* we actually get the *great vintages* – the vintages which are passed down to us in the history of viticulture as the great vintages.

7. Quantity always means a loss of quality. Large production means, therefore, wines with less body, thinner wines (see also under 3).

The chemical analysis of the must can already give us some idea of the wine's future. If the grapes have not reached full ripeness, we know that the wine has to be improved by the addition of sugar. What nature has not given, the cellar master has to add. This is not an idea to be rejected – on the contrary; if it is done well and the treatment is correct, and the fermentation is guided, the product is a very good table wine.

The first factor in the evaluation of young must is the 'Mostgewicht', the specific gravity of the must. It indicates the number of grams by which one litre of must is heavier than one litre of water, the sugar content representing about 25 per cent of this calibration. Thus, with a reading of 100° Oechsle, 100 litres will contain about 25 kg of sugar. The so-called Oechsle weight shows the specific gravity in an abridged form. When we speak of an Oechsle degree of 72, we mean that the specific gravity of the must is 1,072. 118° Oechsle would be 1,118. Oechsle was the name of the inventor, a German physicist.

The degrees of Oechsle also show us the potential alcohol content of the future wine. I say 'potential alcohol', because most wines have some remnant of unfermented sugar (Restsuesse) and there are wines the sugar content of which cannot be fully converted into alcohol, such as the Auslesen, Beerenauslesen and Trockenbeerenauslesen.

The specific gravity of the must is equal to the grams of alcohol per litre. In other words, a must of 76° Oechsle will produce a wine of 76g alcohol per litre. This calculation is not quite exact, because it is only correct in the middle range of the scale; with a higher Oechsle degree the alcohol content will become higher, with lower sugar content the alcohol will be lower, but this is only a very small fraction and of no great significance. For the conversion table of Oechsle degrees into percentage per volume see Appendix 6.

In this connection I would like to mention that in general, when speaking of the alcohol content of a wine in the English-speaking countries, we do not refer to the weight of alcohol per litre, but to the percentage per volume (for calculation see Appendix 7).

Here now are some specifications which are the minimum requirements of a good wine: a correct balance of sugar and acidity combined with fine fruity aroma and bouquet. The ripening of the grapes actually begins at the moment that the grapes start to become soft and change colour. From that moment on, the size of the grape remains approximately the same, though it may swell. During the ripening process the sugar content of the grape increases, whereas the amount of acidity is reduced. In other words, a really ripe grape has a high content of sugar and a low content of acidity. If the sugar content is too low and the grape is unripe, it produces a wine which not only tastes bad, but falls an easy prey to acetobacter and other infections, and it is also unpalatable because alcohol and acidity are found in the wrong proportions and there is a lack of body. Sugar may be added to such musts. Generally speaking, a must of less than 70° Oechsle has to be enriched.

Formerly, Germans used not to take into account the degrees of alcohol of a wine. But now everything is based on this measurement. In Germany the foundation of this calculation is the sugar content, the Oechsle degree of the must, the so-called must-weight.

The question of enrichment by the addition of sugar is an old one, but the fact that the 'concentrated grape must' can be used is new, and furthermore Tafelweine may be partly concentrated in order to give the wine body, though this is only permitted for Tafelweine. According to many experts, the prohibition against using sugar solution is likely in lean years to lead to wines which will not reach the same quality as deacidification.

Moreover, the question of '*suessung*' which means the adding of unfermented grape must of the same origin just before bottling in order to make the wine milder and softer in taste, is not new but it has created enormous problems for the German grower who has to do everything to keep the grape must unfermented and stable, but also this method of improvement will give quite a different product.

Whereas some countries have the problem of too much sugar in their wines so that the question of enrichment never arises, they have, on the other hand, the problem of insufficient acidity in their wines. Therefore in their wine laws the question of addition of citric acid or tannic acid has to be covered, as well as whether this is to be declared on the label or not. German wines, however, have so much acidity as a rule that such treatment is unnecessary and the addition of acid substances is in fact prohibited.

Acidity is a most important and astonishing factor in evaluating a must and its future. The amount of acidity can easily be corrected and is being corrected in good wine-growing countries.

In a hot climate the acidity is so much reduced during the ripening process that the grapes must be gathered before they reach full ripeness. Wines with too low acidity taste dull and are uninspiring; wines with too much acidity taste sour, but what the sophisticated wine drinker wants is a refreshing wine, and to be refreshing it must have a fruity acidity in harmonious proportion to the sugar content, the body, the bouquet and fruit of the wine. It is this factor which gives German wines their special position in the wide range of the world's wines.

The body of the wine is the foundation; sound acidity, bouquet, fruitiness build it up. A wine which lacks the freshness of acidity tells us less and is shortened (it has no 'tail'); without sufficient fruity acidity the wine loses its elegance, its race and its real character.

We must also remember that the acidity content is a major factor in the staying and keeping power of a table wine. Generally speaking wines with too low an acid content do not last long, but, of course, in the final analysis it is the balance of acidity, sugar and alcohol which counts.

Too much acidity never produces a good wine – it means a sour wine – hard, sharp, biting and unpleasant. The grape in its unripe state contains a considerable proportion of malic acidity, say as much as 20 grams per litre. During the ripening this goes down to perhaps 3 to 6 grams per litre in the must. The expert often calls the malic acid 'unripe acidity'. The proportion of malic acidity to tartaric acidity changes all the time during the ripening process, always in favour of the tartaric acid. In the great vintages malic acid is left only in a very minute quantity.

As well as the loss of acidity from the must through the precipitation of tartaric acid, there is a measurable loss through biological degradation. Malolactic fermentation is the result of the action of bacteria upon malic acid, resulting in lactic acid.

The following table shows the total acidity of the must and also the reduction of acidity through fermentation and accompanying bacterial action.

Total acidity of must g/l	*Reduction in per cent of total acidity*
6·0 to 6·9	22
7·0 to 7·9	31
8·0 to 8·9	37
9·0 to 9·9	42
10·0 to 10·9	43
11·0 to 11·9	47
12·0 to 12·9	48
13·0 to 13·9	50

and perhaps more

The acidity in must can be as low as 6 to 10 grams per litre, but in very ripe years must can be poor in acidity – as low as 3 to 4 grams per litre. In a *very* bad vintage with *very* unripe grapes, such as the vintages of 1954 and 1965, it may be as high as 30 grams per litre! The acidity of such musts consists of tartaric acid, 3 to 5 grams; malic acid, up to 20 grams; and a small amount of tannic acid.

To give an example of an outstanding vintage, 1921 is still considered perhaps the best vintage of the century. In that year acidity was down to 3 to 4 grams per litre. But in a year like 1912, when there was frost, the content of acidity in Mosel must went up to 28 grams per litre. In good vintages, German musts, when they are ripe, show acidity of between 8 and 12 grams per litre, in medium vintages between 10 and 14 grams per litre.

Judgement of the future harmony of the wine is a question of intuition and of memory. Though all vintages are different, experience shows how much acidity will be lost during development. Furthermore, the cellar master can assist the wine in its development. As soon as he examines the must he can decide whether the acidity content is too high and should be reduced. This must be done before fermentation if quality is to be maintained. The cellar master can postpone his decision until 16 March following the vintage, and this is the last day on which this procedure is permitted.

The regulation of the European Community recognizes that acidity is an appraisal factor of the quality, as well as a care factor of wine. It lays down that fresh grapes, grape must, grape must in fermentation and new wine still in fermentation may be the subject of partial deacidification in the wine-producing areas of Germany, Luxembourg, and some areas of France. This has to be carried out as a single operation and has to take place before the first racking of the wine. The regulation is that deacidification may be carried out only with neutral potassium tartrate or with calcium carbonate, the latter containing if necessary small quantities of double calcium salt of d-tartaric and l-malic acids.

Incidentally, during fermentation some acids are newly formed but only in very small and unimportant quantities.

One more important factor which we have to look for in the must is the bouquet. The composition of the mixture of different kinds of grapes has a very great bearing on the character of the future wine. Some kinds of grapes, even when fully ripe, do not have much sugar, but have high acidity and little bouquet, and these grapes produce small wines only.

Other kinds, such as Silvaner, Ruländer and Pinot Gris are of importance just on account of their high potential sugar content and can produce quality wines as acidity is not too high. Of course, the bouquet of these grapes is of significance but it is not very pronounced.

The bouquet of the grapes is most apparent in such grapes as the Muscat, the Traminer and Gewürztraminer and in the new grapes which have been developed over the last decades, the Müller-Thurgau and the Scheurebe. But the bouquet constituents only develop with the progressive ripening of the grape. The unripe Riesling, for instance, does not show any bouquet whatsoever, and only the fully ripe Riesling shows us a very good grape bouquet. In any event, if we can find bouquet in the young must we know for certain that the wine will show an even stronger bouquet of the same kind. We must not forget that during fermentation, through the influence of the yeast, new bouquet compounds are formed but the original bouquet of the grape influences the bouquet of the wine.

Summing up we can say, therefore, that even on the first day when we meet the must we can predict the potential of the future wine. We know the analysis so far as acidity and sugar content are concerned, and by our own tasting we can find out how much extract there is in the bouquet, how ripe it is and if some grape bouquet has been developed during the ripening process. We know that if the quantity produced is too high, it will always reduce the quality. Add to this the location of origin, its local climate, the actual weather, the time of blossoming, the time of ripening and harvesting, and we can draw further conclusions by comparing past vintages. Last but not least, the character of the grower plays its part; does he work hard, and does he invest enough and give the vineyard enough, or too much, nourishment (fertilizer)?

Tables which deal with hours of sunshine and amounts of rainfall etc. in various German vineyards are to be found in Appendix 2.

The sampling of old vintages proves again and again that each vintage has its own character, and the student of wines recognizes these characteristics. It does not matter whether it is an ordinary table wine, a Spätlese or an Auslese, the specific character of the vintage shows. Perhaps one might say the higher one goes in the scale of wine, e.g. Beerenauslese, Trockenbeerenauslese, the more difficult it becomes to recognize the vintage.

Each kind of grape has its particular need if it is to grow and to become famous. The Riesling, for instance, needs very fine weather during blossoming time, and especially during the harvest – warm weather with sufficient dampness. There is no better Riesling wine produced than in the valleys of the Mosel or in the Rheingau when the grapes have reached the state of ripeness or even full ripeness. There should be mist in the early morning, sunshine in the morning and afternoon and mist again in the evening. Actually when the Riesling grape has reached this state, the *botrytis* fungus which it needs can only be produced if there is also dampness. This is one of the reasons why in 1959 only very few noble Trockenbeerenauslesen were made – the *botrytis* had no opportunity to act – the weather was fine, fine all the time, and the dampness and the early mist were missing. So one has to watch the weather conditions throughout the year to be able to judge the quality of the newly harvested must. On the other hand, the Burgundy grapes, the red grapes, would be destroyed, or at least their colour would, by an attack of the *botrytis* fungus, and therefore a very late dry summer and dry harvesting time are the best growing conditions for the Pinot Noir grapes.

As I have shown, we can judge from the *must* what the qualities of the *wine* will be when it is three, five, ten or fifteen years old, but, and this is a very important 'but', the must can only develop into fine wine, if it has the necessary '*élévation*', if the cellar master looks after it and guides fermentation, giving it the final treatment and taking each step at the right time, including the bottling. Incidentally, perhaps at the time of birth, before or just after the pressing of the grapes, a very important job has to be done to avoid disappointment: in a year which has produced grapes attacked by *botrytis gris* or even *botrytis noble*, it may become necessary to cleanse the must. If that is forgotten, all other conditions in which the young wine has grown have little or no influence. If the must has a fault, and if the fault is not noticed and treated immediately, it will remain and appear later in the wine. A fault may obliterate all qualities, even the finest characteristics of a great wine, even of a great vintage.

GRAPE CRUSHING

Some growers destalk white and black grapes when they are crushed to reduce the amount of tannin and to prevent residues of sprays of insecticides and dirt from getting into the grape must.

In order to reduce the amount of sludge, turbidity-forming matter, dirt and undesired micro-organisms the white grapes are 'desludged', i.e. cleansed (see Chapter 11). Pure cultured yeast is added to start the fermentation and to ensure a clean – preferably slow – fermentation. The slower and cooler the fermentation, the cleaner and healthier the wine will be.

Many people believed that yeast would transfer the taste and flavour of its origin to the wine; for example if a French champagne yeast were to be used in a German wine, this wine would adopt some champagne characteristics. However, this is not the case. I found this happen only once, in a Steinberger Trockenbeerenauslese which was so difficult to bring to fermentation that as a last resort sherry yeast was used. Nobody was told about this, but at the first public tasting experts considered that the Steinberg Trockenbeerenauslese had a special unusual character. There is no doubt, the sherry yeast had made its impression!

OXIDATION

In order to reduce oxidation to a minimum the must is processed quickly and pumped immediately into fermentation vats.

At all times one endeavours to exclude all possibility of oxidation and to preserve the natural carbonic acid content of the wine. The sulphurous acid content must be checked, and the wine protected against contact with air when racking and filling up.

When grape juice is transformed into wine by fermentation, the most noteworthy chemical change is the transformation of the sugar content into roughly equal quantities of alcohol and carbon dioxide. The alcohol content of any wine is somewhat less than half the sugar content of the must.

Carbonic acid is produced in large quantities during alcoholic fermentation. A cask of 1,200 litres (i.e. one *Stück*) of average quality produces 40,000 litres of carbonic acid. Normal wines contain 0·1 to 0·5 g/l carbonic acid, *spritzig* wines 1 g/l. A wine is called '*spritzig*' when one feels a slight prickle on tongue and palate (slightly effervescent). 1·5 per cent carbonic acid by weight at 15° C equals a pressure of 7·7 atmospheres.

Some, not all German wines undergo a *malolactic fermentation.* This fermentation may take place during or shortly after the primary alcoholic fermentation, or it may be delayed for months or even years, sometimes even after the bottling of the wine. When it occurs the wine may become cloudy and evolution of carbon dioxide may make the wine slightly *spritzig*. Some people enjoy the wine in this state; it can in any case be drunk and under no circumstances should it be thrown away.

Malolactic fermentation is a bacterial fermentation, i.e. decarboxidation of malic acid to lactic acid and carbon dioxide. It occurs naturally in most red wines, less often in white wines. Only a very small percentage of German wines undergo this process. Many growers find it undesirable and will do everything possible to avoid it.

Malolactic fermentation should of course take place while the wine is in cask, but it has been found desirable only for red table wines and not for all white wines. If a wine needs reduction of acidity, the German '*éleveur*' deacidifies the grape must and by the special methods applied produces a wine with a fine fruity acidity and a refreshing taste.

10

Categories of wine

Let us imagine we enter a cellar in which we can find examples of all types and classes of wine which Germany produces. We shall find the following inscriptions on vats and casks of various sizes:

Weisswein
Rotwein
Roseewein
Rotling
Schillerwein
Weissherbst

and beside these names we might find the following remarks:

Kabinett?
Spätlese?
Auslese?
Beerenauslese?
Trockenbeerenauslese?
Eiswein Kabinett?
" Spätlese?
" Auslese?

This list gives the kinds of wine (*Weinarten*) recognized by the new wine law as German wines. The reason for the question marks is explained below.

1. WEISSWEIN (White wine) A wine produced from 100 per cent white grapes.

2. ROTWEIN (Red wine) (a) A wine produced exclusively from red (black) grapes as a red must, or (b) a 100 per cent German red wine to which German Roseewein has been added.

It may sound strange that in alternative (b) the law should emphasize the 100 per cent German origin of the red wine, but in some vintages German red wines need the addition of imported red wine (Deckrotwein) to give them the correct red colour. This addition will be permitted until 1979, eight years after the coming into force of the new wine law.

Red grapes need not necessarily produce red wine only. The colour particles are part of the inside skin of the grape, the flesh and juice are white. If therefore the grapes are pressed immediately, the must is white or only slightly tinged with pink or grey. It is laid down that must made from Portugieser grapes pressed as just described must be sold as rosé wine.

3. ROSEEWEIN (*Rosé* wine) A wine produced from red grapes pressed as white wine.
Weissherbst is a Roseewein produced from one kind of grape only, the name of which has to be stated on the label in the same print and size as the name Weissherbst. Blending with red wine is not permitted. The denomination Weissherbst is permitted for quality wines (see below p. 103) from the Ahr, Rheinhessen, Rheingau and Nahe.

4. ROTLING Rotling might appear to be a new denomination, but it has already been in use in some German districts for white-red blends. It can be produced from mixed plantations of white and red grapes, or by mixing red and white grapes, or red and white mash, but the mixing or blending of white and red wine is prohibited. The grower has to make up his mind early – once the mash stage is passed it is no longer permitted to blend the two kinds.
Schillerwein is a Rotling, permitted in Württemberg only. These are pale red to pink coloured wines produced from the mixture of unfermented mash or from the unfermented mixed juice of white and red wine grapes or from red wine grapes alone.

The grower has marked the casks with a question mark following attributes such as Kabinett or Spätlese. It means that the grape must has fulfilled the first conditions for such an attribute. After the picking of the grapes the grower knows if the wine will reach the necessary requirements for the various classes.

Whether he will finally be permitted to use them depends on the further treatment of the wine. The final decision is made only after a rigorous tasting and retasting of the wine after bottling. If the chemical analysis shows the correct treatment, the wine is submitted to the official examination committee for a certificate of quality and the official examination number.

The conditions are as follows:

German wine may be called Kabinett, Spätlese, Auslese, Beerenauslese, Trockenbeerenauslese and Eiswein only when (a) on application the 'Prädikat' has been attributed to it, (b) an examination number has been allotted to the wine certifying that the quality of the wine is up to this standard, namely the minimum sugar content in Oechsle degrees at harvesting time, as can be seen from the facing table showing the various attributes for different grapes in the different wine-producing German federal states.

The minimum requirements with regard to sugar content of the must for 'Qualitaetsweine mit Praedikat' have been fixed by the various governments of the German federal states, see table on facing page.

The federal states can fix the maximum permitted crop per hectare for the production of quality wine. This has been done so far by two federal states:

Baden-Württemberg
1. for the vines Roter Gutedel, Weisser Gutedel, Heroldrebe, Blauer Limberger, Müller-Thurgau, Blauer Portugieser, Grüner Silvaner and Blauer Trollinger
as 95 hl must per ha
2. for all other vines including new varieties
as 75 hl must per ha
and by
Bavaria (Bayern)
generally 100 hl must per ha.

The lowest potential of alcoholic strength of the predicate wines will be found in the Kabinett, i.e. 70° Oechsle before fermentation; the minimum degrees for all predicate wines are regulated by by-laws of the federal states.

KABINETT The predicate 'Kabinett' will be attributed to a wine provided that:

1. the grapes used in its production are exclusively from recommended vines, harvested in one single *Bereich*. It must have a minimum natural alcohol content as laid down in by-laws by the governments of the wine-producing federal states.
2. the wine as such has not been deacidified; the *must* can be deacidified.
3. the wine is not a Perlwein. It is considered that carbonic acid might disturb the harmony of a predicate wine.
4. no sugar or concentrated must has been added and the wine has not been concentrated.
5. the wine has been made in the wine-producing district, in other words, the *grapes* have not been moved away to another district for pressing. Once the grapes have been pressed, the must can be moved, treated and blended with *Süssreserve* (see p. 125) immediately before bottling without losing the right to a 'Prädikat'.

	Ahr	Hessische Bergstrasse	Mittel-Rhein	Mosel-Saar-Ruwer	Nahe	Rheingau	Rheinhessen	Rheinpfalz	Franken	Württemberg*	Baden*
	1	2	3	4	5	6	7	8	9	10	11
Kabinett											
Riesling	70	73	70	70	70	73	73	73	76	72	72
Müller-Thurgau & Silvaner		80				80	73	73	76	72	72
All others	73		73	73	73		76	76	76	75/78	75/81*
All red grapes including Weissherbst		78				78			80		72/75*
Elbling			70								
Spätlese											
Riesling	76	85	76	76	78	85	85	90	85	85	85
Ruländer Traminer							90	90	90		
Scheurebe Rieslaner										88	
All other White	80		80	80	82		90	90	85	85/88*	85/91*
All Red	85	90				90	90	90	90		85/88*
Auslese											
Riesling	83	95	83	83	85	95	92	92	100	95	98
All other White	88	100	88	88	92	100	95	95	100	95	101
All Red						105	100	100	100		101
Weissherbst		105				105					
Beerenauslese											
All	110	125	110	110	120	125	120	120	125	124	124
Trockenbeerenauslese											
All	150	150	150	150	150	150	150	150	150	150	150

* For full particulars see under the respective headings in Chapter 21.

6. the wine in colour, bouquet and taste is free of all faults. It must be typical of wines of the geographical district and of the grape, if a grape is to be mentioned on the label.

To sum up, Kabinett will cover those wines which can be left unsweetened, and are produced from grapes which are ripe or just ripe, but not fully ripe, for otherwise the grower would ask for a higher predicate certificate.

SPÄTLESE and AUSLESE The new law contains many safeguards against the misuse of the Spätlese classification. First of all the grower has to advise the authorities that he wants to harvest a Spätlese or a higher grade (not the Kabinett). The authorities can immediately start to function, and examine the grapes in the vineyard and the must in the pressing house of the cellar.

A Spätlese wine must not be deacidified as *wine*. If the grower finds that the fully ripe grapes still have too high acidity, he is allowed to deacidify the *must*, i.e. before fermentation, but he cannot do this to the finished product – the fermented wine.

The most important point is that even after all conditions are fulfilled only the result of the actual tasting by the examination committee and the allocation of an examination number decides finally whether the wine is a Spätlese. Colour, bouquet and taste must be faultless and typical of the origin and grape used.

In order to enhance the quality of wine still further, special procedures are habitually applied during the harvesting. A Spätlese is produced from grapes in a *late* harvesting and in a state full of *ripeness*. For an Auslese only fully ripe grapes can be used, when all unripe and diseased grapes have been removed.

There are great differences between the law of 1930 and the new law regarding Spätlese and Auslese. In the old law the wording is nearly identical. The Spätlese was defined as an unsweetened wine harvested *after* the general harvesting time and when fully ripe. In the new law they are harvested *in* a late picking. A late harvesting can fall within the general picking time if the harvest as such starts late. If during the general harvesting time the grapes are fully ripe the conditions for a Spätlese are fulfilled.

From these facts it is apparent that in future, picking dates (for example St. Barbarawein, St. Nikolauswein, Sylvesterwein) cannot be stated on the label any more. The wine is either a Spätlese or it is not. The picking dates were a curiosity, but quite interesting, when for instance the earliest and only real frost occurred on St. Nikolaus Day and ice wine could be produced by those who could afford to risk leaving some grapes ungathered and whose gamble paid off.

Though it is specifically stated in the case of an Auslese that all damaged, diseased and not fully ripe grapes must be removed from the bunch, this is not so for the Spätlese if, as a whole, the bunch appears fully ripe.

One must stress the point that the sugar content is not the only factor necessary to the production of fine wines. A tasting in addition to the chemical analysis must show that the other components of the wine, especially the extract, are there in sufficient quantity, and that acidity is in not too high a concentration, so that all is a picture of harmony and fullness and the wine represents a true Spätlese wine as desired by the consumer.

In the past grapes have been gathered at the end of November, or the beginning of December, or even in the following year (the so-called 'Three Kings' Day wine', i.e. Twelfth Night wine) and one wonders whether these very late-gathered grapes are really better in comparison with grapes 'late gathered' within the harvesting time.

It is well known that in many years bad weather and especially rain wash out the quality of the Spätlese, and the quality of wines gathered very, very late is often far below the quality of the late-gathered grapes harvested earlier. Mr. Walter Hillebrand's article 'Considerations about the time of gathering of the Riesling' (*Weinberg und Keller*, 1969, p. 31) deals with this question and is an important contribution towards the evaluation of wine and vintage.

The harmony of the Oechsle degrees and the acidity and the quality and intensity of the aroma constituents are of great importance. This harmony depends very much upon the choice of the right time for picking the grapes.

One is generally of the opinion that the wine will be better the later the gathering takes place. Generally speaking, wine made from grapes gathered late tastes better, even if there should be no increase in the sugar content of the must, because the aroma will be finer and will present itself more delicately. Furthermore, with wines containing more acidity, such as Riesling and Scheurebe, the unripe acidity will be reduced thereby giving more harmony. In years when the grapes ripen very early, the acidity can fall under the harmonious optimum if the grapes are gathered late. Vintages with such weather conditions are very rare in Germany so far as Riesling is concerned, so that late gathering is usually advantageous.

Spätlese is a specification of quality, also very important from the financial point of view. Many estates try to gather their grapes as late as possible. This presents no difficulties with the early ripening of average vines, but with the late-ripening Riesling, a very late gathering can bring no advantages in many a vintage, but on the contrary can mean a loss as weather conditions are often very unfavourable.

One tries to choose a time for gathering when the proportion of sugar and acidity in the grapes is at its most favourable. The sugar value is regarded more highly than the acidity, and the result is often a reduction in the quantity of the harvest. Losses which one suffers with late gatherings and which one cannot prevent, cannot always be compensated by a better quality. A late gathering can also bring problems from the labour point of view; it is very difficult to find the necessary labour for the grape picking in a damp cold season.

All these reasons force growers today to fix the dates for the gathering far more precisely than, say, thirty to fifty years ago.

Mr. Hillebrand, basing his argument on special data and graphs regarding ripeness and weather, shows from which date on the average, over a period, a very late gathering can present risks. He states that in the period from 1950 to 1966, the sugar content, calculated in Oechsle degrees, increased between 1 and 10 October by an average of 5°, between 11 and 20 October by 3°, and between 21 and 31 October by only 0·5° Oechsle. He comes to the conclusion that after 25 October there can even be an occasional reduction in the sugar content. Even in the very best vintages, such as 1953, 1959 and 1964, he found that there was no increase in the sugar content after the 20 October. His graphs show that ripening progresses very fast during September (during September one can count on very good weather). The length of the days is still sufficient to allow very considerable warming of the soil in good weather.

In an average year acidity is reduced rapidly during September, but in October the further reduction is far less. On the average it is only 6·1 per cent. But this reduction is important, because an acidity of more than 15 per cent is not welcome even with the Riesling. The reduction after 20 October is about 2 per cent and this, being so small, cannot be used as an argument for a very late picking of the grapes.

Hillebrand considers that after 20 October a very decisive increase in the ripening process with the Riesling is impossible, and deduces this from the weather statistics. Rainfall and the number of rainy days increase after 20 October. He finds therefore that on average over thirty years the best conditions for the gathering of grapes obtain between 20 September and 20 October.

BEERENAUSLESE Only berries with noble rot or *at least over-ripe berries* must be used.

TROCKENBEERENAUSLESE Only completely shrunk noble-rotten berries may be used. But should no noble rottenness have started, on account of special characteristics in the vine or because of particular weather conditions, *over-ripeness of the over-ripe grapes will be sufficient.*

In the definition of Beeren- and Trockenbeerenauslese the words in italics are new. This alteration in the law is the result of experience acquired in *dry* vintages such as 1921, 1934 and 1959, when lack of dampness prevented the formation of noble rot.

Eiswein: If a wine has been produced exclusively from grapes which at the time of picking and pressing were frozen, the predicate 'Eiswein' is given in addition to the basic predicate. If, however, the grapes were frozen, but at the tasting the characteristics of a Spätlese or Auslese do not show, the wine is rejected; it could theoretically be a Kabinett wine, but never an Eiswein.

This is quite important – it puts an end to the 'Frost-wines' which have been offered in abundance. If a wine does not fulfil the conditions of a quality wine with predicate it cannot be an ice wine!

The way to improve the quality of German wines has always been to leave the grapes on the vine as long as possible (within the limits indicated above), but the great danger was last-minute destruction by attacks by bees and birds which could lead to great losses. Birds and insects soon find the ripest grapes and vintners who leave grapes ungathered in vineyards suffer.

If the grower has used special care during harvesting it is his aim to make the best and to avoid any treatment which would disqualify and declassify his wines. The group of wines which I have just dealt with are a speciality of Germany. These wines are known as : 'Qualitätsweine mit Prädikat' (quality wines with predicate). The remaining still wines in our imaginary cellar may belong to the other two categories – Tafelwein or Qualitätswein or may not be considered 'wine' at all.

It can happen that the grape does not reach a sugar content of 44°, or 50° in Baden. The must resulting from the pressing of these grapes cannot be used for the production of wine for sale or distribution. It can be used as the 'family drink' (*Haustrunk*) or for the vineyard workers.

The following are the three categories of quality into which all German wines are divided, according to the wine law of 1971:

1. Ordinary table wine: Tafelwein, Deutscher Tafelwein
2. Quality wine: Qualitätswein
3. Quality wine with predicate: Qualitätswein mit Prädikat (which merits high marks).

All wines must fall into one of these three categories.

Whereas in France and other wine-producing countries, quality is, in the first instance, connected with the place of origin, Germany has not used this criterion in her legislation. Quality wines can be produced in any village or district, and no village is legally excluded from this possibility of producing quality wines.

Quality wines, however, must originate from one specific region. A Palatinate quality wine is not allowed to contain any wine from another district. A Rheinhessen quality wine with predicate must originate from one single *Bereich*, and both quality wine and quality wine with predicate must have been produced from 'recommended' grapes (see page 62). The quality wines must be produced (i.e. the grapes must have been pressed and the must and young wine treated) in the wine-producing districts. The governments of the federal states can decree until 31 August 1976 that vinification may take place outside the wine-producing district. After that date grapes must be pressed within the vine-growing districts. The quality wines with predicate have even now to be vinified in the wine-producing district.

They must have a minimum potential alcoholic strength. The minimum alcoholic strength may differ in the various federal states or in the various wine-growing districts, and, of course, it will be different in the various grades of quality, depending upon climate, soil and vine. The overall minimum, however, is 57° Oechsle – of the natural juice before enrichment.

The study of the minimum requirements for quality wines shows that the various federal governments each have a different approach. It very much depends on the kind of vine and how it flourishes in the various districts. The lists shown on facing page will illustrate this point:

In exceptional vintages the minimum degree may be changed. For example in 1972 the wines were generally lighter in alcohol and the permitted minima were reduced by about 4°.

There is something definitely new and more in line with the French law when we see that Germany now permits – in certain circumstances – some 'improved' wines to be sold as quality wines. These are wines which must have been improved by the addition of pure sugar, not sugar solution. However, in special circumstances and in the case of certain districts, the addition of sugar solutions will be permitted, again by by-law, but sweetening by sugar solution must not amount to an increase of more than 10 per cent in volume.

Quality wines with predicate must not contain any added sugar. They must be natural wines, but, as already explained, 'natural' or '*naturrein*' no longer appears on the label.

And last, but not least, quality wines with and without predicate, are subject to examination by the control board and the issue of an examination number, and a number has to be obtained for each separate cask of wine (see page 378).

	natural min. content of alcohol °Alcohol	(°Oechsle)
BADEN		
1. White Riesling	7·5	(60)
2. All white vines not mentioned in 1, 3 and 4	8·4	(66)
3. Auxerrois, white Burgundy, Kerner, all red vines (except blue Spätburgunder for production of red wine), wines not naming vine, new crossings of red vines not yet entered in vine register according to para. 1	8·9	(69)
4. Freisamer, Gewürztraminer, Ruländer, blue Spätburgunder for production of red wine, red Traminer, new crossings of white vines not yet entered in vine register para. 1	9·4	(72)
WÜRTTEMBERG		
1. Blue Limberger, White Riesling, green Silvaner, blue Trollinger	7·0	(57)
2. All vines not mentioned in 1 and 3 and wine without specification of vine	7·5	(60)
3. Ehrenfelser, Kerner, Morio-Muskat, Perle, Rieslaner, Scheurebe, Freisamer, Gewürztraminer, Ruländer, red Traminer, new crossings not yet entered in vine register as per para. 1	8·0	(63)
HESSIA—HESSEN		
1. Rheingau		
a. all white wines	7·5	(60)
b. Spätburgunder	8·8	(68)
c. all other red wines	7·5	(60)
2. Hessische Bergstrasse for all wines	7·5	(60)
RHEINLAND-PFALZ		
1. Riesling cultivated in Ahr, Mittelrhein, Mosel-Saar-Ruwer and Nahe except in Bereich Sued of the Nahe district, also the vine Elbling cultivated in Mosel-Saar-Ruwer district	7·0	(57)
all other vines of these districts	7·5	(60)
2. Riesling, Morio-Muskat and Portugieser of the districts Rheinpfalz, Rheinhessen and in the Bereich Sued of the Nahe district	7·5	(60)
all other vines in these districts	7·8	(62)
3. Deviation from nos. 1 and 2 for the 1971 Portugieser	7·0	(57)
BAVARIA (Bayern)		
Anbaugebiet Franken and Landkreis Lindau all vines	7·5	(60)

An English translation for 'Qualitätswein' and 'Qualitätswein mit Prädikat' which not only the taster but also the general public can understand is:

Qualitätswein = quality wine = quality controlled
Qualitätswein mit Prädikat = quality wine with predicate, i.e. superior quality controlled or special harvesting and quality controlled.

If one really wants to evaluate Germany as a wine-growing country and bears in mind these qualities which can be produced every year, then we must say that the strength of German viticulture does not lie in the top-grade wines, but in the quality wines, the Kabinett and Spätlese wines. The quantities of Auslesen, Beerenauslesen and Trockenbeerenauslesen which have been produced over the last few years are proportionally very small and the costs of production are very high if one considers Auslese wines of other countries.

There is no doubt that Trockenbeerenauslesen of this quality and with this finesse and elegance cannot be produced in any other part of the world. At many tastings I have shown the finest Château Yquem and other Sauternes against German Beeren- and Trockenbeerenauslesen, and witnessed that whilst opinions may vary as to whether Château Yquem can stand up against a Beerenauslese, a Trockenbeerenauslese is unbeatable; it is far above anything Château Yquem can produce.

It is easier to find in the Bordelais or Loire districts wines which can stand comparison with Auslesen and Beerenauslesen as for example the Quarts de Chaume of the Loire. They may be stronger in alcohol, but they are not much less enjoyable than the German similar wines. German grapes and German methods of vinification have made these wines specialities which are very difficult to match.

On account of climatic conditions in Germany it is much more difficult to produce these wines in Germany than anywhere else. These 'showpieces' are evidence of what can be achieved, but we must also admit that nearly 90 per cent of an average vintage consists of Tafelweine, quality wines and wines up to the Spätlese standard.

But there are other reasons why the German wines of this class are better, and the most important of these is the question of rainfall in the wine districts, and this means rainfall at the time of year when the vine needs water to nourish the growing grapes. During the period of vegetation the vine needs nourishment, needs water. In districts round the Mediterranean, rain falls during the winter months, whereas in the German wine districts there is more rainfall during the summer than in winter. (Similar conditions exist in the Champagne, Loire and Alsace districts of France, and also in Austria.) One would be unjust if one did not mention here the high-class Auslese and Beerenauslese wines which Austria produces. The Trockenbeerenauslesen of Austria cannot, however, be compared with those of Germany, but one can compare an Austrian Trockenbeerenauslese with a German Beerenauslese, an Austrian Beerenauslese with a German Auslese. Quality for quality the Austrian wines are cheaper, because they are cheaper to produce in large quantities.

11

Grading and vinification

Even in indifferent vintages the wine drinker wants his favourite wine in perfect condition. Here begins the art of the expert, the French speak of the '*Négociant éleveur*' – I like the expression.

After the cellar master has sorted out the must in the various categories, the grower or merchant uses all information at his disposal and plans the vinification and further treatment accordingly.

He will of course conform strictly to the regulations, bearing in mind that what is not actually allowed is forbidden. His plans, in the first instance, will refer to:

1. Cleansing of the must
2. Deacidification, when not already done – see page 99.
3. Enrichment (*Anreicherung*)

if he has confirmed that in its natural state the must can produce wine at all.

Treatments 1 and 2 are allowed for *all* musts.

Treatment 3 is allowed for Tafelweine and Qualitätsweine only.

CLEANSING OF THE MUST (*Entschleimen*)

The freshly pressed must is allowed to stand for some time. It becomes clear when all solid and flocculent sediments from the flesh of the grapes or attributable to fungi, particles of dirt and other foreign bodies have settled. If the grapes taken off the vines contain many rotten or diseased berries, or if they are very dirty, it is necessary to remove the sludge from the must to enable it to clarify in such a manner as to obtain a final product entirely free from flocculence. 15 to 20 g of potassium pyrosulphite or $7\frac{1}{2}$ to 10 g of liquefied sulphurous acid are added to each 100 litres of must when they are delivered from the wine press. This delays fermentation for several days and the must is left in a cool room to settle. The sulphur also kills all wild ferments which would accelerate fermentation and thereby damage the quality of the future wine.

This method is mainly used by the smaller growers. The estates and co-operatives use the centrifuge for the same purpose. Here the must coming from the press is driven through a centrifuge. The use of the centrifuge has, of course, been known for a long time for the cleansing of milk, beer and other beverages, but it is only in the last few years that its use has become an important factor in vinification.

The centrifuge consists of a metal chamber fitted with cylindrical secondary compartments around its circumference. The chamber is rotated at a speed of 150 revolutions per second. The centrifugal force set up by the rotation drives the particles contained in the must to the wall of the chamber where they remain, the must being collected in the innermost compartment. The must is therefore delivered from the centrifuge free of particles.

ANREICHERUNG – ENRICHMENT – CHAPTALIZATION

for Tafelweine and Qualitätsweine.

Anreicherung or improvement of the wine is the expression used in the new law for what was hitherto known as *Zuckerung*, or *Verbesserung* (sugaring, or improvement).

Let me explain at this point the difference between *Anreicherung*, *Süssung*, *Süssreserve* and *Restsüsse*, as I have found that many people, even wine men, cannot always distinguish between these terms.

Anreicherung (enrichment) increases the alcohol content. Its meaning is actually the same as *Verbesserung* (improvement).

Süssreserve is the liquid which is used for *Süssung*, e.g. a Testwein, Dosagenwein. It is a grape must 'reserved' for adding to the final product.

Süssung means the process of adding *Süssreserve* to wine otherwise ready for bottling. Exactly how this is done will be described later. The time for use is when the wine is ready for bottling, a short time before the bottling date. Only growers and wholesalers are allowed to perform *Süssung*; it is forbidden to retailers.

Restsüsse or *Restzucker* = residual sugar. This is the unfermented sugar in the bottled wine: it may be a residue of unfermented sugar in the original grape must, or arise from the *Süssung* dosage before bottling.

Let us now examine the various treatments of wines which the grower has to consider applying.

Unfavourable climatic conditions in many German wine-growing districts often prevent a (varying) proportion of the grapes from reaching full maturity. In most years, therefore, many German wine growers are unfortunately compelled to take steps to improve a large part of the crop. This consists in adding sugar or sugar solution to the defective juice up to 15 per cent of its quantity for Tafelweine, 10 per cent for Quality wines. The use of sugar solutions is not allowed in Bayern and Baden-Württemberg.

In order to understand the important changes brought about by the new law, let me first state the situation before 1971.

The addition of sugar to German wines was regulated by the wine law of 25 July 1930. Article 3 states that sugar (or sugar dissolved in pure water) may be added to grape must or wines (in the case of red wine, also to grape mash) derived from home-grown grapes, provided that this is done 'for the purpose of supplementing a natural lack of sugar or alcohol, or counteracting a natural excess of acid, to an extent sufficient to produce in the said wine, a composition equal to that of wines derived in a good year from grapes of the same kind and origin without extraneous additions. Such addition may, however, in no case make up more than one-fourth of the whole quantity of the liquid.'

The legality of the proceeding by which a lack of sugar or alcohol or an excess of acids might be cured through the addition of dry sugar or an aqueous sugar solution was dependent on the fact that these defects were 'due to natural causes'. Intentional unnecessary premature grape-gathering debarred the use of any such improvement measures. In Germany the law limited the amount of extraneous sugar (or sugar solution) to a quantity which made the composition of the improved product equal in alcohol and acid content to that of wines derived in a good year from grapes of the same kind from the same site without extraneous addition.

In the case of sugar solution, a further limit was imposed, that in no case – however high the acid content of the original produce – might more than one-quarter of the total liquid be made up of added sugar solution; in other words not more than one-third of the quantity of the defective must or wine could be added. The highest permissible ratio of sugar solution to wine (or must) was thus 250 litres of the former to 750 litres of the original liquid.

In order to simplify the calculations attendant on the sweetening process, the various grape-growing districts in the Rhineland had been divided into three categories, each with its own sweetening maximum.

Until 1958, this maximum was fixed according to the Oechsle standard. The addition of sugar solution was permitted up to a maximum content of 95° Oechsle for category 1. For category 2 the limit was 92°, and for category 3, 85°. Poorer vineyards in these districts were restricted to a limit still lower than that of their category, while particularly good sites in categories 2 and 3 might exceed by a small margin the limits of their respective categories.

Since 1958, the maximum sugar content has been expressed in grams of alcohol per litre, and it is a well-known fact that, particularly in good vintages, 95° Oechsle in the must produces approximately 97, or even a little more, grams of alcohol per litre. Generally speaking, one can therefore assume that sweetened wines had the same composition as before. There is no need to emphasize that the calculation of the potential alcohol content cannot always be correct. After all, fermentation is a biological process which cannot be precisely estimated or forecast, as the yeast – a micro-organism – cannot be dictated to by the grower; and for this reason the law courts have generally allowed an additional 5 grams, even when this was not expressed by statute.

In 1958 the German Government published a by-law to the wine law and this, up to a point, contained a classification of German vineyards – a classification which had been overdue for some years. This law was based on many years of observation, and one can therefore say that it contained a useful classification of German vineyards at least where the classification was a purely geographical one.

For some districts it laid down the classification according to the kind of grape, in other cases it was based on geographical origin. Sometimes whole districts were sub-divided into three classes – as in the case of Franconia, Rhinehessia and the Palatinate – in other districts individual villages were sub-divided into three classes – as in the Rheingau and Bergstrasse.

Where the classification was not based on the geographical situation of the vineyard, but on the grape, namely, for Baden, Württemberg, Lake Constance, Mosel, Saar, Ruwer, Ahr and Middle Rhine, the Riesling grape was invariably considered to produce the best wines.

1. Wines made from the Riesling grape formed the first class, and all other wines made from non-Riesling grapes, the second class.

2. For Baden, Württemberg and Lake Constance, all grapes were considered first class with the exception of Müller-Thurgau, Gutedel (second class) and Elbling and Raeuschling (third class).

This did not apply to white wines from Franconia, Palatinate, Rhinehessia, Nahe, Rheingau and Bergstrasse. In the first four districts, all grapes were considered equal for each village. In the latter two districts the Lage was the decisive factor. *Each* Rheingau village was divided into *three* classes.

The 'grape principle' applied also to red wines: those made of Burgundy and Limberger grapes were supposed to attain 105 g, and all other grapes with the exception of the Portugieser grapes, 100 g, and the Portugieser grape, 95 g, of alcohol in a good vintage.

While it was illegal to re-sugar a must or wine which had already been treated, pure wines of previous vintages could be 'improved' in the period between 1 October and 31 January. After 31 January sugaring was forbidden, but a special extension to 31 March was possible and was actually granted in some bad vintages.

Other regulations laid down in the wine law of 1930 aimed at simplifying control. Thus, sweetening might only be carried out within the German wine regions, and the authorities had to be notified of the proposed sugaring of all grape mash, must or wine. In the case of natural wines, such notification must be given at least eight days in advance, while a single 'block' notification was sufficient to cover the whole produce of a new crop. The sugar used had to be pure and free from colouring matter; subject to this condition it might be the product of cane, beet, starch, or a mixture of fruit sugar and grape sugar ('invert' sugar) such as is often used for the purpose. As already stated, no wines could be put on the market as wines if there had been any contravention of the law in their treatment. Such wines were also liable to confiscation.

THE 'NEW' SITUATION

The first big change brought about by the new wine law is that there has been a departure from the idea of allowing enrichment up to the quality of a good (not an excellent) vintage for the same site and the same kind of grape.

The new law brings in regulations about quantitative enrichment and qualitative enrichment and both rules are absolute:

1. Quantitative enrichment: the quantity of sugar allowed must not increase the alcoholic strength for white wine by more than 30g and for red wine by more than 35g per litre.

1972 produced grapes with a special high acidity and low sugar content. The European wine laws had provided for such vintages permitting a higher degree of enrichment. The degree of enrichment has been increased by 1° alcohol = 8g sugar, i.e.

Zone A White wine by 4·5° = 36g alcohol per 100 litres
Zone B White wine by 3·5° = 28g alcohol per 100 litres
Portugieser red wines by 5° = 40g alcohol per 100 litres

2. Qualitative Limit: white wine 95g, red wine 106g.

In other words, a wine containing 65g alcohol can be enriched by sugar increasing the alcohol by 30g, if it contains 75g alcohol by 20g of alcohol, if 85g, by 10g. And theoretically, though no grower in his senses would do so, 90g by 5g of alcohol.

Should the wine in a very inferior vintage have less than 58g of alcohol, it may still be enriched so that the final product contains 88g of alcohol; it is theoretically possible that in a bad vintage the 'added' alcohol would be equal to the naturally produced alcohol.

There is one more important point to remember: the sugar to be used for improving must be technically clean, non-coloured Saccharose or Dextrose of the same quality, and must contain at least 99·5 per cent fermentable sugar. Sugar containing starch is no longer permitted; this was the sugar usually used by growers to give their wine more extract (body) and make it taste rounder and more natural. This was jokingly known as 'sweetened *Naturwein*' (*gezuckerter Naturwein*).

Here again we have one of those laws which are difficult to understand. In all industries one makes great efforts to get the best out of the raw material available – not so in the wine industry. Instead one prohibits the use of a sugar containing starch, which is not harmful in any way; on the contrary, it produces a better wine. The reason behind this is supposed to be the protection of the consumer, who on account of the effect of the *Stärkezucker* might assume the wine to be an originally better product (*Ausgangsstoff*) and be asked to pay too much.

Incidentally the use of syrup is not permitted. The sugar must be dissolved in the grower's or merchant's cellar; he must not buy dissolved sugar, as this could also contain other ingredients not allowed as *Zusatzstoff* (additive), though sugar solution is permitted for a limited period.

A new method of enrichment is the use of *Traubensaftkonzentrat* (grape must concentrate). This can in future be used for the enrichment of Tafel wines, i.e. it cannot be used for quality wines of defined regions. The concentrate can be used for the increase of the alcohol content or for the enrichment or sweetening of the wine.

However, the final product, the Tafelwein, must not be increased by more than 11 per cent in Zone A and 8 per cent in Zone B.

The total alcohol content of a Tafelwein must not be more than 11·5 per cent in Zone A, 12 per cent in Zone B.

The residual unfermented sugar is, generally speaking, not allowed to be more than one-third in weight of the actual alcohol.

Finally, it should be mentioned that the enrichment of old wine will no longer be permitted. In the past the grower could always postpone the enrichment and try to sell his natural wine. If this proved to be unsaleable he could, from September onwards following the new vintage, enrich the one-year-old wine. Now, he has to decide, before 1 April, if he wants to enrich the wine. If he does not do so, he might have to use his wine for the production of sparkling wine or Branntwein (brandy). Of course he could always use it for blending with a younger vintage, especially if this has perhaps too little acidity and the natural older vintage is too acid.

Another, and for Germany quite new, way of enrichment is part concentration of the grape must or the wine. We know the value of concentration. Ice wine is made by natural refrigeration in the vineyard, enrichment by artificial part concentration in the pressing house or cellar.

This method can also be used for the finished article to reduce the water content, and by concentration increase all other components proportionally.

Incidentally concentration can also be effected by heat: a part of the water is evaporated under vacuum conditions. These procedures are of course not new. They have been used for many years in the U.S.A., Italy, France and other countries, where concentrated grape juice has been added to improve grape musts and also for the manufacture of liqueurs.

If concentration is chosen as the best way of enrichment, the volume must not be decreased by more than 20 per cent. Enrichment and *süssung* have to be reported to the local office forty-eight hours before work starts. If forbidden procedures are applied, sale of the wine is a punishable offence.

The minimum alcohol content of a Tafelwein at the time of sale is 67 g/l = 8·5 per cent alcohol by volume. The basic grape must has a minimum sugar content of over 44° Oechsle (see Appendix 8).

In a normal vintage it can be enriched by 28 g/l alcohol and in exceptionally wet and bad vintages by 36 g/l alcohol. The enrichment must not bring the final product to more than 92 g/l alcohol.

The cellar master has to observe the development of the wine in all its stages. He is aware that some treatments are absolutely necessary and he must use them at the right time. Others may become necessary. A wine may get 'sick'; it may develop faults or hidden faults may show. A faulty wine is unsaleable. The consumer must be protected.

The cellar master must in any treatment procedures consider the protection of the quality of the wine and the protection of the health of the consumer. He therefore makes sure that the means he uses are actually permissible, and he must therefore ensure control of all procedures. Only treatments and additives which have been expressly included in the regulations are permitted, and all others are strictly forbidden. Treatments which are forbidden now, but were previously allowed, include the use of agar-agar, aferrin, albumen, Spanish earth and oxygen.

Sulphur in various forms, such as sulphur dioxide in solution (sulphurous acid) has been used since time immemorial in all wine-producing countries to prevent oxidation in all fruit juices as well as grape must and wine. The use of sulphur dioxide is strictly controlled in all wine-producing countries and to the present day there is no substitute for it. Its use is necessitated by the requirements of good cellarage; it is needed to keep the wines sound and to prevent the formation of organisms which might cause decomposition. The necessary quantity depends upon the type of wine but it is essential for the quality of the wine that a maximum be set for the use of sulphur.

The regulation regarding sulphurization is based on the opinions of chemists who had to consider whether the ingestion of certain quantities of sulphur might influence bodily well-being quite apart from wine tasters, who detest an excess. Whereas formerly the highest possible sulphur content had always been allowed, now it is reduced to the minimum sufficient for the technically correct nurturing of the wine.

The E.E.C. law lays down the various quantities of sulphurous acid allowed for different qualities.

At the time when the wine is ready for immediate consumption and is intended for distribution the content of sulphurous acid must at present not exceed the following quantities per litre (the figures in brackets give the maximum total content of sulphurous acid *after* 1 September 1976).

1. Beerenauslesen and Trockenbeerenauslesen: 75 mg and 400 mg total (400).
2. Auslesen, Eiswein and other wines with alcoholic strength of more than 110 mg total alcohol – 60 mg free and 350 mg total.
3. *White wines:* 300 mg per litre if the wine contains residual sugar of 5 g per litre or more, and 250 mg per litre, if it contains less than 5 g per litre.

Red wines: 200 mg per litre.

At first sight these quantities appear higher than hitherto allowed, but this is not so. Some people are of the opinion that it means a reduction in the quantity of sulphur allowed. The reason given is that a different procedure for the analysis has been established. In future the amount of sulphur has to be found by distillation only; in the past, it was by titration. The process of distillation gives an exact figure for the analysis and I have been told that the difference in the method of titration and distillation amounts to the difference between the amounts of sulphur allowed in the old and the new laws.

It must again be noted that certain materials are permitted for use and no others. Some have been used for centuries, such as isinglass, gelatine, albumen, sulphur and charcoal. Others are new and, after experimentation and investigation, have been admitted for the treatment of wine.

Before I enumerate the various permitted treatments, and to avoid creating a wrong impression – especially with inexperienced readers who might find them alarming – I would like to emphasize certain aspects.

Treatment of wine is only necessary if it does not develop as expected. Just as a human being falls ill and requires treatment to recover, so it is with wine. Some wines will not require any treatment at all from vine to glass, others will need one or the other of these 'medicines', but of course by no means all these substances are used in every wine. In the main they are only exceptionally required for a particular process of treatment. Most wines will normally never come into contact with any of them. All have their justification and are completely harmless in every way. As a rule they are eliminated from the wine in conjunction with turbid substances or faulty taste substances or the natural components of the development of the wine.

The following, besides sulphur, are permitted:

Carbonic Acid is the by-product of every fermentation, and when wines are cellared cool, often a slight residual trace of carbon dioxide is found in the wine (*spritz*). The addition of carbon dioxide to a wine before or at bottling very often refreshes it, and will help it retain its youth in bottle.

Ascorbic Acid is chemically pure vitamin C, sometimes used to refresh tired wine before bottling.

Gelatine is used sometimes to precipitate cloudiness in wines, particularly impurities which cannot be removed by filtration.

Tannic Acid is present in all types of wines in varying amounts from stalks and pips and also from wooden casks. Tannin is a particularly important ingredient of a fine red wine. Tannin can be used to precipitate certain partially soluble unwanted materials in wine as part of the clarification process before bottling.

Silicic Acid is another pure compound which is used to precipitate unwanted materials from wine.

Bentonite sand is a specially pure soil which is also used to precipitate unwanted materials from wine, mainly proteins whose presence gives the wine an unpleasant cloudiness.

Potassium Ferrocyanide. All grape musts contain traces of metal especially iron and frequently a certain amount of copper from brass taps, etc. In order to avoid later turbidity it is important to remove the metals from the wine and they are conveniently precipitated by using potassium ferrocyanide which forms an insoluble blue precipitate so that treatment is often called 'blue fining'. Most German wines require this treatment.

Filtering Aids. Asbestos, diatomaceous earth and cellulose are used for filtering wine which is a mechanical removal of all turbid substances. The process used is very similar to the normal filtering of coffee grounds at home.

Active Carbon. If a wine takes on unpleasant tastes or smells, active carbon may be used to absorb them. The power of active carbon is such, however, that many good flavours are also absorbed and the treatment certainly reduces the quality of the wine and can bleach it to the colour of water.

Polyvinyl Polypyorolidone. This has been used for many years in the manufacture of pharmaceuticals and also in brewing and is used for the treatment of red wines which have a very high tannin content. The product is insoluble and precipitates with the excess tannin.

Silver Chloride. If unpleasant sulphur products (mercaptans and hydrogen sulphide) are formed in wines, the addition of silver chloride eliminates them by precipitations.

Nitrogen which is a main gaseous component of air is chemically absolutely neutral and is frequently used in filling storage containers to avoid the presence of oxygen which can affect the wine.

Metatartaric Acid. This is sometimes used to stabilize wines by ensuring that the essential tartaric acid remains in solution.

For treatment by the addition of any material the principle is: everything which is not specifically allowed is prohibited. For procedures it is the other way round: procedures by which no material is added to the wine are allowed, if they are not *expressis verbis* prohibited by law. Ion exchangers and the use of ultraviolet rays are, generally speaking, prohibited by law.

Ion exchangers work by selectively exchanging matter in wine with that of the resin. In this way they can reduce acidity or remove tartrates or metals and other impurities. To go further into the actual theory behind the process is beyond the scope of a book on wine.

There are different resins, however, which are used in the ion exchange columns and science has not yet spoken the last word. In the wine law, it is specifically laid down that 'ion exchangers, ultraviolet rays and ionizing rays may be used only when the law permits it'. A by-law may give such authority (due consideration having been given in the first instance to the protection of the wine drinker) for the following purposes:

1. rectification of mistakes
2. amelioration of quality
3. to allow proper ageing and transport, and
4. for certain diet purposes

which covers a very great deal.

'Processes in the preparation of wine' are all those processes by which neither the material nor the wine itself is influenced in composition or appearance, and by which no other material is added.

If we heat a wine, use refrigeration or ultrasonic waves we do not add anything to the wine, but we know that the wine is changed in some way. Pasteur introduced pasteurization, but since that time heat has come to be used in a quite different way. We might kill the yeast by bringing the wine to a temperature of 65°C; we might use heat to induce fermentation; we might use heat instead of bentonite to free the wine from albumen.

Refrigeration, known as 'ultra cooling', has been used – especially in wines for ordinary consumption – to free wines from tartaric acid by precipitating tartaric acid crystals. We know that refrigeration has also been used for the concentration of must, as has heat. Many British wines are made from concentrated must, and concentration of must for Tafelwein is a way of enriching it.

12

Further treatment of the wines

Fermentation is a gradual process. By the time it ceases the sugar has been broken down and the expiring yeast precipitated to the bottom of the vessel. Now the young wine can be separated from this sediment and can be racked off, i.e. drained off into another cask.

RACKING

Racking is a very important treatment, the process of drawing off the clear wine from the lees, the deposits consisting of micro-organisms and unstable substances which have formed during fermentation and which have fallen to the bottom of the fermentation vat. German wines have seldom more than two rackings. The first racking takes place at the end of fermentation, the second between one and three months later.

As soon as the wine has settled after the first racking, it is examined analytically and organoleptically to find out what other treatments are necessary to make it ready for bottling. Whenever possible, all necessary treatments are combined. Racking is usually combined with sulphurization, which is always necessary to keep the vat into which the wine is being racked, free of germs.

The racking of the deposits as a result of fining takes place two to three weeks after the treatment, in many cases combined with a light filtration. In most rackings all possible steps are taken to keep air away from the wine. Any contact with air may lead to an earlier oxidation and ageing.

BLENDING

Blending is the mixing of wine and must originating from:

1. different countries
   different viticultural zones, regions or districts, villages, sites
2. from different grape varieties
3. from different vintages
4. from different categories of quality.

In the Rheingau, the principal wine-growing centres of Rhinehessia, the Palatinate and the central Mosel region, most growers keep the wines produced by each vineyard separated from each other. Some of them even go so far as to keep in different casks the wine made from grapes gathered on different days. Thus the individuality of the wines is meticulously preserved.

It is, however, obvious that the quality of the grape harvest varies from year to year, even in one locality. Nevertheless, once the wine-drinking public has become accustomed to a wine with particular qualities, it is apt to expect the wine merchant to continue delivering the same wine. Sometimes the blending of various wines may achieve the desired result, and this has been found to be the best way of meeting the wishes of consumers. Accordingly the law permits the blending of wines of different origins.

Speaking in general terms, it is always possible to blend wines from all over the world from all countries and districts to make one product. I can imagine that with careful planning one could get an acceptable drink. But wine-producing countries have restricted this liberty for various reasons, to protect their own wine growers and also the consumer. In Germany it is generally prohibited to blend red and white wines, exceptions to the rule being that red and white Tafelweine can be blended, if the end product still has the characteristics of red Tafelwein; and Rotling, which is a blend of white and red wine.

Permission to blend *rosé* and red wine is the result of conditions in the German vineyards. In a damp year red grapes may start to rot, and even when they are gathered and quickly pressed, the must does not show a red colour. It is a Roseewein in its natural state, and this wine may be blended with red wine to make red wine.

There is an exception to this exception: Roseewein from Portugieser grapes may be blended with Roseewein only; to blend Portugieser Roseewein with red wine is prohibited.

As can be seen, blending serves various purposes. It is one of the ways of improving the quality of little wines which, by the addition of fuller wines, can be made into harmonious end products with good flavour and bouquet. A wine with a too high acidity content mixed with a low acidity wine can – without high expenditure – be converted into an acceptable quality wine, whereas either wine on its own would have been a second-rate product.

The same purpose is behind the blending of wines which are too rich in alcohol, produced in great vintages, with wines of secondary vintage, as was done to some extent by the blending of 1959 wines with either 1958 or 1960 wines. Blending by the expert is often the best way to produce a harmonious product, and is particularly useful in the case of type wines or branded wines. To a smaller extent blending becomes necessary when filling up casks and other containers to make good the natural loss by evaporation, or by racking, filtration, etc.

Blending is a very difficult and intricate part of cellar work, an art that requires many years' experience and a first-class sense of smell and taste. It is undertaken in order to make possible the delivery of wines of consistent quality; it is also a method by which prices may be regulated and inequalities adjusted.

Unfortunately blending has often been misused to enlarge the output of a small vineyard or the quantity of a wine in great demand. The blending of Bernkasteler Doktor and Graben comes to my mind. The small Doktor vineyard of 1·32 ha could not satisfy the demand from Texas, and now the Doctor has been enlarged, incorporating the Bernkasteler Graben vineyard and bringing the new Doctor vineyard to just over 5 ha, with the possibility of a 25 per cent blend from the Bereich Bernkastel!

SÜSSUNG – SÜSSRESERVE – RESTSÜSSE

When the wine is ready for bottling, the proprietor, be he grower or wine merchant, has to make a most important unalterable decision: can the wine be bottled as it is, or does it require some *Süssung* (sweetening).

It is actually a longstanding practice to cater for the taste of some consumers by maintaining certain wines as far as possible at a consistent level of sweetness. The technique of cellar work has now reached a point where this is possible.

To add to completely fermented wine small percentages of sterilized sweet must, or partly fermented wine, sufficient to attain the desired standard of sweetness, has been permitted for more than four decades, and is called 'dosage'. Under no circumstances, however, was the residual sugar of the resultant blend to contain more sugar in weight than 33⅓ per cent in relation to the alcohol. Each wine contains approximately 1 g unfermentable sugar (Arabinose) which could be taken into account.

Now the Süssreserve may consist of unsweetened or of sweetened grape must, if the actual alcohol content of the latter is at least 15 g per litre. A small part of the must is fermented in hermetically sealed vats, a great proportion of the grape sugar being left unfermented. This partly fermented wine is kept in reserve (*Süssreserve*) and added, before bottling, to the fully fermented wine of the same vineyards and vintage, to meet the consumers' tastes. Only by this method has it been possible to keep some wines of the 1957, 1958, 1960, 1961, 1963, 1967 and 1968 vintages natural and unsweetened.

70	g/l	alcohol	may	have	23·5	g	unfermented	sugar
72	,,	,,	,,	,,	25	,,	,,	,,
76	,,	,,	,,	,,	26	,,	,,	,,
80	,,	,,	,,	,,	27	,,	,,	,,
84	,,	,,	,,	,,	29	,,	,,	,,
88	,,	,,	,,	,,	30	,,	,,	,,

The new law has generally speaking adopted the regulations which were formerly in force but those restrictions regarding a residual of unfermented sugar do not apply to the quality wines with predicate, i.e. Kabinett, Spätlese, Auslese, Beerenauslese and Trockenbeerenauslese wines. The reason is obvious in the case of the last three categories because they are produced from grape juice which is very strongly concentrated, where yeast cannot ferment the whole of the sugar. Actually a further fermentation would be undesirable because these high-class 'Spitzenweine' would not be harmonious if they were to contain more alcohol; they would be spirity. (For Perlwein there is a limitation of 40 g per litre.)

Appendices 9 and 10 demonstrate this; see especially the Bavarian restrictions for predicate wines and red wines, and the liberality of Rheinhessen-Pfalz for Rieslings!

The experience one had with *Süssung* in smaller vintages and with little wines was tried out on better-class wine. The fact that the greater part of the greater wines was fully fermented, and that the partly fermented wine of the same vineyard and vintage was added only a short time before bottling, led to the realization that less preservative was needed to let the wine mature in cask.

Today *Süssung* is allowed and used for all wines, including quality wines and quality wines with predicate, up to the Spätlese quality. I have observed that it has even been tried with Auslese wines! I personally consider that an Auslese wine which needs treatment of this kind is not really the kind of Auslese wine which the law or connoisseurs had in mind.

It must be noted that when the wine has reached this state there is only the *Süssung* as described above as a means of sweetening. One cannot at this stage of development of the wine start the addition of sugar.

Incidentally a Spätlese must be sweetened with a Spätlese *Süssreserve*, an Auslese with an Auslese and a Kabinett with a Kabinett *Süssreserve.* One can always use a better-class *Süssreserve* but not an inferior class.

In earlier laws it was laid down that there need be no limitations on the use of *Restsüsse* for Auslese, Beeren- and Trockenbeerenauslese wines. This arose because of the nature of these wines: it is quite impossible to ferment all the sugar contained in the grapes. For all other wines the proportion was 3:1, and the analytical picture of such wines was as shown above.

The federal state authorities have published decrees laying down the proportion of residual sugar and alcohol (see Appendix 9) and I draw attention especially to the fact that Bavaria (Appendix 10) has also laid down a fixed proportion for quality wines with predicate, Kabinett and Spätlese, in the same proportions as for Tafelweine, 1:3 for red wine and for Rotling even less (1:5).

When drinking French wines one expects red wine to be dry, i.e. fully fermented, but that is not so in Germany. The German growers apply exactly the same principle to red wine as to white wine and the German expects the red wine to be on the 'sweet' side. It is therefore pleasing to see that Bavaria – advised by great experts – not only keeps down the sugar content of red wines, but restricts the proportion to 1:5. If one looks, on the other hand, at the treatment of wines in Rheinland-Pfalz, namely for their Mosel wines, even a Tafelwein can, under special circumstances, have the same proportion of *Restsüsse* and alcohol as quality wines of defined areas. This means that a Mosel wine Bereich Bernkastel, can have *Restsüsse* of half the weight of its alcohol content. Such wines are not showing their real character; the Mosel character is completely destroyed by this method. Whoever likes such a sugar-drink can prepare it cheaply for himself – mix the cheapest available dry wine from anywhere with half the quantity of grape juice from anywhere, possibly with a special grape flavour such as Muscat.

One has of course to ask oneself, what will be the result of all this for the wine drinker? Will he get a better product or a product of inferior quality and value? So far as the taste of the final product is concerned it appears that if the proportion of residual sugar is restricted by law, it does not make a great difference or any difference at all to the sweetening of the product – whichever way one looks at it. There is no doubt that wines which are sweetened with concentrated grape juice from the same vineyard or from the same grape or from the same vintage will be better wines, with more body, and fuller. After all the concentrate contains less water than a *Süssreserve*. For many years the dosage for various sparkling wines was produced from grape concentrate, and there is no doubt that this produces a much fuller and more powerful sparkling wine than if ordinary sweetened wine had been used. Most interesting developments will be seen when concentrate is used in vintages with low acidity, or perhaps in all years in the southern part of the European Community where the wines show a certain lack of acidity. The grape-must concentrate will contain more acidity, because the acidity is concentrated as well as all the other components of the must.

Incidentally it is permitted to deacidify grape must which is destined to be made into concentrate. This of course has led to wonderful results in years with high acidity.

If *Süssreserve* contains only a very small quantity of acidity, much more harmonious and more drinkable wines will be produced. There is no doubt that the wine drinkers of the future will have many opportunities to study the developments in vinification and to develop their own tastes, their own preference.

At this time one can only hint at the various possibilities and very much hope that the wine drinker looks at coming vintages with critical eyes and critical palate, and moreover that the wine trade and wine growers will listen to what the wine-drinking public has to tell them, because in the end the wine drinker is the master and the teacher of wine grower and wine merchant.

It must be the task of every wine grower and wine merchant to make the very best possible out of the raw material which nature has given him. His actions are limited only by the regulations of the wine law.

Seven million gallons of German wines were exported in 1970 – 21 per cent more than in 1969 – and fifteen million gallons in 1973. It has quadrupled within a decade – not a bad growth rate. The question exporters and importers are now asking themselves is this: are the provisions of the new wine act to apply to wines for export as strictly as they do to those consumed in Germany?

The new act, like the act of 1930, proceeds from the principle that export wines are subject to the same regulations as to production and labelling as wines for consumption at home. It expressly excludes wine from any of the concessions made to exporters of food in the Food Act according to which foodstuffs merely had to comply with the regulations of the recipient country. On the other hand, the new wine act contains some provisions which in some ways make the export of wine easier while at the same time insisting on still stricter rules in other respects. The stricter regulations are designed to ensure the high quality of German wine abroad.

The most important special provisions governing the export of wine are the following:

The wine act of 1969 allowed the addition of alcohol to export wines for the purpose of stabilizing them, provided such attention did not contravene any law of the country of destination. This concession was intended to strengthen the competitive position of the German wine exporter in foreign markets. The 1971 act, however, contains no such provision. The question of the addition of alcohol has already been settled in an E.E.C. regulation which has the force of law. This regulation forbids the addition of alcohol to all wines other than 'Brennwein' (wine distillate) and 'Likörwein' – the French 'vin de liqueur' – in order to ensure that the natural character of the wine is as far as possible preserved. This has now been modified by allowing the addition of alcohol (wine distillate) in the case of table wines and quality wines from certain regions, if these wines are exported to countries *outside* the E.E.C. and if the climatic conditions and consumer habits in these countries necessitate such addition. By partially relaxing their original ban the authorities wanted to make sure that the quality of the wine does not suffer through climatic conditions during shipment. The regulation does insist, however, that on no account must the total alcohol content be increased by more than 2° – 16 g/l.

In certain circumstances the new wine law allows exporters to use descriptions and forms of presentation that are inadmissible in Germany. But these concessions are subject to stringent conditions. Firstly, description and presentation must strictly conform to the regulations obtaining in the country of destination, and secondly, they must not be against the public interest.

In allowing wine exporters this degree of latitude, the law givers have acted on the principle that it is only fair to take account of the legal requirements of the recipient country. Admittedly, these concessions do not go very far, for they are limited to the labelling and presentation of the wine. Moreover, the recipient country must expressly request these facilities; mere tacit consent is not enough.

Importing German wines depends therefore on the observance of the regulations prevailing in the particular country for which the shipment is destined. In addition, the shipment must not be 'against the public interest'. What is to be understood by 'public interest?' In using the term in this context, the wine act simply aims at protecting the interests of the consuming public.

The act further empowers the federal government to direct by by-law that wines for export are to be stored separately from other products, and that certain descriptions and forms of presentation must not be used.

So far no by-law to this effect has been issued. Should the government, however, decide to do so, it would be tantamount to introducing a kind of export control.

There would seem to be no need for such a step, for export certificates already exist; they are issued by specialist establishments for export wines, acting on the authority of their respective state governments, and seem to answer the purpose. In addition, there are also the certificates of origin which the Chamber of Industry and Commerce frequently issues in respect of wines to be shipped abroad.

Apart from the above-mentioned few exceptions, the same motto applies to German wine abroad as at home: 'Better quality; more information; greater reliability'. This motto expresses the German wine growers' desire to be equal to the increasing demand the world over for better quality and more information, and this in turn means greater reliability for the foreign trader and consumer alike.

BOTTLING

Bottling is a very important process, and the method of bottling can very often decide the future quality and the life of the wine.

When the wine is ready for bottling, the way of bottling depends upon the aim of the bottler: if the wine is to be for immediate consumption, for drinking in a year or two, or for laying down for later. He must try to conserve the quality and, if the wine is not meant for immediate consumption, he must assure its development when bottled. This means it must be protected against attacks of micro-biological organisms. The bottler must be sure that the wine does not contain any matter which might make it cloudy in bottle, as for instance albumen or metals. He must know that it has sufficient, but not more than the legal amount of sulphurous acid. Wine with too much sulphurous acid will lose colour, will develop very, very slowly, and only when the free sulphur disappears will it begin to show more character, more body and more flavour. The bottler should also know the quantity of oxygen and carbonic acid. We learn more and more about the significance of carbonic acid in wine. All wines contain some carbonic acid in solution, even very old and dark wines, even red wines, but the largest quantities are found in white wines, especially when they are very young. The amount of carbonic acid has a great influence on evaluation of the quality of the wine. Often very small differences in the quantity of CO_2 in the same wine have a marked effect on the taste buds. Most wine tasters cannot taste a content of less than 1 g per litre CO_2, and such a small quantity does not change the appearance of the wine – it does not produce more pearls.

I have seen wines returned by the consumer only because, when the bottle was opened, the wine showed a small trace of effervescence caused by carbonic acid. The consumer believed that the wine was fermenting! One can distinguish quite easily: wine in fermentation has a yeasty smell, a yeasty taste and shows cloudiness. If these three factors are not apparent, one should not reject a wine. Carbonic acid is refreshing and keeps the wine fresh, and the bottler therefore aims to keep the carbonic acid in the wine. Strangely, the public has always accepted carbonic acid in Mosel, Saar and Ruwer wines which one expects to be '*spritzig*'.

THE BOTTLING SYSTEM

In order to cater for the taste of the ordinary wine drinker the wines contain *Restsüsse*, some residue of unfermented sugar. In these wines there always exists a danger of secondary fermentation in bottle. To forestall this one can add certain chemicals, but some countries do not permit the use of some of them. Such a chemical is Baycovin whose use is now prohibited in Germany; many countries also forbid the import of wines treated with this substance. An alternative is sorbic acid, again one of those substances not permitted in some countries.

Apart from chemical treatment, there are various ways of pasteurization. Pasteurization of the wines on their way from vat to bottle can be followed by a cooling process, or sterile bottling can take place by pasteurization of the bottled wine, a system based on the sterilization of bottled beer. An improved system of pasteurization in use today is one in which sterile bottling is combined with short-time heating, the wine running through a special apparatus, bringing it for a short while to a temperature of 55° to 65°C in order to kill any yeast which it might contain. It then runs through a sterile filter.

The most acceptable method is just bottling through sterilizing filters (cold method). Obviously the filter used for this purpose cannot be one of the ordinary asbestos filters used for clearing the wine of impurities, but must be specially constructed. Sterilizing filters are made on the model of the cellar presses which were formerly in common use in wine cellars. Sealed off between two covers there is a fixed number of so-called 'clear' and 'turbid' chambers, arranged alternately. Separating the chambers are so-called 'sterilizing sheets' held in place by a simple device. It is these sheets that give the filter its peculiar character. They have minute pores that not even the smallest microscopic particles can penetrate, which means that they are capable of excluding from wines or other filterable liquids even bacteria and active ferments. This method makes it possible to sterilize liquids without heating them. The replacement of the pasteurizing apparatus (till lately employed for sterilizing wines) by these filters represents an immense improvement. The pasteurization of wine meant heating, but the filter achieves the same object at normal cellar temperature, thus removing the risk of change in the character of the wine inseparable from the application of heat.

The opinion that filtration would kill a wine as dead as pasteurization has been proved wrong; filtration only takes out those particles which are suspended in the wine, but nothing whatsoever dissolved in the wine. Therefore filtration cannot do any harm to it. The development of the wine will not be hampered by the use of sterilizing filters. When making port, the wine growers use brandy to stop the fermentation and kill any remaining ferments; for table wines sterilization filters serve the same purpose without altering the character of the wine.

Immediately after bottling there is a great loss of quality and in this connection we have to go into the question of *bottle sickness.* Wine which has been newly bottled shows some reluctance to express its character during the first month. Only after the wine has had time to recover for four to six weeks will it come slowly back and reveal itself. We must remember that all German wines today are bottled through filters. Furthermore, as I have explained, most are blended with *Süssreserve* of their own origin but with some remnant sweetness shortly before bottling. Each blend is like a marriage and harmony must develop. Even if the added wine is of the same origin there are two different developments and two different components. During bottling some carbonic acid will usually escape, and so the wine comes in contact with air, in other words with oxygen. Thus the whole character of the wine will change for some time until it develops in the bottle and is regenerated. Once that happens development goes slowly forward. There are some wines which will be at their best after a year or fifteen months, others will take two, three, four years, and some will take ten, twenty or thirty years. Of course when I give the latter figures I am thinking of the Beerenauslese and Trockenbeerenauslese. Incidentally, I cannot subscribe to the theory that the sweeter the wine the longer its life. After all, the sweetness must be harmonious, but the most decisive point, the strongest factor in giving 'keeping power' is actually the acidity. Good German wines have a fine fruity acidity consisting mostly of tartaric acid. It is this acidity that keeps the wine alive for many, many years. Perhaps that is the reason why Eisweine will keep for so long. When one tastes them after a year or two one finds them in most cases too astringent, too harsh, the result of the concentration of all components of the grape. When the grape freezes it also multiplies the acidity percentage-wise. Not only the sugar but the acidity also is concentrated. They need many years before the acidity is reduced to harmonious level.

CORKS

Last but not least I would like to say a few words about corks. The ideal corks are used in England for bottling vintage ports. These corks very often remain in the bottle for forty or fifty years, and are still strong and fresh. They are the best to be found. Unfortunately the Germans are not quite as clever in the selection of their corks, and many estates are too mean to spend a few extra pfennigs to put the best corks into their bottles. If one remembers all the work and expense involved until the moment when the wine goes into the bottle, one would expect that people would also be more careful in their selection of corks; after all, a bad cork can destroy all the enjoyment of a fine bottle of wine. Generally speaking I would not leave the original cork of a German-bottled wine in the bottle for more than twelve to fifteen years. Even the greatest estates like the Hessian State Domain re-cork their wines very often after twelve or fifteen years. If they only selected the same quality of corks as those used for vintage ports this would certainly not be necessary.

Very often one asks oneself why corks are still used at all, especially for these fine wines, and particularly as since we started to use plastic 'corks' for sparkling wines, we have never had any complaint about the 'corkiness' of the wine. I believe that we like tradition too much and maybe a little snobbery is involved in the way we still adhere to ancient methods. There is so much progress around us in vinification, treatment and bottling where only the most modern and best machines are accepted, why should we stop just at the very last stage, the corking, and retain the natural cork?

A most interesting experiment by the Viticultural College in Geisenheim has recently been published (*Deutscher Weinbau* 1973, p. 788): 'The quality of bottled wine with screwcap closure can surpass the quality of the wine in a bottle closed with a cork. A 1970 Silvaner wine, bottled in February 1971, was bottled and corked in both ways. It was submitted to blind tastings of four groups of tasters with the following result:

Three groups gave preference in a unanimous decision to the screwcap bottled wine. The fourth group was divided: 7 were for the screwcap wine, 4 were for the wine 'that had been corked and 1 considered both wines of equal quality'.

The screwcap bottle has an airtight closure and does not allow air (oxygen) to enter. When bottles are standing upright, as is often the case in cellars and stores, the cork may dry and get smaller and allow the air to enter the bottle. The result is oxidization, ageing and disappearance of freshness.

13

Examination of quality wines

When all conditions for the production of quality wines have been fulfilled, the producer, if he has tasted the wine and found it in order, has to apply for an examination. His wine has to be analysed at an officially recognized oenological laboratory and the analysis submitted with the wine as evidence of minimum quality standards. This personal obligation must make the grower careful in the first instance. After all the quality and value of any wine depends first of all on its chemically ascertainable components. Much might be written on this question, but here it will perhaps be sufficient to give a typical analysis of a German Rhine wine, and, as a matter of interest, I give two analyses of the same wine, one produced by fermentation in an hermetically sealed tank, the other by the old-fashioned method of fermentation (as reported by Dr. Geiss in *Wein und Rebe* 15 September 1950).

	Tank Wine	Vat Wine
Specific gravity	1·0027	0·9954
Alcohol, g/l	82·5	81·8
Alcohol, volume	10·45(a)	10·36
Extract, indirect, g/l	43·1	24·0
Sugar, g/l	16·0	< 1·0
Sugar-free extract, g/l	28·1	24·0
Volatile acid, g/l	0·19	0·28
Total acid as tartaric, g/l	7·6	8·1
Free sulphurous acid, mg/l	16·6	6·4
Total sulphurous acid, mg/l	79·3	56·3
Original gravity (Oechsle°)	85·0	85·0
Original gravity calculated	90·4	82·0

(a) 18·2° Sikes,
g/l = grams per litre,
mg/l = milligrams per litre.

Further components are tartaric, malic or lactic acid, glycerine, ash and nitrogen.

In many countries it is customary for ordinary table wines to be marketed exclusively according to their alcohol content. But it must be stated that the tasting test is preferable to the chemical method and is decisive. A chemical analysis can never succeed in conveying a wine's essential overall quality. In Germany it is the expert taster with his tried and experienced palate who assesses the value of a wine, judging it by its intrinsic qualities – especially its bouquet and flavour, to which of course its alcohol content and the rest of its chemical make-up contribute.

I have tasted thousands of wines over the course of nearly sixty years, and in all blind tastings have rejected all those wines with less than 8·5 grams potential alcohol, which proves to me that the alcohol content is an important factor in the evaluation of German wines. The sugar content of those grapes which produce wines of a lesser degree shows that their degree of ripeness was low. The new German wine law has prohibited the sale of wine under 67 grams actual (= 8·5 by volume) alcohol per litre as a safeguard to the consumer who, relying on the quality of the 'natural estate bottled wine' with the name of a big grower, has sometimes actually received a third-rate wine of less value than a *vin ordinaire*. Furthermore, if according to analysis the wine is not in order – for instance it may contain too much sulphur, or it may be cloudy – he will not bother the Control Committee with a hopeless application.

Each application has to be submitted together with the analysis and three bottles of the wine to the Board of Examination. After these formal requirements have been fulfilled, the wine is subject to an organoleptic examination in which a team of expert tasters judge the wine, in a blind tasting, according to an official points system.

Points are awarded in four categories (see also Appendix 11):

Colour: has to be in character with the wine in question, i.e. white, red, *rosé*, etc.

Clarity: the wine has to be clear. Two points may be awarded, but at least 1 point must be achieved.

Bouquet: to be called 'clean-cut' 4 points may be awarded but 2 points at least must be achieved.

Flavour: this is most important of all, and 12 points may be awarded, but 6 points must be achieved.

For quality wines with predicate the minimum number of points they must reach to qualify is of course higher. Kabinett needs 13 points, Spätlese 14 points, Auslese 15 points, Beerenauslese 16 points and Trockenbeerenauslese 17 points.

Analysis and the committee of tasters have to prove that all legal requirements have been fulfilled, then an examination number (*Prüfungsnummer*) is issued. The number consists of several figures, thus making it easy for the authorities to discover the origin of the wine and to trace a potential culprit in case of complaints about the wine.

The number consists of five parts:

1. number of examination committee (Koblenz = 1; Bernkastel = 2; Trier = 3; Alzey = 4; Neustadt = 5; Eltville = 6)
2. the bottler's village code (Nierstein = 382; Piesport = 596; Bernkastel = 907)
3. the grower's or bottler's own code number
4. the grower's or bottler's application number
5. the year of application.

If the Examination Board is not satisfied with the quality, it can, for example, demote a proffered 'Spätlese' to a lower grade Kabinett or QbA. If the producer disagrees with the verdict of the committee, he can appeal to two higher committees to safeguard his rights.

In respect of branded wines or where vast quantities of one wine are bottled the number is valid for one year. This is necessary since production cannot be laid down exactly one year in advance – on the contrary, this is determined by the consumer demand. Such an exemption permit is in turn liable to re-examination either by the Wine Board of Control or from the Committee of Examination. The 'examination number' is solely an interim authorization, and can be withdrawn should spot-checks from the authorities prove that wine numbers have been forged, or that wines being sold no longer represent the quality presented for examination. Such identity comparisons are possible for a period of up to two years following issue of the number since two or three samples are retained by the authorities.

The sensible application of this system together with the close co-operation of all the authorities involved in the examination of wines which are already on sale ensures that the certificate of approval is genuine, enabling the consumer to purchase the wine of his choice in the certainty that the description on the label corresponds to the contents of the bottle. Not only the consumer but also the wine producer can reap benefits from this new system. Due to the multiplicity of the samples submitted for approval, the Board of Examination has a unique opportunity to follow the trend of German viticulture from year to year, as well as to see the mistakes made by individual producers in the care and preparation of their wines. For the first time it is possible to guide and advise wine producers, both large and small, to eliminate mistakes and to improve their wine-making techniques. This is not only to their own advantage but also to the advantage of the consumer, since there is now absolutely no justification for bringing a wine of mediocre quality on to the market, under false pretences.

The following statistics give an indication of the work involved and the results and benefits for the wine drinker:

11 Examination Officers examined nearly 118,000 samples from 1 January 1972 to 31 March 1973. 4 per cent of the wines submitted were refused altogether and 5 per cent received a lower predicate than expected by the applicant.

The most interesting statistics are those published by the examination committee for Franconia, covering applications from 1 January 1973 to the end of September 1973.

Category	*Vintage*	*No. of applications accepted*	*Litres*	*Down graded*	*Rejected*
Qualitätswein	1971	28	43,256	—	—
	1972	1,545	10,196,546	—	90
	Total	1,573	10,239,802		
Kabinett	1971	103	369,488		
	1972	134	319,518	17	20
	Total	237	689,006		
Spätlese	1971	231	823,521		
	1972	15	22,235	44	21
	Total	246	845,756		
Auslese	1971	42	61,500		
	1972	4	1,280	13	11
	Total	46	62,780		
Beerenauslese	1971	4	644		
	1972	—	—	2	—
Trockenbeerenauslese	1971	3	349		
	1972	—	—	—	1
	Total	3	349		
Altogether		2,109	11,838,337	76	143

Several points are worth noting, in particular the proportion in quantity of the quality wines with predicate to ordinary quality wines, their rarity and therefore their exceptional value; Trockenbeerenauslese 3‰, Auslese 6‰. No 1972 vintage Beeren- or Trockenbeerenauslesen! Four different Beerenauslesen produced 644 litres = just over 70 dozen. 3 Trockenbeerenauslesen produced 349 litres = 38 dozen!

Secondly, the number of quality wines with predicate rejected means the grower is not allowed to sell – he can only blend. Thirdly, the protection awarded to the consumer is enormous: in 1972 all submitted Beeren- and Trockenbeerenauslesen were rejected, 100 per cent, Auslesen 86 per cent, Spätlesen 80 per cent! In the past much of the work had to be done by the 'good' wine merchant; these were the wines the good wine taster and merchant would reject and these statistics show how important it is to have a good wine merchant and expert taster: he has still to sort out and there is no pre-tasting by a committee for Tafelweine.

14

Further development of bottled wine

Once wine has been bottled it still remains subject to alterations and changes. These changes take place especially in colour and bouquet and of course also in the chemical analysis of the wine. We know that red wines need many years to develop and mature and to be ready for drinking. I remember very well that just a few years ago wine merchants were arguing when the 1928 château-bottled clarets would be ready for drinking. This in fact is something I heard discussed on the first day I entered the English wine trade (1933). At that time the question was, would the 1929 be ready for drinking earlier than the 1928 or vice versa. As it happened, the 1929s after ten years in bottle were reaching their peak, and the 1928s remained harsh. Most of these wines have been drunk now, but occasionally an odd remaining bottle can be found, and even now one sometimes hears the comment that it would have done the wine a lot of good if one had waited another few years!

But let us turn to German white wine. In its youth it has a yellowish-green colour and with bottle age it turns first yellow, then gold-yellow, next it declines to light brown and at the end, so to speak before it dies, it becomes a darkish brown. I am not saying that all wines which have a gold-yellow or a darkish colour are old. Colour alone will not tell the age, because there are wines which are born with a dark colour, as for instance the Ruländer, the Traminer, and especially all those wines which are produced from noble rotten grapes. They are, very often, very golden and perhaps even brown in their youngest days, and this applies particularly to the very high quality Beerenauslesen and Trockenbeerenauslesen. Therefore when you see a wine, do not pass judgement on it by its colour alone. But of course great wines smell differently in the bottle than in the glass. Tasting and swirling the wine in the tasting glass, we find that the wine leaves on the glass a pointed shape which in popular German wine language is called 'Church window' as it has the shape of a Gothic window. This residue may be thick or thin and is an indication of the strength of the wine extract and body.

The wine undergoes a great change in its bouquet. Chemical reactions have not finished with the bottling of the wine; development continues to take place. At the end of its life the wine becomes what the Germans call '*firn*', with a bouquet which reminds one of Madeira, and therefore we speak of such a wine as 'madeirized'.

The time wine will take to acquire such colours and bouquet can never be predicted. It very much depends in what surroundings and at what temperature the wine is kept. Evaporation and ageing of the wines is accelerated if the wine is kept at a higher temperature. If one therefore has a good vintage wine and wishes to taste it and get the best out of it earlier, then one must not keep it in too cool a place, but must let it develop quicker and so reach its peak earlier and show its full capacity and finesse; but if you require the wine to keep a long time, say if you give a cask of wine to your child or grandchild, intending that they should enjoy the wine on their coming of age or wedding day, or a day when he or she passes an important examination, then keep it in a very cold place – the cooler the storage room the longer the life of the wine. I must, however, warn you that the room should not be too cold. I would never recommend a temperature lower than 9°C, or, say, 8°C. My advice is, therefore: always keep red wines in a warmer and white wines in a cooler place if there is a choice so that you may see each wine at its best, at the peak of its quality.

Exactly as the quality of a wine depends to a large extent on the first act of planting the vine, so the duration and life of the wine depends very much upon the way the wine has been bottled, in other words, upon the technological treatment given to it. Different kinds of wine and the different kinds of grapes and different qualities behave differently in bottle. And whether the wine is dry, medium dry, medium sweet or sweet also has an influence on the development of the wine.

In this connection the question of crystallization, the forming of crystals of tartaric acid, must be mentioned. Tartaric acid crystals only appear in a wine of quality and you should be pleased to have such a wine set before you. In any case, when you see large tartaric acid crystals in the wine, remember the bottle acts as a magnifying glass and the crystals appear much bigger than they actually are.

Your wine may have passed its best, it may be on its way down. We know there are factors which have an influence on the wines which is not a good one, which lead to cloudiness, to 'madeirized' taste or to 'corkiness', a taste of a foul cork. Many of these accidents happen if the wine has not been treated and bottled by an expert, but others are unavoidable and the wine drinker must accept these as a consequence of the development of the wine as a living organism.

The question of how long a white wine will last is not asked as often today as it used to be some twenty or thirty years ago. When speaking of laying down wines for investment or for maturing, one usually thinks of red wines. But great white wines are increasing in value as much as red wines do, and it is quite worth while considering them for laying down or keeping them in order to enjoy their full finesse and elegance. The question of how long a wine lasts is not easily answered. Those of us who know vineyards, grapes and growers and who have a lifelong experience of various wines, can estimate the development of a wine by intuition. We know that various factors have a great influence on the development and maturation of a wine. We know for instance that various soils produce wines which last longer than others. We know that wines produced in very young vineyards do not have the staying power of those wines from vineyards which are seven or eight years old. We know also that the temperature of the storage place is of very great influence and if the same wine is stored in cellars at 25°, 20°, 10° and 5°C, we know that the wine in the cellar at 5° will last much longer (perhaps five times as long) as the wine matured in the cellar at 25°. Wine is a living product and its life depends on how it is looked after by its cellar master (doctor) and by its housekeeper.

I remember the occasion when I visited a new customer in 1936 and showed him wines of the 1934 and 1935 vintages. He liked very many of them, but when making his budget for buying he asked about each wine: 'How long will it last?' And when I spoke of eight or ten years, or even twelve years, he appeared very doubtful. Finally a very substantial order was placed, but I had to guarantee a staying power of five years. I have tasted some of these wines in 1969 with the same client when they were not five but thirty-five years old, and we were both amazed at how young and fresh they were.

I can give many similar examples.

Generally I would say that ordinary table wines will certainly keep for between two and three years. Kabinett wines and lower-grade Spätlesen will reach their best at about five years old. Auslesen, Beerenauslesen and Trockenbeerenauslesen will reach at least the age of twelve years on account of their high concentration of acidity, sweetness and alcohol. But many of them as I have said, will reach twenty, thirty or fifty years of age.

In a recent tasting in honour of Count Matuschka-Greiffenclau of Schloss Vollrads, on the occasion of his eightieth birthday, some really old wines were tasted including a 1727 Rüdesheimer Apostelwein Bremer Ratskeller. 'Apostelwein' means that twelve men must drink one glass without getting drunk. This referred to the strength of the wine. It was donated by the Director of the Ratskeller at Bremen, himself a son of Winkel (Rheingau). This is one of those wines which on account of their great quality at vintage time were kept by the

Bremer Ratskeller in cask over centuries. There is no doubt that the wine is not fully original: in my opinion the Solera system was used every year to fill up the cask so that not too much air could come in touch with the wine; but whatever happened there must be some drops of 1727 left in the mixture which was actually bottled immediately after the War. The Director told us that when he returned to the cellar of the Bremer Ratskeller (the Mansion House Cellar) after the occupation, he found that most wines had gone, but on a few casks of really old wines, such as the 1727, he found notices fixed by the occupation authorities to the effect that it was dangerous to health to drink that wine and so they had survived. He himself had tasted it immediately, found it was a typical old wine, and had it analysed. It still showed 13·30 alcohol by volume then and very good other components so he decided to bottle it, and if we consider that this wine has been in bottle for twenty-five years, even if diffused by the Solera system, it was an enormous specimen. It was madeirized but still fresh in some sense. Only a Riesling wine could have withstood all this treatment.

An 1893 Schloss Vollrads Kabinett followed this wine, a wine of the best vintage of the last century. And in its state and its composition it was similar to the 1727, in spite of the enormous difference in age.

The crowning glory of the meeting was 1947 Schloss Vollrads Trockenbeerenauslese which I had tasted last with the late André Simon on 26 April 1961. We were preparing our book *The Great Wines of Germany*, and a tasting of Schloss Vollrads Trockenbeerenauslesen of the vintages 1911–59 took place. Then the 1947 received the following judgement: '170° Oechsle, bottled 20 May 1950. A medium, deep golden colour which makes the wine appear older than its three predecessors (these were 1937, 1934 and 1933) and although the bouquet is fully developed, or perhaps overdeveloped, and the flavour which is medium sweetness and medium ripeness, is well developed, there is still a firmness towards the end, but it has less life and future than the 1933, 1934 or the 1937. It will be senile soon.'

When I saw the 1947 at the top of the list at Count Matuschka-Greiffenclau's tasting, I wondered, but the only judgement I can give about our tasting in 1961 is that we must have been very unlucky in the bottle we opened, because this 1947 Schloss Vollrads Trockenbeerenauslese still had an enormous quality, still had life for many years, with delicate acidity – a really noble wine.

I do not think I am wrong in saying that generally speaking it is the acidity which gives the wine its staying power. Wines which are of a lower acidity show much less staying power than those with higher acid content. Therefore the Riesling will show much longer life than any of the early-ripening grapes.

My readers will perhaps be surprised when I say that Auslesen,

Beerenauslesen and Trockenbeerenauslesen can have a high degree of acidity. One might not taste it but it is there, covered up by the richness and sweetness of these wines. It is this acidity which keeps them fresh and elegant and still able to quench thirst in spite of their sweetness. It is true that many people when drinking white wines want young, fresh and often 'green' wines. These are certainly enjoyable, but how much more pleasure does one derive from a matured wine even if it shows some age, just a 'few grey hairs'.

CORKSCREWS

Nothing is more annoying than if a bottle of wine, aged and matured in the cellar, the owner's pride and joy, and which is in good condition, is spoilt at the last minute only because the cork is not removed in the right way. So many people just do not know which corkscrew to use and how to use it properly.

First of all one must remember that wines which have been lying in the cellar undisturbed perhaps for decades, maybe in a damp place, may have formed some fungi on top of the cork or between the cork and the capsule. Some dirt may have gathered. If the cork were to be drawn without attention to this fact, the wine poured out of the bottle would touch the dirt and would suffer in bouquet and flavour.

The first task therefore must be to clean the outside of the cork and surrounding bottle and to scrape the cork or even wash it, wash the lip of the bottle, dry it and then dry the cork.

Then remove part of the metal capsule so that the wine when poured does not come into contact with it.

Before selecting the right corkscrew we must remember that the cork may have been in the bottle for many years. It has taken the shape of the opening of the bottle, it will have shrunk, it will have become harder and more narrow, just to fit the bottle neck. If you try to push the corkscrew into the cork, you might push the cork into the bottle which is certainly not what you intend. Should this, however, happen by accident, you have not lost the wine; decant it immediately into a decanter or into another clean bottle and the wine will be none the worse for it. A cork which has thus slipped into the bottle does not make the wine corky or bad. There are actually some special instruments to pull out a cork which has been pushed into the bottle. If you have one of these, you can forget the accident.

There are many corkscrews in use. The easiest to use is the Bell Corkscrew which can be used without strength or effort. Another good corkscrew is the 'Waiter's Knife'. A good corkscrew should be wider at the pointed end than near the handle. The spiral of the screw should be big enough so that you can see the beginning of the screw when using it, and you should be able to push a match through the gaps in the spiral. The screw should end in a sharp point which should be put softly on the middle of the cork and screwed in slowly, until it has penetrated far enough to assist in lifting the cork from the bottle. If you insert the corkscrew only half or three-quarters of the length of the cork, there is a danger that you will tear off this part and some of the cork will be left in the bottle which you cannot reach with your corkscrew, and which will be difficult to extract. You may of course push it into the bottle, as it is clean, having never been in contact with cellar air or dirt, and start serving from it, but it does not look too nice with the cork swimming on top of the wine, and it is better to decant. When buying a corkscrew, the only point to look for is the screw; if this is good the corkscrew is good. Too often the value and price of a corkscrew are determined by the material of which the handle is made; this is of no importance as far as serving the wine is concerned.

15

Naming of the wines

1. QUALITY WINES

The purpose of the division of German vinelands into *Weinbaugebiete* and *Anbaugebiete*, which in their essence are identical and congruent, lies in the naming of the wines. The term '*bestimmte Anbaugebiete*' (specific regions) is used in the case of quality wines. All quality wines have to fall into one of the eleven defined (designated) specific wine-producing regions.

2. TAFELWEINE

The Tafelweine are named according to the river along or nearby which they are produced.

The region is the largest division and may be subdivided into subregions. This subdivision only happens in the case of Tafelweine, and this in a strange way. Rhein and Mosel count as one region for the designation of Tafelweine. Should the Tafelwein originate from the Rhine, the subregion 'Rhein' can be used.

To give a few examples, if Wehlener Sonnenuhr produced Qualitätswein and Tafelwein, the labels would read:

Qualitätswein Mosel-Saar-Ruwer	or	Deutscher Tafelwein Mosel
Wehlener Sonnenuhr		Wehlener

A Qualitätswein from the Saar will be labelled:

Qualitätswein
Mosel-Saar-Ruwer

A Tafelwein:

Deutscher Tafelwein
Mosel

Such is the law.

The Ahrwine, if a Tafelwein, becomes a Rhine wine, and this

applies also to the Hessische Bergstrasse. Under the 1930 law the denomination 'Rheinwein' was important, because all Rhine wines could be sold as Liebfraumilch and 'Rheinwein' meant wine from Rheinhessen, Rheinpfalz, Nahe, Mittelrhein and Rheingau. This break with tradition is just not understandable and is not logical either.

If there are 'Mainweine' for Tafelweine, why make the Main from Hochheim to Frankfurt part of the Rheinweinbaugebiet – the famous 'Anbaugebiet Rheingau' for Qualitätsweine?

NOMENCLATURE: THE LABEL

Very strict regulations control the naming and marking of wines intended for sale. The overriding principle is embodied in a regulation forbidding misleading nomenclature and all deceptive marketing devices. A second regulation is founded on the basic rule that topographical designations of wines may be used solely for indicating their origins. The principle of labelling is: 'Wahrheit und Klarheit', Verity and Clarity.

Only the following statements are permitted in giving the geographical origin of a wine:

1. Names of registered sites of *Bereiche*.
2. Names of villages or parts of villages (*Ortsteile*, suburbs).
3. Names of areas or sub-areas.
4. The word '*deutsch*' (German).
5. Special denomination admitted for types of wine such as Liebfraumilch and Affenthaler.

And in future *all* wines must be marketed with a permitted geographical denomination which must be *one* of the following:

Deutsch (German)
Specific region or subregion
Bereich, community or village
Name of site (*Lage* or *Grosslage* with name of village)

There exist a number of villages with identical names, for example:

Rüdesheim (Rheingau), Rüdesheim (Nahe)
Zell (Mosel), Zell (Rheinpfalz), Zell-Weierbach (Baden), Zell (Franconia)
Alsenz (Nahe), Alsenz (Rheinpfalz)
Beilstein (Mosel), Beilstein (Württemberg).

Quality wines and quality wines with predicate show of course the *Anbaugebiet*; this is a distinction to avoid misleading the public. In this case it becomes necessary to add a further word of identification, namely the name of the *Anbaugebiet.*

Tafelwein	Tafelwein
Rhein	Rhein
Rüdesheim (Nahe)	Rüdesheim (Rheingau)

Objections may be raised to the use of the name of an *Anbaugebiet* for such purposes, but I cannot see any other way. The use of the post code may be easier, but how many people would understand this on a wine label?

There are even cases where the same village name appears twice in the same Anbaugebiet, for example Herxheim (Rheinpfalz). In this case they may have a mark of identity in the official name 'Herxheim am Berg', 'Herxheim bei Landau'. Or they may not have such a mark of identification, for example two villages Burgen on the Moselle. In the first case the full name is necessary and sufficient, in the latter case the addition of the name of the *Bereich* may be the easiest way for differentiation. If one should object to these suggestions regarding Rüdesheim (Nahe) for Tafelwein, the name of the *Bereich* would be the best solution as the alternative.

The most famous and most used generic names under the 1930 law were:

PLACE	*GENERAL NAME*
Mosel	
Berncastel and Graach	Braunes
Dhron and Neumagen	Hofberg
Graach and Wehlen	*Muenzlay
Longuich and Schweich	Probstberg
Oberfell and Alken	Rosenberg
Piesport and Niederemmel	Taubengarten
Senheim and Mesenich	Lay, Kolay, Rosenberg and Kuckukslay
Wiltingen and Oberemmel	*Scharzberg
Nahe	
Kreuznach and Hargesheim	Kronenberg
Rüdesheim and Mandel	*Rosengarten
Palatinate	
Diedesfeld and Hambach	Hartkopf, Steppenwiese
Bad Dürkheim and Ungstein	Spielberg
Bad Dürkheim and Wachenheim	Fuchsmantel, Schenkenboehl
Ungstein and Karlstadt	*Kobnert

PLACE	*GENERAL NAME*
Rheingau	
Eltville and Kiedrich	Sandgrub
Eltville and Rauenthal	*Steinmaecher, Wagenkehr, Ehr
Geisenheim and Winkel	Steinacker
Hallgarten and Hattenheim	*Deitelsberg, *Mehrhoelzchen
Hochheim and Kostheim	*Daubhaus
Rüdesheim and Eibingen	Kiesel, Haeuserweg
Winkel and Johannisberg	*Erntebringer
Rhinehessia	
Alsheim and Mettenheim	Goldberg
Dienheim and Oppenheim	*Kroetenbrunnen, Goldberg, Saar
Nierstein and Schwabsburg	Domthal, Schnappenberg

* These have become *Grosslagen.*

These were the thorn in the flesh of those who wanted verity and who did not like the idea that a wine labelled Kreuznachet Kronenberg actually originated in a neighbouring village. The creation of the *Grosslage* was to replace the *Gattungslage*, the generic site. Alas, the result is that one is even further away from the truth! A *Grosslage* may cover a range of villages.

Any wine grown within the *Grosslage* may carry the name of the *Grosslage and* any village within it. The Grosslage Kloster Liebfrauenberg within the Bereich Suedliche Weinstrasse covers 1340·20 ha, and seventeen villages, among which Bad Bergzabern is the leading one. This wine may be offered as Bad Bergzaberner Kloster Liebfrauenberg. . . . One has the choice between seventeen villages. . . . Other *Grosslagen* cover only part of the vineyards of one village, for example Niersteiner Auflangen, and there are many which cover the vineyards of a few neighbouring villages. Quite a number of the former generic names have become *Grosslagen* (those marked with an asterisk on the list), others have disappeared. One or two have become *Einzellagen* (single sites) as for example Kiedricher Sandgrub – the Niersteiner Domtal has become the Grosslage 'Niersteiner Gutes Domtal' and covers one vineyard of Nierstein plus those of a dozen villages.

A single *Lage* which is part of two, three or more villages can be used in connection with any one of the village names. Thus can a Wachenheimer Fuchsmantel be sold as Bad Duerkheimer Fuchsmantel, even if the grapes originate 100 per cent from Wachenheim.

The wine drinker must in future look more and more to the shipper's name, if he likes identity of quality. Continuity means continuity of name, vintage and shipper.

The name of a site on its own is not permitted; it must be accompanied by the name of the village. The best example for this was

Marcobrunn

a site in Erbach (Rheingau) with wine marketed by some as

Erbacher Marcobrunn

by others as

Marcobrunner

Marcobrunn is of course a vineyard in Erbach, but for many decades one grower sold some Hattenheimer wine situated a few hundred yards from the Marcobrunn vineyards as 'Marcobrunner'.

The name of a *Bereich* must be preceded by the word 'Bereich', e.g. Bereich Bernkastel.

A wine from the famous Steinberg vineyard will be labelled Steinberger as in the past, but it means 'from the suburb Steinberg', exactly as a Niersteiner comes from Nierstein.

This is again one of the absurd results of a law made by bureaucrats. I had said in my book *Wine Law 1969* (p. 57): 'Steinberger will in future be Hattenheimer Steinberg. Wines which were in the past sold under the name of an estate will have to add a geographical denomination, or they may try to have the name of the estate entered in the vineyard register as a site name: Schloss Vollrads, Schloss Johannisberg, or new Ortsteile.' The owners of these vineyards succeeded in having their vineyards or estates made into an 'Ortsteil', i.e. part of the village.

As I have said one of the guiding principles of the new wine law is that everything is prohibited which is not expressly permitted. This applies also to the label. We know that in the past there were many misunderstandings as by-laws were interpreted in different ways by different people.

From now on there will no longer be a '*feine*', '*feinste*', or '*hochfeinste*' Spätlese or Auslese, and there will be no more '*edel*', or Goldbeerenauslese, only Spätlese, or Auslese or Beerenauslese. There will be no more descriptions such as '*Naturwein*', '*Ungezuckerter Wein*', '*rein*', '*naturrein*', '*echt*', '*Originalwein*', '*Durchgegoren*' (fully fermented), '*Wachstum*', '*Kreszenz*' (own vineyard), '*Originalabfüllung*' or '*Originalabzug*' (bottled in the cellar of the proprietor), '*Schlossabzug*' (castle-bottled), '*Fass no.*' (cask no.), '*Fuder No.*' (cask no.). Even the '*allerfeinste*' Trockenbeerenauslese has to go. Other now obsolete inscriptions are: Kellerabfüllung, Hochgewächs, Edelgewächs, Edelauslese, Spätauslese, and many more. Nor will there be any more St. Nikolaus wine in the future, or St. Barbara, Christmas or Sylvester wine. This is a sad blow for some American importers who used to insist on having the wording, 'best cask' on every label. This also is now prohibited. Even the printing of the characteristics of a wine has to be stopped, for example 'body', 'agreeable', 'very dry', 'bone dry'. '*Trocken*' (dry) is permitted, however, if the wine contains not more than 4 g unfermented sugar per litre.

The new wine law puts an end to these endless fancy descriptions just as it puts an end to different names for the same thing. The Riesling will in future be the Riesling and not the Klingelberger (as it used to be called in Baden), the Klevner will be the Traminer in Baden, too, and there are no exceptions.

May I emphasize once more the regulation that the statement '*natur*' alone or in any other form or shape is prohibited. Furthermore the same applies to the statement that 'no sugar has been added in the production of the wine'.

LABELLING OF QUALITY WINE

A label for a 'Qualitätswein' wine must show the number of examination and must state its geographical origin, viz: for Qualitätswein at least the specified region, for Qualitätswein mit Prädikat at least the *bereich*, registered in the Vineyard Register (*Weinbergsrolle*) *or* a special denomination admitted by special by-law.

In addition to all regulations about classification of quality there is a special clause which is meant to open the way for special names for types of wine. Here such names as Liebfraumilch, Moselblümchen, and Affentaler come to mind. I shall deal with these later, on our wine journey.

I could imagine a Rheingau or Rheinhessen type name to be created for district or subdistrict wine, or for Rheinhessen or Palatinate red wine. I have no doubt that this question will be clarified in due course. In the end everybody will offer his own type wine. After all, branded wines are often type wines with a geographical indication as Kellergeist-Bereich Bernkastel.

In future the combinations 'Spätlese Kabinett', 'Auslese Kabinett', 'Trockenbeerenauslese Kabinett' must and will disappear; the wine is either a Spätlese, or a Kabinett and so on. Estates such as Schloss Johannisberg with a special range of Kabinett wines have either to find a different denomination for a second range or give it up altogether. The use of different seals or capsules is of course still allowed.

Some growers have made a start with equalization of their wines, but have not gone the whole way, for instance Schloss Johannisberg, which formerly produced three different *cuvées* (blendings). The better wines, the Auslese, the Beerenauslese and Trockenbeerenauslese, were individually treated and sold. In actual fact, part of these *cuvées* were sold with the designation 'Kabinett' and the same quality was sold with different labels, it depended how the wines were marketed. The estate bottlings were generally all sold through wholesale houses, whereas the Kabinett wines went through appointed agents – there was even an agent for Germany! The classification table read as follows:

Schloss Johannisberger

Estate bottling	*Kabinett bottling*
Red seal	Orange seal
Green seal	White seal (Spätlese)
Pink seal (Spätlese or Auslese)	Blue seal (Auslese)
Pink seal (Beerenauslese)	Gold seal (Beerenauslese)
Pink seal (Trockenbeerenauslese)	Gold seal (Trockenbeerenauslese)

In future the classification will be as follows: Schloss Johannisberg quality wine will carry a yellow seal. Their quality wine with predicate will be subdivided into two ranges to keep up the old tradition. As 'Kabinett' is now a predicate, the range of Kabinett wines becomes a second range of predicate wines. The second range will carry the old Kabinett label, and the classification is as follows:

	Crest label	*Picture label*
Qualitätswein	yellow	
Qualitätswein mit Prädikat		
Kabinett	red	orange
Spätlese	green	white
Auslese	pink	sky-blue
Eiswein	silver	
Beeren- and Trockenbeerenauslese	gold	

The classification of Schloss Vollrads has changed in a similar way.

Past:

Originalabfüllung: green, green-silver
Schlossabzug: red, red-silver, red-gold
Kabinett: blue, blue-silver, blue-gold
Auslese: pink, pink-gold, pink-white
Beerenauslese: white
Trockenbeerenauslese: white-gold

Present: Schlossabzug is prohibited, and these seals disappear.

Qualitätswein: green and green-silver
Kabinett: blue and blue-gold

Spätlese: pink and pink-gold
Auslese and Beerenauslese } white
Trockenbeerenauslese: white-gold

The fact of having one examination number for one container may lead to difficulties and may make some growers' policies change. A container of wine can receive only one examination number – not two numbers for one wine.

Some of the *Prädikatsweinversteigerer* (formerly *Naturweinversteigerer*) (growers who sell their natural wine by auction) still sell by the half *Stueck*. A *Stueck* cask is therefore sold under two numbers, and a double *Stueck* under four numbers, which makes it possible to sell the identical wine under different *Fassnummern* (cask numbers). This will – in my opinion – no longer be possible as the words '*Fassnummer*' and 'Best cask' are not allowed on the label. 'Best cask' belongs to the past.

The title 'Qualitätswein mit Prädikat' carries with it special obligations:

1. It must not be bottled before the 1 January following the gathering of the grapes. This will help to prevent the over-zealous from offering, a few weeks after harvest, distinguished wines of the latest vintage.
2. It must be sold giving its full birth certificate: the registered name of the site or *Bereich*, and the name of the wine-producing community.

If I read this regulation correctly, a wine sold under a type name, say Liebfraumilch, cannot be sold as Spätlese or Auslese wine, although a special by-law allows the use of Liebfraumilch Kabinett and Spätlese for a very short transitional period. It follows that wines under type names, and certainly under brand names, cannot be 'Prädikatsweine'. Some of the Qualitätsweine mit Prädikat enjoy privileges regarding sulphur and alcohol content. I have dealt with these elsewhere (Chapter 11).

The many new names, phrases, and hints on labels have created so much confusion in Germany and in foreign countries that everybody must welcome the fact that in future all those names, descriptive phrases and so on which are not expressly permitted are prohibited. Some time ago I was asked what the name – all on one label – Eiswein-Christwein-Strohwein meant. All this nonsense will be impossible in future. An Eiswein cannot be a Strohwein, and the new law does not recognize 'Strohwein' (straw wine) in any event.

Finally, in order to protect the public from confusion special by-laws may be issued. For instance:

1. The use of certain names or the way the names are used may be laid down.

2. Special containers may be reserved for special products (this has been done for the *Bocksbeutel*).

The principle I repeat is '*Wahrheit und Klarheit*', i.e. true and understandable. Fancy names can still be used, but they must not create the impression of being a geographical denomination, and they must not contain a geographical hint, if the conditions for such a geographical denomination are not fulfilled. If used on a label with a geographical name, it must not be capable of being wrongly understood to be part of the place named.

All labels must show the name of the bottler or the name of the person or firm for whom the wine has been bottled. The new German denomination reads as follows: '*Aus dem Lesegut*', which might be roughly translated as 'produced from the picking or gathering or harvesting' and it is distinct from '*aus dem eigenen Lesegut*' which means 'from his own harvest', a phrase used by the grower who has made wine exclusively from grapes produced by him, and who has bottled it himself. '*Aus eigenem Lesegut – Erzeugerabfüllung*' means producer's bottling, estate bottling.

If a wine has not been vinified by the grower or has not been bottled by him, the wine may be labelled '*aus dem Lesegut*' with the addition of the name of the firm of the producer provided that the grapes for this particular wine have been exclusively produced by the named producer and if this producer has consented to the use of his name. The law emphasizes that the *Erzeuger* (producer) may only be the person who has harvested the grapes from vineyards which are in his own possession. In this case for English-speaking countries the term 'growth' or 'grower' appears to me a good solution.

If the grower is a member of an association, a society, a limited company, or a co-operative society whose only purpose is the production of wine from the grapes of their members, this legal entity is called '*Zusammenschluss*'. Wines bottled by such a legal entity may also be marked '*aus dem Lesegut*' or '*Erzeugerabfüllung*' (estate bottling).

For this purpose it does not matter whether the wines are ordinary table wines or quality wines.

To sum up:

1. If grower, producer and bottler are identical: '*Erzeugerabfuellung*' or '*Aus eigenem Lesegut*' (estate bottling).

2. If grower and producer/bottler are two different persons, the bottler can state (with the permission of the grower) 'Growth X' or 'Grower X', bottled by or shipped by . . . , but in this case *both* names must be shown on the label.

The trade in the English-speaking world can, in my opinion, continue to use the well-known expressions 'estate bottling' and 'growth', and in this way give wine drinkers the correct information. I can, however, imagine that others might hold divergent opinions and I foresee that problems may arise in the future. In the past these expressions guaranteed natural wines, and it will be quite understandable if somebody insists that as in Germany, new expressions could be used here too for other than the quality wines with predicate.

The following examples illustrate the German wine label (all quality wine labels show also the examination number, see page 108):

FRIEND FRITZ WINE CO Winkel/Rheingau TAFELWEIN aus den Laendern der EWG Produce of the E.E.C.	Tafelwein of the E.E.C. according to decree 2133/74 which indicates that the Tafelwein is a blend of products either originating in different member states or which were not turned into wine in the member states in which the grapes used were harvested.
FRIEND FRITZ WINE CO Winkel/Rheingau Qualitätswein Rheinhessen 'Fritzengold' Bereich Nierstein Bottled and produced in Germany	QbA from *Bereich.*
FRIEND FRITZ WINE CO Winkel/Rheingau DEUTSCHER TAFELWEIN Produced and bottled in Germany	100 per cent German wine, a blend from as many German districts as the shippers select.
FRIEND FRITZ WINE CO Winkel/Rheingau Qualitätswein Rheinhessen NIERSTEINER GUTES DOMTAL Bottled and produced in Germany	Qualitätswein from *Grosslage.*

FRIEND FRITZ WINE CO Winkel/Rheingau Qualitätswein Rheinhessen NIERSTEINER GLOECK Bottled and produced in Germany	Qualitätswein from a single site. The label does not give indication of *Grosslage* or *Einzellage*, the knowledge counts.
FRIEND FRITZ WINE CO Winkel/Rheingau LIEBFRAUMILCH Qualitätswein Bottled and produced in Germany	Liebfraumilch as quality wine has to originate from one specific region – Rheinpfalz, Rheinhessen, Nahe, Rheingau, in other words there may be four types of Liebfraumilch, but changes are being considered and blending of wines of the four regions is 'admitted'. The label does not show any specific region.
Erzeugerabfuellung	treated and bottled in the producer's cellars = Estate Bottled = aus eigenem Lesegut.
Aus dem Lesegut von XYZ	bottled by a merchant. The producer must have given permission, when selling the cask, that his name as the producer can be stated.
Riesling, Müller-Thurgau, Scheurebe	three kinds of grapes have been used in the production of the blend, of which Riesling constitutes a larger part than Müller-Thurgau, Müller-Thurgau a larger or at least part than Müller-Thurgau, Mül-
Niersteiner Kranzberg Riesling Trockenbeerenauslese	This denomination of Kranzberg is allowed, if the Trockenbeerenauslese originates over 50 per cent from this vineyard.

Niersteiner Riesling Trockenbeerenauslese	This indicates that the grapes originate from Nierstein from various vineyards and less than 50 per cent of any one vineyard.

NAME-GIVING ORTSTEILE (suburbs)

STEINBERG	*Ortsteil* of Hattenheim, no single site
SCHLOSS VOLLRADS	*Ortsteil* of Winkel, Schlossberg Site
SCHLOSS JOHANNISBERG	*Ortsteil* of Geisenheim, partly Klaus (a small part)
SCHARZHOFBERG	*Ortsteil* of Wiltingen (Saar)

I am sure many lovers of German wine will regret the disappearance of such expressions as '*Originalabfüllung*' and '*Kellerabfüllung*', expressions which have been used for many decades and have been understood inside and outside Germany for what they were, i.e.wines produced, treated and bottled by the grower.

'*Originalabfüllung*' was more than just a term. As the word says, it was a guarantee that everything in the bottle was 'original', the vintage was 100 per cent vintage, the geographical origin was 100 per cent correct. Some growers stopped using '*Originalabfüllung*' and replaced it by '*Kellerabzug*'. Leading in this field was the Hessian Domain in Eltville.

A 1959 Steinberger Originalabfüllung had to be a Steinberg wine of the vintage 1959. But a Steinberger 1959 Kellerabzug might contain 33⅓ per cent of another vintage or another vineyard. This had great advantages for the grower. It was a way of getting rid of lesser vintages and wines of lesser vineyards.

Another way the grower could achieve this was by blending and giving two names. The best example of this was the Berncasteler Doctor blended with wine of the neighbouring Graben which became Doktor und Graben Originalabfüllung. The bottle contained a very high proportion of wine from Graben – the customer paid 100 per cent for Doctor.

Unfortunately this practice will not continue, to the great disadvantage of the wine drinker, if he is silly enough to buy and drink labels, because '*Erzeugerabfüllung*' allows the grower to blend in 25 per cent of another vintage, 25 per cent of another vineyard, or 25 per cent of another grape. This is a bad enough result for the buyer. But the new vineyard register has enlarged many famous vineyards. The 1·32 – undersized – Doctor has been enlarged to 5 ha, incorporating the lesser Graben vineyard. The former 'Doktor und Graben', which contained a few drops of Doktor, now becomes 100 per cent 'Doctor', and the grower can, under '*Erzeugerabfüllung*', blend in 25 per cent of a lesser vintage, or 25 per cent of a vineyard from the Bereich Bernkastel belonging to him and is thus in a position to offer a much greater quantity of 'Doctor' than he had been able to sell in previous years as 'Doctor und Graben'. The canny buyer will hesitate long before he or she pays the same or similar prices. Unscrupulous growers, unscrupulous brokers and unscrupulous shippers can and will try to confuse the issue. I hope however that this warning will save my readers a lot of money. Beware of some names – leave them to the snobs!

TAFELWEIN

The catalogue on pp. 154–5 shows that a bottle labelled 'Tafelwein' does not contain German wine. Tafelwein is a blend of wines from countries of the E.E.C. and can as such contain some German wine, but need not. 'Deutscher Tafelwein' is the name for a 100 per cent German wine.

The E.E.C. has four wine-producing and wine-exporting countries (not counting the small amount grown in this country and, for instance, in Belgium) and any blended wine from these countries is Tafelwein, when the components of the blend originate from the same zone of the E.E.C. If the imported wine is just *one* unblended wine, it is an '*auslaendischer*' (foreign) Tafelwein.

One might ask, why should anybody consider importing wine from two foreign countries to blend and bottle them in Germany. Where is the advantage? The advantage lies in the chance to produce a better wine at a lower price. The region of one of the wines to be blended may lack a certain component and one therefore has to find a wine from another country which fills this gap, one wine complements the other and the end product is a perfect Tafelwein, 'from the countries of the E.E.C.'

As soon as I heard of this regulation, I tasted dozens of 'imperfect wines' and tried to find the ideal 'partners'. A wine can, however, only be called 'Tafelwein' if all wines used for the blend originate in the same E.E.C. zones. If the wines originate in different zones – even if all districts are regions of the E.E.C. – the denomination 'Tafelwein' is lost and the wine becomes just 'wine'.

Some such blends of French and German wines have astonished some of my friends – wines of Spätlese or sometimes even Auslese character could be named just 'Friend Fritz Tafelwein' or 'Tischwein', depending on the components of the blend, and were in price the best bargains available on the wine market.

These international blends are nothing new. Until 1909 it was a custom of German merchants to make good wine from an inferior vintage by adding foreign wine. Some unscrupulous shippers have never stopped this practice and have been rash enough to name the wines according to quality and not according to their origin. They can even be sold with the name of a *Weinbaugebiet*, if 85 per cent of the wine originates from it and when the blend consists of wine of Zones A or A + B. If the blend contains wine from Zone C it can be sold under an invented or fancy name.

Now that economically all E.E.C. countries are one unit, interesting new developments can be expected for the wine lover who goes for quality independent of origin and name.

BLENDING

Any one of the regulations about blending may be changed at any time by the E.E.C. authorities. Basically I am of the opinion that if a wine is blended it is only right to choose a name which covers all components. If the wine contains wines of two villages of the same *Bereich*, then the name of the *Bereich* must appear, if it contains the wines of various *Bereiche* of the same region or subregion, then the name of the region or subregion should be given. If it contains components of various regions, then the only designation allowed is that the wine is 'of German origin'. In any case, my own view is that a proportion of 75:25 per cent of grape, of vintage, of name will eventually be reduced to 85:15* per cent. And so far as naming is concerned a blend is not harmful if the blending is done of must grapes or young wine. In other words, wine which has not yet been racked.

NAMING OF BLENDS

In the case of a vintage blend a vintage may only be stated if the blend contains at least 75 per cent of grapes of that vintage. As already indicated the blend has an influence on the naming of the wine: the names of vintage and grapes are lost if the blend does not contain 75 per cent of a particular kind.

If a range of grapes has been used in the blend, their names may be given if none of them impregnates the wine with its character, but

* See new Regulations 2133/74.

each kind of grape must be stated on the label in a correct sequence from the largest to the smallest proportion in the blend.

Restrictions on the naming of the blends are standardized for quality wines and quality wines with predicate.

Quality wines must originate 75 per cent from a 'site' or 'village' or 'district' and must give the wine its local character. The balance of 25 per cent must originate exclusively from the *same* defined area (i.e. Palatinate, Rheingau, etc.), and must be of equal value.

After 1976 no quality wine can originate from two districts even if the vineyards from which the grapes originate should be situated side by side. The only exception is Liebfraumilch.

The federal governments are authorized to allow '*uebergebietliche*' blends ('multi-regional' blends). Rheinland-Pfalz has given this concession until vintage 1975, but information of such blends must be supplied to the authorities.

Blends of quality wines with predicate must originate from the same *Bereich.*

There is no possibility that blending may result in a cheaper wine, as all parts of the blend must be of equal value – otherwise the wine is a Tafelwein and not a quality wine.

Beerenauslesen and Trockenbeerenauslesen which are produced from grapes of more than one site may be labelled with the name of the site from which more than 50 per cent of the grapes originate. If the share of any site does not reach 50 per cent, no site name can be given.

DETAILED POINTS ON NAMING OF BLENDS

1. A 'general blend' of wines from various wine-growing German districts is to take the lowest grade 'Deutscher Tafelwein' (German table wine).

2. A geographical denomination can be taken, if the grapes used originate at least to the extent of 75 per cent from the naming 'area', if that part gives the wine its character and the raw material of other origin is equal in value and also exclusively from the same district.

If the wine has no district name, just '*deutsch*' (German) it may be a blend of wines from all German districts, i.e. a blend of Palatinate, Rhinehessia and Mosel would be called '*Deutsch*'.

It is interesting to note that after rackings, etc. the '*füllwein*' (topping-up wine) must be of identical origin as the bulk to which it is being added. The topping-up operation is classified as 'blending' and an error here may lead to declassification and consequent loss of value.

A blend of German *red* wine containing Deckrotwein – allowed until 1979 – can never be a quality wine with predicate: if it contains 15 per cent Deckrotwein it is a Tafelwein, if it contains 10 per cent it can be a quality wine if all other conditions are fulfilled.

Adding *Süssreserve* does not count as blending and has no influence on the naming of the product but this may be changed by an E.E.C. law which is under consideration.

However, should the *Süssreserve* not originate in the same vineyard, or not be from the same vintage, then the rule of blending has to be used for the naming of the wine. If for instance the *Süssreserve* for Spätlese wines should not come from the same *Bereich*, it would lead to the loss of the predicate 'Spätlese'.

The latest development in blending is the 'European blend' from the countries of the E.E.C. (*aus den Ländern der E.W.G.*). Blends of this kind are 'Tafelwein', even if all its components are quality wines. Such a wine may contain wines of all the wine-producing countries of the E.E.C., containing of course German wines too.

Blends with wines from countries outside the E.E.C. are prohibited.

BRANDS (INVENTED NAMES)

Phantasienamen, Markennamen

Vineyard names are so numerous and the possibilities of offending against the wine law as described previously so great, that many wines are sold under invented or fancy names – not that the wine law had nothing to say about this too. Thousands of invented names have been registered and more are being registered every week. A shipper may just offer his X's 'Weinzauber' without any indication of the geographical origin of the wine – perhaps just as 'German white wine' (Deutscher Weisswein).

Invented names must not be used in conjunction with a geographical designation, as this might be taken to indicate a district of origin. Therefore the invented name has to be printed on the label in such a position that the invented name cannot be misunderstood and taken as a geographical denomination. Invented names may not be so formed as to mislead the purchaser, i.e. the quality of the wine must not be inferior to that which the purchaser is entitled to expect from the label. If a wine should be sold as Mother Mosel, it must be a Mosel wine; if under the name Rheinliebchen, a Rhine wine.

Formerly Liebfraumilch counted as an invented name for a good quality wine, but it has now become a 'wine type' name.

In one category of fancy names is the 'branded' wine. Wine merchants strive to offer wines or blends of wines under one name, the brand, whatever the origin of the product, with the aim that each bottling should be equal to the next bottling in bouquet, taste, colour, alcoholic strength and body; in other words all bottlings theoretically have to be the same in their chemical analysis, brought about by the blender's art – even in different quality vintages.

What I have just described would be the ideal branded wine. It exists only in theory. In practice, it is quite impossible to reach a single result in two blends. Even if all parts are identical in quantity and quality, small differences can occur depending for instance on how much later the last blending was made after the first, how much the wine was exposed to air and how much treatment it required.

The idea of the branding of wines is to give the consumer 'the same as previously supplied'. But this means in practice that he should expect a similar, but not an identical wine. To produce an exactly similar blend independent of vintage differences is simply impossible. I am therefore of the opinion that a wine which, if sold under geographical denomination would be entitled to a vintage, should have the same right if the wine is sold as branded wine.

RESTRICTIONS IN NOMENCLATURE

Here is the full name of a wine:

Mosel-Saar-Ruwer	
Qualitätswein b.A.	
Bereich Bernkastel	(*Bereich*)
Piesporter Michelsberg	(*Grosslage* greater site)
Brauneberger Juffer	(single site *Einzellage*)

As the examination numbers are given to bottled wines only, the proprietor can offer the wine in cask under various names, but must inform the customer accordingly. In other words, he can offer it as

Bereich Bernkastel
or Piesporter Michelsberg
or Brauneberger Juffer

but after the customer has made his choice, he applies with *this* name for the examination number.

In my opinion nobody can be prevented from printing the full true statement on the label. At present the authorities take the view that the applicant for the examination number makes his choice. His choice (baptism) fixes the name. If later on he would like to rename the part he has bought, he must apply for a new examination number.

Under no circumstances may a proprietor sell the same wine under *two* different names, even though the wine may be entitled to both. This was already a regulation under the old law to prevent a grower or merchant from appearing to hold a larger stock than he really did.

CLASSIFICATION AND VINTAGES

In France, the *Chambre Syndicale des Courtiers* in Bordeaux have classified the wines of Bordeaux in order of merit – the red wines in five growths, the white wines in two. Nothing of the kind is possible with German wines. The French château as a rule produces one *cuvée* only.

In Germany, the situation is quite different. German growers, large and small, stow their wines in individual casks as they come from the press. On the Mosel they usually use *Fuders* (960 litres) and half-*Fuders*; *Stücks* (1,200 litres), half-*Stücks* and quarter-*Stücks* are customary in Rhinehessia and the Rheingau; while in the Palatinate they use *Fuders* of 1,000 litre capacity. The wines mature in the casks and keep their individuality at least as long as they remain in the wine grower's cellar. For this reason wines from the same growers differ greatly in quality. The differences are due to various circumstances: the grapes may have been gathered in the early or the late harvest period; they may have been gathered with particular care, for instance by the selection of special bunches of the fruit, or even of specially ripe or overripe single berries, etc.

The *Lagen* (sites) are divided into a great many smallholdings of various sizes. Only a few large or sizeable *Lagen* are in the hands of one owner, the best of these being the Steinberger (State Domain). The few sites under 5 ha are generally speaking of no importance. These subdivisions afford another reason for the differences in wines from the same *Lage*. One owner may tend his vineyard more carefully than the other, and may manure it at shorter intervals, and this makes for great differences in taste – quite apart from the different dates and selective methods of gathering the fruit already mentioned.

Some growers have for these reasons adopted a method of classifying their own wines by furnishing them with different labels, caps or seals, and some have used the word 'Cabinet' (or Kabinett) to designate wines which fetch a certain price (laid down by the individual grower). This, as I have already pointed out, has been changed by the 1971 wine law. Kabinett – and this is the right spelling – has become the attribute of a Prädikatswein.

The change-over to fermentation and storage in large vessels has already brought about a change in this kind of classification. Schloss Johannisberg had in any case begun after the 1950 vintage to use tanks of 5,000 litres each, and the State Domain in the Rheingau uses tanks of 8,500 litres and of 21,000 litres, the balance of the crop still being kept in casks of 1,200 litres.

The growers themselves are well aware how misleading it is for the consumer when two wines of the same name vary as greatly in all their characteristics as I have shown above. In future they will be distinguishable, because each individual cask will have its own examination number on the label. Wines of the same cask and the same bottling must have the same number.

It has been suggested in some quarters that German growers should accept the French method. It would certainly deprive us of the Auslese, the Beeren- and Trockenbeerenauslese wines, but it would increase the average overall quality to a high degree. Those who are of this opinion are thinking in particular of the Steinberger wines. If you taste the whole range, you will find that the 'Steinberger' is no more than a *vin ordinaire* – hardly worth drinking – because all that is best in the vineyard has gone into the Auslese, the Beerenauslese and the Trockenbeerenauslese, and the latter is considered the best wine of the Rheingau. They argue what a grand wine the 'Steinberger' would be if all the vineyard products were to be used for one *cuvée*, and it would help to bring an exquisite wine within range of thousands instead of the few who can afford to buy the extract, the Trockenbeerenauslese. And what is true of the Steinberger applies, of course, to all vineyards. As I said in *Rhineland-Wineland* price differences are sometimes colossal. At the auctions in January 1951, for example, the best cask of 1949 Steinberger (the ordinary Steinberger) cost 50 per cent more than the cheapest. When bottled, they look exactly alike, therefore, the argument goes on, the unfortunate consumer who, having had and enjoyed one consignment of bottles from the best cask, may get his next consignment from the cheapest, is due for a sad disappointment. Is it false pride on the part of the German grower when he boasts of the high price his best cask has attained, if at the same time his other wines are the poorer for it? Anyone who has tasted the Auslese, Beerenauslese and Trockenbeerenauslese wines cannot and will not agree with these arguments. These wines are the nectar of the gods, wines to be sipped on a festive occasion, and they represent the finest Nature can produce.

It is of course true that this method reduces the average quality, as was only too clear when too many Beerenauslesen were made in 1959 in the Steinberg vineyard, reducing the quality of most of the 1959 Spätlese and Auslese wines of this vineyard to below standard.

But it would be a loss should we ever be deprived of these delights, and it is not likely that growers will listen to such arguments. They may reduce the ordinary wines to one or two *cuvées* but will never give up their efforts to produce the best. The competitions arranged by Government bodies and viticultural associations will stimulate the growers' ambitions still further.

First of all there is the legal classification, Tafelwein, Qualitätswein mit Prädikat, etc. The new wine law has forced many estates to change their own classification of their growths. I have already referred to Schloss Vollrads and Schloss Johannisberg.

One must strongly warn against the concept that because a wine is produced by Mr. X or comes from this or that site (*Lage*) or village, it *must* be good. It would be still less justifiable to speak of a grower as *the* leading grower, and therefore expect the best only. Such ideas lead to great disappointment.

The Steinberg vineyard is considered the best site of the Rheingau, a most impressive site, but the qualities of its wines, coming from one grower – the State Domain – differ as much between themselves as do the Clos de Vougeot wines in Burgundy, belonging to more than a dozen growers. The 1961 Steinberger should never have been bottled; its Kabinett was just good enough to be an aperitif. The 1959s were all good – ranging from ordinary table wine to the Feinste Trockenbeerenauslese.

Changes have taken place in the vinification, in the blending. The great estates have started to equalize their wines. The ordinary Steinberger is being chaptalized and marketed as 'Qualitätswein' and one can expect under one label one Qualitätswein with very small differences. Wherever possible, Tafelweine, Quality wines and Kabinett wines are equalized by all estates. One will seldom find two different qualities under the same label. But if it happens, the wine is marked accordingly and the difference can be seen at least from the different official examination number. At the spring sale of 1975 the Steinberger Riesling QbA and Kabinett were presented in such two qualities, one quality as 'dry', without the addition of Süssreserve, and the other with Süssreserve. At the press conference the administrator asked me for my opinion of the dry Steinberger Kabinett wine and my answer was quite simple, 'Where is the wine?'; it did not show any vinosity and fruit.

One grower was especially successful with his 1949, 1950 and 1953 wines and soon he was called 'the leading grower'. 1954–63 were not all successful, even including the 1959, with the exception of a few casks, but he received much higher prices for all his wines because somebody had stamped him as the leading grower. His Spätlesen and Auslesen were rejected by me as fakes.

It gives the greatest pleasure to find in poor vintages the really good and excellent wines; it is an even greater pleasure to find in the cellars of the medium-sized growers qualities which beat those of their aristocratic larger neighbours. Individual care and skill often produce qualities in wines without pedigree which are far above those of the Doctors, Sonnenuhrs or Steinbergers.

To sum up: I am strictly against any personal cult.

Only his own palate and purse can decide for any individual wine lover which wine is best for him. So long as he is inexperienced, he cannot do better than follow the advice of his wine merchant who has tasted and selected the wines on his list with a view to satisfying his clients' needs. One cannot classify village against village, and site name against site name. If comparison is wanted, one should only compare ordinary with ordinary wines, Spätlese with Spätlese, and Auslese with Auslese. The classifications in the olden days were mostly made on the basis of the best cask which was produced. If one vineyard produced the best cask, it was considered the best vineyard.

As already indicated, the only classification possible is by the taste and value of each single cask. There are of course specially favoured *Lagen* which enjoy suitable soil and much sunshine and therefore produce genuinely good wines, provided nature in the relevant vintage has ripened the grapes. Knowledge of these factors will assist the consumer and help to avoid disappointment. We shall meet them on our wine journey.

The new Vineyard Register has in many cases increased existing sites. Why not be adventurous, try the unknown or less known wines, the unknown village, the unknown site, the unknown merchant?

As a general guide, Spätlese or Auslese wine is always apt to give full satisfaction on account of its special ripeness and fruitiness, especially today when as a result of the official examination a minimum quality and a wine free of faults are guaranteed.

Some enthusiastic wine drinkers, and not by any means the least knowledgeable, prefer old well-seasoned wines to any others. Nowadays such wines are difficult to find.

I wrote in 1963: 'One of my friends still has a good stock of 1933, 1934, 1935 and 1937 wines which we tasted in spring 1963. In our tasting result we placed the 1934 the highest and came to the conclusion that the 1934 proved to be a finer vintage than the much praised 1921. The staying power of the 1934 is astonishing. A Hallgartener Jungfer Riesling Spätlese 1934 showed such light fresh colour and taste that it may have another 20 to 30 years and still be enjoyed.'

Even the most fastidious taste should be satisfied with the 1964, 1966 and 1971 wines. The last decades truly have given us a fine range of vintages. If you can still find wines of the 1949, 1952, 1953 or 1959 vintages you will be surprised about the staying power of German wines. There is, however, one condition which must be mentioned: the wines must have been stored at a temperature not exceeding approximately 11°C.

Personally I am of the opinion that the connoisseur has abandoned the idea of valuing wine according to age. It is certainly interesting to observe a wine ageing and its development, but a young wine can give so much pleasure; it has finesse and elegance so that it outclasses older wine of the same vineyards – it is as if you compared a young girl, just coming of age, in all her freshness and beauty, with a more mature woman. In exactly the same way as we become wrinkled when we get older, so do wines after having reached their best. The 1921, 1934, 1937, 1945, 1949, 1952, 1953, 1959, 1964, 1966 and 1971 wines have, of course, great names. The 1961 vintage which was a great vintage in France, but not in Germany, still produced unique Eisweine of great quality and in good quantities, too.

It has generally been considered that Mosels keep in flourishing condition for seven years – but I have drunk much older Mosels which had lost nothing of their vigour. On the whole, however, I prefer younger wines with their freshness and delicate flavour – a two-to three-year-old Mosel or a four- to ten-year-old Rhine wine should be able to satisfy fully even the most capricious palate.

Wines are living organisms and must be treated as such: account must be taken of their individual peculiarities. Rheingau, Rhine-hessian and Palatinate wines often reach a ripe old age without deteriorating.

Bottled wines do not stay static in quality, but are subject to alteration and change. They continue their development until it reaches its peak. Having reached this stage, the wines remain at their best for years, or even for decades, and then gradually deteriorate.

Great wines deteriorate very slowly. Some retain their good qualities for thirty, fifty, even more years. The Museum of Bottled Wines in the Kurhaus, Wiesbaden, which was destroyed in 1945, showed Rheingau wines (*Original- und Hochgewaechs*) which were over 200 years old (the oldest was a 1706 vintage). In the autumn of 1941 the owner had tasted his collection and rearranged it according to the current value of the individual exhibits. He then published a little brochure of the results of his 'probe'. Here is an extract from his booklet: 'From the year 1859 onwards some of the wines have retained their original noble sweetness; together with the delicate acidity characteristic of Rheingau products and the bouquet which in the course of the years has been wonderfully enhanced, their present qualities combine to give the wines a flavour which may be designed as "fluid", fruity and highly aristocratic.' The collection included wines from all Rheingau communities. The Museum of Bottled Wines in Deidesheim, belonging to the well-known writer on wines and vineyard owner Geheimrat Dr. von Bassermann-Jordan, is still in undisturbed existence. Here we find remainders of every vintage since 1889. A few specimens (not a complete collection) go back to an 1811 Forster Ungeheuer Estate Bottling. The oldest estate bottled wines are from the year 1706.

There are a few such collections left in Germany; others were destroyed during the war. The State Wine Cellars of Assmannshausen, Eltville, and Kloster Eberbach still exist and count among their treasures wines which go back to 1893. The collections of the State Wine Domains, Rüdesheim and Hochheim were on the other hand destroyed to the last bottle.

In the same way the Museum of Bottled Wines at the Pfortenhaus in Kloster Eberbach was destroyed. Before the war its wine list included vintages going back to 1857.

Some estates and collectors have now begun to restock their collections. The vintages of 1945 to 1972 now have an honoured place in these and are likely to rejoice the hearts of future generations. In the whole history of German viticulture, there have never been so many good years in succession, as the vintage chart shows (see p. 171). It should be noted, however, that vintage charts can only give a general survey of annual production and may be incorrect in regard to some districts and *Lagen*. In some places good wines have been produced in bad years, while poor wines may be brought forth from time to time even in the best years.

In general the 1921 vintage may be described as 'excellent', and 1920 as 'good', but in Rüdesheim (Rheingau) it was the other way round. In other places too – particularly in the Palatinate – some of the 1920 wines outshone by far those produced in the 'peak' year of 1921.

The 1939 wine was 'inferior' owing to frost damage just before the grapes ripened. And yet some sheltered *Lagen* produced wines of particular elegance and finesse in that same season.

How unpredictable wines may be was proved by the so-called ice wines in 1890. These constituted an extraordinary phenomenon, because – despite all prophecies to the contrary – they turned out to be exquisite. The ripe berries on the vines had been frozen by an 'ice-rain', i.e. by a rainfall when the temperature was below freezing point. The water in the berries turned to ice and this left the remaining grape juice more concentrated and proportionally richer in sugar content. The wines made from this thick syrup were so sweet and fine as to be comparable to outstanding Auslesen.

Some of the 1949 wines had similar qualities. In 1950 Schloss Johannisberg produced one cask of 'ice wine' by pure accident. A great number of ice wines was produced in 1961 and 1962 in all districts, and in nearly every year since some growers have tried. 1973 was just such a successful vintage. For the ordinary consumer 'museum' wines are not of great interest. For the last 25 years I have been laying aside a few bottles of certain good wines, in order to observe their development over a long period and to test their durability and the age to which they can attain. But sometimes, moved by curiosity – or because I was particularly fond of some particular wine – I have raided these stores until all the 'museum' relics of the vintage in question were consumed. On the whole it is certainly better to drink wines before they reach their peak, rather than wait until their decline has set in.

Stored wines must be examined from time to time, and in particular it must be ascertained whether the corks of the bottles are still intact.

16

Recent vintages

The fact that wines are designated by their *Lagen* and by the year of origin shows that in all stages of their development in cask and in bottle the results depend on Nature. Anyone therefore who expects the wine grower to deliver identical products year after year, as if they were machine-made, is depriving himself of the exquisite enjoyment that can be provided only through the great variety of the offerings from different sites under the changing conditions of different seasons. No vintage is the same as the next – the degree of sunshine varies and with it the characteristics of that season's wines. The real wine connoisseur makes it his aim and his pride to pick out the finest product among the manifold kinds set before him, and – renewing this delightful occupation every season – to enjoy these 'peak' wines to the full. His cultivated wine palate may be compared to the finely attuned sound-sense of the musician or the colour-conscious eye of the artist, and affords him similar opportunities for artistic appreciation.

The general quality of German wines in recent years – to which we now turn our attention – has been very good. Nature has been very kind to German viticulture. The 1945 and 1946 vintages were fully satisfactory in quality, particularly in view of the fact that the war took heavy toll of German vineyards. During the war, little labour was available and there was a great shortage of everything, such as the things needed for protecting the plants. This makes the reasonably good quality of the wines little short of astonishing. In 1945 there were late frosts during the first days of May and the late summer was fine and sunny, but it was July that brought the storms and sudden showers to which we owe the exceptional qualities of that year's in quantity small vintage, the velvety taste, fruity richness and bouquet. Unhappily the vintage was even smaller than it need have been as there was a serious shortage of labour for picking the grapes and making the wine.

The weather in 1946 was very similar in many respects; the wines of that year owe their characteristic traits to the autumn. Full of body but fruity, they contained more acidity than usual, but were well-balanced and elegant and in general, fully representative of the typical Rhine wine flavour.

Next came the great year 1947 noted for what was almost excessive sunshine. All wine growers had fine harvests and produced heavy wines of a very pronounced character whose delicious bouquet was the delight of every wine connoisseur, even though many wines of the vintage showed a lack of acidity. It was an outstanding year, in which the specific gravity of the must was particularly high. It should, however, be noted in passing that this quality alone is not sufficient indication of the greatness of a wine. In the harmonious blending of sweetness with sufficient acidity the 1947 was a worthy successor to the famous 1921 vintage, and altogether a wine that will long be remembered by producers and consumers.

The 1948 harvest produced a wine which in some places outshone the 1947 in its harmony and raciness. Its quality may be described as great, and quantitatively the crops were outstanding. Both quality and quantity were due to the beautiful weather which prevailed while the vines were in flower. The summer was followed by a mild and sunny autumn. The delightful flavour of the 1948 wines coupled with their general harmony and delicate bouquet have been greatly appreciated by connoisseurs.

It is well known that a rich – and still more an excessively rich – crop is in general obtained at the expense of quality. Despite this undoubted fact, the 1948 can compete on equal terms with its predecessors, even in some cases being preferred to them. Thus 1945 to 1948 constitute four successive good years, and the 1949 bid fair to equal them. Wherever the grapes were able to ripen undisturbed by natural phenomena and wherever their subterranean store or supply of moisture was sufficient to offset the lack of rain in that year, the wine produced had an elegant fullness and harmony that may make it the wine of the century. On the other hand, dry sites produced wines of only medium quality which can at best be compared with the 1928 vintage. A notable feature of the year 1949 was the frequent appearance of the Edelfäule – *botritys cinerea* – on the berries, some of which had shrivelled to raisinlike consistency. Whenever this happened and the berries which had been so attacked were gathered or pressed separately and the wine appropriately treated, a really superb product was achieved.

The 1950 wines were high in quantity, but qualitatively they fall far below those of previous years. When sunshine was needed there were rainfalls, and many berries began to rot before they had reached the required maturity. In consequence they could only be made durable and drinkable by the addition of sugar.

The 1951 vintage was the worst since 1941 and was similar in quality to the 1931; it has been surpassed by the 1954 – a vintage which the grower will remember for a long time, because everything went wrong with the weather – spring frosts, much rain and no sunshine, a vintage which the wine lover will not seek out. If wine is captured sunshine, there was no 'wine' in 1954.

This made the two vintages of 1952 and 1953 all the more enjoyable. 1952 was a satisfactory vintage and some really good wines were made. After a fine July and August many people expected a fine year and one even dreamt of better wines than 1949 and 1921. Unfortunately the weather in September and October was disappointing, but an Indian summer brought us if not great yet still good Spätlese and Auslese wines, similar in quality to the 1948. They are ideal luncheon wines.

1953 was a fine successor to the 1949 and everything I have said about 1949 applies to 1953. These are ripe wines, with fruit, finesse and elegance.

There is a saying that a good vintage needs 'thirteen months' good weather', and good weather means rain and sun always at the right time and in the right quantity.

The vintages 1955 to 1958 are not worth mentioning; they are in any case overshadowed by the vintage of the century, the 1959.

The Statistical Office which receives detailed reports on the quality of the grapes during harvests, has issued very interesting comparative figures. One of the most important parts of the report is always the evaluation of the vintage. Let the figures speak for themselves (in percentages).

	Very Good	Good	Average	Inferior
1954	1	18	49	32
1955	3	27	49	21
1956	1	17	43	39
1957	6	37	46	11
1958	16	74	6	4
1959	50	45	5	0
1960	6	35	45	14
1961	13	46	34	7
1962	14	46	30	10
1963	8	36	41	15
1964	23	49	26	2
1965	1	14	44	41
1966	22	55	21	2
1967	12	41	37	10
1968	0	11	44	45
1969	10	39	44	7
1970	8	40	42	10

The evaluation was always based on the Oechsle degrees, i.e. if the must had

less than 60°	Oechsle	it was	'very inferior'
60 – 70°	,,	,,	'inferior'
70 – 80°	,,	,,	'average'
80 – 90°	,,	,,	'good'
90° and more	,,	,,	'very good'.

This method has now been discontinued, and the report is based on the new classification of German wines into Tafelweine, Qualitätsweine, and Qualitätsweine mit Prädikat. Therefore the evaluation is based on whether a must has the potential of producing Tafelwein, Qualitätswein or a Qualitätswein mit Prädikat. Of course the statistics cannot give us a definite quantity for the classes, because the definite classification depends upon the attribution of an examination number after the wine has been chemically analysed and tasted by the Tasting Committee, and passed by them in its specific class.

The figures for 1973 are:

1. *White Wines* (expressed in hectolitres)
   Tafelweine: 274,715 hl with an average sugar content of 55° Oechsle
   Qualitätsweine: 5,460,654 hl with an average sugar content of 68° Oechsle
   Qualitätsweine mit Prädikat: 3,350,050 hl with an average sugar content of 79° Oechsle

2. *Red Wines*
   Tafelweine: 144,256 hl with an average sugar content of 58° Oechsle
   Qualitätsweine: 1,034,458 hl with an average sugar content of 67° Oechsle
   Qualitätsweine mit Prädikat: 330,647 hl with an average sugar content of 83° Oechsle

It might astonish my readers that when we compare the former with the new evaluation we find that the Tafelweine are all those which in previous years have been considered very inferior, and that the Qualitätsweine are those wines which in previous years were considered 'inferior'. Even the Prädikatsweine under the old evaluation were only considered to be of 'medium' quality and higher.

The old evaluation was based on the must, i.e. how nature had produced it in the various vintages. The new evaluation states clearly that the must is apt to become Tafelwein or Qualitätswein, etc. and therefore takes into consideration what can become of the must – with the help of the cellarmaster, enrichment and fair vinification.

It was a principle of the old German wine law to allow the wines to be enriched to such an extent that they became equal to wines of a good vintage. The new method is therefore better. Formerly the wine drinker was more or less unable to assess the merits of a vintage. The new method gives him the guidance which was lacking under the former system.

The new method is a very useful type of classification. It shows realistically there are good wines produced in 'bad' years and bad wines in 'good' years. It highlights a great vintage such as the 1959 – no inferior and only five average wines. Conversely, it shows why 1965 might well be a candidate for the 'negative' vintage of the century.

Shortly before completing the first edition of my book *Rhineland Wineland* in 1951, I came across a little booklet called *Wine Chronicle, A thousand years of wine on the Moselle, the Rhine and the Main* by Deichmann and Wolf, published by Rauschenbusch, Stollhamm, Berlin. This book surveys the whole range of the centuries from A.D. 300 to 1949, and leaves the reader breathless with astonishment at the wealth of knowledge of times long past and the painstaking research of the authors.

Arranged in chronological order, the seasons are presented with a description of the weather in each year and a short description of the quantity and quality of the vintage produced. For example, 1125: Vineyards, people and cattle frozen to death. Dead birds fell to the ground out of the air. Quantity and quality of wine poor. 1166: Favourable wine year, but famine in the land. In Franconia wine was used in place of water for mixing the mortar for building. 1296: Favourable weather, good and plentiful wine, so that much of the old wine was poured away. 1529: A poor wine. In 1530 the wine caused the 'Christian Chancellor' an attack of the colic. In 1628 the wine was so bad that even the vinegar was ruined by it. If there were any need to prove that wine growing is a risky business, this book would furnish sufficient evidence.

The great vintages of this century are:

1904, 1911, 1915, 1917, 1920, 1921, 1929, 1933, 1934, 1935, 1937, 1945, 1947, 1949, 1953, 1959, 1964, 1971.

The vintage of 1971 deserves special mention as it was the first under the new law. If we look back to the harvest of 1970, we find that the weather at harvesting time was very favourable and lasted nearly until Christmas. The average temperature was 7·5°C where the normal average is considered to be 5·4°C. We still recall that on account of the good weather and the good and healthy state of the grapes, the growers left them on the vine so that just before Christmas, and on December 31 and even on 6 January 1971 they were able to produce Eiswein. The prior conditions for a good 1971 were certainly fulfilled.

The cold weather lasted for approximately four weeks and reached, at lowest, a temperature of −17·9°C, which was actually 'Three Kings' Day' 16 January when some Eiswein was harvested. If these grapes had been left quite in the open, they would have become food for the birds, but the German growers protected the grapes against birds and weather (because rain could have washed away the ripe grapes) by covering the vineyards with foil. Experts are still studying the best ways of doing this but, in any event, they succeeded in 1970. This is an expensive procedure but if it succeeds, it pays for the extra labour and material. The winter was not very cold but the temperature was below average, and even in March the second spell of cold weather brought the temperature down to −11·2°C. Rainfall was far below average, with only 175 mm of rain. The start of vegetation was therefore retarded, and this took place at the beginning of April. This month was also a very dry month with rain 33 per cent below average.

Budding started in the last third of April, and on some sites only in the first week of May. Development was very different in various types of vine and one sees the cause of it in the large crop of 1970 and the hard winter with its dryness. The long-desired rain came in the last week of May. Hail also damaged some vineyards. Blossoming was very irregular. Whereas the first blossoms were found on the best sites at the end of May, in other vineyards it started only at the end of June and ended there at the beginning of July.

June was too cool with too much rain. The latter part of June was again cool and damp, but July brought the great change. Its warm and dry weather contributed to quick and dry development of the grapes and at the end of July vegetation was approximately ten days ahead of an average year. Very little damage was done by the diseases and enemies of the vine. At the beginning of August the early-ripening grapes and even the Riesling on the best sites showed the first signs of the ripening process. Only in sites where there was insufficient underground water supply was some damage noticeable.

Some 'Vorlesen' (early gathering before the official harvest) were authorized when the Morio-Muskat were likely to have fallen off the vine – the degree of ripeness is best shown by the Oechsle degree of 72–90°. The official harvest started in the Palatinate for the Portugieser on 20 September, and for Müller-Thurgau in Rheinhessen on 20 September in some parts, and in other parts on 23 September. The quantity of the early-ripening grapes harvested was so much smaller than expected that the 1971 crop was not more than 5 million hectolitres, half that of 1970!

There is an old saying 'Little Rhine Great Wine' – 'Kleiner Rhein Grosser Wein' and in 1971 we had the experience of the water of the Rhine getting lower every day. The rocks – Hunger rocks – (Hungersteine) were again visible in the middle of the Rhine on the Binger Loch near Assmannshausen. Navigation on the Rhine suffered and boats could only move half-loaded. The Rhine reached its lowest for over 153 years and grapes reached their highest degree of sugar. A great vintage not only producing great wines, but a lot of great wines. A year with problems, too!

We did not need 'the best of the century' but were pleased and grateful to have a good vintage once more. The grapes had reached ripeness throughout and the Oechsle degrees were very satisfactory. They lay generally for all early-ripening grapes between 70° and 80° and Morio-Muskat reached 90°. I should mention that as usual in such vintages with lack of rain, some vineyards had suffered through a lack of water, the effect of the dryness being a slowing down in the development of the sugar content in the grapes. Such grapes are ripe, but had lower Oechsle degrees than expected.

Here, by way of comparison, are details of other '71 vintages over the centuries:

871 Good vintage – fine grapes and wine.
1171 Great heat – great wine.
1271 Very fertile vintage – noble rot throughout, great quantity and great quality.
1371 Not much wine – bad, but expensive.
1471 Not much wine, but very great wine; unfavourable weather during blossoming but a warm summer and a fine Indian summer.
1571 A very severe winter, a year of much hail. Quantity small and wine sour.
1671 Quite a lot of wine made of satisfactory quality with some exceptions. Middle-Rhine vineyards suffered from early cold and there was not much wine produced.
1771 Not much wine produced – wet weather and poor blossoming in mid June. Many diseases of the vine, and frost a week before harvesting started.
1871 Small quantity (1/3 of average) and inferior quality. The chronicler states: Must had 60–95°. Harvesting started on 23 October in very favourable weather.

It is interesting to note: 'Inferior quality, must of 60–95°'.

From this remark we can see the progress which science has brought to viticulture. Today a must with 57° Oechsle becomes a quality wine and 95° means Auslese or at least Spätlese as the table on p. 103 shows.

The vintage of 1971 has exceeded all expectations, and a contributory factor may be the small quantity, approximately half that of the 1970 vintage. From the start reports about the sugar and acid content of the young must were all enthusiastic. The quantity of Spitzenweine in the Beeren- and Trockenbeerenauslese class was larger than ever before. The great wines were not scarce in 1971, but the ordinary table wines were. A great preparation of the harvest were Kabinett and Spätleseweine. Here are some details district by district:

Mosel – Saar – Ruwer

Many growers produced Beerenauslese (up to 135° Oechsle) and Trockenbeerenauslesen from 160° to well above 200° Oechsle. Auslese and Spätlese come to 70 per cent in quantity of the harvest.

Wines are well balanced and have a great future.

Rheingau

Kabinettwines 73–84° Oechsle 20 per cent
Spätlese 50 per cent
Auslese 15 per cent to Beeren- and Trockenbeerenauslese 5 per cent with very good balancing fruity acidity.

The Mosel-Saar-Ruwer and Rheingau are nearly all Riesling wines.

Nahe

Kabinett
Spätlese
Auslese
were produced from different grapes: Müller-Thurgau, Silvaner, Riesling, Scheurebe and Pinot Chardonnay, Weissburgunder and new crossings.

The first four mentioned produced Beerenauslese to a degree formerly unknown:

Silvaner 1 per cent Beerenauslesen

Riesling 7 per cent Beerenauslesen, 1 per cent Trockenbeerenauslesen

Scheurebe 2 per cent Beerenauslesen

Weissburgunder 8 per cent Beerenauslesen, 2 per cent Trockenbeerenauslesen

The balance all Auslesen! These 'white Burgundies' are therefore quite different from the white Burgundies of Burgundy!

Rheinhessen

Here the Auslesen and Beerenauslesen with approximately 15 per cent are the outstanding grades produced, which include 'White Burgundy' and Gewürztraminer. The Kabinett and Spätlese wines with 15 per cent and 50 per cent respectively are the wines to look for.

Rheinpfalz

A great quantity of Beerenauslesen and Trockenbeerenauslesen and, what is remarkable, with the highest Oechsle ever reported and from new grapes:

Huxelrebe 202°
Scheurebe 118–247°
Siegerrebe 283–327°

These wines deserve to be included in one's cellar for laying down.

Kabinett 40 per cent
Spätlese 30 per cent
Auslesen 10 per cent

I should like to refer to *Franken* as the area which presents great wines from new crossings in great variety, such as Ortega, Mariensteiner, Perle, Albalonga, Rieslaner and Kerner:

Auslesen with 110°–130° Oechsle
Beerenauslesen 130°–160°
Trockenbeerenauslesen up to 200°

were harvested, among them Perle with 194°. In terms of grape varieties, the Oechsle figures were:

Müller-Thurgau	210°
Silvaner	260
Rieslaner	238
Ortega	204

and a Siegerrebe of 347° Oechsle, the highest degree ever reached! In most districts the proportions of acidity and sugar content were very favourable.

Eisweine of the vintage deserve a special place in this report. First of all because special efforts were made by many growers, by leaving a part of their vineyards unharvested and covering up the grapes, and secondly, the latest ever gathered Eisweine were made.

The first night with sufficient frost to produce Eiswein was the night from 17/18 November 1971 and the second was on 16/17 January 1972. By the second date the fully ripe grapes had been dehydrated to such an extent that there was not much juice left in the grape to freeze. The concentration of the frozen grapes produced must with 140° Oechsle sugar content, in other words Beerenauslese quality!

All in all 1971 is a vintage to taste, to select, to lay down and to enjoy for the next decades; and so far as the Spitzenweine – the top-class Beeren- Trockenbeerenauslesen – are concerned, for the year 2000!

Every year the German vintage is baptized. That does not mean that water is added to the wine but that the vintage is given its name. Everybody is allowed to submit suggestions and all suggestions received for the 1971 vintage contained the word Sonne – sun in various combinations being a hint that this was a year of sunshine especially during the autumn when there was plenty of it. The name adopted was Sonnenfürst.

17

Schaumweine, Sekt and Prädikatssekt

When in 1815 the actor Ludwig Devrient came to the Berlin Court Theatre, he would often play Falstaff in *Henry IV*. In the scene at the 'Wild Boar's Head' when he ordered a cup of sack, Devrient used the German word *Sekt* to denote 'sack'. Obviously this was not meant for Champagne, a beverage unknown in Shakespeare's day, but for sherry. The translator had, however, rendered sack with *Sekt*. From the stage Devrient carried this nomenclature into his private life, and when he was drinking with his crony and friend, the poet E. T. A. Hoffman at the wine restaurant Lutter and Wegner, he used to call out to the waiter: 'Hey villain, bring me a glass of *Sekt*'. Since then the word has established itself in Germany as the correct name for sparkling wine.

This, however, is no longer correct under the new German wine law. The name Sekt is now reserved for a special 'Qualitätsschaumwein' only. The lower grade which is not entitled to the denomination Sekt is now known as Schaumwein (literally 'foaming wine').

'Sekt' or 'Sect' Champagne and Schaumwein have been used in Germany since the middle of the nineteenth century as synonymous for all sparkling wines, a translation of 'Vin Mousseux'. When the Treaty of Versailles prohibited to Germany the denomination of 'Champagne' for German sparkling wine, Sekt became the name for it.

The production of Schaumwein starts generally with the blending of the basic wines, the formation of the *cuvée*; here lies the decisive element, the know-how. These *cuvées* are often the result of the studies and tastings of generations.

The blender must have the end product in mind. As will be explained later, the naming of the product depends on its components; one may aim at a 'world wine', containing a proportion of wines from all wine-producing countries of the world; one may want a product with the name of the country, or the region or the district or even of a single vineyard! Tasting, memory, knowledge of the quality and character of different wines are the factors important to the creator of the *cuvée*.

Schaumwein is a manufactured article produced from wine or grape must. The finished product must contain carbonic acid as a result of alcoholic fermentation and a minimum of 70 grams actual alcohol per litre (8·85 per cent by volume), which at a temperature of 20°C shows in containers of quarter-bottle size a carbonic acid pressure of 3·0 atü* and in larger containers a minimum of 3·5 atü. Perlwein, in contrast, is allowed only 2·5 atü carbonic acid.

The alcohol can have been produced by the first fermentation – a second fermentation is not absolutely necessary. Schaumwein can be produced purely and simply by the addition of carbonic acid (impregnation process). The best-known method, however, is of course, the *Méthode Champenoise*, originated by Dom Perignon, the only method allowed for the production of the protected original 'Champagne'. A further method is much used in Germany, the 'Transvasion' method: the wine goes through a second fermentation in bottle but to free it from the lees it is transferred into a vat where it is kept under carbonic acid pressure and from there filtered into the bottle, ready for sale. A final method is to collect the carbonic acid which is formed during the first fermentation of the grape must. After the fermentation and treatment of the still wine is finished the collected carbonic acid is used to produce Schaumwein. This is an impregnation method, where only the wine's own carbonic acid is used and no carbonic acid from another source.

Schaumwein must never be bottled in containers larger than 3·2 litres. At present Schaumwein is being bottled in 0·250 l, 0·375 l, 0·75 l, 1 l, 1·5 l, 2 l, and 3 l bottles. The reason for the lower pressure in the small bottles is the different closure which is used for these.

There is no doubt that the production of sparkling wine was felt to be a way of making use of otherwise undrinkable wine – wine with such a low alcoholic content that it had no staying power, but had on the other hand so much acidity that it was not good enough for human consumption. To manufacture a better and drinkable product other ingredients are necessary, and those which are allowed to be used, and their quantity, has been fixed by law. They are:

1. Sugar of the same kind as in the enrichment of wine.
2. Citric acid up to 1·5 g per litre, but the total allowed content of acids is limited to 7·5 g per litre.
3. Distillate of wine up to 5 g per litre of the total fluid.
4. Sulphurous acid, as in wine, 50 g free and 300 g total sulphurous acid.
5. The whole production, be it fermentation in vat, tank or bottles has to be done in one and the same factory.

* atü denotes the pressure above normal air pressure, i.e. above 1 atmosphere (1 atm).

Exactly as the law stipulates full information for the consumer about the quality of still wine, so it does for Schaumwein. Schaumwein produced by the addition of carbonic acid must be labelled '*mit zugestzter Kohlensaeure*' (with added carbonic acid). '*Méthode Champenoise*' is only allowed if the fermentation took place in bottle and the wine has remained on lees in the bottle for a minimum of six months. The label must show the name of the producer or distributor or exporter, but the latter only if he can show documents with exact proof about the producer.

These regulations refer to '*inländischem Schaumwein*', which may be produced in Germany from any wine, red, white or *rosé*, from any part of the world. The data given are those for the minimum quality. To protect the consumer and give him full information, various quality classes were created. The classification is similar to that for still wine:

1. Inländischer Schaumwein
2. Quality Schaumwein or Sekt (German Sekt)
3. Deutscher Prädikatssekt (German predicate Sekt) a better class of quality Schaumwein.

'Inland' Qualitätsschaumwein or Sekt are identical but the Government was empowered to issue a by-law and make the denomination 'Sekt' conditional upon a certain proportion of the basic wine being of German origin (i.e. 60 per cent).

QUALITÄTSSCHAUMWEIN = SEKT

1. contains a minimum of 10 g actual alcohol and not more than 35 g free and 250 mg total sulphurous acid;
2. has been produced without addition of carbonic acid and by a second fermentation;
3. has remained at least 60 days (or in containers 3 weeks) on the lees and has been stored in the same factory for a minimum of nine months under the carbonic pressure of 3·5 atü at 20°C;
4. is free of all faults with regard to colour, smell and taste; and
5. has been awarded a control number (*Prüfungsnummer*).

This is the explanation: carbonic acid which gives sparkling wine its sparkle, its effervescence, should be married with the wine, and in order that this should be effected, some time has to pass. These are the characteristics which are of importance if a sparkling wine is to be considered a Qualitätsschaumwein: less sulphurous acid for the higher quality wine, and longer storage on the lees and in the bottle before sale.

The designation Sekt is only allowed for German Schaumwein. Foreign Schaumweine can be offered as quality Schaumwines under the same conditions as German quality Schaumwines. But this denomination can only be replaced by the word 'Sekt' if in the whole country of origin the German language is an official State language. This is Germany's answer to the Treaty of Versailles, which prohibited Germany from using the words Champagne and Cognac. Germany wants to prevent countries where the German language is used in one or two regions only from allowing these districts to establish rights for themselves and their country. The Court of Justice of the E.E.C. in Luxembourg has decided that the designation Sekt is a generic name for all quality sparkling wines and cannot be restricted to those produced in Germany (March 1975).

The same applies to Prädikatssekt. The German wine law will be altered to bring it in line with the instructions to the German Government by the Court.

At present regulations 2893/2894/74 cover production and denomination of Sparkling Wines and Sparkling Quality Wines in the E.E.C.

Qualitätsschaumwein, Sekt, and Prädikatssekt, all these distinctions owe their birth to Germany's association with the E.E.C.

France and Italy insisted that quality originated in the first instance from an *appellation contrôlée*, such as Champagne, or Asti, and they liked their monopoly for quality sparkling wines; they specially used the argument that German Schaumwein or Sekt was produced to a large extent not from German but from imported wines. Germany's counter-argument, and rightly so, was simple: the quality of the raw material and particularly the quality of the end product was the most important and decisive point. Unfortunately Germany has not followed this argument, as will be shown in the next paragraph.

PRÄDIKATSSEKT

Prädikatssekt or Deutscher Prädikatssekt is a Sekt which has been recognized as a Sekt. There is no other condition as far as the quality is concerned, but the *cuvée* must contain 60 per cent German wine! It may be that the Prädikatssekt shows more than the character of the basic German wine, especially if it is a Riesling wine, but this is not absolutely necessary.

Why must a Prädikatssekt be produced with a minimum of 60 per cent German wine? The protection of the German wine grower, and not the required quality is the basis of this clause in the wine law. The grower is given a wonderful opportunity to dispose of wine which would only produce a second-rate still wine, for, as every member of the wine trade knows, only those wines are used for the manufacture and production of sparkling wines which in their natural state are just undrinkable.

The geographical origin of the vine may only be stated for quality Schaumwein, Sekt and Prädikatssekt, and on condition that 75 per cent of the raw material used must be entitled to the denomination. Any such geographical statements must be in accordance with the wine law. A non-existent site, a fancy village name cannot be used. The geographical denomination must have been registered in the vineyard register and the vine must have been registered in the vine register.

For example, 'Moselriesling Schaumwein' must contain 75 per cent of Moselriesling wines to be 'Deutscher Prädikatssekt'; 'Sparkling Bereich Johannisberger Sekt' must contain 75 per cent of wines from that Bereich; Sparkling Bernkasteler Sekt must originate 75 per cent from Bernkastel and a '1964 vintage Rheinsekt' must contain 75 per cent of vintage 1964 and 75 per cent of the wine must come from the Rhine. It is noteworthy that the balance can consist of imported wines.

Not more than one kind of grape or vintage may be stated. If the Sekt is a vintage Sekt then one vintage, if it is a 'vine' Sekt then only one kind of grape may be stated.

The general rules for the control and examination of quality sparkling wines are stricter than any that have been laid down in any other country.

The control is based on the obligatory control number, which can only be awarded when the sparkling wine has actually been presented to the committee for examination and when the committee has recognized the Schaumwein as a quality product (see Appendix 12). Prädikatssekt need not contain a Prädikat *wine* – it can contain the poorest of the German wines. This is a discrimination against real quality wines. Here is one of those cases where the Government had to give in to the wine growers. In the mind of the ordinary consumer, however, the fact that a sparkling wine is named 'German Prädikatssekt' is sufficient to create the idea that it contains or is of special quality.

As can be seen from the above, the fact that a wine has had added carbonic acid is considered (and rightly so) as something which makes the wine 'inferior' to other sparkling wines. But the same cannot be said regarding sparkling wine which ferments in tank, and wine where fermentation takes place in bottle. So far the German law goes along with the micro-biologists who contend that the larger surface area and the more vigorous mixing of the ingredients are a guarantee of *better quality*. In any case experiments and tastings have shown that even 'experts' who have to deal with sparkling wines in their everyday business have not detected the difference between those wines which have been fermented in tank and those fermented in bottle.

So long as the wine fermented in tank has enough bottle age, the pearls resulting from the carbonic acid are very small and are not different from those of bottle-fermented sparkling wine. The German wine law, therefore, recognizes the fact that bottle age has an important role to play in the quality of sparkling wine; provided the wine has nine months bottle age in the sparkling wine factory it becomes a Qualitätsschaumwein or Sekt, so long as all the other conditions of such a quality are fulfilled, and an examination number has been given to the wine. Of course there are still some sparkling-wine manufacturers who in very small quantities use the *Méthode Champenoise* – the second fermentation in the bottle – to make their Sekt. But this alone is not sufficient reason to call it a wine of the higher quality, a predicate Sekt.

'Dosage' is the sugar solution which is injected into Sekt near the end of the production process, because its quantity determines the various types of Sekt. According to decree 2893/74 *Brut Sekt* (naturally dry) contains up to 15 g of sugar per litre, *Extra Dry* may have between 12 and 20 g, *Dry* or *Sec* up to 35 g, *Semi-dry* (semi-sekt) up to 50 g and sweet Sekt (*doux*, or *goût américain*) over 50 g per litre. For 'dry' the German language uses the equivalent '*trocken*'.

Sekt will keep best when stored in a dry cellar with temperatures of between 10 to 15°C (50 to 61°F). Most Sekt bottles now have plastic stoppers, and these may be stored in an upright position. However, Sekt bottles which are closed by natural corks must be stored lying on their sides so that the cork will always be kept moist by the wine.

When opening a bottle the stopper should be pulled slowly and come out with only a soft plop. To achieve this, one first peels the metal foil from the stopper to uncover the loop of wire threaded over and round it. One must bend the loop forwards towards oneself and wiggle it carefully right and left to break the wire. Then one takes off the steel clasp holding the stopper in position and one turns the stopper slowly to pull it out. If the Sekt is too warm, it may happen that the stopper is pushed from the neck of the bottle by the pressure of the carbon dioxide inside. If this threatens to occur, one holds it down, after having drawn the steel clasp, with one finger to make it come out gradually.

White Sekt, to show its quality best, should be poured out at a temperature of about 12°C (54°F) but red Sekt will display its flowery fragrance to the full only at about 15°C (61°F).

The regulation regarding the shape of the bottles for Schaumwein is new: 'Schaumwein must be bottled and distributed in sparkling-wine bottles of the traditional form and furthermore, such bottles may only be used for Schaumwein and for no other beverage.'

We know that there are differences in the shapes of bottles used and this law might lead to cases where the courts will have to decide which is 'traditional' and which is not, just as we have various shapes for champagne bottles.

Last but not least, it is important to choose the correct glasses for

Sekt, to bring out in the best way the pearly sparkle of the drink. The tall and narrow champagne glasses known as *'flûtes'* are the most suitable ones for, whilst wide shallow goblets may look attractive, they have the disadvantage that the carbon dioxide dissolved in the Sekt evaporates too swiftly from their larger surface, and this kills the Sekt's flavour before it can really be appreciated.

To conclude: German Sekt manufacturers have shown the way to produce from typical German grapes sparkling wines of such quality that they will and must take the first place in the world among all sparkling wines, just as the German still wines have no equal in other countries. The fact that they are not restricted to one district of cultivation (i.e. the size of Champagne) gives Germany great opportunities. I look forward to the day when someone will hold a blind tasting of really well-selected fine Prädikatssekts against sparkling wines from other countries, including the Grandes Marques of Champagne. Here is a challenge: who will organize the competition, who will be the judges?

A report of the Chamber of Agriculture of Bad Kreuznach gives the following interesting statistics:

453 applications for examination were made between 1 October 1971 and 31 December 1972, covering

	%	litres
White Sekt	44·9	22,799,342
Red Sekt	3·2	1,617,100
White Prädikatssekt	50·7	25,713,065
Red	0·8	409,300
Rosée Sekt	0·3	149,000
Rosée Prädikatssekt	0·1	58,500

Of these only 16 per cent or 8,240,875 litres were produced by fermentation in bottle. 84 per cent or 42,505,432 litres were tank fermented.

Ordinary Sekt does not show any statement about grape, origin or vintage and of the Prädikatssekt, these statements are:

	%
Grapes	7·05
Geographical origin	0·44
Grapes and geographical origin	2·56
Vintage	1·86

BOOK II

Wine Journey

18

Wine roads and wine museums

To visit the German vinelands, we shall wander along the *Weinstrassen* – wine roads. The first and original wine road, also called the German wine road, covers the Palatinate from the French frontier to Rheinhessen. Today, however, most districts have their wine road. Rheinhessen has the Liebfraumilch road, and is very proud of it, then there are the Nahe road, the Schwaebische Weinstrasse (Württemberg) and the Baden Weinstrasse. The Rheingau-Riesling route was opened in 1973.

In addition, many towns compete against each other in starting a so-called '*Weinlehrpfad*' (wine education walk, or nature trail). In Trier, which claims to be the oldest town of Germany, it starts behind the Roman amphitheatre in the vineyards of the Viticultural College and leads through vineyards to the suburb Trier-Olewig. Forty notice-boards along the trail tell the wanderer everything he should know about wine, within a comfortable walk of forty-five minutes. In addition to learning his lessons he has also a magnificent view across the Mosel valley. The walk finds its fitting end in a wine cellar where he can taste the wines of the vineyards he has just so much admired.

Now we can start our journey through the various wine districts in Germany in order to learn more about the manifold characteristics of their wines. Let us once more remind ourselves that wine is the product of climate, soil, the grapes which were planted and the techniques used in its making, hence the great differences in quality.

At the beginning of our wine journey I would like to emphasize one more point: often visitors to the wine districts find that they can buy very cheaply, and then on returning home, expect to buy wines at similar prices. They overlook the enormous expenses connected with the distribution of wine; time taken for packing and cartoning for export as well as charges for shipping and insurance always increase the cost of the wines, and therefore the further the distance between the place of production and the place of consumption the higher the price. The many people who are involved in this process must of course have their fair share of profit or wages and when the State has taken its share in duty and tax the price is many times the price paid 'where the wine was grown'.

If one is really interested in drinking at home a wine which one enjoyed on holiday, one should try to find out all details, and best of all secure a label and arrange shipment on the spot to one's wine merchant who will be only too pleased to oblige an old customer against an appropriate commission.

A visit to one or more of the wine museums will be a great pleasure for people who are interested in antiquities connected with wine. As we have no family trees of Rhenish viticulture, we have to look around for other facts to give us an indication of German viticulture in ancient times. In the wine museum at Speyer, which is well worth a visit, we find illustrated the whole history of German winelands and their age-old culture. Until the city of Speyer was destroyed in 1689 it was the main centre of the wine trade, and it was in recognition of this that the museum was established there. It contains striking proofs of Roman viticulture in the Palatinate: in particular Roman tools that originated in Greece and were found in Palatinate soil and knives of the Gallo-Roman period from Marseilles. Incidentally similarly shaped tools are still used in Greece today. Tools, documents and coats of arms of the Palatinate communities are exhibited in the museum, so are old wine-casks, presses and wine vessels. They include an amphora, a vessel with two handles, from the third century, which was found still filled with wine in a Speyer sarcophagus, and which occupies the place of honour in the exhibition.

The wine museum at Trier (created in 1925) used to contain exhibits from all German wine regions and from places all over Germany. Its viticultural and statistical material was unique and it specialized in cultural history. It took hours even to glance only at the wealth of exhibits illustrating everything connected with wine. But to our eternal regret the contents of the museum were wantonly destroyed by the retreating German army at the end of the Second World War and looted by local inhabitants. Invaluable material for research was lost. The historic wine presses were burnt and the rest of the collection stolen. Nothing remains but the building itself which is intact and the books of the library, most of which survived. There are plans afoot for restocking the museum.

Two further museums have been established since the war: the wine museum in the Broemserburg at Rüdesheim (Rhine) and the Museum of Würzburg.

At Rüdesheim students of wine can attend impressive lectures and see exhibits from the 2,000-year-old history of viticulture on the Rhine.

The Museum of Würzburg is housed in a castle, the Fortress Marienburg, on a hill overlooking the town. It was the residence of the Prince Bishops of Würzburg and the Dukes of Franconia for nearly 500 years. This one-time arsenal with impressive halls and high vaulted ceilings provides the ideal backcloth for priceless works of art and traditional antiquities. Visitors enter the room through a magnificent wrought-iron door which was originally made as a cellar entrance in 1716. The flags of the craftsmen's guilds lend a splash of colour to this impressive exhibition, and a collection of beautifully decorated guild chests pays honour to Würzburg's crafts and trades.

In the great hall are no fewer than seven old wine presses, surrounded by sculptured heads of casks, sculptured taps, coopers' tools, crests, containers of all kinds, coloured and ornamented wine cups of china and pewter, jugs, wooden drinking cups and the Franken *roemer* glass as well as *Bocksbeutels* in the varying shapes of the centuries.

There are many smaller museums dealing with wine and culture connected with wine. In Meersburg, on Lake Constance, we find the famous Turkish barrel, and there are special exhibits in the arts and crafts departments of many city museums with unique collections of glasses, for example in Duesseldorf, Cologne, Hamburg and Munich.

19

Rheinland-Pfalz

Our first visit is to the federal state of Rheinland-Pfalz. Its *Anbaugebiete* (specific regions) are:

Rheinpfalz
Rheinhessen
Nahe
Mittelrhein
Mosel-Saar-Ruwer
Ahr (see Chapter 23)

within which are the following districts (1970 figures):

	Ha
Mittelrhein, incl. Lahn	918
Nahe district, Koblenz	3,134
Mosel: Obermosel	880
Saar	1,014
Ruwer	330
Mittelmosel	5,688
Untermosel	2,718
Ahr	197
Rhinehessia: Worms	4,844
Oppenheim	1,396
Mainz	991
Ingelheim	1,102
Wiesbach	1,757
Bingen	291
Nahe (Rheinhessen)	642
Alzey	5,267
Palatinate: Mittelhaardt	4,374
Oberhaardt	9,879
Unterhaardt with Zellertal	1,444
Nahe district, Pfalz	471
Rheinland-Pfalz Total:	47,337

Rheinland-Pfalz has the following proportion of vines, expressed in percentages of all the German vineyards/vines (with acknowledgement to Dr. Schubring, Wiesbaden):

White wines	73 per cent
Red wines	39 per cent
Of all wines	70 per cent

THE STATE-OWNED VITICULTURAL DOMAINS

(*Staatliche Domaene*)

These were started up around the turn of the century. The reason was the great demand for Riesling wines and the difficult economic situation of viticulture caused by the increase in the diseases and enemies of the vine which had resulted in tremendous damage.

The vineyards of the domains were founded in the northern part of the state, mostly on land which had previously been planted uneconomically with bushes. This, of course, was only done where the soil appeared suitable for the planting of vineyards. Large areas were bought in Rheinhessen, particularly in villages known for their quality along the Rhine and around Bingen.

The founders had great hopes for the success of this venture and most hopes were fulfilled, not only because good progress was made and high-class wines were produced. The influence of the domains soon made itself felt in the acceptance of their methods by other growers. This led to the purchase of the estate of Kloster Marienthal in the Ahr Region in 1925, and in 1927 the estate of the Lower Nahe was bought after many of the communities had suffered phylloxera. For the same reason another estate was bought in 1953 in the Alsenz Valley.

The controlled domains are:

(a) the state domains of Trier – this includes the properties of Ockfen (14 ha), Avelsbach (27 ha) and Serrig (34 ha), with a total viticulture area of 75 ha. The wines are stored in the main cellars in Trier.

(b) the state domains of Niederhausen-Schlossboeckelheim (25 ha), Lower Nahe (10 ha) and Altenbamberg in the Alsenz Valley, with a total viticulture area of 40 ha. The wines are stored in the main cellars in Niederhausen-Schlossboeckelheim and now include the Bingen Rheinhessen (14·7 ha) wines of the 1975 liquidated state domains of Mainz. The properties of Oppenheim (16·3 ha), Nierstein (16·7 ha) and Bodenheim (12·1 ha) have been partly transferred to the viticultural college in Oppenheim and partly leased out. They were formerly members of a co-operative and these wines are co-operative Erzeugerabfuellung up to the vintage 1974. As the co-operative could not dispose of the quantities of high-class wine at the high prices of a famous estate the arrangement was terminated and the domain liquidated.

(c) the state vineyard of Marienthal (Ahr) with a total viticulture surface of 14 ha, which on account of the great distance between Marienthal and Niederhausen was made separate and annexed to the teaching establishment Ahrweiler as an independent red-wine property. The wines are stored in the Marienthal cellars.

We shall start our journey on the left bank of the Rhine, in the south, and travel to the north. Our wine journey begins in the

PALATINATE

Area 18,839 ha
84 per cent white wine
Average crop 1·7 hl/ha
Silvaner 33 per cent Riesling 14 per cent
Müller-Thurgau 23 per cent Portugieser 16 per cent

Coming from the Rhine into the Palatinate, the traveller sees a fertile plain spread out before him. This is, so to speak, the advance guard of the Palatinate – known as the 'forward' (Vorder-) Palatinate. Towards the west this plain is separated from the Western Palatinate by a long chain of hills which (at its southern end) is a continuation of the Vosges mountains, while to the north it is known as the 'Haardt' range, or simply the 'Haardt'.

The English designation 'Palatinate' for the German 'Pfalz' is linguistically and historically well founded, for 'Pfalz' is derived from the Latin 'Palatinus', the name of the first of the seven Roman hills to be inhabited and the one on which the Imperial Palace was built under Augustus. This, the site of the first Imperial Palace, then gave its specific name to the whole genus of royal residences. Wherever a Roman Emperor rested his head in the course of his Imperial travels, the building that housed him became a palatium. And hence, of course, the English word 'palace', the German word '*palast*', and also the derivative '*Pfalz*'. The person responsible for the administration of the '*Pfalzen*' or royal residences, was known as the *Pfalzgraf* (Count of the Pfalz). The title *Pfalzgraf bei Rhein* (*Pfalzgraf* by the Rhine) first appears in documents of the year 1136. Like other offices, that of the *Pfalzgraf* became hereditary and assumed an increasingly territorial character in the course of years, so that finally it came to include local sovereign rights. From 1354 till 1803 (with the exception of the years 1635 to 1648) the area was known as *Kurpfalz*, and in that period the territory was more extensive than the Palatinate today. On the right bank of the Rhine it stretched beyond Mannheim and Heidelberg to the left bank of the river as far as and including Bacharach. The peace treaties of Campo Formio (1797) between Austria and France, gave all German territory on the left bank of the Rhine to France, and it remained French property under the Republic and the French Empire. In 1814–15, when Napoleon's fate was sealed, a mixed Austrian-Bavarian administration was appointed for the disputed territory to the left of the Rhine, until in 1816 it was handed over to Bavaria. In 1817 it was called *Bayrischer Rheinkreiss* (Bavarian Rhine District). Since 1838 it has been known (geographically speaking) as the *Pfalz*.

The eastern strip of the Palatinate – about 86 km in length and 30 km wide – lies on the left bank of the Rhine. It comprises about 160,000 square kilometres of vineyards with about 160,000,000 vines, tended by about 35,000 growers who are distributed among about 200 communities. The Palatinate alone has more vineyards than the whole of the Rheingau, Mosel-Saar-Ruwer and Nahe territories put together. It also has more vine plantations than Hessia, Baden and Württemberg.

The wine region of the Palatinate lies about 210 metres (630 feet) above the chilly mist-wrapped Rhine valley. The eastern slopes of the Haardt range afford a natural protection against the cold winds from west and north.

The vineyards of the Palatinate are nowadays almost entirely confined to sites which are particularly suitable for grape cultivation and as a rule guarantee a good mature crop.

A good many of the vine plantations are to be found in the plain. In consequence, the inhabitants of the Palatinate seldom speak of their *Weinberge* (lit. Vine hills – the usual German word for 'vineyards'), but mostly of *Wingerten* – i.e. *Weingarten*, meaning wine gardens. The geological and climatic conditions in the Palatinate account for this difference. The Rhine Valley from Muehlhausen to Bingen is like an immense sunken trench. The Vosges and the Haardt on the one side, the Black Forest and the Odenwald on the other, form the sides of this mighty 'ditch' through which the river Rhine flows. In the whole region of the Rhine plains the climate is outstandingly warm and dry, but particularly so in the Palatinate. In the summer there is almost tropical heat, and the winters are mostly mild and free from snow, so that the traveller may well think he has struck a patch of the 'warm

South'. Fine chestnut trees decorate the hills and bear good fruit. Almond trees are scattered about the vineyards, or line long stretches of the roads; mulberries and fig trees flourish in the gardens; peach and apricot trees are weighed down by the weight of the fruit they bear, while other fine fruits are to be found everywhere in great profusion; even lemons are sometimes grown here.

Such a favourable climate obviously promotes the growth of vines, which here put out their shoots and blossom earlier and bring their grapes to an earlier maturity than in any other German district.

Particularly in years when the sun has been sparing of its rays do the wines of the Palatinate usually outshine their rivals in other German wine regions, as for example in the vintage of 1970. As a rule they are milder, have less acidity and are somewhat mellower but on the other hand richer than the comparable products of different regions. Anyone therefore whose digestion is inclined to be intolerant of acids will find that these wines suit him better than others. The tendency to prefer sweeter, richer wines has enlarged the market for Palatinate products.

The nature of the soil in the whole of this Palatinate wine region varies considerably, sometimes changing more than once within a very short space. The vineyards in the southern part of the Vorderpfalz are mostly constructed on loess soil, i.e. a diluvial deposit of fine loam. This, sometimes light, sometimes heavy, frequently forms in such immense deposits that cave-like cellars can be dug in it. Along the Haardt, which has a coloured sandstone soil, vineyards are to be found on its detritus, i.e. a rather poor, dry sand. But sandy soils of older origin also occur, as well as shingle and gravel soil. The sites built thereon often take their names from the soil – that is why we find Kieselberg (meaning shingle hill, gravel hill). Excellent wines are produced on such ground.

Then again within the same region we find limestone soils, sometimes only as small reefs of tertiary lime, interrupting the loess or sand stretches. In these cases it may happen that we find a vine plantation of only a few acres. There is, however, a more extensive stretch of limestone soil bearing north from Bad Dürkheim via Ungstein, Kallstadt and Leistadt to Harxheim. Other lime sites of considerable extent are to be found in the Zellerthal (Harxheim, Zell, Niefernheim). In some places almost every site lies on different soil – sand, clay, slate and porphyry. And finally there is the soil composed of a younger eruptive rock, viz. basalt. This is found near Forst.

It has long been the custom of wine growers to take away for their own use the so-called 'pitch-stone deposit', i.e. the rubble found in basalt quarries. This substance, on account of its potassium content and its dark colour, has been found very useful for improving vineyard soil. Large tracts of the Forster and Deidesheimer vineyards have been so treated, and the high quality of their wines may well be due partly to this.

The main species of grape to be found here are the Silvaner (in this district known as *Oesterreicher* or *Franken-* ('Austrian' or 'Franconian'); then the Riesling, which is grown in large quantities, mainly in the finest production region of the Middle Haardt. The Traminer and the Gewürztraminer, which used to be the main product of the Palatinate, are now only sparsely grown as a pure strain; and then there is the blue Portugieser, from which a light red wine is made.

We pass through the Weintor (wine gate) near Schweigen. The frontier of France and Germany runs through the vineyards of Schweigen, so that the greatest part of the Schweigen vineyards is situated in France. The Schweigen growers have been allowed to visit and work their vineyards in France, and they have built new roads so that they can reach their vineyards more easily. They have spent millions of marks on this and on new wiring, etc. for their vineyards. The grapes are, of course, gathered by the German growers, transported to Germany and sold as German wine. Should it be called French, should it be called Alsatian wine? A most interesting and intriguing situation has been solved by the new wine law.

At this point the road begins which takes its name from the millions of vines lining its borders: *die Deutsche Weinstrasse.*

Whilst in the Rheingau and in the Mosel districts the landscape of the grape country is dominated by the river, here it is the road – the Wine Highway – that, taking the place of the flowing stream, guides the traveller though the fertile winelands.

The Weinstrasse runs for more than fifty miles to Bockenheim, its northernmost point. As a result of the favourable geographic conditions – the protective mountains in the west and the fertile Rhine plain in the east – wine has been produced in this area for the past 2,000 years. The area also produces wonderful fruit: figs and almonds ripen here, as well as chestnuts. The road runs through more than 200 wine-producing villages; it has not been widened and runs between vineyards or round vineyards, through a village street, or over the top of a hill with a fine view. This is a journey on which to relax, to admire old houses, handsome old town halls, and, last but not least, inviting ancient inns where the good wine is matched by good food.

OBERHAARDT (UPPER HAARDT) The Upper Haardt is the wine cellar of the Palatinate, or rather of the whole of Germany, for nowhere are such record harvests gathered as here.

In *Rhineland Wineland* I said: 'Medium wines are produced which are marketed as "small" to "medium", mostly in cask, but sometimes in bottle. A goodly proportion is devoted to the preparation of sparkling wine. A few sites in the upper country may be said to produce medium – more rarely good – table and bottle wines (Hambach, St. Martin, and a few sites in Weyher and Burrweiler, in Edenkoben and Maikammer have a good reputation), but for the German exporter and the foreign importer the wines are uninteresting and classed as "mass-produced". During the last few years, many of these wines have been shipped as cheap Liebfraumilch to the U.S.A. Should any drinker of cheap Liebfraumilch read this paragraph, I would advise him to buy next time a wine with a geographical denomination exported by a reputable house so that his impression of German wine is rectified.'

This statement has now been made obsolete by the new Vineyard Register, and the area is called the *Bereich Südliche Weinstrasse* which covers the following *Grosslagen*, *Einzellagen* and villages (the principal among which are given in italics):

Grosslage	*Villages*
Guttenberg	*Schweigen-Rechtenbach*
521·75 ha	Steinfeld
	Dierbach
	Vollmersweiler
	Niederotterbach
	Kapsweyer
	Freckenfeld
	Schaidt
	Kandel
	Dörrenbach
	Minfeld
	Schweighofen
	Oberotterbach

Dörrenbach has many old houses and the fortified church still has its old towers and arrow slits. The timbered hall was built at the end of the sixteenth century and lies at the foot of these impressive fortifications.

Grosslage	*Villages*
Kloster Liebrauenberg	*Bad-Bergzabern*
1340·20 ha	Klingenmünster
	Gleiszellen
	Gleishorbach
	Pleisweiler-Oberhofen
	Niederhorbach

Grosslage	*Villages*
Kloster Liebrauenberg 1340·20 ha	Kapellen-Drusweiler Oberhausen Babelroth Hergersweiler Winden Steinweiler Rohrbach Billigheim-Ingenheim Mühlhofen-Appenhofen Heuchelheim Klingen

Bad-Bergzabern, a quiet little spa, was already known to the Romans who called it 'Taberna Montanae', i.e. the Inn in the Mountains.

Grosslage	*Villages*
Herrlich 1290·20 ha	*Eschbach* Leinsweiler Göcklingen Ilbesheim Wollmesheim Mörzheim Impflingen Insheim Herxheim Herxheim-Weyher

At Leinsweiler the landscape is dominated by two ruined castles, the Madenburg and the castle of Landeck. Not far away is Annweiler which is famous for its three castles, Trifels, Anebos and Mimz. Trifels was the pride of the Salic and Hohenstauffen emperors who built one of their strongest fortifications here. King Richard the Lionheart was once held captive here by Emperor Henry VI.

Grosslage	*Villages*
Königsgarten 1271·50 ha	*Godramstein* *Landau* Queichheim Moriheim Arzheim Ranschbach Birkweiler Frankweiler Albersweiler

Grosslagen	*Villages*
Königsgarten 1271·50 ha	Queichhambach
	Gräfenhausen
	Siebeldingen
Trappenberg 1441·22 ha	*Hochstadt*
	Offenbach
	Ottersheim
	Knittelsheim
	Bellheim
	Bornheim
	Essingen
	Zeiskam
	Lustadt
	Weingarten
	Schwegenheim
	Commersheim
	Böbingen
	Freisbach
	Freimersheim
	Altdorf
	Venningen with Einzellage 'Doktor'
	Gross- und Kleinfischlingen
Bischofskreuz 1547·60 ha	*Walsheim*
	Burrweiler
	Gleisweiler
	Flemlingen
	Böchingen
	Roschbach
	Nussdorf
	Dammheim
	Knöringen
Ordensgut 1121·03 ha	*Rhodt*
	Weyher
	Hainfeld
	Edesheim
Schloss Ludwigshohe 786·58 ha	*Edenkoben*
	St. Martin
Mandelhöhe 1120·00 ha	*Maikammer*
	Kirrweiler

Hugh Johnson, speaking about the Upper Rheinpfalz, remarks: 'Almost all their production is café wine, handsomely served in thick trunked glasses called Pokale, but not bottled.'

The 1971 vintage provides reason enough to look at this district as a potential producer of great wines. First of all, the new plantations, often with new varieties of grapes, stand the chance of producing fuller and more elegant wines. In 1971 the Suedliche Weinstrasse produced wines of outstanding quality, Spätlesen, Auslesen and even Beeren- and Trockenbeerenauslesen which in quality are the equals of the Mittel Haardt and sometimes even better.

A Walsheimer Bischofskreuz (*Grosslage*) Auslese containing a blend of Silvaner and Ruländer grapes has all the characteristics of a Beerenauslese and with a reputation as stated by Hugh Johnson, the wine was proportionately the cheapest I ever bought and sold.

The highest sugar content of grapes reached in Germany in 1971 was in this district, though only a very small quantity of Trockenbeerenauslese was produced, in a Nussdorf vineyard, but at 326° Oechsle this was a remarkable success. Bischofskreuz and Herrlich are the *Grosslagen* in greatest demand. The highest Oechsle degree of the 1959 vintage wines was found in a Bernkasteler wine.

North of the Upper Haardt and adjoining it, we find Bereich Middle Haardt – Deutsche Weinstrasse. This is the district north of Neustadt and the Haardt range. It is the region where the quality wines of the Palatinate are produced.

Less rain falls in the country between Neustadt and Bad Dürkheim than anywhere else in Germany and it has more sunshine than any other part. Moreover, this soil is unsuitable for anything but the growing of vines, so that the whole region has been turned into what seems to be one vast vineyard. The main species grown is the Riesling, cultivated as a pure strain and selectively gathered, and producing Auslese wines, Beeren- and Trockenbeerenauslesen of superb quality. Gewürztraminer and white muscatels are also cultivated here. In the lower, moister sites there are Silvaner plantations.

The communities between Neustadt and Bad Dürkheim and their sites are all worth knowing:

Neustadt has become an important town since many wine villages have been incorporated. It is the central focus of the Palatinate wine trade, and also lies at the centre point of the Weinstrasse. Here also the German Grape Festival takes place, culminating in the election of a German Wine Queen, a gay occasion which is held every year.

The following villages were incorporated into Neustadt and now form *Ortsteile*: Diedesfeld, Geinsheim, Lachen-Speyerdorf, Hambach Gimmeldingen, Haardt, Koeningsbach and Mussbach. Therefore, a wine from the vineyard of Gimmeldingen called Schloessel may be labelled: Gimmeldinger Schloessel, or Neustadt Gimmeldinger Schloessel, or Neustadter Schloessel.

The growers, proud of their former independent villages, will choose the first alternative, but we have to be prepared to meet all three possible labels!

In Neustadt three *Grosslagen* meet, enclosing some single sites of importance:

Grosslagen	*Vineyards and areas in ha**	
Pfaffengrund	Neustadter Berg	180
679 ha	Duttweiler Kreuzberg	100
Rebstöckel	Neustadter Grain	85
673 ha	Hambacher Schlossberg (formerly part of Upper Haardt)	138
	Hambacher Kirchberg	79
Meerspinne	Gimmeldinger Biengarten	40
850·50 ha	Haardter Herzog	48
	and Mandelring	69
	Koenigsbacher Idig	22
	Jesuitengarten	17
	and Oelberg	30
	Mussbacher Eselshaut	293·05
	Kurfuerst	50
	and Bischofsweg	45

From here we enter a region which grows wines of famous quality and ranking.

Our next stop is Deidesheim. One of the important estates belongs to the Bassermann-Jordan family, to whose late father, Dr. Friedrich von Bassermann-Jordan, we are indebted for a historical survey of German viticulture.

The soil in Deidesheim is suitable for fine quality wines, consisting of volcanic primary rock, shingle, sand and lime. Deidesheim is the centre of the highest-grade wine production in the Rhine-Palatinate state. The 'peak' wines in the world prosper here.

Grosslage Hofstück (1,181 ha) covers the vineyard Deidesheimer Nonnenstück (125 ha), and all vineyards of the villages: Niederkirchen, Meckenheim, Gormheim, Friedelsheim, Ellerstadt, Hochdorf-Assenheim, Rödersheim-Gronau and of the following single sites of Ruppertsberg:

Vineyards and areas in ha	
Linsenbusch	187·05
Nussbien	78

* Where no area is given no figure is available. In some towns and villages the final limits of sites have not yet been fixed.

	Vineyards and areas in ha
Reiterpfad	81
Spiess	5·07
Hoheburg	20
Gaisboehl	7·08

Grosslage Mariengarten (399·37 ha) covers all the other Deidesheim single sites, viz:

	Vineyards and areas in ha
Herrgottsack	120
Maushoehle	20
Kieselberg	20
Kalkofen	5
Grainhuebel	12
Hohenmorgen	1·90
Leinhöehle	20
Langenmorgen	4
Paradiesgarten	50

and the following sites of Forst and Wachenheim:

Villages	*Vineyards and areas in ha*	
Forst	Kirchenstuck	4·05
	Freundstuck	4·23
	Jesuitengarten	6·10
	Ungeheuer	38·39
	Elster	11·82
	Musenhang	19·97
	Pechstein	21·01
Wachenheim	Altenburg	10
	Belz Boehlig	8·50
	Gerümpel	13
	Rechbaechel	
	Goldbaechel	4·30

The next *Grosslage* is Schnepfenflug an der Weinstrasse. It is necessary to quote this title in full, because there is a second Schnepfenflug, viz. Schnepfenflug vom Zellertal. There was a great 'fight' between the owners of the vineyards called Schnepfenflug as to who would carry off the right to the name. Nobody but they knows why. *Schnepfe* is a bird, *flug* mean flight. *Schnepfe*, however, is also local slang for 'prostitute'. The reasoning lies, I suppose, in the hidden meaning!

And here are the single sites of Grosslage Schnepfenflug an der Weinstrasse:

Villages	*Vineyards and areas in ha*	
Deidcsheim	Letten	122
Forst	Stift	18.79
	Süsskopf	40
Forst Wachenheim and Friedelsheim	Bischofsgarten	200
Friedelsheim	Kreuz	25
	Schlossgarten	50
Wachenheim	Luginsland	

Bischofsgarten is a single site situated in three neighbouring villages and the grower has the choice of three village names.

Grosslage Schenkenboehl (555 ha) covers the vineyards of Wachenheim and Bad Dürkheim as follows:

Villages	*Vineyards and areas in ha*	
Wachenheim	Koenigswingert	155
	Mandelgarten	190
	Schlossberg	15
Bad Dürkheim	Fuchsmantel	92
	Fronhof	95
	Abtsfronhof	3·20

Bad Dürkheim, a health resort long known for its arsenic-brine springs, is now – since 1960 – also visited for its sodium-calcium chloride warm springs. These can be used for inhalations, bathing and drinking. The Dürkheimer Sausage Market is world famous.

Grosslage Hochmess (1142·2 ha) covers Dürkheim sites, although the Michelsberg site is also part of Ungstein.

Villages	*Vineyards and areas in ha*	
Dürkheim	Michelsberg	8·20
	Spielberg	24
	Hochbenn	56
	Rittergarten	26

Grosslage Feuerberg (1017 ha) extends into Dürkheim, Kallstadt, Weisenheim am Berg, Goennheim, Bobenheim am Berg and Ellerstadt.

Village	*Vineyards and areas in ha*	
Dürkheim	Herrenmorgen	100
	Nonnengarten	395
	Steinberg	75

Villages	*Vineyards and areas in ha*	
Bobenheim am Berg	Kieselberg	42·35
	Ohligpfad	41·50
Ellerstadt	Bubeneck	35
	Dickkop	25
	Sonnenberg	85
Goennheim	Martinshoehe	60
Kallstadt	Kreidekeller	46
	Annaberg	7·37
Weisenheim am Berg	Vogelsang	105

Grosslage Honigsaeckel (155 ha) covers the excellent sites of the neighbouring and very ancient village Ungstein. Zones of a similar character are:

Village	*Vineyards and areas in ha*	
Ungstein	Weilberg	45
	Herrenberg	45
	Nussriegel	65

Grosslage Kobnert (1,512 ha) covers sites in Herxheim, Freinsheim, Kallstadt and Ungstein, and the villages Dackenheim, Erpolzheim and Leistadt.

Villages	*Vineyards and areas in ha*	
Herxheim	Kirchenstueck	45
	Himmelreich	31
	Honigsack	130
Kallstadt	Kronenberg	60
	Steinacker	120
Ungstein	Bettelhaus	58
	Osterberg	75
Dackenheim	Liebesbrunnen	56
	Mandelroeth	45
	Kapellgarten	3
Erpolzheim	Kirschgarten	80
Leistadt	Kirchenstueck	20
	Kalkofen	90
Freinsheim	Musikantenbuckel	180
	Oschelskopf	105
	Schwarzes Kreuz	135
	Hochgewann Honigsack	

The Grosslage Saumagen (50 ha) covers sites in Kallstadt.

Village	*Vineyards and areas in ha*	
Kallstadt	Horn	10
	Nill	20
	Kirchenstueck	20

Kallstadt's most famous vineyards are the 'Saumagen' and the Annaberg Estate. The chalky soil and clay produce wines of exquisite quality. Wine has been produced here since Roman times.

Grosslage Rosenbuehl (557 ha) covers the district formerly known as Unterhaardt (Lower Haardt) which is now part of the Bereich Mittelhaardt Deutsche Weinstrasse. It includes vineyards in Erpolzneim, Freinsheim, Weisenheim and Lambsheim.

Villages	*Vineyards and areas in ha*	
Erpolzheim	Kieselberg	45
	Goldberg	23
Freinsheim	Goldberg	170
Weisenheim am Sand	Altenberg	80
	Hahnen	80
	Halde	45
	Hasenzeile	65
	Burweg	49
Lambsheim and Weisenheim	Burgweg	49

Merging into the fertile Rhinehessian plain the German Weinstrasse comes to an end. The soil on which the Unterhaardt vines grow is heavy and rich in lime (clay, loess and sand). This tends to produce milder wines, less elegant and patrician and with less body than those from the Middle Haardt, but nevertheless fruity and refined and extremely pleasing to some palates.

Grosslage Hoellenpfad (569·82 ha) includes the viticultural area of the villages Battenberg, Kleinkarlbach, Mertesheim and Neuleiningen but especially that of Gruenstadt. Gruenstadt is distinguished by a wine-marketing association. The wines produced by members of this organization are judged annually during the Gruenstadt Wine Festival by a special panel of experts and are drunk in enormous quantities by tens of thousands of visitors to the Festival.

Gruenstadt sees the end of the Weinstrasse, but not of the viticultural area of the Palatinate. Adjacent to it lie the vineyards of the Northern Palatinate.

Grosslage Grafenstueck (660·98 ha) covers sites in Bockenheim, Kindenheim and Obrigheim.

Villages	*Vineyards and areas in ha*	
Bockenheim	Schlossberg	63·38
	Klosterschaffnerei	7·71
	Burggarten	6·21
	Heiligenkirche	24·28
	Goldgrube	
Bockenheim and Kindenheim	Vogelsang	162
Kindenheim	Katzenstein	17
	Burgweg	29
Obrigheim	Benn	30
	Hochgericht	40
	Schloss	20
	Rosengarten	20
	Mandelpfad	30

There in the Zell valley, on lime soil mixed with clay, grows a wine very different from all other Palatinate wines, a wine both robust and steely. The Zell product known as Schwarzer Herrgott has an excellent reputation in Germany itself, but is so far unknown in other countries. The place of production is Harxheim-Zell.

Grosslage Schnepfenflug vom Zellertal. We have mentioned this before as not being the same as Schnepfenflug an der Weinstrasse. The following villages and sites lie in this *Grosslage*:

Villages	*Vineyards and areas in ha*	
Albisheim	Heiligenborn	42
Bubenheim	Hahnekamm	5·43
Bolanden	Schlossberg	2
Gauersheim	Schuetzenhuette	6·90
Harxheim	Goldloch	26
Kirchheimbolanden	Schlossgarten	3·70
Ruessingen	Breinsberg	2·53
Rittersheim	Am hohen Stein	3
Stetten	Heilighaeuschen	7·50
Zell	Schwarzer Herrgott	11·20
Einselthum u. Zell	Klosterstueck	136
Zell u. Niefernheim	Koenigsweg	30·89
Niefernheim, Zell and Einselthum	Kreuzberg	116·04
Morschheim	Im Heubusch	13

Villages	*Vineyards and areas in ha*	
Kerzenheim	Esper	2·30
Immesheim	Sonnenstueck	12·34
Ottersheim	Zeller Brauensberg	6·47

The last *Grosslage* is Schwarzerde with sites in Kirchheim, Bissersheim, Grosskarlbach, Laumersheim, Obersuelzen, Dirmstein, Gerolsheim, Hessheim, Heuchelheim/Frankenthal, Grossniedesheim and Kleinniedesheim.

Villages	*Vineyards and areas in ha*	
Bissersheim	Goldberg	20
	Held	25
	Orlenberg	15
	Steig	30
Kirchheim	Geisskopf	60
	Steinacker	50
	Roemerstrasse	27
	Kreuz	33
Grosskarlbach	Burgweg	60
	Osterberg	120
Laumersheim	Kirschgarten	39
	Mandelberg	36
	Sonnengarten	28
Obersuelzen	Schnepp	6·50
Dirmstein	Herrgottsacker	130
	Jesuitenhofgarten	4·50
	Madelpfad	110
Gerolsheim	Klosterweg	30
	Lerchenspiel	47
Hessheim	Lange Els	19
Heuchelheim/Frankenthal	Steinkopf	56
Grossniedesheim	Schafberg	13·26
Kleinniedesheim	Schlossgarten	6
	Vorderberg	42

In conclusion it may be said that of all Palatinate wines those from the following communities are in the top class:

Forst
Deidesheim
Koenigsbach
Ruppertsberg
Wachenheim

The second class is composed of those from:

Dürkheim
Ungstein
Gimmeldingen
Haardt
Kallstadt
Mussbach
Neustadt
Winzingen
Niederkirchen

and other villages. It is worth tasting a large range to draw up your own classification.

IMPORTANT GROWERS IN THE PALATINATE

von Buhl	Deidesheim
von Bassermann-Jordan	Deidesheim
Buerklin-Wolf	Wachenheim
Annaberg	Bad Dürkheim
Wilhelm Spindler	Forst
Herbert Giessen Erben	Deidesheim
Lehmann-Hilgard	Freinsheim
Jul. Ferd Kimich	Deidesheim
Dr. Fleischmann	Bad Dürkheim
F. Motzenbaecker	Ruppertsberg

RHEINHESSEN

Area 17,384 ha
92 per cent white wine
8 per cent red
Average crop 1·5 hl/ha
Silvaner 39 per cent   Riesling 6 per cent
Müller-Thurgau 26 per cent   Portugieser 7 per cent

Emerging from the Palatinate we immediately find ourselves near Worms, in the wine district of Rhinehessia. The designation Rhinehessia is used to denote the origin of all wines grown in the county of Rhinehessia with the exception of a small area along the river Nahe.

It is often forgotten that Rhinehessia once formed part of the French Republic (1797–1816). Rhinehessia is today part of the Federal Republic 'Rheinland-Pfalz', the greatest wine-growing state of Western Germany.

Round the east and north of Rhinehessia the river Rhine flows in a wide semi-circle (Worms-Mainz-Bingen), while the Nahe flows to the west of the province. The region comprises over 17,000 hectares of cultivated vinelands, and here we find the greatest possible variety of wines – ranging from 'small' table wines to the most exquisite 'peak' wines (Spitzenweine) comparable to any others produced not only in Germany, but all over the world.

Rhinehessia has been called 'God's Garden'. The fertility and wealth of this strip of land has been famous from time immemorial.

Rheinhessen actually lies in a valley, protected by surrounding mountains. In the north the Taunus, in the west the Hunsrueck and in the south-west the Haardt, in the south-east the Black Forest, and in the east the Odenwald and Spessart ranges. This is – climatically – a splendid position for viticulture. One can count on 180 to 200 frost-free days with high average temperatures (in Mainz 10·3°C, Worms 9·8°C, Oppenheim 9·8°C, Alzey 9°C). The rainfall is an average of only 510 mm, in 1959 and 1964 it was only 415 and 380 mm respectively. Rheinhessen is poor in forests and therefore it is a district of dryness. Rainfall is very irregular, but in a way very favourable for viticulture. Long, warm and dry autumns are very frequent. The steep hills near Nackenheim and Nierstein lie about 100 to 150 metres above sea level, the Rhine valley 80 to 90 m and the high plateau, the 'Rheinhessen hinterland', 150 to 300 m.

Of the growers about 6,200 have less than half a hectare, 4,500 hold between one half and one hectare, 3,400 hold between 1 and 2 hectares, 1,500 between 2 and 5 hectares and 275 own over 5 hectares. That means that 64 per cent of the growers own land under 5 hectares, and one-third of the growers own 70 per cent of the viticultural area.

The Carolingians made sure of owning large tracts of land here, whereon they built their royal castles. Their successors took over the estates as imperial property and were well aware of the treasures they secured thereby. A '*Vogt*' – governor – administered these estates and collected tithes and other dues for the imperial household from tenants and neighbouring landowners.

As we have seen while discussing other German wine regions, the quality of a wine depends not only on the climate, the species of grape, the degree of attention devoted to caring for the vines, and the treatment of the wine itself when it has reached the cellars, but also on the kind of *soil* on which the vines are planted. The soil exercises a decisive influence on the quality of the wine and is responsible for innumerable differences in taste which the wine connoisseur knows how to appreciate. The same species of grape planted on various soils produces entirely different wines; in particular, it is the bouquet – that indefinable quality – that is dependent, not only on the kind of grape but also on the kind of soil on which such grape is grown. Different soils contain different kinds of nutriment – the varieties in even neighbouring patches of land are sometimes astonishing – and that is what ties the taste of the wine so closely to the nature of the soil.

In considering the wines of Rhinehessia with its 165 wine-growing communities from the point of view of the soil, it is necessary to distinguish between the wines of the 'Rhine Front' from Worms to Oppenheim and Nierstein-Nackenheim, the wines that originate near Bingen on the Rhine, and those from the high plateau lying farther back, and those of Alzey and Gau-Bickelheim. All this was taken into consideration when the new *Bereiche* and *Grosslagen* were created.

Based on geological factors, Rheinhessen with its 165 wine growing communities is divided into three *Bereiche*: Wonnegau, Nierstein and Bingen.

BEREICH WONNEGAU On arriving at Worms, we find – near the Rhine bridge – the Church of our Lady (Liebfrauenkirche) which is surrounded by a few vineyards. It has already been mentioned that the wine marketed under the designation Liebfraumilch does not come from these vineyards. Incidentally, the entire annual output amounts to only about 110,000 litres. The wine is of medium quality and has a decidedly earthy taste to which most wine drinkers object.

The *Grosslage* for Worms, Pfeddersheim and all other '*Ortsteile*' is Liebfrauenmorgen, a name chosen to come as close as possible to the well-known name!

Villages	*Sites*
Worms (including Pfeddersheim and Wies-Oppenheim)	Hochberg
	Kreuzblick
	St. Georgenberg
	Am Heiligen Häuschen
	Affenberg
	Bildstock
	Goldpfad
	Kapellenstueck
	Klausenberg
	Lerchelsberg
	Liebfrauenstift-Kirchenstueck
	Liebfrauenring
	Remeyerhof
	Rheinberg
	Roemersteg
	St. Annaberg
	Schneckenberg
	St. Cyriakusberg

Villages	*Sites*
Worms-Horchheim	Goldberg
Worms-Leiselheim	Nonnenwingert
Worms-Weinsheim	Burgweg

LIEBFRAUMILCH Here is the place to halt and discuss Liebfraumilch wines.

None of the wine laws of 1893, 1909 and 1930 contained any mention of Liebfraumilch, the name which is known to every wine drinker, a wine which is in great demand. In *Rhineland Wineland* I could therefore write as follows: 'Contrary to popular belief, Liebfraumilch is not a district at all, but an invented name which may be applied to any pleasant Rhine wine of good quality. The name is derived from the Liebfrauenkirche (Church of our Lady) at Worms, which is surrounded by vineyards.'

We meet the name in various spellings:

1562 A statement about planting of vines by 'Canonicus of our lieben Frawenstift'
1703 Liebfrauen Milch
1718 Lieben-Frauen-Milch
1744 In the *Rheinische Antiquarius*, p. 16, the famous Lieben Frauen Milch at Worms is compared with nobler wines.
1769 A book dealing with viticulture speaks of the wine of Worms 'Lieben Frauenmilch'. It grows on the Kirchhof (churchyard) which shows the original use of the land as a burial ground.
1776 In *Rheinische Antiquarius*: 'Liebfrauen Milch'.
1810 The official Land Register contains the name Liebfrauenmilch for the whole vineyard which appeared later as Liebfrauenstift and Liebfrauenbuckel.
1972 Wormser Liebfrauenstift-Kirchenstueck.

'Liebfraumilch' was originally 'Liebfrauminch'. '*Minch*' is an old word for '*Moench*', German for monk. 'Liebfrauminch' wines were the wines which belonged to the monks of the Liebfrauenkirche. Incidentally the whole district round the church was known as the 'Minch'. The natural development of the language has changed the consonant 'n' to 'l' and Liebfrauminch to Liebfraumilch (milk).

The vineyards round Worms church, known as Liebfrauenstift, produce an average of 12,000 dozen bottles a year, a quantity which is obviously insufficient to cover the demand for Liebfraumilch.

The new wine law of 1971 now fixes the geographical area for the real Liebfraumilch.

Many people when they use the expression 'real' Liebfraumilch refer to the vineyard round the Liebfrauenstift church. The wines from this district always showed some special characteristics, but not pleasant ones. I have always found them too earthy, and other writers even speak of a 'straw' flavour. H. Warner Allan referred to them as having a faintly unpleasant tang of some of the outlying Cognacs. The name 'Liebfraumilch' certainly originated from there. I find that the Liebfraumilch wines – especially many branded Liebfraumilch wines – are much more harmonious than the Liebfrauenstiftsweine. Liebfraumilch might have originated there, but the Liebfrauenstiftsweine are not the 'original Liebfraumilch wines'.

Until 1971 a wine sold as Liebfraumilch could have been a Rhine wine from any Rhine district whatsoever. It could have come from the Rheingau, from Rhinehessia, from the Rheinpfalz or from the Nahe and the Middle Rhine (as far as Koblenz).

As Liebfraumilch was an invented name, nothing could be added to it that might be interpreted as an indication of origin. On the other hand, additions such as 'Spätlese' and 'Auslese' were of course permissible where the implications coincided with the facts.

To distinguish their choice of Liebfraumilch, shippers create their own brand. This may either be just an additional fancy name, or perhaps a distinguishing label.

New limitations have been placed on the use of Liebfraumilch as follows:

1. Liebfraumilch cannot be a Tafelwein. It must be a quality wine which has passed the test and has an official examination number.
2. Liebfraumilch can only be used for quality wine from Rheinpfalz, Rheinhessen, Nahe and Rheingau; it is not now permissible to use a wine from the Middle Rhine for Liebfraumilch.
3. The must for a Liebfraumilch must have a sugar content of at least 60° Oechsle.
4. The wine must be of pleasing character (*liebliche* character), delicious taste and good quality, and its major part must be produced from the Riesling, Silvaner or Müller-Thurgau grape, and must possess the taste characteristics of one of these types.
5. The names of vines may *not* be used with Liebfraumilch (i.e. there will be no more Liebfraumilch Riesling or Liebfraumilch Scheurebe).
6. The 'alcohol-residual sugar' proportions must not be less than 2·5:1 for Riesling and 3:1 for other grapes. It sounds paradoxical to prohibit naming according to the grapes used, although the taste must be dictated by their character and the residual sugar is based on the grape!
7. Liebfraumilch must not be sold with a predicate, i.e. no more Liebfraumilch Auslese. As a concession Liebfraumilch Spätlese or Kabinett were allowed up to and including the 1974 vintage.

Actually what had developed by custom and by law over the last sixty years is now laid down in the special legislation about Liebfraumilch. In other words: that which was done has now been legalized and has been found to be correct.

There is an important restriction. After long debates in which Rhinehessia claimed Liebfraumilch as its own, it was laid down that Liebfraumilch as a quality wine had to originate in one defined region. It can be a blend but only from one region; it cannot be a blend of wines from all or even two defined regions, but only from one area. It can of course also originate in an *Einzellage*. There is nothing in law which lays down that Liebfraumilch must be a blend. If one decides that a wine from a well-known estate is just the wine one wants to sell as Liebfraumilch, an unblended single vineyard wine, one can go ahead, and my former company has done so in the past. As regards the defined regions for Liebfraumilch, there are four: Rhinehessia, Nahe, Palatinate and Rheingau. I hope that this clears up any misunderstandings.

Let me explain what is meant by 'pleasing character' (under No. 4) i.e. *liebliche Art*. This means pleasing to the senses, delicious taste, delightful. Most wines with residual sugar show this, but good quality cannot be found in many Liebfraumilch wines during the last few years. After 1950 it became the fashion to look for cheaper and cheaper wine for Liebfraumilch, and finally only the cheapest wines sailed under the flag 'Liebfraumilch', if only to satisfy the demand of the supermarkets for the lowest price. Some extensively advertised Liebfraumilch became popular – but in blind tastings did not show well.

Now the '*liebliche Art*' is guaranteed by the regulation that Liebfraumilch must have some residual sugar and this therefore spells the end of 'dry' Liebfraumilch, and perhaps of Liebfraumilch altogether. Wine lovers will turn to good quality wine of guaranteed geographical origin.

In the extensive vine-covered hill country to be found on the left bank of the Rhine, vines are planted almost exclusively on loess.

Grosslage covers the villages and their sites:

Grosslage	*Village*	*Vineyards*
Bergkloster	Westhofen	Morstein,
		Brunnhaeuschen
		Steingrube
		Kirchspiel
		Benn
		Aulerde
		Rotenstein

Grosslagen	*Villages*	*Vineyards*
Bergkloster	Gundheim	Sonnenberg
		Hungerbiene
		Mandelbrunnen
	Gundersheim	Koenigstuhl
		Hoellenbrand
	Hangen-Weisheim	Sommerwende
	Eppelsheim	
	inc. Dintesheim	Felsen
	Flomborn	Goldberg,
		Feuerberg
	Esselborn	Goldberg
	Bermersheim/Wo	Hasenlauf
Pilgerpfad	Monzernheim	Goldberg
		Steinboehl
	Dittelsheim	Kloppberg
		Moenchhube
		Geiersberg
		Pfaffen-muetze
		Leckerberg
	Frettenheim	Heil
	Hessloch	Liebfrauenberg
		Mondschein
		Edle Weingaerten
	Bechtheim	Hasensprung
		Heilig
		Kreuz
	Osthofen	Rheinberg
		Kirchberg
		Lienberg
		Klosterberg

Part of the vineyards of Bechtheim and Osthofen form the Grosslage,

Gotteshilfe	Bechtheim	Geyersberg
		Rosengarten
		Stein
	Osthofen	Goldberg
		Hasenbiss
		Leckzapfen

The vineyards of Alzey are to be found widely scattered over the sites of the Selz valley and the plains of the Alzey plateau. The wines produced are: Silvaner and Müller-Thurgau (white) and St. Laurent (red). Their quality varies. The district is cold and windy and therefore unfavourable for the production of quality wines. It is 'little wines' which are cultivated here, those sold '*en carafe*'. They are seldom bottled (except when blended with other wines). It is here too that grapes for the table are produced and sold to health resorts for grape cures.

Grosslagen	*Villages*	*Vineyards*
Sybillenstein	Alzey incl. Heimersheim	Kapellenberg
		Rotenfels
		Roemerberg
		Pfaffenhalde
		Wartberg
		Sonnenberg
	Dautenheim	Himmelacker
	Wahlheim	Schelmen
	Freimersheim	Frankenstein
	Mauchenheim	Sioner
		Klosterberg
	Weinheim	Kapellenberg
		Mandelberg
		Hlg. Blutberg
		Kirchenstueck
		Hoelle
	Offenheim	Mandelberg
	Bechenheim	Froehlich
Domblick	Moelsheim	Silberberg
		Zellerweg Am Schwarzen Herrgott
	Wachenheim	Horn
		Rotenberg
	Monsheim incl. Kriegsheim	Silberberg
		Rosenberg
	Hohen-Suelzen	Kirchenstueck
		Sonnenberg
	Offstein	Engelsberg
		Schlossgarten

We now come to the most important *Bereich* of Rhinehessia and a very important German district, the *Bereich Nierstein* and its *Grosslagen*:

1. *Sankt Alban*

   Mainz, Bodenheim, Gau-Bischofsheim, Harxheim, Klein-Winternheim, Ober-Olm. Part of Lörzweiler.

2. *Domherr*
   The Mainz suburbs, Mainz-Finthen and Drais, and a few villages:
   Essenheim, Gabsheim, Klein-Winterheim, Ober-Olm, Saulheim, Schornsheim, Stadecken-Elsheim, Udenheim, Badenheim.
3. *Gutes Domtal*
   Vineyards of the villages: Nieder-Olm, Sörgenloch, Zornheim, Mommenheim, Selzen, Hahnheim, Köngernheim, Undenheim, Friesenheim, Weinolsheim, Dalheim, Dexheim. Parts of Nierstein, Nackenheim and Lörzweiler.
4. *Petersberg*
   Villages Albig, Biebelnheim, Bechtolsheim, Gau-Odernheim, Framersheim, Gau-Heppenheim, Spiesheim. Parts of Alzey.
5. *Krötenbrunnen*
   Dolgesheim, Hillesheim, Wintersheim, Eimsheim, Eich, Gimbsheim, and part of the following villages: Oppenheim, Dienheim, Ludwigshöhe, Guntersblum, Alsheim, Mettenheim. Part of Ulversheim.
6. *Güldenmorgen*
   Parts of Oppenheim and Dienheim. Ülversheim.
7. *Vögelsgärten*
   Parts of Guntersblum and Ludwigshöhe
8. *Rheinblick*
   Dorn-Dürkheim and part of Alsheim and Mettenheim.

Let us start with Mainz. Even in Roman days Mainz was a wine city. Until the nineteenth century vines were grown inside the city's walls. Then the town expanded, and where vineyards stretched at one time, new suburbs arose. Nevertheless Mainz retained its reputation as a viticultural metropolis, and wine continued to play an important part in the municipal economy. Wine taverns in the old lanes and alleys went on cultivating an interest in wines. However, since the enlargement of the urban area, vines have once again been planted within the boundaries of Mainz. Thus Mainz, the wine city, has resumed its status as a vine-growing community by the incorporation of suburbs, as this list shows.

Grosslage	*Villages*	*Vineyards*
St. Alban	*Mainz*-Laubenheim	Johannisberg
		Klosterberg
		Edelmann
	Mainz-Ebersheim	Huettberg
		Weinkeller
		Sand

Grosslage	*Villages*	*Vineyards*
St. Alban	*Mainz*-Hechtsheim	Kirchenstueck
	Lörzweiler	Hohberg
		Oelgild
	Bodenheim	Kreuzberg
		Kapelle
		Leidhecke
		Silberberg
		Westrum
		Burgweg
		Heitersbruennchen
		Hoch
		Ebersberg
		Moenchspfad
	Gau Bischofsheim	Kellersberg
		Herrenberg

The complete cultivated area is 264 ha which it is intended to increase by another 196 ha in the suburbs of Hechtsheim, Laubenheim and Ebersheim.

Mild wines with a fine bouquet are produced in this *Bereich*. They are good wholesome wines, though they never attain the excellence of a top-quality Niersteiner.

Moving now to the Grosslage Petersberg, we have:

Villages	*Vineyards*
Albig	Homberg
	Hundskopf
	Schloss Hammerstein
Bechtolsheim	Homberg
	Klosterberg
	Sonnenberg
	Wingertstor
Biebenheim	Pilgerstein
	Rosenberg
Framersheim	Hornsberg
	Kreuzberg
	Zeshberg
Gau-Heppenheim	Pfarrgarten
	Schlossberg
Gau-Odernheim	Fuchsloch
	Herrgottspfad
	Ölberg
	Vogelsang
Spiesheim	Osterberg

From these wines originate many of the Rhinehessian Liebfraumilch. The Schloss Hammerstein from Albig has become better known by its production of new crossings.

Where the Rhinehessian hills draw quite close to the Rhine, we come upon Nackenheim, clustered around its vineyards in the form of a horseshoe – at one point the well-known Rothenberg, at another the Engelsberg with an old mountain chapel, both in Grosslage Niersteiner Spiegelberg, and, pushing right down into the village, the Schmittkapellchen in Grosslage Niersteiner Gutes Domtal. The houses are built down to the very bank of the river, crowded close together, and among them are imposing homesteads all with stone-arched gateways.

It was not till the end of the eighteenth century when the growers were freed from serfdom, that the whole of the land to the last patch became dedicated to the cultivation of the vine.

Today there is no room for the cultivation of any but the highest-quality products. Climate, situation, nature of the soil, those are the three main determinants of the character and quality of a wine, and all are so favourable in Nackenheim that nothing but the best need be or is produced. Sun-kissed slopes and hills of red sandstone and clay slate (so-called '*Rotliegendes*') are here the homes of the Riesling and Silvaner grape which are also favoured by the evaporation, reflected light, and warmth-conveying influence of the broad stream of the Rhine. Small wonder that they bring forth a wine which combines depth, fire, spiciness and delicacy in marvellous and noble harmony. But hard work is needed to attain these results. In an average year the quantitative yield in this region is less than in any other part of Rhinehessia.

For a long time – far too long – Nackenheim wines were used for blending with others. In bestowing their maturity and sweetness on wines from other regions which were deficient in these qualities, they descended into anonymity – the name of Nackenheim was lost. It is only in recent years that people have begun to recognize the individuality, the special qualities and the exquisite taste of the wines fathered on the Nackenheim slopes. The estates of Gunderloch-Lange produce wines which, showing all the finesse of the best Rhinehessian wines, have some of the characteristics of good Rheingau wines.

And now at last we come to Nierstein (see plan, p. 354). As in Schwabsburg and Nackenheim we find in Nierstein clayey, sandy soils of violet-red colour (*Rotliegendes*).

NIERSTEIN boasts a population whose ancestors have been settled there for many generations, and all its families are dependent either directly or indirectly on the cultivation of vines. There are about 500 individual owners of vineyards – both large and small plantations. Almost every Nierstein family owns at least part of a vineyard, but only about twenty per cent of the wine estates play a significant part as producers of world-famous 'peak' wines. It is almost entirely owing to them that the name Nierstein has such a good reputation as designating the place of origin of superb vintages.

Literary allusions to the quality of Niersteiner wines are not infrequent. In Goethe's *Ur-Faust* for instance, where the scene is laid in Auerbach's cellar, one of the 'jolly topers' calls for a glass of 'genuine Niersteiner'. Then there was K. J. Weber (1767–1832), who wrote in his slim volume *Demokritos* under the heading 'The Delights of Drinking': 'In my opinion *Niersteiner* heads the list. If, now that I am old, I could drink a bottle of it a day, I am certain I should live ten years longer.'

The wines from the single site Nackenheimer Engelsberg may be sold under a Niersteiner Grosslage name as Spiegelberg.

The Nierstein sites include three sites under the normal size of 5 ha as concessions to growers who had introduced their wines under these names:

Goldene Luft	0·5685 ha
Brudersberg	1·3300 ha
Gloeck	2·1074 ha

Several estates have a colourful and well-documented history. One of the oldest buildings is the Kurfuerstenhof in Nierstein. The origin goes back to the Roman Emperor Valentinian. Charlemagne enjoyed the wines when visiting Nierstein. Later, in 1375, after having suffered many vicissitudes, it was given by the Emperor Charles IV to the Kurfuerst von der Pfalz (Elector of the Palatinate), when it received the name 'Kurfuerstenhof' (Elector's Estate).

Finally we come to the Grosslage 'Gutes Domtal'. Some explanation is required here: Niersteiner Domtal was the most famous generic vineyard name for Rhinehessian Rhine wines – unfortunately a much misused generic name. This was the reason why the Council of Nierstein some years ago registered 'Gutes Domtal' as a trade mark and generic name for all Nierstein wines proper.

In future 'Gutes Domtal' covers only one vineyard site of Nierstein, Niersteiner Pfaffenkappe, but includes the vineyards of a dozen villages. Gutes Domtal has changed its meaning and implications. Single sites of interest in this *Grosslage* are Dexheimer Doktor where excellent 1971 Spätlese and Auslese wines were produced, also Nackenheimer Schmittskapellchen. The following are other sites in this *Grosslage*:

Grosslage	*Villages*	*Vineyards*
Gutes Domtal	Dalheim	Altdoerr
		Kranzberg
		Steinberg
	Friesenheim	Altdoerr
		Bergpfad
		Knopf
	Hahnheim	Knopf
		Moosberg
	Koengernheim	Goldgrube
	Loerzweiler	Koenigstuhl
	Mommenheim	Kloppenberg
		Osterberg
		Silbergrube
	Nieder-Olm	Goldberg
		Klosterberg
		Sonnenberg
	Selzen	Gottesgarten
		Osterberg
		Rheinpforte
	Soergenloch	Moosberg
	Undenheim	Goldberg
	Weinolsheim	Hohberg
		Kehr
	Zornheim	Dachgewann
		Guldenmorgen
		Moenchbaeumchen
		Pilgerweg
		Vogelsang

Not less important are the vineyards south of Nierstein. Here the tertiary marl and lime assist the growth of first-quality wines, particularly in dry years as this kind of soil is capable of storing considerable quantities of finely distributed moisture. Red sandstone striated with sandy clays is also found. It is easily warmed by the sun's rays, and in wet seasons stores superfluous moisture in such a way that the vines are not harmed.

Most of these vineyards were formerly within a 15 km radius of the generic name Oppenheimer Krötenbrunnen which was in great demand inside Germany, even more than abroad. This formerly generic name now gives the name to a *Grosslage* which is much too small to support the demand. As the following list of other *Grosslagen* shows, parts of those well-known villages which contributed to the fame of the name 'Krötenbrunnen' have been excluded. The lesser known villages in the Grosslage Krötenbrunnen, and the good and best sites of Oppenheim and Dienheim in the Grosslage Gueldenmorgen have been included.

OPPENHEIM This is a 1,200-year-old town, once upon a time a free Reichstadt, which has the church of St. Catherine and the ruin of the Landskrone fortress. It is also known as the town of the 'Gothic and the wine'.

Grosslagen	*Villages*	*Vineyards*
Krötenbrunnen	Dolgesheim	Kreuzberg
		Schuetzenhuette
	Hillesheim	Altenberg
		Sonnenheil
	Wintersheim	Fraugarten
	Eimsheim	Sonnenhang
		Hexelberg
		Roemerschanze
	Uelversheim	Aulenberg
		Schloss
	Gimbsheim	Liebfrauenthal
		Sonnenweg
	Oppenheim	Herrengarten
		Paterhof
		Schloss
		Schlossberg
	Dienheim	Herrengarten
		Paterhof
		Schloss
	Ludwigshoehe	Honigberg
	Guntersblum	Sonnenberg
		Eiserne Hand
		St. Julianenbrunen
		Steinberg
	Eich	Goldberg
	Mettenheim	Goldberg
	Alsheim	Goldberg
Gueldenmorgen	Oppenheim	Daubhaus
		Guthenhaus
		Herrenberg
		Sacktraeger
		Schuetzenhuette
		Kreuz
		Zuckerberg

Grosslagen	*Villages*	*Vineyards*
Gueldenmorgen	Dienheim	Kreuz
		Herrenberg
		Silius-Brunnen
		Tafelstein
		Falkenberg
Vogelsgaerten	Guntersblum	Auenthal
		Himmeltal
		Steig-Terassen
		Bornpfad
		Kreuzkapelle
	Ludwigshoehe	Teufelskopf
Rheinblick	Dorn-Duerkheim	Hasensprung
		Roemerberg
	Alsheim	Fischerpfad
		Fruehmesse
		Roemerberg
		Sonnenberg

BEREICH BINGEN The municipality of Bingen-Rhine lies actually on the Rhine and Nahe.

The new Vine Register has brought great changes to the Nahe. There need to be eleven districts but they have been reduced for the wines of the valley of the right bank of the Nahe up to where the Nahe meets the Rhine have been added to Rheinhessen:

Hackenheim
Bosenheim
Planig
Ippesheim
Gensingen
Grolsheim
Dietersheim
Buedesheim
Bingen

Furthermore the following eight villages, though physically part of Kreuznach (Nahe), have been transferred 'viticulturally' to Rheinhessen:

Biebelsheim
Frei-Laubersheim
Fuerfeld
Neu-Bamberg
Pfaffen-Schwabenheim

Pleitersheim
Tiefenthal
Volxheim

The Grosslage St. Rochuskapelle covers these and all vineyards of Bingen-Stadt.

Villages	*Vineyards*
Bingen	Bubenstück
	Kapellenberg
	Kirchberg
	Osterberg
	Pfarrgarten
	Rosengarten
	Scharlachberg
	Schelmenstück
	Schlossberg-Schwätzerchen
	Schwarzenberg
Sponsheim	Palmenstein
Grolsheim	Ölberg
Gensingen	Goldberg
Horrweiler	Gewürzgärtchen
	Goldberg
Welgesheim	Kirchgärtchen
Biebelsheim	Honigberg
	Kieselberg
Pfaffen-Schwabenheim	Hölle
	Mandelbaum
	Sonnenberg
Zotzenheim	Johannisberg
	Klostergarten
Badenheim	Galgenberg
	Römerberg
Aspisheim	Johannisberg
	Sonnenberg
Dromersheim	Honigberg
	Kapellenberg
	Klosterweg
	Mainzerweg
Ockenheim	Hockenmühle
	Klosterweg
	Kreuz
	Laberstall
	St. Jakobsberg
	Schönhölle

Although the Bingen vineyards are separated from the Rheingau only by the width of the river, they produce quite different wines. The wines along the railway line and on the slopes around Bingen used to be distinguished by a certain 'smokiness' derived from the smoke of the engines. I myself do not care for the taste, but the wine found many lovers. The change to electrical engines has led to cleaner wines.

Bingen is a city with a long wine tradition going back to the fourteenth century. One of the many anecdotes originating from this city tells that one day the Bishop of Mainz called a meeting of the clergy in Bingen. During the meeting the Bishop wanted to make a note and asked someone to lend him a pencil. Hastily all present scrabbled in their pockets and each one of them brought out – a corkscrew. Since then corkscrews have been dubbed 'Bingen pencils'. A popular saying is: 'I've done no "bing-ing" today,' meaning, 'I haven't been intoxicated today.' Curiously enough, this could be expressed in English by 'I haven't been on the *binge* today,' although Partridge's *Dictionary of Slang* gives no indication that the English and German expressions could be etymologically connected.

On the Rochusberg near Bingen we find clay slate, lightly mixed with Devonian quartz. The slate disintegrates easily, producing a clayey soil which, though poor in lime, is rich in vegetable mould and has a medium potassium and high nitrogen content. The large dark slabs of slate and the quartz keep the soil loose, which is a good quality because it permits the passage of air, the easy circulation of water and the rapid assimilation of warmth – all of which have an excellent and characteristic effect on the surface soil of these vineyards.

The Rochusberg is crowned with a chapel which was rebuilt in 1814. Its consecration was celebrated by a popular festival (which incidentally is now repeated annually). Goethe, who was present at the consecration, has given us a description of the festival, including the sermon preached on that occasion by a suffragan Bishop. An extract from it seems both appropriate and amusing enough to be included here.

The Bishop had been preaching on the vice of drunkenness. After he had described it in drastic terms, he ended the sermon as follows:

'You, my devout hearers, who have already been pardoned and directed to show repentance and do penance, will realize from all that I have said that he who abuses God's glorious gifts in such a manner commits the greatest sin. But abuse is by no means the same thing as use. Has it not been written that wine delighteth the heart of man! That shows that we can and should enjoy wine, in order to give pleasure to ourselves and others. Now, among you here today there is possibly no one who could take unto himself two measures of wine without thereby causing his senses to become confused. But if anyone who has taken but three or four measures should so far forget himself as not to recognize his own wife and children, as to wound them by abusive words, by blows or kicks, in fact, if he should treat his dearest and nearest as if they were his greatest enemies. then let him immediately take counsel with himself and in future refrain from such excess, for it causes him to become unpleasing and contemptible in the sight of God and his own fellow-men.

'But should anyone after taking four measures, yea, five or six, still remain unaffected – should he still be able to give kindly assistance to his fellow Christians, to regulate his own household; should he even still be capable of carrying out the orders of his clerical and lay superiors – then let him enjoy his modest portion and thankfully accept it. But let him beware of going forward without further tests, for here as a rule weak humans reach their limit. It is very rarely that our Gracious Heavenly Father grants anyone the special gift of being able to consume eight measures, as He has granted it to me, his faithful servant. Since, however, no one can say of me that I have attacked anyone in an unjust fit of wrath, or that I have failed to recognize the members of my own household or my relations, or still less that I have failed to perform any of my spiritual duties or offices – since indeed you will all testify that I am at all times prepared to act in praise of and to the honour of God Almighty and to the benefit and advantage of my neighbours – therefore I may with a good conscience and in sincere gratitude continue in future to enjoy this gift which has been vouchsafed to me.

'And you, my devout hearers – each and every one of you – take your modest portion, in order that you may be refreshed in body and rejoiced in spirit, according to the Will of the All-Highest Giver. And in order that you may do this and on the other hand banish all excesses, I beg you all to act according to the command of the Holy Apostle who has said: Examine all and retain the best.'

At that time the 1811 vintage enjoyed the reputation of being about the best that had been produced for several years. This is what Goethe said of it on that occasion:

'Gazing on the fruitful vineyards all around me, I feel moved to do honour to our great 1811. The name of that wine is like the name of a great and beneficent ruler. When praise is due for anything that befalls this country, it is the name of the ruler that is on everyone's lips. And so it is with a good vintage. The people who dwell on the Nahe greatly praise a wine that grows on their land, and to which they have given the name Monsignor. It is said of this wine that it is pleasant and easy to drink, but that before a man is aware of it, it goes to his head. We were invited to partake of its delights and it has been so highly recommended that we are all eagerness to taste it in such good company and to put ourselves to the test, even though the experiment may be attended with some risk.'

FROM BINGEN TO MAINZ Not very much need be said about the wines of Rheinhessen between Bingen and Mainz and the plateau lying to the south of this strip. Names connected with this region are:

Grosslage	*Villages*	*Vineyards*
Abtei	Gau-Algesheim	Goldberg Steinert

Grosslagen	*Villages*	*Vineyards*
Abtei	Gau-Algesheim	Rothenberg
		St. Laurenzikapelle
		Johannesberg
	Appenheim	Daubhaus
		Drosselborn
		Hundertgulden
		Eselspfad
	Nieder-Hilbersheim	Honigberg
		Steinacker
	Ober-Hilbersheim	Moenchpforte
	Sprendlingen	Sonnenberg
		Wissberg
		Hoelle
		Klostergarten
	St. Johann	Klostergarten
		Steinberg
		Geyersberg
	Wolfsheim	St. Kathrin
		Osterberg
		Goetzenborn
	Partenheim	St. Georgen
		Steinberg
Kaiserpfalz	Ingelheim (the red-wine centre of Rheinhessen)	Burgberg
		Hoellenweg
		Horn
		Kirchenstueck
		Lottenstueck
		Rabenkopf
		Rheinhoehe
		Pares
		Rotes Kreuz
		Sonnenberg
		Sonnenhang
		Schlossberg
		Schloss Westerhaus
		Steinacker
		Täuscherspfad
	Heidesheim	Geissberg
		Hoellenberg
		Steinacker
	Wackernheim	Rabenkopf
		Schwalben
		Steinberg

Grosslagen	*Villages*	*Vineyards*
Kaiserpfalz	Gross-Winternheim *Ortsteil* of Ingelheim	Bockstein
		Heilighaeuschen
		Klosterbruder
		Schlossberg
	Engelstadt	Adelpfad
		Roemerberg
	Schwabenheim	Sonnenberg
		Klostergarten
		Schlossberg
	Bubenheim	Honigberg
		Kallenberg
	Jugenheim	Goldberg
		Hasensprung
		Heiligenhaeuschen
		St. Georgenberg
Adelberg	Woerrstadt	Kachelberg
		Rheingrafenberg
	Wendelsheim	Heiligenpfad
		Steigerberg
	Armsheim	Geiersberg
		Goldstueckchen
		Leckerberg
	Bermersheim v.d.H	Hildegardisberg
		Klosterberg
	Bornheim	Haehnchen
		Huette-Terassen
		Kirchenstueck
		Schoenberg
	Ensheim	Kachelberg
	Erbes-Buedesheim	Geisterberg
		Vogelsang
	Flonheim	Klostergarten
		La Roche
		Pfaffenberg
		Rotenpfad
		Bingerberg
	Lonsheim	Mandelberg
		Schoenberg
	Nack	Ahrenberg
	Nieder-Wiesen	Wingertsberg
	Sulzheim	Greifenberg
		Schildberg
		Honigberg

Grosslagen	*Villages*	*Vineyards*
Kurfuerstenstueck	Gau Bickelheim	Kapelle
		Saukopf
		Bockshaut
	Gau-Weinheim	Kaisergarten
		Geyersberg
		Wissberg
	Vendersheim	Sonnenberg
		Goldberg
	Wallertheim	Vogelsang
		Heil
	Gumbsheim	Schlosshoelle
Rheingrafenstein	Hackenheim	Klostergarten
		Gewuerzgarten
		Kirchberg
		Sonnenberg
		Galgenberg
	Volxheim	Liebfrau
		Moenchberg
		Alte Roemerstrasse
	Pleitersheim	Sternberg
	Tiefenthal	Graukatz
	Neu-Bamberg	Heerkretz
		Eichelberg
		Kirschwingert
		Kletterberg
	Woellstein	Aeffchen
		Haarberg-Katzen-steg
		Hoelle
		Oelberg
	Siefersheim	Hoellberg
		Goldenes Horn
		Heerkretz
		Martinzberg
	Eckelsheim	Sonnenkoepfchen
		Kirchberg
		Eselstreiber
	Wonsheim	Sonnenberg
		Hoelle
	Stein-Bockenheim	Sonnenberg
	Freilaubersheim	Rheingrafenberg
		Kirchberg
		Reichskeller

Grosslage	*Villages*	*Vineyards*
Rheingrafenstein	Freilaubersheim Fuerfeld	Fels Eichelberg Kapellenberg Steige

There is no doubt that some of the hitherto unknown villages will appear in future on labels, if not with *Einzellagen* then with *Grosslagen.* As site names must be accompanied by village names, I considered it best to include all.

IMPORTANT GROWERS IN RHEINHESSEN:

1.	Kommerzienrat P. A. Ohler'sches Weingut Inh. H. Becker Wwe.	6530 Bingen
2.	Weingut Oberst Schultz-Werner Inh. F. R. Schultz	6501 Gaubischofsheim
3.	Oberstlt. Liebrecht'sche Weinguts-verwaltung Inh. F. Nacke	6501 Bodenheim
4.	Weingut Gunderloch-Lange Nachf. Inh. R. Hörner	6506 Nackenheim
5.	Weingut Gunderloch-Usinger Inh. K. O. Usinger	6506 Nackenheim
6.	Weingut Freiherr Heyl zu Herrnsheim Inh. I. von Weymarn	6505 Nierstein
7.	Weingut Geschw. Schuch Inh. H. Günther	6505 Nierstein
8.	Weingut Reinhold Senfter Inh. I. Nix	6505 Nierstein
9.	Gräfl. Wolff Metternich'sches Weingut Verwaltung: Rentmeister F. Ruhs	6505 Nierstein 5071 Blecher
10.	Weingut Brüder Dr. Becker	6501 Ludwigshöhe
11.	Weingut Rappenhof Inh. Dr. Reinhard Muth	6526 Alsheim
12.	Weingut Burgermeister Balbach	6505 Nierstein
13.	Weingut Franz Karl Schmitt	6503 Nierstein

NAHE

Area 5,644 ha
90 per cent white wine
Average crop 70 hl/ha
Silvaner 32 per cent Riesling 25 per cent
Müller-Thurgau 30 per cent

Leafing through an old book of student drinking songs, I found one commending the wines of the Nahe. This is how it begins:

> Here's to Monzinger – smooth and fine,
> Like satin (only wetter),
> First cousin to a Rhenish wine –
> I don't know which tastes better.

The song might have added that the Nahe wines are also first cousins to the Mosel wines, though Nahe wines are reminiscent both of Rhine and Mosel wines. It is really not surprising if one looks at the map: the geographical position is between the two rivers.

Nahe wines yield an annual average of 400,000 hectolitres, produced by 83 wine-growing communities.

Looking down from the Rüdesheimerberg vineyards towards the opposite bank of the Rhine, you will see a little stream slipping past the two watchful hills known as the Scharlachkopf and the Elisenhöhe and winding its peaceful way towards the Rhine. That is the Nahe river. Its source is near Birkenfeld on the Hunsrück saddle and its path to the Rhine takes it through one of the most beautiful valleys in the region. The products of this valley, however, are not the only ones sold under the name of 'Nahe wines'. The name includes those from the districts of Baumolder and the Alsenz valley.

Far back along the valley where the Nahe flows into the Rhine almost all of its banks (at least those with a southern aspect) are planted with vines. Nahe wines are comparatively little known, though in olden days they appear to have been popular. Many stories tell of imposing drinking tournaments held in the vinelands of the Nahe, as a result of which entire estates were often wagered and lost. The lords of the castles, the heads of monasteries, and the mayors of the cities, all interested in cherishing and protecting the Nahe vineyards were involved in these gambles.

Nowadays rivalry takes a more peaceable form; quality counts before quantity and there the Nahe wines can certainly hold their own in competition with other German wine regions. Both the Domain and the carefully cultivated ancient private estates produce wines which have a distinctive character. They are racy, fiery and patrician. But more of this subject later.

What does the Nahe region look like? Dominating the landscape is the height known as the Burgklopp, rising up from the town of Bingen and standing out behind the vine-covered Scharlachkopf. The ancient Roman Drusus Bridge that once spanned the Nahe was destroyed by the Nazis during their retreat in 1945, but it has been rebuilt in the old style.

Not all villages along the Nahe belong to the 'Anbaugebiet Nahe'. Moving up the river Nahe from its mouth, the villages on the right bank of Büdesheim, Dietersheim, Sponsheim, Grolsheim and Gensingen up to the suburbs of Kreuznach belong to the 'Anbaugebiet Rheinhessen'. Therefore the most famous Nahe vineyard Binger Scharlachberg, formerly a Büdesheimer, was amalgamated into Bingen and is now a Rhinehessian wine!

The Nahe has also its *Weinstrasse* (wine road). We cross the Drusus Bridge at Bingen, where we reach the western bank with its many picturesque villages. The first is Bingerbrueck, an *Ortsteil* of Bingen which it is prohibited to make use of for viticultural purposes. Bingerbruecker wines (17·47 ha) must be sold as such without any mention of Bingen.

The Nahe Weinstrasse leads us through two *Bereiche*, the Bereich Kreuznuch and the Bereich Schloss Boeckelheim. Please note the spelling, the *Bereich* Schloss Boeckelheim is written in two words, both needing capital letters, but the *village* Schlossboeckelheim is written in one word.

Starting with Bereich Kreuznach:

Grosslage	*Villages*	*Vineyards*
	Muenster-Sarmsheim	Dautenpflaenzer
Schlosskapelle		Trollberg
		Hapellenberg
		Koenigschloss
		Liebehoell
		Pittersberg
		Rheinberg
		Roemerberg
		Steinkopf
	Laubenheim	Fuchsen
		Hoernchen
		Junker
		Karthaeuser
		Krone
		St. Remigiusberg
		Vogelsang

This Laubenheim must not be confused with Laubenheim near Nierstein.

	Windesheim	Dreiselberg
		Fels
		Hausgiebel
		Hoelle
		Roemerberg
		Rosenberg
		Saukopf

Grosslage	*Villages*	*Vineyards*
	Windesheim	Schaefchen
Schlosskapelle		Sonnenmorgen
	Guldental	Apostelberg
		Hippereich
		Hoelle
		Honigberg
		Rosenteich
		St. Martin
		Sonnenberg
		Teufelskueche

Guldental is the new name for the villages Heddesheim and Waldhilbersheim.

Then we come to the Grosslage Sonnenborn with its sites in one village Langenlonsheim, with its rich sun-drenched slopes. At Langenlonsheim the Guldenbach valley rises to Stromberg and on to the Hunsrueck range.

	Langenlonsheim	Bergborn
		Koenigschild
		Lauerweg
		Steinchen
		Loehrer Berg
		Rothenberg
		St. Antoniusweg

We approach the Grosslage Kronenberg with sites in the villages of Bretzenheim, Hargesheim and of course Bad Kreuznach. Winzenheim now forms part of Kreuznach with its famous sites Rosenheck and Honigberg.

And now we reach Bad Kreuznach with its great vine plantation which has been called the city 'of roses and nightingales'. Bad Kreuznach is not only a very pleasant spa, but also the centre of Nahe viticulture. It is a good place to stay when visiting the Palatinate, Mosel, Rheingau and Middle Rhine regions. The Kurhaus is an excellent place to stay and relax, the Trollmuehle to taste wines.

The Kreuznach sites are:

Agnesienberg	Gutental	Honigberg
Berg	Himmelgarten	Hungriger Wolf
Breitenweg	Hinkelstein	In den Mauern
Brueckes	Hirtenhain	In den 17 Morgen
Forst	Hofgarten	Junker
Galgenberg	Hoellenbrand	Kahlenberg

Kapellenberg	Nonnengarten	Schloss Kauzenberg
Katzenhoelle	Osterhoell	St. Martin
Kroetenpfuhl	Paradies	Steinberg
Moenchberg	Roemerhalde	Steinweg
Mollenbrunnen	Rosenberg	Tilgesbrunnen
Monhard	Rosenheck	Vogelsang
Narrenkappe	Rosenhuegel	

BEREICH SCHLOSS BÖCKELHEIM Vines are also widely cultivated in the lateral valleys branching out from the Kreuznach district. Here for example is the territory of the *Grosslage* Rosengarten, the best-known place in which is Rüdesheim (Nahe). It lies in the heart of the Nahe vineyards, about ten miles as the crow flies from the even more famous Rüdesheim (Rhine). Its wines are of good quality and the former generic name Rüdesheimer Rosengarten was so popular that it did not come as a surprise that the *Grosslage* was named Rosengarten.

The leading communities are:

Villages	*Vineyards*
Rüdesheim	Goldgrube
	Wiesberg
Mandel	Alte Roemerstrasse
	Becherbrunnen
	Dellchen
	Palmengarten
	Schlossberg

all with pleasant wines. The other vineyards in this district produce wines of the same or very similar quality. They are

Hueffelsheim	Gutenhoelle
	Moenchberg
	Steyer

which once changed hands as the result of a wager when a knight, Ritter Boos von Waldeck, drank a whole bootful of must in one draught.

Weinsheim	Katergrube
	Kellerberg
	Steinkaut

This is the wine village *par excellence* as its name indicates, with vineyards named after the hills, here rather grandiosely called 'mountains'.

We now come to Roxheim:		*Vineyards*
		Berg
		Birkenberg
		Hoellenpfad
		Huettenberg
		Muehlenberg
		Sonneberg
and to St. Katharinen:		
		Fels
		Klostergarten
		Steinkreuz
Other villages are:	Bockenau	Geisberg
		Im Felseneck
		Im Neuberg
		Stromberg
	Braunweiler	Hellenpfad
		Michaeliskapelle
		Schlossberg
		Wetterkreuz
	Burgsponheim	Hoellenpfad
		Pfaffenberg
		Schlossberg
	Sponheim	Abtei
		Grafenberg
		Klostergarten
		Muehlberg

To this '*Amtsbezirk*' Rüdesheim (local government centre) belong twelve communities, of which the most important is Niederhausen an der Nahe, in the Bereich Schloss Boeckelheim and the Grosslage Burgweg.

The other famous village is Schlossboeckelheim.

Its sites:	Heimberg
	In den Felsen
	Kuperfergrube
	Felsenburg
	Muehlberg
	Koenigsfels

are among the best to be found along the whole of the Nahe.

The viticultural Domain is world famous and worth a visit. The administrative buildings of the Domain are picturesquely situated on the western spur of the hill and afford a delightful view of the river Nahe framed in vine-covered banks.

Straight ahead lie vineyards rising in a series of terraces to the highest point of the Kupferberg (copper mountain) and comprising the sites Schlossboeckelheimer Kupfergrube and Niederhauser Herrmannshoehle.

The terraces are separated from each other and buttressed by strong fortress-like walls; they run from north to south so as to catch every ray of sunlight, thus giving the grapes the best possible chance of ripening.

I visited Director Goedecke in 1949. He was born in the Nahe region and is an expert in viticulture and the treatment of wines. He showed me an old painting of the Kupferberg as it was before 1902. At that date not a single vine grew there. Its slopes, now so harmoniously covered with beautifully cultivated vineyards, were then a mass of oak scrub and brushwood, cleft by deep gorges. The Prussian State, using convict labour, later planted these model vineyards.

Director Goedecke invited me to a tasting session. We started in the cellar where the 1948 and 1949 wines in cask came under review and then went on to his office where we began with wines in bottle dating from the years 1947 and 1948 and ended with the pride of the Domain – the 1945 Schloss Boeckelheimer Kupfergrube Trockenbeerenauslese which, at the 1948 auction had sold for 66 DM per bottle (£5·50p) – the 1959, 1964, 1971 are of outstanding quality. Director Raquet has now taken over the administration including the Rhinehessian vineyards of Bingen of the State Domain.

Its copper content has given the soil of the 'Kupfergrube' a curious earthy colour. (The 'Kupfergrube' (copper mine) was at one time actually mined, but uneconomically.) The wine has a taste which is reminiscent of blackcurrants. The earthy element gives the beverage a certain delicate piquancy. To be understood and enjoyed this particular wine must be sipped rather than drunk in the normal way.

The vineyards on these slopes are now at the height of their productive capacity.

In addition to the State Domain there are other estates such as Weingut Paul Anheuser, Bad Kreuznach, Weingut Haus Grutus, Traisen, August Anhaeuser or Anheuser and smaller growers, proprietors of vineyards in the village of Schlossboeckelheim (that is what it really is, in spite of its name: a village and not a weatherbeaten old castle – and not state-owned).

The Niederhauser sites:	Pfingstweide
	Hermannshoehle
	Klamm

The Niederhauser sites (*cont.*):

Kertz
Rosenheck
Felsenstever
Pfaffenstein
Stollenberg
Steinberg
Rosenberg
Steinwingert
Hermannsberg

Close by are Norheim, with its sites:

Dellchen
Goetzenfels
Kafels
Kirschheck
Klosterberg
Oberberg
Onkelchen
Sonnenberg

and Traisen am Rotenfels, where some glorious vines grow among porphyry rocks. Sites:

Bastei
Kickelskopf
Nonnengarten
Rotenfels

Still in the Grosslage Burgweg, through the beautiful Salinen valley, we come to Bad Münster am Stein, a delightfully pretty spa with its sites:

Erzgruppe
Felseneck
Feuerberg
Goetzenfels
Hoell
Koehler-Koepfchen
Luisengarten
Schlossberg
Rotenfelser im Winkel
Steigerdell
Stephansberg

On the heights of the opposite bank we see the ruins of the Ebernburg, the mighty fortress that belonged to Franz von Sickingen. Ebernburg and Bad Münster am Stein have been amalgamated into one viticultural community in the Grosslage Burgweg. On their sites grow the vines that produce Silvaner, Riesling, Traminer and Portugieser grapes.

On the warm slopes of the porphyry rocks we find sites that bear signs of high-grade cultivation. The wines produced are peculiarly racy, have an individual bouquet, are steely, fruity and, in the case of Rieslings, of a fine piquancy.

Farther south, in the valley of the lively Alsenz, there are many more vine-cultivating areas, among which Altenbamberg deserves mention (still in the Grosslage Burgweg).

Waldboeckelheim, slightly off the route along the river, is known for its good sites, exemplified by:

	Drachenbrunnen
	Hamm
	Marienpforter Klosterberg
	Kronenfels
	Roemerberg
	Kirchberg
	Muckerhoelle
	Muehlberg

Other villages in this *Grosslage* are:

Duchroth	Felsenberg
	Feuerberg
	Kaiserberg
	Koenigsfels
	Rothenberg
	Vogelschlag
Oberhausen	Felsenberg
	Kieselberg
	Leistenberg
	Rotenberg

We come now to the end of the Grosslage Burgweg, and enter Grosslage Paradiesgarten.

At Monzingen we enter a new viticultural region of good repute. This fairly extensive district, which includes Weiler and Martinstein, is practically the end of the Nahe wine lands.

Villages	*Vineyards*
Monzingen	Fruehlingsplaetzchen
	Halenberg
	Rosenberg
Weiler	Herrenzehntel
	Heiligenberg

In the valleys on both sides of the Nahe, there are many more places with a thriving wine culture – for example, on the Glan near Offenbach, and Odernheim. Although the vine centres on the Alsenz and some of those on the Glan, are politically speaking in the Palatinate, their wines belong to the Nahe category.

In the first edition of *Rhineland Wineland* I wrote: 'The winelands on the Nahe cater for all tastes. The high-grade wines of the vintage year 1949 from this region are the equals of the best anywhere. In fact, they attained higher prices from German wine merchants than many kinds from other districts.

'In conclusion it may be said of the Nahe wines that their value for export is certain to rise.'

The 1953 and even more the 1959 Nahe wines were real beauties. They had the charm of a good Mosel, the aroma of a Rheingau and the fruit of Rhinehessian wines. The 1961 and 1962 ice wines of the Nahe were great wines which never reached their best – most of them were drunk too young. The 1971s are worthy successors.

THE VILLAGES ALONG THE NAHE WEINSTRASSE

	Cultivated area in ha
Bingerbrück	17·47
Münster-Sarmsheim	220·00
Burg Layen	(*see* Rümmelsheim)
Waldlaubersheim	80·00
Genheim	33·26
Schweppenhausen	52·15
Windesheim	163·22
Guldental	500·00
Gutenberg	68·01
Wallhausen	237·86
Sommerloch	42·25
Braunweiler	72·00
St. Katharinen	31·81
Mandel	120·00
Sponheim	46.51
Burg Sponheim	32·35
Bockenau	37·40
Daubach	
Auen	21·00
Monzingen	193·00
Martinstein	10·00
Merxheim	57·00

	Cultivated area in ha
Meddersheim	127·00
Sobernheim	25·00
Staudernheim	8·00
Odernheim	50·00
Duchroth	93·03
Oberhausen	37·26
Niederhausen	110·37
Norheim	75·00
Bad Münster a. St.-Ebernburg	111·21
Bad Kreuznach	391·14
Bretzenheim	106·07
Langenlonsheim	250·00
Laubenheim	98·32

THE VILLAGES AROUND THE NAHE WEINSTRASSE

	Cultivated area in ha
Rümmelsheim	191·75
Dorsheim	73·20
Eckenroth	11·93
Schöneberg	20·69
Hergenfeld	28·82
Hargesheim	45·19
Dalberg	21·06
Roxheim	66·28
Rüdesheim	43·20
Weinsheim	69·87
Waldböckelheim	87·80
Traisen	37·97
Hüffelsheim	37·26
Schlossböckelheim	20·43
Oberstreit	5·15
Boos	10·39
Nussbaum	23·00
Weiler b. Monzingen	60·00
Kirschroth	43·00
Abtweiler	2·00
Raumbach	28·30
Meisenheim	35·09
Rehborn	36·00

	Cultivated area in ha
Callbach	3·00
Feilbingert	62·90
Hallgarten	6·16
Obermoschel	51·00
Niedermoschel	38·00
Hochstätten	36·50
Altenbamberg	36·56
Bad Kreuznach, Winzenheim	45·93
Steinhardt	(*see* Sobernheim)
Ippesheim, Planig, Bosenheim } Bad Kreuznach	300·00

MITTELRHEIN

Part of this region does not belong to Rheinland-Pfalz for the most northern wine-growing district of the Middle Rhine belongs to the federal state of Nordrhein-Westfalen. The vines cover 23 hectares and are planted on the hillside of the legendary Siebengebirge – the Seven Mountains. There are five full-time growers and a few others here and in 1971 they harvested 750 and in 1970 800 hectolitres of wine. They are proud of their product. The statistics for this area are

Area 848 ha
98 per cent white wine
Average crop 70,000 hl
Riesling 83 per cent   Silvaner 4 per cent
Müller-Thurgau 9 per cent

We now return to the main area of the Middle Rhine – the district extending along the left bank of the Rhine from Bingerbrück to Rolandseck, and on the right bank from Caub to Königswinter.

There cannot be many river valleys in the world whose natural beauty rivals that of this stretch of the Rhine. This is where the beautiful Rhine really begins, and anyone singing the praises of the Rhine is almost sure to be thinking of the Rhine valley from Bingen to Bonn. But unfortunately, the same cannot be said of the wines of the Middle Rhine. The surface structure and the geological composition of the soil differ from that of the Rheingau. The vines grow on quartzite and Devonian slate and at best produce wines of medium quality. These are either drunk locally, or else they find their way into the sparkling-wine factories, where they are welcome for their steely taste.

The main wine locality on the Middle Rhine is Bacharach on the left bank; it gives its name to the Bereich Bacharach (229 ha). At one time there was a popular saying:

> At Würzburg on Stein, and at Bach'rach on Rhine,
> You will find the best wine.

That alone would show that in earlier days Bacharach wine was famous. But the town of Bacharach owes this reputation less to its good vineyards than to the circumstance that it was a reloading station for the big ships. Only little ships could pass through the rapids of the so-called Binger Loch ('Bingen Hole'). And so it came about that the Bacharach warehouses were a general repository for the Rhine wines from Rhinehessia, the Rheingau, and the Rhenish Palatinate – and these wines were then sent into the world as *Bacharacher*.

Closely connected with Bacharach – in fact, always mentioned in one breath, as it were, with that city – are Steeg and Oberdiebach. Their 'Four Valley Wines' are among the best produced by the Middle Rhine. That these wines used to find favour even with very pampered drinkers, is shown by the story told about the Emperor Wenzel (deprived of his throne at Koenigstuhl in Rhense in the year 1400) who is said to have estimated the value of the Freedom of the City of Nuremberg at about four casks of Bacharach Muscatel.

Bacharach and Steeg sites are situated in the Grosslage Schloss Stahleck which also covers the villages of Oberdiebach and Manubach.

Next – but on the right bank of the Rhine – comes Kaub:
Grosslage Herrenberg, with sites:

Bluechertal
Rauschelay
Backofen
Pfalzgrafenstein
Rossstein
Burg Gutenfels

The late Dr. C. Spielmann, the Municipal archivist at Wiesbaden, compiled a record of the wine-market toll-book of the town of Kaub in the years 1544 to 1677. This, it appears, stated that at that time wine merchants from the Netherlands came with their ships to Kaub and there bought up the entire stock of locally produced wine. This they then re-sold to North Germany, the Netherlands and England.

Soon we pass the famous Lorelei rock, and should you make an excursion by steamer on this delightful and romantic stretch of the Rhine you can be sure that however happy the German passengers may be – empty bottles may indicate the degree of their happiness –

they will sing Heine's song of the 'Lorelei' – 'Ich weiss nicht was soll es bedeuten.'

In vain would I seek to discover
Why sad and mournful am I,
My thoughts without ceasing brood over
A tale of the times gone by.

As a formidable stream, the Rhine races past Boppard.

The waves are then broken on the Altenberg, where the river turns sharply to the east, forming (in the Boppard Hamm) its biggest bend north of Bingen. Looking down from the Schuetzen we can survey 'wine-soaked' Hamm which – more than five km long and facing due south all the way – is (next to the Rheingau) the best situated tract of wine country on the Middle Rhine. Strong Riesling wines with a fine bouquet flourish here on the upper Koblenz levels. This is the Grosslage Gedeonseck.

Kloster Eberbach in the Rheingau, whose wines are world-famous, used to possess more than 64,000 vines in the Boppard Hamm. The 'Eberbacherhof' – the memory of which is kept alive by the picturesque 'Ebertor' on the Rhine – attended to the cultivation of the vines, and pressed and matured the wines in its own cellars which incidentally still exist.

Before we pass on to the Mosel, which we are now about to reach at Koblenz, it should be noted that the Middle Rhine wine lands extend farther to the north; here they comprise – in particular – Linz, with its sites in the Grosslage Burg Hammerstein (165 ha) and the Bereich Rhein-Burgengau (1,062 ha).

The other *Grosslagen* in it are:

Burg Rheinfels	(St. Goar-Werlan)
Gedeonseck	(Boppard, Rhens)
Loreleyfelsen	(249 ha)
Marksburg	(49 ha)
Schloss Schoenburg	(179 ha)

and finally the Grosslage Lahntal – covering the vineyards of the river Lahn.

When one passes through this beautiful river district, one can see small vineyards on terraces cultivated here and there, and knowing that the maintenance of these vineyards must include to some extent knowledge of mountaineering, one wonders how much longer viticulture can and will continue here. The whole of this viticultural area is economically insignificant, although the landscape would be far less picturesque without the terraced vineyards. There are also many terraces overgrown with grass since phylloxera destroyed the vines.

MOSEL-SAAR-RUWER

The source of the river Moselle is in France. It flows through Luxembourg and forms part of the frontier between Luxembourg and Germany and then flows through Germany as the 'Mosel' until it meets the Rhine in Koblenz. Some years ago it was suggested that German wines from the river Moselle should be called 'Mosel' (the German name) to emphasize their German origin. It is advisable that this should be done forthwith. When French or Luxembourg wines are sold in Germany under the name of the district, these names have to appear in two languages on the label, e.g. a wine from Alsace has to be labelled 'Vin du Rhin = Rheinwein' a wine from Luxembourg 'Vin de la Moselle = Moselwein'. The same applies to Schaumwein (sparkling wine).

'Mosel-Saar-Ruwer 'was the flag under which all wines of the Mosel and her tributaries sailed under the 1930 law, but one was permitted to state on the label only the one from which the wine originated. This has been changed under the new law. We meet denominations such as:

Mosel
Mosel und Rhein
Mosel-Saar-Ruwer
Bereich Saar und Ruwer

and if ever confusion was created, here it is!

Let me explain:

Mosel-Saar-Ruwer is the name of a clearly defined, specific region, the denomination for quality wine and quality wine with predicate.

The area of origin *Mosel* is for Tafelweine only and covers the Tafelweine from Mosel, Saar and Ruwer.

Mosel und Rhein hints (!) at a blend of Tafelweine covered by the area of origin – again Mosel and Rhein.

Saar und Ruwer is a *Bereich* and 'Bereich' will always precede Saar amd Ruwer, so: Bereich Saar und Ruwer, a denomination which can be used for quality wine and Tafelwein. Therefore you may find the following two labels side by side:

Qualitätswein Mosel-Saar-Ruwer
  Bereich Saar-Ruwer
    Trierer Thiergarten Riesling

Tafelwein Mosel
  Bereich Saar-Ruwer
    Trierer Riesling or Ayler Riesling

Logical?

And so back to our topic: 'Mosels'.

MOSEL WINES

Mosel-Saar-Ruwer:

Area 10,714 ha
Average crop 900,000 hl/ha
Only white wines 74 hl/ha
Riesling 74 per cent Müller-Thurgau 13 per cent
Elbling 11 per cent

The Rhine provides us with wines which may be described as weighty, massive and full. His daughter, Moselle, supplements his gifts with wines which vary in character according to their place of origin. These wines have had a change of fate on foreign markets.

Unfortunately, soon after the war particularly, many natural wines (especially of the 1946 vintage) were shipped which ought to have remained in their country of origin, for a scarcity of sugar had prevented the growers from supplementing the lack of sugar in the grapes, and many lovers of Mosel wines got very suspicious of them. The vintages 1947, 1948, 1949, 1953 and especially 1959 made up for it and these wines have now become fashionable. The sixties were particularly successful vintages, and the 1971 vintage was even better.

The Mosel valley from Trier to Koblenz is a very long and narrow strip of land, 100 km in length, but when measured across from the vine-covered slopes on one side of the valley to those on the other, the average width works out at no more than 7½ km. The whole area therefore comprises about 750 square km.

But the Mosel, after joining the Saar near Trier, winds in and out so much that the distance from Trier to Koblenz – 100 km as the crow flies – is just about doubled, giving that much more space for wine cultivation. To this must be added the vineyards of the Saar and Ruwer, where there are at least 200 inhabited places – towns, hamlets, villages, parishes, castles, monasteries – and 176 communities grow wine. The general direction of the flow of the river is toward the north-east, but some of its bends are at such an acute angle that in some places the flow is actually in the opposite direction. Most of these bends are very short; in nearly all cases the river very soon turns back to continue its original course. The bends result in the formation of a number of peninsulas which jut out from the mainland into the river. Most of the tongues of land are broad-tipped and are sometimes very long.

If the Mosel from Trier to Koblenz had kept to a straight line in a north-easterly direction instead of indulging in all these fluctuations, it would have had a left bank facing south-east and thus continuously turned to the sun, whilst its right bank would have faced north-west and have been just as consistently deprived of much sunshine. But owing to the multitude of curves, the banks of the river on both sides show the greatest possible variety of aspects, so that climatic conditions on the riverside and in the valley vary from point to point, often at very short intervals. Here you may have a little hillock the slopes of which face south, where the rays of the sun caught in rock crevices are thrown back, their intensive collected warmth being of the greatest possible benefit to the vines. On such slopes vines are planted in every available space, and not a corner is left free. At one point a favoured hillock may be on the right bank whilst the next is found on the left bank. The best wines are derived from slopes such as these which face due south. There are other rocky promontories with slopes facing south-east and east, or south-west and west, which in the course of the seasons are exposed to the rays of the sun in all sort of crannies and crevices. It is here that the medium grades of wine are obtained. And finally there are the slopes which, turned away from the south, get no sun at all. They are cold and useless for wine-growing purposes.

Owing to this curious natural conformation, the inhabitants of the region usually have their villages and dwellings on one side of the river and their vineyards on the other. This has given rise to a complicated system of property-ownership on both banks and also explains the very large number of bridges over the Mosel. Nearly all these bridges were destroyed by the Nazis in their retreat, but have since been replaced.

The slopes bordering the Mosel are much higher than those on the Rhine, or for that matter, on any other German river. Up and up go the steps, innumerable are the terraces, one above the other, and even the topmost level is covered with vines. This means hard work for the wine grower.

The Mosel wine grower has one task peculiar to this region. Throughout the whole winter he has to prise slabs of slate out of the rocks, chop them up small and distribute the pieces in the vineyards – right up to the top level. These slates not only give the Mosel wines their basic taste, but the slabs hewn from the rock have a certain vital energy which they communicate to the vines. They help to keep the soil moist and act as fertilizing agents when they disintegrate. But of course their disintegration means that they have to be constantly replaced. Their usefulness does not end there. In the summer-time – on hot days – the slate stores up the heat of the sun during the day, and when evening comes, the warmth is radiated back on to the grapes, so that even by night the vines – through the action of the slate – indirectly get the benefit of the 'sunshine' they need to complete the maturing process.

Another hard task for the Mosel wine growers is the transportation of loads of fertilizer from the riverside to all the vineyards, including those at the top of the long slopes.

It seems likely that within a reasonable time these tasks will be lessened. Plans have been mooted to build funicular railways modelled on the Swiss ski-lifts – some indeed have already been constructed, notably at Enkirch – which, by connecting the valley with the mountain paths, will make both slate distribution and the transportation of fertilizer a much less strenuous job of work.

On the Mosel they cultivate nothing but vines, market nothing but the wine they produce. They have hardly any cornfields. In so far as they have meadows or keep cattle, it is only in the interests of their viticulture.

At the beginning of the section I said that 11 per cent are Elbling grapes. These are found in the Upper Mosel only, and without exception used for the production of Mosel Schaumwein and Sekt. For a long time the only kind of grape grown was the Riesling, even though this species has only been cultivated there since the sixteenth century. Its triumphant progress on the Mosel, to the final exclusion of all other species, was on the one hand due to the much appreciated taste which it imparts to its wines and its allegedly health-giving properties – it is jokingly known as 'Riesling tea' – and on the other hand to the reliability of its yield.

Unfortunately the Riesling cannot ripen on the higher slopes of the Mosel hills. It is here and also along the Lower Mosel that the Müller-Thurgau has made its appearance and occupies at present 13 per cent of the whole area. Experiments are going on with other new varieties.

On the whole the climate is favourable to grape growing, with a good average temperature and good atmospheric conditions. Apart from evaporation from the river, the vines obtain moisture from a varying rainfall, and warmth from the heat-absorbing action of the slate stone.

This northern district has an average temperature of 9–10°C. Spring arrives during the last third of April. Measured over the last fifty years, the average hours of sunshine during the time of vegetation (from the beginning of May to the end of October) are 1,047 hours. Rainfall is comparatively low: the average is 600–700 millimetres per annum, as the region is situated between two mountain ranges, the Hunsrück and the Eifel, and thus protected.

Discussions have been in progress in Germany for many years on the canalization of the Mosel, and many were afraid that the landscape would be spoilt by this industrialization. In spite of these misgivings, the work was put in hand. Many locks were built to make navigation on the Mosel possible. Now we are hearing about the first effects of canalization on viticulture. The area of water on the lower Mosel was increased by the dams, and the result is an increase in the quality of the wines produced there.

The dams were actually started in 1951 and extend over 15 km long. During various tastings of Mosel wines of the lower Mosel, experts who had observed these wines for many years found that the quality of the wines, the body, the fullness and finesse, had certainly altered, and that they had attained qualities never reached before. The increase in the area of water caused by damming the Mosel has improved the climate of the river valley, as the water is a kind of sun-reflector. Furthermore fog was formed when most wanted during and before the ripening process of the grapes, and increases of temperature were also observed. It is on record that similar effects were observed after the canalization of the Main in the Franconian district.

Now that the canalization of the Mosel is completed, we know that other parts of the Mosel have also benefited from this industrialization. The increase in quality does not of course affect all the Mosel wines, because we have to remember that the increase in the water area is only between two dams which are situated in such a way that a kind of lake is formed between them. These lakes only fill one-third of the Mosel, not the entire length. Therefore, in one-third of the Mosel regions we find better wines, and perhaps in the near future we shall mention villages as producing first quality wines which were previously unknown, at least to foreign wine drinkers.

I give here the names and distances (starting from Koblenz) of the locks:

	km
Koblenz (Moselkur)	1·96
Lehmen	20·83
Mueden	30·09
Fankel	59·38
St. Aldegund	78·30
Enkirch	102·97
Zeltingen	123·85
Wintrich	141·40
Detzem	166·83
Trier	195·83
Grevenmacher (Luxembourg)	212·85

Between 1949 and 1970 *agriculture* decreased in the district of Koblenz by 44·4 per cent and in the district of Trier by 28·3 per cent. From 1950 to 1971 the *viticultural* production area on the Mosel, on the other hand, has increased from 7,265 ha to 10,869 ha.

In the years 1953 to 1957, the average annual wine production was 469,400 hl. Out of this the Middle Mosel produced 254,200 hl = 54·2 per cent, the Lower Mosel 239,600 hl = 27·6 per cent, the Upper Mosel 34,800 hl = 7·4 per cent, the Saar 37,200 hl = 7·9 per cent and the Ruwer 13,500 hl = 2·9 per cent. During the period 1958–71 the wine yield of the Middle Mosel rose by 123 per cent. Its proportion to the total yield of the Mosel, Saar and Ruwer amounted to 53·1 per cent. On the Lower Mosel production was doubled (107·8 per cent), whereas the Upper Mosel showed an increase of over 200 per cent, the Saar of 160 per cent and the Ruwer of 113·7 per cent.

During the years 1953 to 1957 the Middle Mosel had average hectare-yields of 65·9 hl, the Lower Mosel 54·3 hl, Upper Mosel 71·5 hl, Saar 41·7 hl and the Ruwer 46·3 hl. From 1966 to 1970 these amounts increased considerably and, through the rich harvest during 1970 the five-year average for the Middle Mosel came to 107·2 hl/ha, Lower Mosel 100·1 hl/ha, Upper Mosel 129 hl/ha, Saar 94·3 hl/ha and Ruwer 86·6 hl/ha (see table on p. 251).

The different yields depend largely on the ecological conditions but also on the kinds of grapes grown. A picture of the development of the ha-yields of the two most important grapes, Riesling and Müller-Thurgau, can be obtained by studying the table on p. 251.

The increased returns of the Müller-Thurgau as opposed to the Riesling in the period from 1960 to 1970 are the most important cause of the extended cultivation of this grape. Only in 1966 the yield of the Müller-Thurgau on the Middle Mosel was below the Riesling. In all other years it was much higher than the yield of the Riesling. This applies also to the three other areas. It is also interesting to observe the development of various vines, such as Müller-Thurgau, Scheurebe and other crossings in districts formerly known for the cultivation of 100 per cent Riesling wines!

Any analysis of viticulture on the Mosel without taking account of the cost of labour and production would be incomplete. During the last few years some of the vine-growing enterprises on the Lower and Middle Mosel have been examined to obtain their cost structure and labour costs. Over several years labour varied on an average from between 2,300 and 2,400 hrs/ha of yield area. However, in 1970, in spite of the high output, for the first time there was a reduction in the average hours worked by the enterprises under examination. During that year 1,950 hrs per hectare of yield area were the average. Compare this with labour of 800–900 hrs/ha in enterprises being examined in Rhinehessia and the Palatinate.

In those vineyards where quality wines are produced, the vines are mostly kept close to the ground so that the grapes may ripen earlier and more evenly.

Change in viticultural area from 1950 to 1971

	1950* ha	1953 ha	1955 ha	1968 ha	1970 ha	1971 ha
Mittelmosel		3,726	3,868	5,247	5,690	5,789
Untermosel		2,330	2,442	2,687	2,720	2,821
Obermosel		389	489	808	880	898
Saar		842	881	1,034	1,015	1,044
Ruwer		304	287	304	330	317
Mosel, Saar, Ruwer	7,265	7,591	7,967	10,080	10,635	10,869

* No detailed figures available.

Wine production in hl on the Mosel-Saar-Ruwer 1953–1957 to 1966–1970

	1953	1954	1955	1956	1957	ø 1953–57
Mittelmosel	262,683	285,205	242,910	236,073	244,155	254,205
Untermosel	156,784	140,185	141,392	109,248	100,278	129,577
Obermosel	26,724	35,912	53,546	19,077	38,859	34,824
Saar	26,691	47,950	37,531	42,682	31,193	37,209
Ruwer	13,775	17,605	13,747	13,306	9,271	13,541
Mosel, Saar, Ruwer	486,657	526,857	489,126	420,386	423,756	469,356

1966	1967	1968	1969	1970	ø 1966–70
533,993	494,759	490,898	496,849	819,736	567,247
238,934	244,899	250,695	243,506	368,304	269,268
104,520	70,166	91,405	91,717	174,084	106,378
96,235	80,271	79,090	95,331	133,098	96,805
24,541	26,904	20,059	34,515	38,845	28,941
998,063	916,999	932,147	961,918	1,534,067	1,068,639

Increase in %: Mittelmosel + 123·1; Untermosel + 107·8; Obermosel + 205·5; Saar + 160·2; Ruwer + 113·7; Mosel, Saar, Ruwer + 127·7
ø = average.

To ensure that the Riesling grapes reach full maturity even in poor seasons, the grapes are harvested as late as possible: in October or even November. The grapes are not left on the vines – as in the Rheingau – until they reach '*Edelfäule*' (noble rot), but only until they have reached full maturity, and are then pressed immediately in order to preserve the racy qualities of the wine and its golden-green colour.

Mosel-Saar-Ruwer: *Development of the spread of grapes in ha from 1964 to 1970*

	Riesling	Müller-Thurgau	Elbling	Silvaner	Auxerrois	Ruländer	Scheurebe	Obhus	Total
Middle Mosel									
1964 ha	4,364	490	74	9	—	—	7	33	4,977
%	87·7	9·8	1·5	0·2	—	—	0·1	0·7	100
1970 ha	4,468	974	75	—	—	—	—	98	5,615
%	79·6	17·4	1·3	—	—	—	—	1·7	100
Lower Mosel									
1964 ha	2,192	246	195	—	—	—	—	8	2,641
%	83·0	9·3	7·4	—	—	—	—	0·3	100
1970 ha	2,223	381	206	—	—	—	—	16	2,826
%	78·7	13·5	7·3	—	—	—	—	0·5	100
Upper Mosel									
1964 ha	4	21	785	—	2	1	—	3	816
%	0·5	2·6	96·2	—	0·2	0·1	—	0·4	100
1970 ha	5	31	865	—	—	—	—	13	914
%	0·6	3·4	94·6	—	—	—	—	1·4	100
Saar									
1964 ha	936	101	5	—	5	—	—	10	1,057
%	88·5	9·6	0·5	—	0·5	—	—	0·9	100
1970 ha	997	181	—	—	—	—	—	50	1,228
%	81·2	14·7	—	—	—	—	—	4·1	100
Ruwer									
1964 ha	274	12	—	—	—	—	—	—	286
%	95·8	4·2	—	—	—	—	—	—	100
1970 ha	284	22	—	—	—	—	—	3	309
%	91·9	7·1	—	—	—	—	—	1·0	100

The vine country falls naturally into three parts, based on the differences in soil and the resultant differences and peculiarities of the vines cultivated thereon: the Upper Mosel, the Middle Mosel and the Lower Mosel.

The region of the Middle Mosel produces a wine which has the lowest alcohol content of any German, or indeed any European wines, but at the same time boasts the greatest wealth in 'bouquet' constituents and has a pleasant refreshing acidity. Praises of the wines of the Mosel have been sung for many centuries, but the first was Ausonius in his *Mosella.* A quotation from this will serve to illuminate the character of the Mosel:

> 'Every wine grown in each small hamlet has its own jealously preserved point of honour. All these wines may resemble each other in that they have been grown on the same steely slate ground, a fact that is immediately perceptible by the tongue (the taste one knew as a schoolboy when one licked one's slate); but each individual sample of liquor with a separate name and from a separate site shows some characteristic that is inimitable elsewhere. Something in each sample rejoices in its own recognizable peculiarity, ranging from something frankly rustic to the finest shades of aristocratic heredity and hedonism. The wine does not make you feel heated – it is cool and pleasant to drink. It is neither heavy, nor has it ill effects. It is light, volatile, fine and clear: like fresh agreeable music which remains in the memory without troubling mind or body, it hardly affects you at all. That is a point of honour with the wine, that is balsam for the shattered nerves of modern man.'

And thus it has come about that not only the wine drinker, but the doctor too has learned to prize the qualities of this wine: doctors take Mosel wines seriously. They attach importance to them as helping to preserve good health and to improve the condition of those who are sick. It has for instance been ascertained that cases of calculus are practically unknown on the Mosel and that Mosel wines have a specific curative influence on kidney stones, bladder stones and gallstones. Ausonius stressed that *vinum mosellanum sanum est.* Among many medical treatises dealing with this subject, Henderson's *History of Wines* (1824) deserves mention. He writes that the lighter Rhine wines and the Mosel wines are far more cooling in their effects than wines imported into England from other districts and countries, and are often prescribed in their own country for promoting urination. 'They have proved very effective for many kinds of fevers in which the patient had a weak pulse and debilitated nerves. They can be prescribed with more confidence than most other kinds of wine, as they contain but little alcohol, the action of what little alcohol there is being weakened by the presence of free acids. They are also said to be effective in reducing adipose tissue.'

At one time no continental ship set sail without a store of Mosel wines as the best and safest cure for scurvy.

Luckily for the Mosel-Saar-Ruwer, under the new vinification, 1964, 1966, 1967 and 1969 developed attractive elegant wines with a fine aroma and bouquet and little alchohol content, ideally made for the driver who likes to enjoy a glass of light wine and drive home in his own car.

When for the first time the great estates offered the 1970s, their authentic but chaptalized wine, many wine drinkers made these wines their first love. I have seldom seen such an enthusiastic reception of something new.

And when I was making notes for this chapter a few days after a tasting of the Hallgarten Selection of 1971s, I could say these wines would in time overtake those from the Rhine. Indeed the 1971 Saar and Ruwer have proved to be the greatest! At the first tasting 70 were selected out of 200 tasted and I can only repeat what James Burgis, the expert wine buyer of Harrods said: 'Never before have I tasted a range of wine where each wine has its merits and I could not mention a single one I should not like and would reject!'

And now let us continue our journey:

BEREICH OBERMOSEL The vines of the Upper Mosel – like those of Champagne – are rooted in shell-limestone. The wines they produce are 'small' wines, mostly sour and – on account of their meagre alcohol content – not suited for consumption in their pure form. As a rule they find their way into cheap blends or the manufacture of sparkling Mosel.

The frontier delimitation of the autonomous Saar district 'Saarland' has cut off the communities of Weis-Nennig, Besch and Perl from the Upper Mosel wine-growing region. The federal state 'Saarland' does not include a single vineyard devoted to the cultivation of Saar wines, so that the three communities of the Upper Mosel represent the modest viticultural efforts of the whole Saarland.

SAARLAND

84 ha
1971 = 110·2 hl/ha
1970 165 hl/ha
1971 3,660 hl
1970 15,818 hl
Some *red* wines are produced
1971 white wine 71° Oechsle
red wine 83°

In the 'Three-Country-Corner' (Germany, Luxembourg, France) the vineyards sustained heavy losses during the war. But the general economic situation, in particular the wine market in the Saarland, has encouraged the growers to devote themselves with greater intensity to cultivating their plantations. A maximum yield of 96 hl/ha for the production of quality wines has been fixed and inter-regional blending is permitted until 31 August 1976. The destroyed vineyards have been restored, while those that escaped damage are being devoutly tended. The region of the Upper Mosel is extremely lucky in its climate so it is reasonable to expect that the efforts of the growers will meet with success. They plant the Silvaner, Ruländer and Auxerrois grapes, and all these wines enjoy popularity on the Upper Mosel, for though they do not yield such large quantities as the Elbling they are of far better quality. In the Saar itself the newly acquired territory on the Upper Mosel is known as the Riviera of the Saar, because many foreign tourists make for this part of the country, and a liking for Mosel wines apparently plays a part in their choice.

The Upper Mosel forms the Bereich Obermosel (1,134·56 ha) with the Grosslagen Mesenicher Königsberg (206·56 ha) and Nitteler Gipfel (928 ha). It is followed by the Bereich Saar-Ruwer which includes, in addition to the villages of the Saar and Ruwer, the Mosel city of Trier.

BEREICH SAAR–RUWER The younger Saar wines in comparison with others may be designated as the playboy of this wine family, being steely, elegant, and volatile with a delicate bouquet; while the youngest scion of the Mosel – the product of the Ruwer – is racy, steely and fragrant.

The vine plantation area comprises 1,000 hectares and stretches from Saarburg to Konz. In the lower reaches of the Saar the soil is slaty, while above Saarburg it consists of shell-limestone. The grape species commonly planted here is the Riesling. Owing to the comparatively high situation of the vineyards (over 600 feet) and the harsh winds coming from Lorraine and Hunsrueck, the average wine produced in this region is of no more than medium quality, but in a good year Saar wines are nevertheless in fairly good demand on account of their distinctive bouquet and flavour, their superior breed and elegance. The 1949 vintage attained unexampled maturity, and the wines were the best ever made then. But May frosts had destroyed two-thirds of the crop, so that only a small quantity of this desirable wine was produced.

The best Saar wines ever made are the 1971s: such harmony, finesse and elegance have never before been witnessed, better even than the 1964 Saar wines which had high quality; and their bouquet is better even than that of the 1959s, and these were great.

Unfortunately the 1971 Saar wine crop was small. Only 3,600 hl were produced (against nearly 36,000 in 1970). A few minutes of hail in August 1971 destroyed the main part of the crop. But the small crop left is the greatest!

The former site Scharzberg which belonged to Wiltingen and Oberemmel and was therefore a generic name covering a radius of 15 km, has been struck off the register as a single site and has become the *Grosslage* for Saar wines. Scharzberg was such a well known name that the wines were often marketed just as 'Scharzberger'. The Grosslage Scharzberg covers the Saar area with 1,555·22 ha.

The State Domains of Serrig and Ockfen own very good sites and produce wines that are much sought after, such as the Ockfener Bockstein.

The largest wine-growing locality in the Saar is Wiltingen. Oberemmel lies in a side-valley of the Saar near Wiltingen and produces good wines. Its sites are:

Agritiusberg
Rauler
Huette
Junkerberg

Grosslage	*Villages*	*Vineyards and areas in ha*	
Scharzberg	Ockfen	Heppenstein	6·6
		Bockstein	55·6
		Kupp	7
		Herrenberg	7·5
		Geisberg	1
		Neuwies	
		Sickelgarten	
	Schoden	Herrenberg	30
		Geisberg	20
		Saarfeilser	
		Marienberg	6
	Wiltingen	Sandberg	2·28
		Hoelle	2·35
		Kupp	7·30
		Braune Kupp	5·80
		Gottesfuss	4·42
		Klosterberg	71·32
		Rosenberg	61·35
		Braunfels	58·48
		Schlangengraben	54·41
		Schlossberg	17·79
		*Scharzhofberg	27·35

* The Scharzhofberger is an *Ortsteil* and will therefore in future be marketed as before, i.e. as 'Scharzhofberger'. This famous vineyard belongs to a few well-known growers: Egon Mueller, Hohe Domkirche, von Volxem, Vereinigt Hospitien, Kessellstatt, Rautenstrauch v. Hoevel, Apollinaris Koch.

Grosslage	*Villages*	*Vineyards and areas in ha*	
Scharzberg	Oberemmel	Altenberg	75
		Karlsberg	42
		Rosenberg	61
		Huette	5·13
		Agritiusberg	5·27
		Raul	2·36
	Kanzem	Altenberg	
		Sonnenberg	25
		Hoerecker	0·73
		Schlossberg	4·27

The great 1964 Kanzemer wines won many permanent friends for this lesser known region.

	Kanzem, Filzen, Hamm	Altenberg	22
	Filzen	Steineberger	10
		Urbelt	12
		Unterberg	20
		Herrenberg	5·5
		Pulchen	4·8
		Liebfrauenberg	5·2
	Koenen	Fels	6·61
		Kirchberg	9·07
	Ayl	Kupp	81
		Scheidterberg	20
		Herrenberger	4·58

Ayler Kupp wines of 1970 and 1971 vintages from various growers are amongst the finest of these vintages.

	Konz	Auf der Kupp	40
		Klosterberg	15
		Falkensteiner	
		Hofberg	18
		Euchariusberg	40
		Brauneberg	18
		Sprung	9
	Mennig	Herrenberg	35
		Sonnenberg	35
		Euchariusberg	40
		Altenberg	40
	Pellingen	Jesuitengarten	4·49
		Herrgottsrock	

Grosslage	*Villages*	*Vineyards and areas in ha*	
Scharzberg	Saarburg	Rausch	12
		Antonius-brunnen	10
		Bergschloesschen	8
		Burgberg	9·07
		Klosterberg	5·08
		Kupp	18·49
		Fuchs	16·5
		Schlossberg	
		Stirn	
		Laurentiusberg	
	Irsch	Vogelsang	22
		Sonnenberg	47
		Hubertusberg	34
	Serrig	Herrenberg	6·5
		Wuertzberg	6·5
		Schloss Saarsteiner	8·3
		Schloss Saarfelser Schlossburg	5·33
		Heiligenborn	7·15
		Hoeppslei	7·07
		*Koenig Johann Berg	8
		Antoniusberg	12
		Kupp	12
		Vogelsang	29·23
	Kastel-Staadt	Maximin Stadt	4·27
		Koenig Johann Berg	5

We leave the Saar and with it the Grosslage Scharzberg and come next to the Grosslage Trierer Roemerlay, which has an area of 736·16 ha.

The Grosslage Trierer Roemerlay embraces all the single sites of Trier and those vineyards of Trier which are not part of any single site and all the sites of the following villages:

* A site of historical – less of quality – interest is the Serriger Koenig Johann Berg near Kastel, also called the 'Klaus'. Close by is the hermitage in which John, the blind King of Bohemia who fell in the battle of Crecy on 26 August 1346, was buried. Since 1947 his grave has been transferred to Luxembourg Cathedral and is now a national memorial.

Villages	*Vineyards and areas in ha*	
Franzenheim (Mosel)	Johannisberg	17·5
Hockweiler (Mosel)	—	5·98
Riveris (Ruwer)	Kuehnchen	8
Pluwig	—	
Sommerau	Schlossberg	5·6
Korlingen	Layakul	
Morscheid	Dominikanerberg	2·22
	Heiligenhäuschen	

and all other 'Ruwer' vineyards.

Between Saar and Ruwer on the Mosel lies the famous Trier (Trèves), the principality of the Mosel, claiming to be the oldest city in Germany and showing proof of its ancient history – the Roman amphitheatre, Roman baths, the Porta Nigra and a museum which possesses many treasures from Roman times. It is also an important viticultural centre, especially now that many surrounding villages have been incorporated into it and the wines originating from them are designated 'Trierer'. Like Stuttgart it can boast that vines grow within its city walls.

Trier is now a city (*Grossstadt*) with approximately 107,000 inhabitants and one of the largest vine-growing communities on the Mosel, 120 ha with one million vines.

The principal *Ortsteil* (suburb) is Olewig with its famous Augenscheiner. Eitelsbach, the well-known village on the Ruwer with the Karthaeuserhofberg site is also part of Trier now. But I doubt very much whether these highly valued wines will ever show Trier as their geographical origin. It also includes Avelsbach and Olewig where during the first weekend in August the Trier Wine Festival is celebrated.

Grosslage	*Town*	*Vineyards*	*ha*
Roemerlay	Trier	Augenscheiner	4·47
		Sonneberg	3·7
		Marienholz	56·41
		Domherrenberg	45·2
		Maximiner	4
		Altenberg	10·20
		Herrenberg	12
		Hammerstein	11·88
		Rotlay	9·41
		St. Maximiner Kreuzberg	10·3

Grosslage	*Town*	*Vineyards*	*ha*
Roemerlay	Trier	Deutschherren-koepfchen	1·64
		Deutschherren-berg	19·65
		Jesuitenwingert	14
		Burgberg	27·65
		Benediktinerberg	5·5
		Kurfuersten-hofberg	6·7
		Thiergarten	14·5
		St. Mattheiser	25
		St. Petrusberg	9
		St. Martiner	24·9
		Andreasberg	13·55
		Leikaul	13·85
		Kupp	9·77

Until 1945 the German *Weinmuseum* was established in Trier but it was lost after the end of the war; plans are in hand, however, to re-establish it, but evidence of viticulture along the Mosel during the Roman occupation can still be seen in the Museum of Trier (*Landesmuseum*), objects in glass, stone and clay.

Karthauerserhofberg is in Trier Eitelsbach. The owner, Mr. Warner Tyrrell, is also the President of the German Viticultural Wine Growers' Association. The history of this estate goes back to 1335, or rather before that year, because it was in 1335 that the Archduke of Trier and the Archbishop Baldrian of Luxembourg, who was the most important sovereign of Kurtrier, bestowed this estate on the Order of the Carthusian monks. For 500 years the monks and a few lay brethren worked the estate and lived there. But in 1803 the estate was secularized like so many others, and in 1811 a Luxembourg citizen bought it; it remained the property of his family for over a century. It is situated in a small valley which begins behind the last houses of the Trierer suburb of Eitelsbach, and the estate has approximately 100 ha, actually the same size as it had under the monks. 18 ha of this are one area of vineyards, planted almost 100 per cent with Riesling, but the estate is taking part in an experiment on new crossings. The production lies between 75 and 175 *Fuder* per year, and the average production is 70 hl/ha. In the old-fashioned way, wooden casks are used for maturing the wine.

Good vintage years are as a rule also good years for the phylloxera. A report from the Mosel gives details about the increase of this insect in the vintage year 1971. 8,665 ha in the county of Trier have proved to be especially infested, and this includes part of the Middle Mosel, the Upper Mosel, the Saar and the Ruwer. The Upper Mosel and Saar have been particularly affected. On the other hand a lesser degree of infestation was noted in that part of the Trier County which belongs to the Middle Mosel, and in particular the areas of Bernkastel and Wittlich of the middle district are little affected. No investigations of phylloxera are being carried on in the districts of the Upper Mosel. This district is planted today on American root stock. In the village of Temmels they found fewer than three vineyards affected in 1970 and 1971, and strangely these were on American root stock. One expected that the root stock would not be affected by phylloxera, but this seems not to be the case. There is one single village in the Saar district, Schloss Kastelstadt, which is free of phylloxera. It is said that the situation of this village is such that the flying phylloxeras do not reach it. The Saar district is 75 per cent planted on root stock.

Phylloxera was newly found in 24 villages which included 107 different vineyards. For the first time the vineyards of Traben-Trarbach and Wehlen had been attacked and there are now only a few villages free from this insect. It is noteworthy that the Lower Mosel is still completely free of phylloxera.

As regards the plantations on American roots I should like to add that in the district of Trier 58 per cent are now on American root stock and approximately 450 ha are added every year. One hopes that by the end of this decade no vineyard will still have pure European vines. Actually the reorganization of the German vineyards is always accompanied by the planting of the new vineyards on root stock, and after the reorganization is complete it will be prohibited to plant any new vineyard without root stock. It is estimated that approximately 440 ha will not be reorganized. These are small parcels of vineyards which are situated in lonely spots, very often surrounded by rocks. These vineyards will continue to be handled and worked as they were a thousand years ago, by manual work only.

In Trier the average highest temperature for the months of May to September is: 23°, 24°, 24°, 23°, 20°C; the duration of sunshine per day is 7, 6, 7, 6, 5, hours; the vineyard area consists of three million vines, 350 ha of vineyards (more than 3 per cent of the area defined as Mosel-Saar-Ruwer).

In Trier the State Domain covers the amalgamated Domains Avelsbach (32 ha), Ockfen (14 ha) and Serrig (34 ha). The cellars are in Trier, between the main railway station and the Porta Nigra, and visitors are welcomed. Here one can still find the wine maturing in hundreds of wooden casks – the cellar covers 5,474 square metres and one can taste to one's heart's content.

These estates were started in 1896. The South-west and South sites were planted where ancient oak forests had stood; they are:

Villages	*Vineyards*
Avelsbacher	Hammerstein
	Kupp
	Rotlei
Ockfener	Bockstein
	Herrenberg
	Heppenstein
Serriger	Vogelsang
	Heiligenborn
	Hoeppslei

The grapes cultivated are:

85 per cent Riesling
3 per cent Müller-Thurgau
1 per cent Ruländer
1 per cent Spätburgunder
10 per cent other vines

Their pride is their 'Schatzkammer' (treasure chamber) which holds a few of the best of all vintages since 1920, including the 1921 Serriger Trockenbeerenauslese (290° Oechsle).

Wine seminars have become fashionable. Many Germans combine the pleasure of a holiday with the pleasure of learning about and tasting and drinking wine. Such seminars are held in the Rheingau, Trier and other places. In Trier they are also given in English. The week-end wine seminars include lectures, excursions, visits to wine cellars and last but not least wine tastings.

They are arranged by Volkshochschule Trier, 55 Trier, Palais Walderdorff, telephone (0651) 718327 and the Verkehrsamt Trier (Tourist Office), telephone (0651) 718446 and 718448 in co-operation with the Weinwerbung (Wine Propaganda Office) Mosel-Saar-Ruwer.

On the narrow slopes of the slate-strewn valley of the Ruwer the Riesling grape seldom reaches full ripeness. The accusation usually levelled against Ruwer wines is perfectly justified and they are in consequence less popular than Mosel wines. But in good years such as 1921, 1934, 1949, 1953, 1959, 1964 and 1971 they rank with the finest. These vintages have a volatile, elegant bouquet reminiscent of blackcurrants combined with a touch of earthiness.

The ordinary 1959 Ruwer wines were the perfection of a fine table wine: light, elegant and dry, whereas the Spätlese and Auslese wines were, on account of their unbalanced richness, most disappointing. In 1964 the Ruwer produced the best of all German wines, the

1966 were good, the 1970 quality wines excellent. 1971 might beat all previous vintages. The staying power of these wines with their ripe bouquet and well-balanced and harmonious character is quite delightful.

Grosslage	*Village*	*Vineyards*	*ha*
Roemerlay	Kasel or Casel	Nieschen	16·8
		Kehrnagel	22·2
		Hitzlay	22
		Herrenberg	8·8
		Paulinsberg	10·2
		Timpert	2·5
		Dominikanerberg	5

Other wine localities in the Ruwer region are Eitelsbach with its world famous Karthaeuserhofberg (Grower Rautenstrauch), Mertesdorf, Waldrach (Weingut Scherfs Muehle) and Petershof with its Waldracher Doktorberg. If one is keen to have a 'Doktor' wine on one's dining table this nearly unknown vineyard will oblige.

Grosslage	*Villages*	*Vineyards*	*ha*
Roemerlay	Trier Ortsteil		
	Karthaeuserhofberg	Stirn Ortsberg Burgberg Kronenberg	18·5
	Mertesdorf	Lorenzhefer-Felslay	2·5
		Herrenberg	30
		Johannisberg	4·2
		Lorenzhofer Maeuerchen	2·7
	Mertesdorf (part of)	Abtsberg	9·83
	Ortsteil	Herrenberg	9·96
	Maximiner Gruenhaus	Bruderberg	2·10

A Maximin-Gruenhaueser Herrenberg of 1933 vintage holds an unforgettable memory for me. When fire-watching one night with two friends we drank a bottle of it and were singing its praises and commenting on its marvellous development when the sirens gave the alarm. That night I lost my whole store of original bottlings, including several cases of the wine we had been drinking. I had to wait until 1959 to find a replacement for the lost treasure. A good parcel was put aside for my own private use but not for long. A repeat order originating from the one person whom one cannot refuse made me open my museum. The 1964 and 1960 were good, the 1971 great wines.

Grosslage	*Villages*	*Vineyards*	*ha*
Roemerlay	Waldrach	Laurentiusberg	5·9
		Hubertusberg	5
		Krone	40
		Meisenberg	31
		Sonneberg	15
		Jungfernberg	5
		Doktorborg	5
		Kurfuerstenberg	1·3
		Jesuitengarten	1·2
		Ehrenberg	
	Waldrach, Morscheid, Riveris	Heiligenhaeuschen	approx. 11

Waldrach, once not considered worth mentioning, now produces wines which are in demand. Waldracher Krone in all classes up to the Auslese and Eiswein has taught some people a lesson.

We now enter the third *Bereich*, the Bereich Bernkastel, which is equal in quality to and covers the famous part of the Mittelmosel, of which Bernkastel has always been considered the centre. To expand the Bereich to this extent was a welcome decision.

Here we find wines that are aristocratic and spicy and have an exquisite bouquet. Best known among Mosel wines is the Berncasteler Doktor which became world-famous after it had been warmly recommended by King Edward VII's personal physician. The vineyard site is not very large and is moreover cut up into three estates (owned respectively by Dr. Thanisch and by Messrs Deinhard and Lauerburg). In a good year the site will produce no more than from 1,500 to 2,000 dozen bottles so it is easy to understand why very high fancy prices – one might almost call them monopoly prices – are paid for them. Sold on the value of the wine alone – despite the fact that the Berncasteler Doktor has by far the greatest 'name' – the wines from other vineyards of Mosel and Saar have often attained prices higher than those achieved by the famous Doktor. Inside Germany the Wehlener Sonnenuhr is reckoned to be easily the best of all Mosel wines. Fifty to seventy years ago it was the Brauneberger Brauneberg. So even vineyards have their changes of fortune! In any case the Berncasteler Doktor of 1921 – the 1·32 ha vineyard situated on the best part of the hill overlooking Bernkastel – is in no way identical with the much enlarged vineyard Bernkasteler Doctor which includes some very much poorer parts (now over 5 ha). I shall have more to say about this on page 270. In the new Register the vineyard is entered as Doctor, whereas Doktor is generally spelt with a k.

As a matter of interest other Doktor vineyards exist at Dexheim near Nierstein (Rhinehessia), at Waldrach (Ruwer), at Ihringen (Baden), at Venningen (Pal.) which I frankly confess to prefer to the Thanisch Doktorwein.

All the wine communities of this region are worthy of mention, but we must content ourselves here with naming the best among so many that are good:

On the left bank:

Traben	Cues
Kroev	Lieser
Uerzig	Piesport
Wehlen	Trittenheim

on the right bank of the river:

Zell	Bernkastel
Enkirch	Muelheim
Trarbach	Brauneberg
Erden	Neumagen
Zeltingen	Dhron (inland, belonging to Neumagen)

The large-scale wine growers of the Middle Mosel have combined to form two associations – the Large Ring – Trierer Ring – and the Small Ring – the Berncasteler Ring. The largest owners are the State and the Church – a remnant of the days of feudal and ecclesiastical power. They are the State Domain and the Bischoefliches Konvict (Episcopal Seminary), the Hohe Domkirche (Cathedral), the Priester Seminar (Priests' Seminary) and the Vereinigte Hospitien – all situated in Trier but owning land in many communities. Then there are a large number of estates of various sizes and many smallholders.

Let us wander along the Mosel.

The first *Grosslage* we meet is Probstberg (1,804 ha) and the most important village is Longuich with the Maximiner Herrenberg (12 ha) and Hirschlay (204 ha) sites which produce amiable, delicate wines of medium quality.

Other villages and vineyards in this *Grosslage* are:

Village	*Vineyards*	*ha*
Kenn	Held	15
	Maximiner Hofgarten	15

Villages	*Vineyards*	*ha*
Schweich	Annaberg	18
	Burgmauer	50
	Herrenberg	37
Riol	Roemerberg	4
Fell	Maximiner	160
	Durgberg	160
Mehring	no single sites	

Now we reach the important *Grosslage* of the Mosel: Piesporter Michelsberg (2,290 ha). The first village within this *Grosslage*, Trittenheim, has the sites Altaerchen (245 ha) and Apotheke (55 ha).

Neumagen is the most ancient wine-growing locality in Germany, the place in which the oldest evidence of German viticulture was discovered, including 'the Wine Ship'. Ausonius sang the praises of this spot under the name 'Nociomagus' – in *Mosella*. It is now amalgamated with Dhron.

Vineyards	*ha*
Engelgrube	47
Laudamusberg	58
Rosengaertchen	37·8

The peculiarities of the Neumagen wines are a flavour of bitter almonds and often a suggestion of the taste of blackcurrants.

Dhron lies on the Mosel at the mouth of the pretty little stream called Dhronbach. The Roman poet Venantius Fortunatus extolled the place in verse.

Sites:

Hofberger (or Dhronhofberger) (110 ha). This takes its name from the court (at the foot of the hill) which was formerly part of the property of the Tholey Monastery (Saar). Its wines are aristocratic, have a noble bouquet and unusual spiciness.

Roterd (125 ha) – which derives its name (meaning 'red earth') from a vein of reddish sand which traverses the slaty soil here.

Dhron wines are distinguished by their most agreeable bouquet.

Vineyards	*ha*
Grafenberg	15
Sonnenuhr	0·9
Grosser Hengelberg	1

Nestling among steep vineyard slopes, in a graceful bend of the Mosel, lies Piesport with its sites in the Grosslage Michelsberg:

Vineyards	*ha*
Goldtroepfchen	104
Falkenberg	30
Günterslay	40
Treppchen	250
Domherr	7
Schubertslay	0·79
Gaertchen	0·40

Of these sites, Günterslay belongs in part to Niederemmel (now part of Piesport) and was therefore used as a collective site designation. Piesport wines are liable to have a slightly tarry flavour which gives them an agreeable fullness.

In Niederemmel Roman remains have also been found. It is the starting-point of the famous Roman road to Bingen. Its vineyard, the Günterslay, which it shares with Piesport, is on the left bank of the Mosel and the wines are called Piesporter.

Piesport has enlarged its Goldtropfchen vineyard and included in it many adjoining vineyards. I was surprised when I read that many of the golden drops had in fact been collected from adjoining vineyards such as Günterslay over many years and therefore the new law 'merely regularizes a *de facto* situation'.

It is astonishing that I had been in the trade for forty years before I observed, too late, why my Piesporter Goldtropfchen was found by so many to be too expensive: it was genuine.

Also in the Grosslage Michelsberg are:

Sehlem	Rotlay	1·25
Rivenich	Niederberg	30
	Geisberg	12
	Rosenberg	35
	Brauneberg	12
Minheim	Günterslay	10
	Rosenberg	60
	Burglay	30
	Kapellchen	40

Formerly the generic site name Piesporter Michelsberg covered a larger area. The trade wanted the new *Grosslage* to cover the identical area, but did not succeed as a large supply can lead to cheaper prices which the growers do not like. Therefore a new *Grosslage*, St. Michael, was created.

Grosslage	*Villages*	*Vineyards*	*ha*
St. Michael	Kluesserath	Bruderschaft	250
		Koenigsberg	100
	Bekond	Brauneberg	38
		Schlossberg	62
	Ensch	Muehlenberg	105
		Sonnenlay	30
		St. Martin	45
	Schleich	Sonnenberg	55
		Klosterberg	20
	Poelich	Held	105
		Suedlay	40
	Thoernich	Ritsch	30
		Enggass	15
	Koewerich	Laurentiuslay	23
		Held	
	Detzem	Maximiner	
		Klosterlay	50
		Wuerzgarten	135
	Leiwen	Klostergarten	420
		Laurentiuslay	19

These wines are more rounded than those of Trittenheim.

Whoever bought Piersporter Michelsberg before, can now, with confidence, order the Detzemer or Leiwener St. Michael – and save money.

The Grosslage Kurfuerstlay: on the Lieserbach, a little way above the Mosel, lies Maring-Noviand with its sites:

	ha
Honigberg	90
Kirchberg	12
Klosterberg	34
Roemerpfad	6
Sonnenuhr	80

Next comes Brauneberg with the sites (still in the Grosslage Kurfuerstlay):

Hasenlaufer	12
Juffer	30
Juffer-Sonnenuhr	11
Mandelgraben	170
Klostergarten	80
Kammer	0·512

Till 1925 the place was called Dusemond, the name being a popular distortion of the Latin *dulcis mons* (sweet mountain). The Romans who planted vines on the Mosel bestowed this name on the place because of the excellence of the Brauneberg wines. In 1806, when Mosel vineyard sites were divided into classes according to the quality of their products, Brauneberg was the only name in the first class.

Brauneberg wines frequently have a strong but pleasing earthy taste which gives them a fullness commended by many drinkers, particularly by those who like a heavy wine with a Mosel bouquet.

The other villages and single sites under the Grosslage Kurfuerstlay (1,770 ha) are:

		ha
Andel		0·18
Wintrich	Ohligsberg	9·73
	Grosser Herrgott	97·64
	Stfanslay	82·87
Veldenz	Sonnesite Kirchberg	94·2
	Grafschafter Sonnenberg	39·35
	Muehlberg	4·8558
	Elisenberg	1·6
	Carlsberg	0·376
Muelheim	Sonnenlay	63
	Helenenkloster	0·7165
	Elisenberg	2·7
	Amtgarten	0·312
Osann-Monzel	Kirchlay	25
	Rosenberg	120
	Paulinslay	25
	Kaetzchen	100
Burgen	Hasenlaeufer	35
	Kirchberg	20
	Roemerberg	10
Kesten	Paulinshofberg	9
	Paulinsberg	40
	Herrenberg	71

Lieser, a locality with a population of 1,500, lies on the river Mosel at the mouth of the little brook called the Lieserbach. Its vineyard Schlossberg (143·30 ha) belongs to the Grosslage Kurfuerstlay; the other vineyards belonging to the Grosslage Beerenlay which has the following sites:

	ha
Niederberg-Helden	24
Rosenlay	22·1
Suessenberg	9

The Lieser wines are justly famed for their wholesome qualities, their excellent flavour and their stimulating 'prickle'.

Bernkastel-Kues: The viticultural area of the town includes that part of it known as Kues, on the left bank of the river. It is among the most valuable vineyard districts on the Mosel and produces wines of superb quality. There are two *Grosslagen* involved.

The Grosslage Badstube (58·8 ha) covers the best-known vineyards on the Bernkastel site of *Bernkastel-Kues*, i.e.

	ha
Graben	14·8
Lay	11
Matheisbildchen	11·4
Bratenhoefchen	18·4
Doctor	3·2528

The name of the site 'Bernkasteler Doctor' is attributed to a legend. Archbishop Boemund II, Elector of Trier 1351–62 (so runs the tale), lord of large tracts of vinelands on the Mosel and the Rhine, and owner of a castle situated on the windy heights above Berncastel, was addicted to spending much of his time in this favoured spot. One day he fell ill there. He was grievously sick and his doctors plied him with medicines in vain. As he lay on what was thought to be his death bed a flask of wine was brought to him from one of the best sites in the neighbourhood. He drank, and a miracle was wrought. The dying prelate recovered, and in gratitude bestowed on the wine – and the site – the appellation 'Berncasteler Doctor'.

On the bank of Kues the sites belong to the Grosslage Kurfuerstlay with the following vineyards:

Weissenstein	14·5
Rosenberg	8·6
Johannisbruenn-chen	33
Kardinalsberg	73

and Schlossberg (50·6 ha) which is also shared by the village of Andel.

The tourist visiting Berncastel-Kues is greeted by a wonderful sight. From where he stands he has a view both up and down the river – of unending rows of vines. Literally millions of the best Rieslings display their wealth to the beholder from this enchanted spot, while, crowning the vine-covered, sun-drenched hillside, the ancient oaks of the Hunsrueck mountains give their dignified blessing to the scene. The town itself has a romantic note, which renders it unique among the small towns of the Mosel. Its centre is the market square on which many medieval streets and alleys converge, and whose most striking feature is a magnificent Renaissance town hall. Built in 1608, it is surrounded by houses of even greater age with pointed gables and wood carvings of great artistic value. Another interesting feature is St. Michael's Fountain splashing merrily in the centre of the square. On the first Sunday in September this has a special function. On that day the citizens of Berncastel-Kues, together with many guests from near and far, celebrate the local wine festival, and the fountain gushes forth wine for their delight. Altogether it is a cheerful festival. Gaily festooned boats ply up and down the river, while from its site on the right bank St. Michael's Tower watches over the whole area as it has done for the past thousand years. At night the festive scene is illuminated by the floodlit ruins of Landshut Castle on the summit of the Schlossberg.

There is so little Berncasteler Doctor produced and the demand is so big that two of the three growers to whom the Doctor vineyard belongs used to gather their grapes together with adjoining vineyards and marketed the wine as Berncasteler Doctor und Graben (Thanisch) and Berncasteler Doctor und Bratenhöfchen (Lauerburg), and the third grower has the same procedure for a part of his crops: Berncasteler Doctor und Badstube (Deinhard).

I have already given my view that none of the wines of German vineyards is so overrated as the *Doctor*. In blind tastings, wines of adjoining vineyards are found to be of equal quality and they cost only half the price.

I give H. C. Wegeler's account of the legal problems raised in connection with the registration of the site name Doctor, beginning with the division between the three original owners of Bernkasteler Doctor:

Deinhard share of original Doctor	55·4 per cent
That of one joint owner (Thanisch)	40·6 per cent
That of another owner (Lauerburg)	4·0 per cent

A site may only be entered in the Vineyard Register if it is at least five hectares in total area. Smaller areas may only be admitted if the formation of a larger site is impossible, either due to the use of the neighbouring land, or because of the very special character of the wine produced from the vineyard in question. The Bernkasteler Doctor is certainly well known, both here in Germany and throughout the world, as one of our most renowned individual sites, and it covers 1·35 hectares.

Naturally, following the vineyard Law of 1 June 1970, we proposed that the Bernkasteler Doktor should be entered at its traditional size (1·32 ha). The committee for the community of Bernkastel discussed many variations in the size of the Doktor vineyard, and once even voted that the Doktor should be extended to cover 15 hectares altogether, on both sides of the Mosel.

Then at the beginning of July the regional committee met in Trier, under the chairmanship of the president of the administrative district of Trier, and now the question of the Bernkasteler Doctor is being pursued in this court. Unfortunately, we still do not have their decision, which must be put to all parties concerned, who then have the right of a final decision from the vineyard committee of the Federal State, with the co-operation of the Minister of Viticulture in Mainz.

Trier has decided that the historic vineyard of Bernkasteler Doctor should be extended by the addition of the Bernkasteler Graben.

In this decision, the committee has let itself be led by the present marketing practice of one of the joint owners of the Doktor, who has always sold a blend 'Doktor und Graben'. 'Doktor' appears in large print on the label, and 'Graben' is in small lettering underneath.

From about 5,000 square metres Doktor and 14,500 square metres Graben, a total of 18 Fuder 'Doktor und Graben' were being marketed. It is easy to see that the contents of the bottle are in opposite proportion to the wording on the label.

'Deinhard could have acted similarly, by following the same policy as Thanisch, and thus putting the adjacent "Badstube" with the Doktor and presenting "Bernkasteler Doktor und Badstube" mixed with part of their crop', Mr. Wegeler said.

'It was our opinion that the consumer should receive the unadulterated product of this renowned vineyard, and we therefore deliberately rejected the production of a *larger* quantity under the label "Doktor und Badstube".'

Mr. Wegeler's calculation may need correction. Miss Thanisch succeeded and had Graben included in the Doctor. This gives the right to add 25 per cent wine of the Bereich Bernkastel and a perfectly honest label would read Berncasteler Doktor! It is always advisable to taste and compare various growers' wines in order to avoid disappointment and expense. The 1971 vintage was still marketed as a blend of Doktor and Graben.

In Bernkastel we are in the heart of the Mittelmosel. The most important neighbouring villages are included in the Grosslage Muenzlay (498 ha):

		ha
Wehlen	Sonnenuhr	65
	Nonnenberg	50
	Klosterberg	
	Rosenberg	
Graach	Himmelreich	86·96
	Domprobst	26·50
	Abtsberg	12·50
	Josephshoefer	5·80

Wehlen (with Machern, now an *Ortsteil* of Bernkastel) sites (Grosslage Muenzlay) are:

Sonnenuhr
Nonnenberg
Klosterberg

Wehlen is situated on the left bank of the Mosel in a grove of fruit trees. It is over a thousand years since the inhabitants of this little community first started to plant vines. The Wehlen wine rejoices in a splendid maturity and a spicy bouquet, due in part to intensive cultivation for quality, but in particular to the soil and the favourable sunny aspect of the sites. The best of the sites (and in my opinion the best site on the Mosel) is the Wehlener Sonnenuhr but the other sites too produce spicy quality wines of great value. The Sonnenuhr is a large vineyard owned by many proprietors. There are great differences in the quality on account of the different positions of parts of the vineyard: vineyards lying in the centre of the hill produce the best wines. I give my preference to the wines of Dr. Zach Bergweiler-Pruem Erben who has the largest holding. They do not produce Beerenauslesen as this takes the best out of their wines, but the Spätlese and Auslese wines are well balanced, harmonious and have finesse and elegance. They cost less than those of other growers who live off the reputation of their 1949 and 1953 vintages.

Graach produces weighty, full, heavy wines that keep well but are coarser, less delicate, than those of the surrounding communities. The sites are:

	ha
Abtsberg	12·50
Josephshoefer	5·80
Domprobat	28·50
Himmelsreich	86·96

The estate known as Josephshof lies between Graach and Wehlen in the heart of the Mittelmosel. It belongs to the Reichsgraf von Kesselstatt. Its wines will in future be labelled as Graacher Josephshoefer.

And this brings us to Zeltingen and to the end of the Mosel bend *par excellence*, on which are situated the best known of all Mosel wine-growing localities, all covered by the Grosslage Muenzlay.

Zeltingen is a charming village with its modern bridge joining the Eifel and the Hunsrueck. Here – beginning far below the place itself – is a veritable parade of vines, stretching farther than the eye can see, well beyond Zeltingen up the river, merging with those of neighbouring communities till they reach Bernkastel, and forming the largest unbroken vineyard area in all Germany. The biggest stretch belongs to Zeltingen itself; in a good year its produce amounts to over

2,000 *Fuder* of wine. The long viticultural tradition of the place and its good slaty soil have given Zeltingen wines their reputation and maintained it. Usually they are the cheapest on the wine list, placed among the smaller, lighter wines of the Middle Mosel, and consequently many drinkers of Mosel look on the Zeltingen products as nothing more than cheap table wines. They are quite wrong, however, because Zeltingen wines are produced in a wide range of qualities, from the simplest to the very best; from the light and volatile to the full and heavy with plenty of body and vigour – wines in fact for everyday use, but also wines to be brought forth as special delights on festive occasions.

One of the most intriguing factors in the nomenclature of German wines is the naming of German vineyards – of which there were no fewer than ten thousand! In view of this enormous number of vineyards, it was good policy on the part of various authorities to try to simplify matters. One of the first decisions was made by the Council of Zeltingen and its sister-town Rachtig. This latter is a Riesling wine-producing village of just over 200 ha, yet the growers marketed their wines under no fewer than nineteen different vineyard names. By the decision of the Council, the Zeltingen and Rachtig vineyard names had already many years ago been reduced to four.

The former Kirchpfad, with its simple, wholesome wines – not exciting, but thoroughly dependable (good foundation, harmonious) – has been incorporated into the much better known site of Sonnenuhr (40 ha).

Himmelreich (130 ha) lies above the village in the best position. The soil is ideal – pure slate, exactly what the vines need. It produces the finest wines of great elegance and with a rich spicy bouquet.

Schlossberg (60 ha) provides high class wines, weighty, heavy and yet aristocratic.

Deutschherrenberg (20 ha): We have nearly reached the end of the élite among Mosel wines, though in the next Grosslage, Schwarzlay, we still find some vineyards with famous names.

Traben-Trarbach extends on the right as well as the left bank of the Mosel, and now also includes the former village of Wolf, a suburb. Trarbach wines are firm, steely and have an agreeable bouquet. The vines grow at the foot of the Grafenburg on these sites:

	ha
Schlossberg	34·4
Burgweg	
Ungsberg	9·1
Huehnerberg	9·3
Kreuzberg	17·9
Taubenhaus	14

Traben wines mature too early and do not keep well; they come from these sites:

	ha
Würzgarten	57
Kraeuterhaus	22·35
Koenigsberg	44·5
Gaispfad	6·5
Zollturm	5·52

Ortsteil Wolf has the following sites:

Auf der Heide	7·5
Goldgrube	14·4
Klosterberg	14·5
Schatzgarten	39
Sonnenlay	21

Traben-Trarbach's last vineyard, Rosengarten, belongs to the suburb Starkenburg.

Uerzig lies on a bend of the Mosel river. It is open to the south, and on its other three sides is cut off and completely sheltered by mountain ridges. On this spot, clay and coloured sandstone from the Eifel, breaking through the slate strata, give the rocks a peculiar red colour and the local wine a characteristic flavour. Uerzig is one of the earliest documented wine-producing communities on the Mosel. In the year 690 the daughter of King Dagobert of the Franks owned a wine estate there. The name, *Ursiacum*, is of Celtic-Latin origin.

The many former Uerziger vineyards have now been amalgamated under the name of Würzgarten, which was formerly the name of its best site. It is situated around a picturesque group of rocks, crowned by a mountain-top, which is one of the most beautiful spots on the Mosel. This is attested by one Von Stramberg who, in 1837, wrote a description of the Mosel. He called Uerzig 'one of the classic places of Germany' on account of its particularly charming situation and the good quality and unique character of its wines. These wines have a bouquet and spiciness which I find astonishing in view of the fact that they are lighter than those of neighbouring communities.

Two groups of castle ruins show where in medieval times certain nobles entrenched themselves on the forbidding rocks. One was owned by the well-known family of the Ritter von der Leyen, and the other belonged to the Von Urleys, the ancestors of the famous Dutch painter Bernaert van Orley (1492–1542). In the year 1066, a sensational political murder was perpetrated on the rocky fastness that belonged to the Urley family: Konrad, Archbishop-Designate of Trier, was thrown from the rocks by his opponents.

Next to and below the Uerzig vineyard we find the famous Erden plantations; most of these, however, are owned by people from Uerzig. The sites come under the same *Grosslage* as Uerzig, namely Schwarzlay:

		ha
Treppchen		45
Praelat	under	1!
Herrenberg		20
Busslay		110

The Erden sites are very sunny, the wines full and spicy, with a pleasant slightly earthy taste.

In the Grosslage Schwarzlay we also find Enkirch. The name is derived from the Latin *ancora* (possibly connected with the Greek *agkura* and means 'anchor'). People began to settle here, below the fastest rapids, as it was the landing-place for Mosel boatmen who were being towed up the river; it was here that they would make their preparations for overcoming the rapids. Enkirch has the largest cultivated vineyard acreage (165 hectares) of any single locality, and in good years produces 1,200 to 1,500 *Fuder*. The only estates which exceed this quantity are those belonging to more than one community with such double names as: Berncastel-Kues, Traben-Trarbach, or Zeltingen-Rachtig.

The most famous of its sites is the Enkircher Steffensberg, with its subsidiary sites:

		ha
Enkirch	Edelberg	30
	Herrenberg	15
	Zeppwingert	17
	Batterieberg	1·0341!!
	Ellergrub	16
	Steffensberg	82
	Weinkammer	22
	Monteneubel	27

Among those who have sung the praises of Enkirch, the 'Anker Inn', and above all of Enkirch wines is the Danzig poet and journalist Johannes Trojan (1837–1915) who, towards the end of his life, was editor-in-chief of the Berlin journal *Kladderadatsch*.

The following sites are also part of the Grosslage Schwarzlay:

Village	*Vineyards*	*ha*
Burg	Wendelstueck	15
	Hahnenschrittchen	28
	Thomasberg	10

Villages	*Vineyards*	*ha*
Burg	Falklay	34
	Schlossberg	33
Kinheim	Hubertuslay	105
	Rosenberg	49
Bausendorf	Herzlay	14
	Hubertuslay	11
Flussbach	Reichelberg	2
Hupperath	Klosterweg	7·15
Platten	Klosterberg	28
	Rotlay	12
Loesnich	Foersterlay	10
	Burgberg	40
Bengel		0·52
Wittlich	Klosterweg	6
	Portnersberg	10
	Rosenberg	5
	Felsentreppchen	3·85
	Bottchen	5
	Lay	14
	Kupp	3

The ancient wine village of Kröv, situated at the foot of a wide range of vine-covered slopes, close to the motorway through the Middle Mosel, has a colourful past. Here we find ancient timbered buildings, picturesque courtyards and quaint corners and, as well, a really beautiful baroque church. As the vineyards of Kröv cover 380 ha, a special Grosslage Nacktarsch has been created and the site names are as follows:

Grosslage	*Vineyards*	*ha*
Kröver Nacktarsch	Paradies	192
(380 ha)	Kirchlay	54
	Steffensberg	45
	Letterslay	49
	Burglay	18
	Herrenberg	22

Although the name 'Nacktarsch' (naked bottom) has indelicate implications, it has, regretfully, to be recorded that this fact has apparently added to its popularity. It is to be found on every wine list in Germany. I foresee a great shortage of Nacktarsch which may drive the prices of the Kröver wines undeservedly high.

Whilst the Grosslage Schwarze Katz belongs to the Bereich Zell/Mosel, the neighbouring Grosslage vom Heissen Stein with its well-known villages of Reil, Briedel and Puenderich still belongs to the Bereich Bernkastel. Single sites of these villages, which produce steely robust wines, are as follows:

Grosslage	*Villages*	*Vineyards*	*ha*
vom Heissen Stein (628 ha)	Reil	Moullay-Hofberg	75
		Falkaley	85
		Goldlay	25
		Sorentberg	12
	Briedel	Nonnengarten	50
		Herzcehn	65
		Schaeferlay	12
		Weisser Berg	34
		Schelm	51
	Puenderich	Marienburg	96
		Goldlay	55
		Nonnengarten	10
		Rosenberg	58

Reil prides itself on having the first nature trail with wine teach-in of the Middle Mosel.

LOWER MOSEL OR BEREICH ZELL On the Lower Mosel from Alf and Bullay to Koblenz we find that ferrous combinations in the crumbling yellow efflorescent soil, which in some parts forms a layer of rubble $1\frac{1}{2}$ to 2 m. deep, have given it a reddish or a yellowish-brown tone. The soil dries out quickly and the layer of yellow, grey or bluish-dark-grey rubble which covers it is very thin. Moreover it has to be supported by numerous buttresses, being very liable to slip on the steep slopes. The wines produced in this district are of a poorer quality than those from the Middle Mosel.

The Silurian stratum is of hard slate with large fragments of rock. Its disintegration is slow, on account of its high content of silicic acid. The slopes are poorly nourished along this area.

The Hunsrueck mountains crowd so far into the valleys along the curving stretches of the Mosel that little space is left for habitation and cultivation. Whenever a community grew up there, it could only manage to straggle along two or three parallel roads.

This applies for instance to the little town of Zell im Hamm (as this bend of the Mosel has been called since time immemorial). Zell (in Latin *cella*) was a Roman settlement. This has been proved by various objects excavated there and now housed in museums at Bonn and Wiesbaden, and is also attested by a Roman sarcophagus erected in the upper part of Zell itself, the part known as Brandenburg.

Although wines from Zell have never been in the top class, Zeller Schwarze Katz is to be found on all German wine lists. Everyone knows the label showing a black cat on a barrel. Zell has never produced as much wine as was sold under the Black Cat label. The name was nothing more than a generic title, and in my opinion a name under which often a better quality of wine was sold than that which originally gave it its designation. It would therefore be unfair if I did not mention that high awards have been presented to two growers of Zeller Schwarze Katz and that the town council of Zell took steps to stop the misuse of this much loved site name.

Now, however, Schwarze Katz is a *Grosslage* covering all Zell vineyards and incorporating the villages of Kaimt and Merl. Their vineyards are as follows:

Grosslage	*Villages*	*Vineyards*	*ha*
Schwarze Katz	Zell	Nussberg	13
(627 ha)		Burglay-Felsen	50
		Petersborn-Kabertchen	31
		Pommerell	22
		Kreuzlay	28
		Geisberg	12
		Domherrenberg	74
	Zell-Kaimt	Roemerquelle	80
		Rosenborn	98
		Marienburger	29
	Zell-Merl	Sonneck	6
		Adler	20
		Koenigslay-Terrassen	10
		Stefansberg	50
		Fettgarten	21
		Klosterberg	83

Zeller Schwarze Katz – one used to say – has a long tail: it reaches both upstream and downstream to Winningen! The new register has restricted the *Grosslage* to wines of Zell only. If the demand continues, there will be an enormous shortage and therefore an even more enormous price.

We have reached the Bereich Zell, Grosslage Zeller Grafschaft, which has the following sites:

Grosslage	*Villages*	*Vineyards*	
Zeller	Nehren	Roemerberg	20

Grosslage	*Villages*	*Vineyards*	*ha*
Grafschaft (656·5 ha)	Ediger-Eller	Calmont	5
		Schuetzenlay	5
		Engelstroepfchen	24
		Bienenlay	7
		Hoell	10
		Pfirsichgarten	35
		Osterlaemmchen	64
		Pfaffenberg	11
		Feuerberg	11·5
		Elzogberg	19·5

Notable among the sites of the Bremm locality is Calmont (part of which belongs to Eller). It is the steepest vineyard I have ever seen and most laborious to cultivate; it is probably the steepest vineyard in the world. It furnished the background scenery for a popular German novel *Die goldenen Berge* (by Clara Viebig). Its sites are:

		ha
Bremm	Calmont	19
	Schlemmertroepfchen	30
	Laurentiusberg	70
	Frauenberg	39·5

One Bremm vineyard belongs to the next *Grosslage*, Rosenhang, viz.

Abtei Klosterstuben	18

Other villages and their vineyards are:

Neef	Rosenberg	80
	Petersberg	15
Beuren	Pelzerberger	1·5
Alf	Kronemberg	9
	Herrenberg	10
	Kapellenberg	15
	Hoelle	2·7
	Burggraf	17·5
	Katzenkopf	5·3
	Arrasburg-Schlossberg	7·5
St. Aldegund	Klosterkammer	40
	Palmberg-Terrassen	13
	Himmelreich	17

Bullay	Graf Beyssel-Herrenberg	17
	Kroneberg	6
	Sonneck	9·5
	Brautrock	10
	Kirchweingarten	10

We come now to the point where there are vineyards on both sides of the river opposite each other but while belonging to the same village are in different *Grosslagen*, different *Grosslagen* having been created for each side of the river.

Grosslage Goldbaeumchen (627 ha)		and	*Grosslage Rosenhang (631 ha)*	*ha*
Senheim			Senheim	
Roemerberg	52		Wahrsager	10·5
			Bienengarten	8
			Vogteiberg	22
			Rosenberg	18
			outside Rosenberg	
			Mesenich	
			Deuslay	14
			Goldgruebchen	34
			Abteiberg	74
Bruttig-Fankel			Bruttig-Fankel	
Goetterlay	20		Pfarrgarten	20
			Rathausberg	30
			Kapellenberg	55
			Martinshorn	35
			Layenberg	10
			Rosenberg	15
Ellenz-Poltersdorf			Ellenz-Poltersdorf	
Altarberg	20		Silberberg	13·5
Kurfuerst	84		Woogberg	6
Briedern			Briedern	
Domherrenberg	52		Roemergarten	56
			Kapellenberg	14
			Servatiusberg	15
			Herrenberg	17
			Beilstein	
			Schlossberg	17
Ernst				
Feuerberg	41			
Kirchlay	30			

Grosslage Goldbaeumchen (627 ha)	and	*Grosslage Rosenhang (631 ha)*	*ha*
		Valwig	
		Herrenberg	27
		Palmberg	15
		Schwarzenberg	15
Cochem		Cochem	
Pinnerkreuzberg	18	Nikolausberg	10
Schlossberg	12	Rosenberg	22
Herrenberg	7	Arzlay	15
Hochlay	7·5		
Klostergarten	11		
Sonnenberg	2·36		
Bischofsstuhl	2·13		

The Cochemer Krampen is 24 km long, the landscape undisturbed by the railway which goes through the 4,213 m-long Kaiser Wilhelm tunnel, the longest in the German railway system.

Klotten			
Brauneberg	25		
Sonnengold	25		
Burg Coreidelsteiner	12		
Rosenberg	20		
Pommern			
Rosenberg	15		
Sonnenuhr	15		
Goldberg	23		
Treis-Karden		Treis-Karden	
Juffermauer	10	Treppchen	15
Muensterberg	6	Greth	8
Dechantsberg	8	Kapellenberg	20
Mueden			
Grosslay	5·5		
St. Castorhoehle	11		
Sonnenring	15		
Lockmauer	5·5		
Funkenberg	6		
Moselkern			
Uebereltzer	11		
Kirchberg	10		
Rosenberg	20		

We continue our journey towards the mouth of the Mosel. The Grosslage Weinhex covers the vineyards on both banks of the river.

Grosslage	*Villages*	*Vineyards*	*ha*
Weinhex (525·05 ha) *left bank:*	Hatzenport	Stolzenberg	5
		Kirchberg	12
		Burg Bischofs-steiner	23
	Loef	Goldblume	12
		Sonnenring	6
	Kattenes	Steinchen	8
	Kattenes and Moselsuersch	Fahrberg	4·5
	Lehmen	Wuerzlay	12
		Klosterberg	6
		Lay	6
		Ausoniusstein	6
	Kobern-Gondorf	Uhlen	10
		Weissenberg	12
		Schlossberg	25
		Fahrberg	7·5
		Gaens	6
		Kehrberg	10
		Fuchshoehle	7
	Winningen	Uhlen	17·4
		Hamm	15·8
		Domgarten	121
		Brueckstueck	10·3
		Im Roettgen	6·6
	Guels	Bienegarten	9·3
		Marienberg	7·25
		Koenigsfels	6·2
		Im Roettgen	5
	Koblenz	Hamm	37·3
		Hubertusborn	18·5
right bank:	Burgen	Bischofstein	7·8
	Alken	Bleidenberg	12
		Hunnenstein	12
		Burgberg	20
	Oberfell	Brauneberg	7
		Rosenberg	6·5
		Goldlay	7
	Niederfell	Faechern	5·5
		Hahllay	5·5
		Goldlay	5
	Dieblich	Heilgraben	4·1

MOSELBLÜMCHEN As we come to the mouth of the Mosel and the end of our Mosel journey I must mention 'Moselblümchen'.

Moselblümchen has been a type of Mosel wine which was offered in a variety of qualities. Under the old laws it could originate in any part of the Mosel. Growers and exporters, whether they used an Upper Mosel wine, or one from the Lower Mosel, or even from the Middle Mosel region, took the fullest advantage of the law permitting the addition of up to one-third of different wine from other districts to give their Moselblümchen just the quality which the customer expected. So one could find Moselblümchen wines varying from very ordinary to really good.

The government of Rheinland-Pfalz, to which the Mosel belongs, has not yet laid down the rules for Moselblümchen as a type of Mosel wine. But the general feeling seems to be that only Tafelwein which is allowed to use the denomination 'Mosel' should be used for Moselblümchen. I cannot myself see any reason why a Moselblümchen cannot therefore be a quality wine, coming from the specific area Mosel-Saar-Ruwer, and be called Moselblümchen with a quality examination number, if the quality of the wine deserves it.

The German Export Association is at present also inclined to the view that only Tafelwein should be sold as Moselblümchen. So those exporters who like to use a better-class wine can of course use quality wine for Moselblümchen, but they must degrade the denomination whilst giving the higher quality. Of course it depends again on how the wine-drinking public will react: will they accept the better class wine at a higher price, yet with the denomination 'Tafelwein'? For many only what is *on* the bottle counts, and not what is *in* the bottle. I would prefer it, if the latter were the case.

IMPORTANT GROWERS OF THE MOSEL, SAAR AND RUWER

Zacharias Bergweiler-Prüm Erben,
Dr. Zacharias Bergweiler.
Zacharias Bergweiler-Prüm Erben,
Dr. Heidemann.
State Domain, Trier.
Viticultural College, Trier.
Bischöfl. Priesterseminar, Trier.
O. van Volxem, Oberemmel/Saar.
Höhe Domkirche, Trier.
Bischfliches Konvikt, Trier.
Seb. Al. Prüm, Wehlen.
Egon Müller, Scharzhof, Wiltingen/Saar.
v. Hövel (Fr. v. Kunow), Oberemmel/Saar.

Carl Rautenstrauch, Kanzem/Saar.
H. Wilh. Rautenstrauch/Eitelsbach.
Gebert, Ockfen/Saar.
Vereinigte Hospitien, Trier.
Erben von Beulwitz, Kasel.
Güterverwaltung des Friedrich-Wilhelm-Gymnasiums, Trier.
P. Licht – Bergweiler Erben, Filzen.
v. Schubert, Maximin Gruenhaus.
Scherfs Mühle, Waldrach.
Gutsverwaltung Karthaeuserhof, vorm. H.Wilh. Rautenstrauch, Eitelsbach (Werner Tyrell).
Fritz v. Nell, Weingut Thiergarten, Trier.
Wwe. Dr. Thanisch, Bernkastel.
Dr. Fischer, Ockfen.
Weingut Piedmont, Filzen (Saar).
St. Johannishof, Dr. Loosen, Bernkastel.

20

Hessen

There is some confusion between Rheinhessen and Hessen which are two quite different political districts.

Many people think, as indeed it is also stated in a well-known encyclopaedia, that: 'Hessia perhaps more properly called Rheinhessen, a German state, as far as wine is concerned a district of Western Germany, bounded on the east and north by the Rhine, and the south by the Pfalz and on the west by the valley of the Nahe.' 'Hessian wines' and 'fine wines of Hessia' are also referred to.

But what is actually described is the administrative district (*Regierungsbezirk*) of Rheinhessen, part of the German federal state of Rheinland-Pfalz. Hessen, however, is a German state (originating from the former Province of Hessen-Nassau) to which the Anbaugebiete Rheingau and Hessische Bergstrasse belong. The capital is Wiesbaden. Until 1918 both Rheinhessen and the Hessische Bergstrasse formed part of the Dukedom of Hessen with the capital Darmstadt!

Bingen is not in Hessen, but in Rheinhessen. It is all very confusing, but let us get the record right.

RHEINGAU

Area 3,047 ha (this figure includes
the Hessian Bergstrasse)
98 per cent white wine
Average crop: 50 hl/ha
Riesling 78 per cent   Silvaner 6 per cent
Müller-Thurgau 11 per cent

'The most beautiful landscape in Germany,' wrote Heinrich von Kleist in 1801, 'which the Great Gardener must have fashioned with the most loving care, rejoiced our eyes as we moved along the Rhine and beheld its banks from Mainz to Coblenz. The whole region resembles a poet's dream and nothing more beautiful could be conjured up by the most fertile imagination than this valley with its changing aspects – now open, now closed, now flowery, now bleak; smiling and frowning in turn. Swift as an arrow flows the Rhine from Mainz, hurrying straight ahead as if its goal were already in view, as if nothing could prevent its arrival there; impatiently it strives to reach it by the shortest route. But a vine-covered hillock, the Rheingau, rises up in its path and diverts its impetuous stream.'

The natural conditions for wine growing are very favourable in this district. The cluster of vineyards on the right bank of the Rhine (which at this point flows from east to west) have a southerly aspect and are protected against the biting east and north winds by the semi-circular wall formed by the thickly-wooded Taunus mountains. The effect of the sun's rays on the more or less steeply inclined vineyard slopes is heightened by their reflection from the surface of the Rhine. Moreover, the high proportion of moisture in the air, caused by the broad surface of the river, has an extremely stimulating influence on the whole development of the plantations, being particularly helpful when the grapes are ripening in the autumn. And finally, the advantages of the site are still further increased by the composition of the soil; this is for the most part very fruitful and particularly well adapted to viticulture.

The designation 'Rheingau' is used for wines originating in the wine-growing communities of the district of Rüdesheim (Rheingaukreis) and is extended to include those from the municipal district of Wiesbaden, the localities Frauenstein and Schierstein, and even the wine-growing centre of Hochheim together with its immediate surroundings; these are situated on the right bank of the river Main and strictly speaking therefore belong to the Main rather than the Rhine.

The most easterly town of the Rheingau is now Frankfurt-am-Main. The Rheingau now includes the following places outside the political county of Rheingau: Wiesbaden with its suburbs Schierstein; Frauenstein; Dotzheim; Mainz-Kostheim; Hochheim; Wicker (42 ha); Floersheim (24 ha); Frankfurt with its single vineyard Lorberger Hang; and Boettiger, an *Ortsteil* of Felsberg near Kassel, where a new vineyard was planted by an enterprising man on his return from France where as a prisoner of war (Second World War) he had gained knowledge of viticulture by working in the vineyards. He has built a restaurant in the vineyards which is most popular and where his wines can be drunk on the spot. This is the most northern vineyard of Germany.

In the Rheingau are the State wine cellars which developed out of the original Nassau, later Prussian Domains and now Hessian Domain. In the best vineyard districts of the Rheingau – and always on the best sites – the Hessian State owns vineyards extending over more than

190 hectares in Hochheim, Rauenthal, Eltville, Kiedrich, Hattenheim, Erbach, Steinberg, Rüdesheim and Assmannshausen. Domain Bensheim of the Bergstrasse (see p. 302) is now included with ten hectares. The vineyard and cellar economy here are excellent and the resultant wines have been known to attain – and in fact still attain – fabulous prices.

Here I should like to repeat categorically that there is no 'German' domain – the German State does not own any of the domains, these are owned by the various federal states.

FRANKFURT am MAIN In about 1850 there were still 300 wine growers in Frankfurt, which is a centre for the production of apple wine today. Now for the first time Frankfurt's name appears again as a wine-growing community. I confess I have never drunk Frankfurter wine, but drank plenty of 'Aepfelwein' – called locally 'Aeppelwoi' – during my student years, the only 'wine' I could afford regularly. I remember, however, an old poem:

Der Wein vom Rhein ist immer gut
Der Moselwein nicht schaden tut
Der Neckarwein ist auch noch recht,
Frankfurt Wein ist immer schlecht.

(Rhine wine is always good
Mosel wine does no harm
Neckar wine is still all right
Frankfurt wine is always bad.)

I am a child of the Rheingau. The Rheingau for us was the land from Lorch to Walluf: these were the boundaries of political and viticultural Rheingau and still are. This was the land where the best wines of the world grew and still grow, and we did not want to know that other areas grew wines, even when we could clearly see the vineyards on the other bank of the Rhine. They just did not exist for us, nor in the eyes of the growers, nor in the eyes of the hoteliers. Even today Rheingau hotels and inns show on their wine lists perhaps one or two Mosels, but seldom can one find a wine from Rheinhessen or the Palatinate.

In early history the Rheingau extended from Kaub to the Bergstrasse. The Hessen Domain, the state, still holds in both areas estates administered from the Rheingau.

Kaiser Otto II donated this district in 983 to the Archbishop of Mainz. After nearly 900 years the Rheingau became part of the Dukedom of Nassau as the result of secularization. In 1866 it was conquered by Prussia and formed the Prussian province of Hessen-Nassau. As a boy I still knew people who had taken part in the war against Prussia, and who remained in their hearts '*Nassauers*' and called themselves '*Musspreussen*' (Must-be-Prussian). After the dissolution of Prussia in 1945 the Rheingau became part of the federal state of Hessen.

There are still many smallholders growing wine in the Rheingau – 2,346 growers cultivate the Rheingau vineyards of 3,148 ha. At the other end of the scale 62 large growers each own more than 10 ha property, 147 growers between 5 and 10 ha. The average annual production of the Rheingau is 33,600 half *Stücks*, equal to 20·1 million litres, and 26 million bottles.

The Rheingau has opened its own *Weinstrasse*, the 'Rheingau Riesling Route', starting in Hochheim. The road is marked with special signs. The wine pilgrim who likes to visit the area and not just drive through its fringes by the motorways, should follow it through the narrow roads of the old villages with their ancient buildings. To take the road along the Rhine from Eltville to Rüdesheim will save him time, but he would miss the beauty spots. Not only his eye is served but also his palate: along the route he will find numerous tasting stands with Rheingau wines ready to be tasted.

The Anbaugebiet Rheingau has only one *Bereich*, Bereich Johannisberg, covering all villages of the region.

Hochheim. It is odd that this place on the River Main should have given the name 'Hock' to Rhine wines as a whole in English-speaking countries. On second thoughts, maybe this is not quite so strange as it appears. The wines of Hochheim have all the typical features of Rheingau products. The sites in Hochheim produce wines which, combined with a slightly earthy taste, are mellow, delicate, and well balanced. The names of the Hochheim sites are:

	ha
Hoelle	36
Reichesthal	
Stein	
Kirchenstueck	15
Domdechaney	10
Herrenberg	
Sommerheil	22
Stielweg	26
Hofmeister	34
Berg	
Königin Viktoria-Berg (Queen Victoria Vineyard)	5

Since the secularization of the Carmelite monasteries in 1803, a large part of the Hochheim estates have been owned by the city of

Frankfurt. To this very day Hochheimer Hoelle is drunk in the Frankfurt *Ratskeller* (town hall – cellar restaurant) as the city's own home-grown wine. Next to be mentioned is Mainz-Kostheim – a suburb of Mainz – with sites:

Weisserd	7
Reichestal	
Steig	15
Berg	

Hochheim and Mainz-Kostheim vineyards belong to the Grosslage Hochheimer Daubhaus, the former generic name for the same vineyards, also the vineyards of Wicker and Floersheim.

The best-known and most advertised single vineyard of Hochheim is the Königin Viktoria-Berg. Not that I think particularly highly of this wine; I have always found its earthy taste so dominant and penetrating that its other qualities are submerged. But this vineyard was christened after Queen Victoria. In 1850 she visited the vineyard, and her visit caused the owner to ask the permission of the Royal Court to rename the *Lage*.

Nor is there anything of special viticultural interest to note about Wiesbaden. It is of world-wide fame as a spa, but less well known as a wine centre. (I advise everybody to let the Wiesbaden local patriots drink their *Neroberger*.) Under the Occupation, Wiesbaden was the home of American Air Force Headquarters.

We can pass over Schierstein (which incidentally possesses one of the oldest and formerly most important Rhine harbours) and the little village of Walluf, which is better known for its horticulture than for its wines. These vineyards, as well as the vineyards of Wiesbaden, are part of the Grosslage Rauenthaler Steinmächer – formerly the generic site name, under which they have been marketed for a long time.

This *Grosslage* (459 ha) also includes the vineyards of:

Kiedrich
Eltville
Rauenthal
Martinsthal

which are part of the Rheingau proper.

Eltville derives its name from the Latin '*alta villa*'. Its vineyard area comprises 740 hectares and is the biggest in the whole Rheingau. Sites belonging to it are:

	ha
Sonnenberg	72
Taubenberg	80
Langenstück	71
Rheinberg	6

Three well-known wine centres, Kiedrich, Martinsthal and Rauenthal, are situated on the heights at the foot of the Taunus mountains.

The sites belonging to Kiedrich are:

	ha
Wasserros	36
Gräfenberg	11
Sandgrube	57
Klosterberg	66

Grosslage Heiligenstock covers the Kiedrich wines.

Wines from these sites are compact and have a fine aroma of spicy herbs. When they have been bottled for some time they are found to have gained in refinement and elegance. At the wine auction in Eberbach in 1906 a Gräfenberg vintage 1893 broke the world price record for any wine sold up to that date.

Wines from the Rauenthal vineyards always cost 10 to 15 per cent more than any other Rheingau products – and rightly so. Here on the steep mountain slopes are produced wines of supreme elegance – mild and aromatic, rose-scented, with a taste suggesting fruits and spices, and often honey-sweet.

In the year 1927 the 1921 Rauenthal Baiken Trockenbeerenauslese attained the price of 101 Reichsmarks (more than £5) per bottle. Quantitatively speaking, Rauenthal produces far less than any other Rheingau locality, and – quality being usually attained at the expense of quantity – this may explain Rauenthal's superiority.

The 1949s kept all the promises they made. In this year Rauenthal produced two-thirds less wine – on an area of equal size – than any of her neighbours. Rauenthal wines of the 1949 vintage proved to be as great as those of 1934 and 1921. Wines of Rauenthal have always kept their early promise, the 1959, 1964 and 1971 are of outstanding quality.

Rauenthal sites:

	ha
Rothenberg	20
Nonnenberg	0·5
Langenstueck	28
Gehrn	18
Wuelfen	14
Baiken	15

Situated in a valley between Rauenthal and Eltville is the community of Martinsthal – known till 1935 as Neudorf. The inhabitants of Neudorf considered that the name Neudorf (new village) was too common; it allowed the distinctive quality of their own wines too little chance of becoming known and appreciated. A 1933 Martinsthal, which had won a special prize for its superb quality, was a wonderful wine – mature, sweet, fruity, with a delicate bouquet.

The sites are:

	ha
Wildsau	31
Langenberg	19
Roedchen	28

The next *Grosslage* is Deutelsberg, which covers the vineyards of Erbach and Hattenheim (453 ha). The sites of Erbach are:

Marcobrunn	5
Honigberg	100
Siegelsberg	16
Hohenrain	18
Michelmark	75
Steinmorgen	50
Schlossberg	5

About ten minutes' walk further on – midway between Erbach and Hattenheim – there is a famous old well. Semicircular in shape, it has four grooved Doric pillars and an inscription in large Roman letters with the words: *Markobrunnen, Gemeinde Erbach* (Marco Well, Community of Erbach). The fact that the Marcobrunnen belongs to Erbach, not to Hattenheim, inspired a humorist to write:

> To solve the thorny question of 'mine versus thine'
> Let Erbach take the water and Hattenheim the wine.

The Marcobrunn vineyard lies in Erbach and always has, though its name in the past has also been applied to wines from the neighbouring Hattenheim.

All this was revealed with the new Vineyard Register. The 1971 wine could not be sold with the vineyard name only, there was no Hattenheimer Marcobrunn and the Hattenheimer wine was therefore sold as Erbacher Marcobrunn – all for the sake of Verity and Clarity!

An application by the owner to enter his Hattenheimer Mannberg vineyard in the vineyard register as Marcobrunn, and so make his marketing practice of the past legal for the future, was rejected. An appeal is pending. Should it be rejected the result will be: the identical wine will be available at a more reasonable price, just because some wine drinkers drink the label and pay for it!

In the year 1788, the third President of the United States, Thomas Jefferson, at that time still American Minister in Paris, undertook a journey to the Rhine. His diary, which was most meticulously kept, mentions many kinds of wine, among which the Marcobrunn enjoyed his especial favour – in fact, he preferred it to all other Rheingau products.

In my opinion, the Marcobrunn wines are neither as elegant nor as fruity as the Rauenthaler; they are particularly robust and spicy and overrated. They are no better in quality than many other Rheingau wines, but much higher in price.

The Marcobrunn vineyard is shared by the estates: Graf Schoenborn, Baron Raitz von Frentz, Baron von Oetinger, the State Domain, Freiherr Langwerth von Simmern, Kohlhaas and Prinz Friedrich von Preussen.

Situated a little higher up is the Nussbrunnen, a well with a gracefully sculptured modern wellhead dedicated to Saint Urban.

Then comes Hattenheim to which belong the sites:

	ha
Engelmannsberg	20
Geiersberg	
Hassel	30
Heiligenberg	36
Pfaffenberg	6
Nussbrunnen	11
Schuetzenhaus	66
Mannberg	12
Wisselbrunnen	18

Incidentally, Hattenheim is the only community in the Rheingau which owns vineyards (the Muller-Stiftung charitable trust).

Equidistant from Hattenheim and Erbach, but farther from the river, idyllically situated in a wooded valley, lies Kloster Eberbach (monastery of the wild-boar stream). It was founded by Augustinian monks in 1116 and built in the shape of a wild boar shown with its tusks. It very soon fell into decay and in 1131 was taken over for a time by the Johannisberg Benedictines, and finally, in 1135, by the Cistercians. Then came a prosperous period for the monastery, the first of the Cisterician Order to be established on the right bank of the Rhine. The monks devoted themselves mainly to viticulture. A hundred years later Eberbach's reputation for the management and extent of its viticulture was second to none. As early as the thirteenth century the monastery had its own ships on the Rhine and a branch in Cologne. This had been established to evade the rule that forbade monks to attend markets or to be absent from the monastery for more than three or four days at a time. The monks managed to obtain special privileges from the Customs, so that they were enabled to buy foreign wines and send them to Cologne free of duty.

In the year 1200, the monks built a wall encircling their whole premises, including the courtyards and gardens. Most of this wall is still standing. Their most famous vineyard was the Steinberg (27 ha) which is still surrounded by a wall 2–2½ m high and nearly 2 km long. The Steinberg vineyard now belongs to the Hessian State Domain. The Steinberg wines were one of the few exceptions to the pre-1971 nomenclature rules – they were sold as Steinberger without the village name 'Hattenheim'. To be able to continue this practice, Steinberg with Kloster Eberbach is entered in the Vineyard Register as Steinberg, an Ortsteil of Hattenheim. The name Steinberg as a famous single site name has not been registered. The Ortsteil Steinberg belongs to the Grosslage Hattenheimer Deutelsberg. The wine can be sold as Steinberger and even as a Tafelwein!

The State Domain has up-to-date equipment and keeps pace with all modern scientific and technical improvements. The cellar alone is worth a visit – it contains nearly 800 half *Stück* (48,000 litres) of wine, but unfortunately special written permission from the Minister of Agriculture is needed and can only be obtained if applied for a good time before the intended visit.

The favourite Rheingau wine in Germany today is the Steinberger, and certainly its Trockenbeerenauslesen represent the noblest and finest of any produced in the whole country.

The 1949 Auslese and Beerenauslese were admired and enjoyed by my friends and their friends. The 1953 was a worthy successor. In 1959 a great quantity of Beeren- and Trockenbeerenauslesen were produced, proportionately too many, so that most (not all!) Spätlesen and Auslesen of this vintage are below the expected quality. In an auction in Frankfurt several single bottles of very old Steinberger were sold on 20 October 1971. These were treated as museum pieces and were knocked down at museum prices. I appreciate more the quality of the 1971 Steinberger Riesling Auslese and the Steinberger Riesling Eiswein Auslese, both gold medal prizewinners in the wine competition in Hessen and the latter also the winner of the Grand Prix of the German Agricultural Association.

Steinberger Neuzucht (new variety) Gm 22–73
intended name: Neuzucht Rabaner
Steinberger Neuzucht Gm 15–114
intended name: Neuzucht Schoenburger
Steinberger Neuzucht Gm 17–52
intended name Gutenborner

have been presented to the trade who showed little enthusiasm preferring tradition – and Riesling.

Eberbach lies at the foot of a mountain known as the Hallgarter Zange (pincers). Its summit is crowned with a massive observation tower giving a magnificent view over the Rheingau, Rhinehessia, the

Hunsrück heights and the Taunus; on a clear day it is possible to see the outlines of the Odenwald and the Vosges foothills.

Sheltering beneath the 'Pincers', lies the village of Hallgarten bathed in sun, glorying in the fertility of its vineyards. My family takes its name from that village, but that is not the only reason why I have a particular penchant for its wines. The growers who live there are born and brought up in the wine tradition and produce the racy and distinguished wines that prove an attraction on any wine list. In the year 1921, that famous year which brought forth fine wines everywhere, the Hallgarten products were superior in body, bouquet and elegance to any others from the Rheingau.

The Hallgarten sites are:

	ha
Jungfer	55
Schönhell	58
Würzgarten	42
Hendelberg	53

Hugh Johnson in his *World Atlas of Wine* writes:

> 'In Hallgarten the Rheingau vineyards reach their highest point. The Hendelberg is 1,000 feet above sea level. There is less mist and less frost up here. In the Würzgarten and Schönhell there is marly soil which gives strong wines of great lasting-power and magnificent bouquet. No single vineyard makes the village name world-famous – though the fact that an excellent shipper has the same name makes it familiar.'

I personally feel very flattered by these statements but I must contradict the author on one point: Hallgarten Jungfer is a vineyard of world renown and I would quote another respected author for Hallgarten's fame and quality.

> 'I shall never forget Hallgarten and whenever I hear such names as Hallgartener Schönhell, Hallgartener Deitelsberg, and others, I can taste again the marvels which they produced in 1921, not over sweet, always the choicest, full of the most glorious flavour and sheer quality. Of all the wines of that famous vintage, and I have known and tried some hundreds, I give pride of place to one or two I have drunk from Hallgarten, which were the acme of perfection.'

So writes Hugh R. Rudd, in his *Hocks and Moselles* (Constable, 1935). Hallgarten will soon become Ortsteil of Oestrich-Winkel.

The former generic site 'Mehrhölzchen' is the *Grosslage* covering in addition to the Hallgarten vineyards the Mittelheim vineyard Eisenkanten and the Oestrich vineyard Klosterberg, the latter in part only, the other part being covered by the Grosslage Gottesthal, which also covers the rest of the Oestrich vineyards.

In Hallgarten most of the growers belong to one of the four local associations, called respectively the 'English', the 'Boers', the 'Germans' and the 'Boxers'. The appellations are now used officially but have a popular origin, dating from their foundation during the Boer War. The poorer growers, having dubbed the large owners 'Englishmen', themselves automatically became the 'Boers'. In 1970 English and Germans amalgamated, and that is the end of the names but not of the tradition of making good wines. In the parish church at Hallgarten stands the famous 'Wine Madonna', a fifteenth-century sculpture and one of the most delightful monuments to Rhenish wine culture.

Nestling close together in the valley are the villages Oestrich, Mittelheim and Winkel. Oestrich, which is blessed with very good vineyards, and Mittelheim share the same railway station, while the Mittelheim-Winkel boundary is practically non-existent. Mittelheim was never marked on any map. In the summer of 1972 the three villages amalgamated into the town Oestrich-Winkel. On the label of all three villages their names will appear independently as *Ortsteile* of the town.

Oestrich's sites are:

	ha
Doosberg	153
Lenchen	145
Klosterberg	142
Rosengarten	
Magdalenengarten	

The Mittelheim sites are called:

Edelmann	93
St. Nikolaus	50
Goldberg	24

The vineyards of this unknown imaginary village are covered by three *Grosslagen*, Johannisberger Erntebringer, Winkeler Honigberg, Hallgartener Mehrhölzchen. The grower who cannot fill his cask with 75 per cent of Mittelheimer Edelmann (noble man) has to adopt the *Grosslage* name.

Winkel has the following sites:

	ha
Gutenberg	51
Jesuitengarten	26
Hasensprung	100
Schlossberg	49
Klaus	

The Winkeler Dachsberg (52 ha) is part of the next Grosslage Johannisberger Erntebringer. The Grosslage Honigberg covers Winkel and Mittelheim vineyards and Ortsteil Schloss Vollrads, above Winkel, tucked away in a little valley half-way up the slope of the wooded Taunus hills. Its wines in addition to the Winkeler Schlossberg grow in other Winkel plus Hattenheim and Mittelheim sites and rank high among the best Rheingau products. Established at the end of the seventeenth century, Schloss Vollrads is justly proud of its press-house. This contains, in addition to some modern presses, one very old press made from the trunks of old oaks on which a coat of arms has been elaborately carved. The castle is owned by Graf Matuschka-Greiffenclau, the leading figure of German viticulture. His family formerly inhabited the oldest existing German residence – the 'Grey House' in Winkel.

Schloss Vollrads' 1933, 1934, 1935, 1945, 1949, 1953 and 1959 vintages are wines of pleasant memories, and its 1959 products are 'grand'. They have an exquisite aroma. Whereas I secured great quantities of the 1959s, I have not bought a bottle of the 1960 and only one *cuvée* each of 1961, 1962 and 1963. The 1964 green seal is a real thirst-quencher, a few *cuvées* of Schlossabzug and Kabinett are good, the Auslese, Beeren- and Trockenbeerenauslese – unfortunately the quantity of these is small – are superb! The Schloss Vollrads Trockenbeerenauslese has always been one of the highlights at auctions. The price of the 1947 Trockenbeerenauslese was the highest paid in the Autumn Auction of 1954. In this connection an early personal experience may be of some interest. The occasion was the bottling of the 1911 Trockenbeerenauslese. Graf Matuschka (grandfather of the present Count) invited my father to taste this. I was even allowed to drink a few drops of the delectable beverage myself. My elders, however, did not content themselves with tasting the 1911. For comparison they had out the finest of the 1904, 1893 and 1868 vintages. My father lived to 87, and that was the only time in his life that he was ever drunk. But to get drunk on wines of such superb quality is apparently not a matter for regret, for again and again my father told the tale whenever a Schloss Vollrads wine was mentioned.

For a tasting when I was researching for my book, *The Great Wines of Germany*, Count Richard Matuschka opened his museum and provided my friends and me with his Trockenbeerenauslesen of 1911, 1917, 1921, 1933, 1934, 1937, 1945, 1947 and 1953, and so we repeated my father's experience. Count Richard died in January 1975 and his son Erwein inherited the estate. His son Ernst has taken over the management and I am sure will continue the tradition of Schloss Vollrads, to produce wines of high quality, in which all members of the Matuschka family, including his mother Eleonore Graefin Matuschka-Greiffenclau, take great interest.

May I just say here that in good vintages, Schloss Vollrads is unbeatable for wines of character, breeding and staying-power. In all vintages they need a long time to mature and too often are drunk too young.

In the sixties Schloss Vollrads kept up its standard and reputation and produced some ice wine also. The 1970 quality wine (green seal) is a great success and the 1971s are superb. The 1970 green seal was the first wine of this estate ever to become enriched. For classification of the wines of Schloss Vollrads, see p. 151.

A little further on we come to Johannisberg, now a suburb of Geisenheim, blessed with fruitful vines. It has had a colourful history. The first Benedictine monastery in the Rheingau was erected at Johannisberg on the initiative of Archbishop Ruthard of Mainz (1088–1109), and the hill was named the *Bischofsberg*. When the monasteries were secularized in 1801, the hill was made over to Prince William of Orange. Five years later, the French Préfecture in Mainz having claimed it as a Domain, Napoleon bestowed both hill and castle as Imperial fief on his Marshal Kellerman. One summer, the Marshal sold the grapes on the vine – the whole yield – to the Mumm concern in Cologne for 32,500 *gulden*. But that happened to be the famous wine year of 1811; the crop yielded 65 *Stück* (one *Stück* holds 1,200 litres), and the merchants obtained 11,000 *gulden* per *Stück* for it! After the fall of Napoleon, the Emperor of Austria (under a clause in the Vienna Act of Congress) came into possession of the estate and bestowed it as fief on Fuerst Metternich – on condition that one-tenth of the wine yield should be surrendered annually to the Austrian Crown. This tribute is still paid to the Habsburgs – in recent years the wine has been sent to Otto von Habsburg in America. Incidentally, in 1815, when the Emperor took over the estate, there was a celebration which Goethe attended.

The Metternich family is still in possession of wine estates – $25\frac{3}{4}$ ha in extent, from which the average crop yield is 200 *Stück*. The vineyard which belongs to Schloss Johannisberg is the 'Klaus' which is partly situated in Geisenheim, Johannisberg and Winkel, an *Einzellage*. As Schloss Johannisberg is now an *Ortsteil* the wine is sold as Schloss Johannisberg without Einzellage.

Beyond the castle lies the village of Johannisberg with its vineyards. The *Grosslage* is Erntebringer, with three small additional vineyards of no great significance:

		ha
	Schwarzenstein	5
	Mittelhoelle	
	Hansenberg	3
and also	Goldatzel	
	Hoelle	
	Vogelsang	
	Klaus	

Johannisberg wines fully deserve their universal popularity.

Johannisberg wine graced the historic occasion when, at the 1858 Berlin Congress, the Russo-Turkish war was brought to its formal conclusion. At the close of the proceedings Bismarck invited the members of the Congress to his house and, raising his glass of 1811 Johannisberger smilingly to Disraeli, gave the toast to 'perpetual world peace and increasing understanding among the European peoples'. He compared the gold of wine to the honest work accomplished by the Congress.

It is this famous village which gives its name to the *Bereich* of the whole Rheingau: Bereich Johannisberg. And this famous village is now only a suburb of the old town which lies close to the river, Geisenheim with its two (dissimilar) open-work Gothic church steeples. Geisenheim is widely known as the home of the largest German training centre for viticulture, fruit-growing and horticulture (see also p. 84). In the castle of Graf Schoenborn at the upper end of the town, in 1648, the Kurfuerst of Mainz, Johann Philipp von Schoenborn, drafted the peace treaty that ended the Thirty Years' War. Here too, he conferred with Leibniz and others on proposals to unite the Catholic and Evangelical Churches.

A memorial to Longfellow in the form of a fountain of Nassau marble, stands on the Bishop Blum place, at the feet of the 'Rheingau Dom' (cathedral church) whose bells inspired Longfellow to write the finale of his 'Golden Legend'. Set into the walls are chiselled marble plaques of the verse:

> 'What bells are those that ring so slow,
> so mellow, musical, and low?'
> 'They are the bells of Geisenheim,
> that with their melancholy chime
> ring out the curfew of the sun.'

Geisenheim sites:

	ha
*Rotenberg	36
Klauserweg	57
*Fuchsberg	68
Kilzberg	56
*Mäuerchen	33
*Moenchspfad	160
Schlossgarten	18
Klaus	15

The vineyards marked with an asterisk are covered by the Grosslage Rüdesheimer Burgweg, the others by Johannisberger Erntebringer. Geisenheim was also the headquarters of my former company. In our spacious tasting room countless wines were tasted including many of those which I later described in my books, and many tastings with friends from England, the U.S.A., Australia, New Zealand and Japan, indeed from all over the world, took place here.

Extending a considerable way along the Rhine lies famous Rüdesheim and its suburb Eibingen. Of its very numerous and far-famed sites, only the following remain:

	ha
Berg Roseneck	29
Berg Rottland	37
Berg Schlossberg	29
Bischofsberg	34
Drachenstein	48
Kirchenpfad	20
Klosterberg	39
Klosterlay	37
Magdalenenkreuz	48
Rosengarten	3(!)

They all belong to the *Grosslage Rüdesheimer Burgweg*, which stretches to the limits of the Rheingau at Lorchhausen.

Here in this district you find the typical Rhenish wine taverns, where all the Rheingau wines may be tasted. The Rheingau is far too proud of its products to serve wines from any other region.

The wines grown on the Rüdesheimer Berg, particularly on the sites Schlossberg, Burgweg and Bischofsberg Roseneck, are famed for their incomparable bouquet and their fruity taste.

The Rüdesheim wines have one characteristic which sets them apart from most others – in so-called 'good years' they are seldom at their best, and vice versa. There is a very simple explanation for this. The Rüdesheim sites, like many on the Mosel, are on steep slopes, consequently the moisture in their soil is apt to leave the higher regions comparatively quickly. The vineyards have little natural moisture, so in a hot summer the warmth is not offset by sufficient water to feed the ripening grapes; this in turn retards the development of their sugar content. The 1921, 1949 and 1959 Rüdesheim wines from the best sites were too dry. Rüdesheim vineyards on their terraces do not produce their best in very sunny years.

The war brought considerable damage to Rüdesheim vineyards. Surveys in the region have shown that about one-quarter of the vineyards were destroyed by bombing. The R.A.F. certainly did its work well on this important target, where many observation posts and anti-aircraft guns had been set up. That the destruction was very far-reaching in its effect, is shown by the case of one vineyard owner who needed 650 tons of earth to repair his thirteen bomb-craters. He employed five workmen eight hours a day for six months to put his vineyard in working order again. The loss of crops in five years must have been somewhere in the region of 1,600 half *Stück* – 1,280,000 bottles.

By now, all damage has been repaired, the layout of the vineyards replanned and new roads built to make the work of the grower easier – though one thunderstorm with cloudburst in the summer of 1973 washed away a lot of ground from some of the reorganized roads and vineyards.

I recommend the traveller to go up the mountain to the *Denkmal* (there is a lift), to view not the ugly monument, but the beautiful landscape; the Rheingau with Schloss Johannisberg and, opposite, the Nahe – a landscape of vineyards.

Assmannshausen with its Ortsteil Aulhausen is famous for its red wines – Grosslage Steil for *red* wines, covering the single sites:

	ha
Frankenthal	45
Hoellenberg	55

Assmannshausen, up to a short time ago the generic name for all Rheingau red wines, now indicates their actual origin. We shall refer to it in the chapter about red hock (see p. 336).

For white wines Hinterkirch (39 ha) and Berg Kaiser-Steinfels (15 ha) are the sites.

Lorch and Lorchhausen – the places immediately following Assmannshausen – belong to the Rheingau though the character of their wines has nothing in common with the products of the Rheingau. We need have no hesitation in including them in our survey of the Middle Rhine.

Lorch, with sites:

	ha
Pfaffenwies	35
Krone	13
Schlossberg	53
Kapellenberg	58
Bodental-Steinberg	28

Lorchhausen with its:

Rosenberg	40
Seligmacher	50

brings us to the Anbaugebiet Mittelrhein. But before visiting it, let us visit the other Hessen-Anbaugebiet, the Hessische Bergstrasse.

ANBAUGEBIET HESSISCHE BERGSTRASSE

Area 350 ha
Average yield 25,000 hl
52 per cent Riesling   26 per cent Silvaner
20 per cent Müller-Thurgau   5 per cent Ruländer
2 per cent Traminer

The old name was 'Strata Montana'. 'Hessische' means part of the state of Hessen, *not* Rheinhessen.

The Hessische Bergstrasse, in contrast to the Badische Bergstrasse, is an independent *Anbaugebiet* situated in the European Zone C, whereas the Badische Bergstrasse is not a Baden-Bereich and is situated in Zone B.

It is known as the '*Fruehlingsgarten*' (spring garden) of Germany. It presents a magnificent sight when the cherry and other fruit trees are in full blossom and people flock there to see it. Soil and climate are ideal.

There are two *Bereiche*: Starkenburg and Umstadt. Heppenheim is the centre, still with a look of the Middle Ages in the Altstadt – the old part of the town – with a historic cellar in the Kurmainzer Amtshof, where one can taste the 'Bergstraesser'.

State-owned 25 ha vineyards are administered by the Hessian State Domain in Eltville, Rheingau, and are situated in the following sites: Heppenheimer Centgericht and Steinkopf, Schoenberger Herrnwingert, Bensheimer Streichling and Kalkgasse.

If the Rheingau could take in the vineyard situated furthest to the north in Germany, 'Böddiger' in the county Melsingen on the river Fulda, one just cannot understand why the Bergstrasse could not have become a *Bereich* of the Anbaugebiet Rheingau.

The wines of Zwingenberg, Bensheim, Auerbach, Heppenheim are comparable to the lesser Rhinehessian wines. They are bottled in the first spring following the grape harvest and are drunk by the thousands who flock to the Bergstrasse to admire the orchards in blossom.

The best wine is the Heppenheimer Steinkopf, generally known as 'Steinkopfer'.

Bereich Starkenburg

Grosslage	*Villages*	*Sites*
Schlossberg (326) ha	Heppenheim (including Erbach and Hambach)	Eckweg Guldenzell Malberg Steinkopf Centgericht Stemmler

Grosslagen	*Villages*	*Sites*	*ha*
Wolfsmagen (268 ha)	Bensheim	Paulus	26
		Hemsberg	71
		Streichling	115
		Kirchberg	9
		Kalgasse	47
Rott (152 ha)	Bensheim-Schoenberg	Herrnwingert	11
	Bensheim-Auerbach	Fuerstenlager	43
		Hoellberg	68
	Zwingenberg	Alte Burg	8
		Steingeroell	22
Bereich Umstadt			
situated within the Odenwald mountains	Seeheim	Mundklingen	15
	Gross-Umstadt	Steingerueck	21
		Herrnberg	61
	Klein-Umstadt	Stachelberg	17
	Rossdorf	Rossberg	

Dieburg and other villages in the county of Darmstadt and Dietzenbach in the county of Offenbach also belong to the Bereich Umstadt.

Important Growers not mentioned in the text

Aschrott'sches Weingut, Hochheim
Schloss Eltz (Graeflich Eltz'sche Gutsverwaltung), Eltville
Weingut Dr. R. Weil, Kiedrich
Viticultural College, Geisenheim
von Brentano, Winkel
Fuerst von Löwenstein-Wertheim-Rosenberg'sches Weingut, Hallgarten
Landgraeflich Hessisches Weingut, Johannisberg
Freiherr von Zwierlein Erben, Geisenheim
von Ritter zu Groenesteyn, Ruedesheim

21

South Germany

This region – like Alsace – produces a great many different kinds of wine, some of which used to bear names other than those used for similar Alsatian products. In South Germany we used to find the *Elbling* white wines (sometimes known as *Raeuschling*), Traminer (sometimes called Clevner) and Riesling (sometimes called Klingelberger). All these wines show the characteristics of the district and can now be labelled only with grape names contained in the official list.

A few words about the region itself and its individual products.

Politically speaking, the region comprises Bavaria, Baden, Württemburg and Hessia. But the law groups the wines from these parts rather differently. The designation *Anbaugebiet Württemberg* is used to denote quality wines originating in Württemberg wine-growing communities (Neckar for Tafelweine).

Baden is used to denote wines from Baden's wine-growing communities including the 'Badische Frankenland' (Badenian Franconia).

The designation *Bodensee* (Lake Constance) is used for part of the vineyards of Baden, Württemberg and Bavaria which are adjacent to the Lake. Each federal state has chosen its own designation. Baden has accepted 'Bereich Bodensee', Bavaria 'Bereich Lindau'.

The designation *Bereich Bergstrasse/Kraichgau* is used for wines from those parts of Baden situated on or near the Bergstrasse from Wiesloch to Weinheim, whereas the wine-growing communities of the Hessian province of Starkenburg form the *Anbaugebiet Hessische Bergstrasse* with which I dealt at the end of the previous chapter.

BADEN-WÜRTTEMBERG

Baden-Württemberg now have 502 single sites and 32 *Grosslagen.* The average size of the *Einzellage* is 40 ha and of the *Grosslage* 600 ha. Baden has 296 *Einzellagen* and 16 *Grosslagen,* Württemberg 206 *Einzellagen* and 16 *Grosslagen.* Whereas Germany consumes 16 litres per head annually, Baden-Württemberg consumes 36 litres!

Baden-Württemberg vineyards in 1878 covered not less than

40,200 ha, but in 1950 there were only 12,374 ha, i.e. 5,966 ha in Baden and 6,408 ha in Württemberg. The reorganization in Baden and Württemberg has brought about great changes. In former centuries they tried to overcome the steepness of the hills by forming terraces and terraced vineyards, and special retaining walls were erected. Now, when it is a matter of making the work less hard and using machines wherever possible, the terraces and walls disappear and we return to the steep-hill viticulture of 1,000 years ago. But remembering the size of the South-German viticultural area of about 100 years ago, we can see that expansion is possible in this particular part of Germany. It is thanks to reorganization that the vineyard area of Baden-Württemberg increases every year by approximately 600 to 800 ha. We have reached a size which is 30 per cent larger than twenty years ago. And as demand is growing all the time, one has to be grateful that all the lost areas are being reclaimed and recultivated.

Vineyard area: 22,000 ha (end of war 17,000 ha)

Wine-producing area: 17,300 ha (end of war 12,700 ha)

The crop has been doubled. This is nearly three times the pre-war crop but this state can hardly cover half of its needs from this production. They 'export' to North Germany and other countries 5 per cent of the Württemberg production and 20 per cent of the Baden production. There are viticultural-conscious dynamic forces working to improve techniques in vineyard and cellar with the most modernized equipment here.

Expressed in percentages, in 1972 Baden-Württemberg had:

17 per cent of all German white-wine vineyards
60 per cent of all German red-wine vineyards
23 per cent of all German vineyards

Red Grapes	*per cent*	*White*	*per cent*
Portugieser	15	Müller-Thurgau	20
Blue Burgundy	88	Riesling	13
Trollinger	100	Silvaner	8
		Ruländer	61

ANBAUGEBIET WÜRTTEMBERG

Weinbaugebiet Neckar
Area 6,295 ha
47 per cent white wine   53 per cent red wine
Average crop 460,000 hl
26 per cent Trollinger   22 per cent Riesling
14 per cent Silvaner   11 per cent Portugieser

6 per cent Müller-Thurgau 6 per cent Limberger
10 per cent Burgunder

The produce of the Württemberg vines were formerly little known outside the state borders, mainly owing to the fact that they barely sufficed for the needs of the local consumers. Moreover, until a short time ago, the quality of these wines was not high enough to tempt external buyers.

When, in 1950, I was discussing with Director Goedecke of the Domain Nierderhausen on the Nahe some questions of viticulture I expressed my amazement at its extraordinary development in the course of the past twenty years. He replied that I should be still more astonished if I were to study viticultural development in Southern Germany, particularly in Württemberg. I must confess that though I had certainly tasted these wines in the course of my travels, as I make a habit of trying the local products wherever I go, they had not impressed me. I could only remember that after drinking the Markgraefler (Baden) I felt weak at the knees and that after the luncheon

Baden-Württemberg Viticulture Table showing its development from 1868 to 1971

	total area ha	producing areas ha	production per ha hl/ha	total production hl
1868/77		38,296	29	
1928/37		22,284	33	
1950	17,377	12,374		
1954	17,936	12,888	37·1	477,795
55	18,663	13,299	29·8	396,714
56	18,420	12,976	9·2	119,099
57	18,330	12,686	28·3	359,257
58	18,332	12,746	70·2	894,835
59	18,339	12,882	56·7	730,770
1960	19,317	14,144	92·5	1,308,393
61	19,388	14,897	42·0	626,404
62	19,449	15,084	56·2	848,455
63	19,500	15,311	85·4	1,307,818
64	19,017	15,348	87·8	1,347,415
65	19,340	15,248	69·0	1,051,785
66	19,530	15,364	79·5	1,222,053
67	19,835	15,165	84·2	1,276,286
68	19,722	15,318	88·1	1,349,822
69	19,969	15,614	74·0	1,154,811
1970	20,407	15,783	132·6	2,092,510
71	22,629	16,548	72·7	1,203,536

at which I partook of it I had to abandon all plans made for the rest of the day. I remember, too, that these wines had been cheap when I was a student at Heidelberg University. We used to mix many of our *Bowlen* (cups) with the help of these inexpensive rather acid wines and large quantities of sugar. Still, I had observed the astonishing development of Alsatian wines and had learnt to enjoy and admire them. So, why should not the South German wines from the right bank of the Rhine at the same geographical level and grown on a soil of very similar nature, be equally capable of attaining world fame?

My reasoning was shared by the growers of Württemberg and of late years Württemberg vineyards and cellars have improved to such a degree that their wines have emerged from their former obscurity and are now very highly esteemed, sometimes attaining higher prices than those from other localities. They have also received publicity of a welcome and effective kind. The late President of the West German Federal Republic, Dr. Theodor Heuss, obtained his doctorate – forty-five years ago – with a thesis on Viticulture and Wine Growers in Heilbronn on the Neckar. In this thesis he surveyed the history and development of Württemberg viticulture from the eighth century. It has been reprinted and – owing to the personality of its author – has contributed in no inconsiderable degree to the popularity of the wines.

In many ways, due to special conditions, Württemberg is unique among German wine-growing regions. For one thing, its climate is poor, for another its soil consists mainly of shell-limestone, red marl and bituminous marl. And these soils do not suit every kind of grape. Similarly the sites have to be carefully chosen to suit the various species. And so, for one reason or another, each little plot in the various wine-producing districts of Württemberg is known for its own particular kind of wine which in many cases is brought to a high state of perfection. There is, for instance, the Silvaner in the Kocher valley and the Tauber valley, the Black Riesling in the Lauffen region on the Neckar, the Trollinger and Limberger in the Heilbronn district, the Riesling in the Rems valley and on the slopes of the Burgberg and the Schemelberg near Weinsberg.

Except perhaps Baden, no German wine region can point to such a large variety of grape species under cultivation as Württemberg which makes both white and red wines. The most important kinds are Gutedel, Müller-Thurgau, Traminer, Ruländer, Silvaner, and above all Riesling, the pride and joy of any wine-grower's heart.

In the course of the last 100 years the viticultural area under cultivation has decreased. After having been badly hit by the phylloxera pest, the wine growers of this region reorganized their plantations by planting vines which are impervious to this noxious insect. The vineyard area decreased considerably (by 61 per cent) partly on account of the phylloxera's depredations and partly as a result of war and post-war conditions. The value of the yield, however, has more than doubled during the same period.

The large wine estates, mostly owned by very old Württemberg families who have always made it their business to produce high-grade wines, play quite a considerable part in ensuring the constant improvement of Württemberg wines. But there are only very few large wine estates in Württemberg; most plantations are on a small scale and have been owned by the same families for generations. In the municipality ot Heilbronn, for instance, there exist 7,950 different vineyard-holdings, making up 445 ha in all, of which 261 are under cultivation. The Württemberg vineyard owner does not depend on his vines alone for his living – he has other lands under cultivation, very often orchards. These 'side-lines' help him over bad times in the vineyards: poor harvests, disappointing quality of the yield and so forth; or unfavourable market conditions.

Good cellarage conditions and the consequent superior quality of Württemberg wines are mainly due to the highly developed co-operatives with, in some cases, first-class equipment for presses and cellars, which are to be found in practically every wine-growing locality worth mentioning.

Passing through Württemberg's wine districts, the traveller cannot fail to notice little houses built in the midst of the vineyards – a sight peculiar to this part of the country. They are used by the wine growers as a resting-place after the day's work where they can take their glasses of wine in ease and comfort.

The commercial centre of Württemberg viticulture is Stuttgart, which is also the seat of the Wine Growers' central organization. Small wonder! The city of Stuttgart is a child of the Neckar, and it is in the valley and side valleys of this river, and beyond them in the valleys of the Rems, Enz, Kocher and Jagst, that most of the Württemberg wine is grown.

The scientific centre of the viticulture of Württemberg is the training and research station of Weinsberg near Heilbronn. Numerous vineyards have been newly planted here since 1946. There is even an irrigation plant, and this may become a model for the whole of German viticulture, for it ensures good yields and good quality even in seasons with meagre rainfalls. The wine growers of Rüdesheim on the Rhine will certainly give a warm welcome to this invention, as their greatest enemy is a dry sunny summer, when the dehydrated soil is incapable of feeding the grapes sufficient water to produce the necessary sugar.

Weinsberg is a government institution covering an area of 33 ha – including plantations and agricultural lands – which overlaps several municipal and site boundaries: Weinsberg, Talheim, Gundelheim and

Burg Wildeck. It has innumerable viticultural and cellarage facilities which, in combination with the ripe experience of its workers and the results of its numerous experiments, enable it to produce wines which serve as examples of what Württemberg can and should bring forth. It is one of the few establishments in Germany which markets only bottled wines and then not before they are fit to drink, i.e. after they have acquired at least a degree of 'bottle maturity'.

Viticulture in Württemberg does not mean a chain of vineyards, but some small vineyard areas situated on the hillsides of the rivers facing south and south-west. Soil and vines vary greatly in the various landscapes. Not only do we find many kinds of wines in the same area, but we also find wines which cannot be found anywhere else. This is the result of a historical development and, most important, Württemberg is the one federal state of Germany in which the cultivation of red wines is larger than that of white wines.

The fact that the Württemberger likes to drink his wine and that he likes to drink a lot of it is one reason why the wines of Württemberg are so little known outside Württemberg. Actually Württemberg imports even more wine from other German and foreign wine districts than they produce themselves. But the Württemberger prefers his Württemberg red wine.

In former centuries the Württemberg wines were not unknown: the Netherlands, England, Austria, Bavaria, Hungary, Bulgaria and even Turkey were customers.

The soil of Württemberg is heavy keuper, and the lower valley of the Neckar, the valley of Weinsberg, the area round Oehringen, Zabergau, and Remstal and the area round Stuttgart have very heavy soil which makes it very difficult for the rain to penetrate. The wines produced on this soil are distinguished by their body, flavour, fruitiness and staying power. Most preferred grapes are Riesling and Trollinger.

The loess soil is quite different and easier for the rain water to penetrate, and the wines produced there are mostly red grapes of the Pinot, Schwarz-Riesling and Samtrot types. Of special interest in the middle Neckar valley are the terraced vineyards, and here as everywhere else they are ideal spots for viticulture. Here we find the Württemberg Trollinger.

In the valleys of the Kocher, Jagst and Tauber rivers where vineyards lie in the plains, Silvaner and Müller-Thurgau vines have been planted.

Every year the amount of rainfall and hours of sunshine during the months of vegetation are excellent for the production of quality wines.

For Württemberg the minimum requirements for quality wines and quality wines with predicate are the following:

QUALITY WINE WITH THE PREDICATE KABINETT

	Oechsle °	*Alcohol*
1. All varieties of vines not mentioned under 2 and 3.	72	9·4
2. White Burgundy, Ehrenfelser, Kerner, Morio-Muskat, Müllerrebe (Schwarz-Riesling), Muskat-Ottonel, Perle, Rieslaner, Scheurebe, Blue Spätburgunder (includ. Clevner and Samtrot), Wine without indication of the kind of vine.	75	9·8
3. Freisamer, Gewürztraminer, Ruländer, Red Traminer, and wines (new varieties) which are not yet entered in the Vine Register according to Par. 1.	78	10·3

QUALITY WINE WITH THE PREDICATE SPÄTLESE

1. All varieties of vines not mentioned under 2.	85	11·4
2. White Burgundy, Ehrenfelser Freisamer, Gewürztraminer, Kerner, Morio-Muskat, Müllerrebe (Schwarz-Riesling), Muskat-Ottonel, Perle, Rieslaner, Ruländer, Scheurebe, Spätburgunder (includ. Clevner and Samtrot), Red Traminer, Wine without indication of the kind of vine, and new varieties which have not yet been entered in the Vine Register according to Par. 1.	88	11·9

QUALITY WINE WITH THE PREDICATE AUSLESE

All varieties of vine, wine without indication of the kind of wine, and wines of new varieties not yet entered in the Vine Register according to Par. 1.	95	13·0

QUALITY WINE WITH THE PREDICATE BEERENAUSLESE

As for Auslese	124	17·5

QUALITY WINE WITH THE PREDICATE TROCKENBEERENAUSLESE

As for Beerenauslese	150	21·5

For those who intend to visit the district I recommended that you follow the route of the 'Schwaebische Weinstrasse', beginning at Gundelsheim. Many of the communities mentioned have more than one vineyard, but I only quote one in each case under the heading of the respective *Grosslage*:

BEREICH WÜRTTEMBERG UNTERLAND

Grosslage: *Staufenberg*
Gundelsheim: Himmelreich
Neckarsulm: Scheuerberg
Heilbronn: Wartberg
Talheim: Stiftsberg

Grosslage: *Kirchenweinberg*
Heilbronn: Sonnenberg (Heilbronn is in fact the largest wine community with 400 ha)
Talheim: Schlossberg
Lauffen: Katzenbeisser
Flein: Eselsberg

Grosslage: *Schalkstein*
Kirchberg: Kelterberg
Gemmrigheim: Neckarberg
Besigheim: Wurmberg
Mundelsheim: Kaesberg
Marbach: Neckarhaelde (the Schiller National Museum is here)
Neckarweihingen: Neckarhaelde

BEREICH REMSTAL-STUTTGART

Grosslage: *Weinsteige*
Fellbach: Laemmler
Bad Cannstatt (suburb of Stuttgart): Zuckerle
Stuttgart: Moenchshalde
Esslingen: Schenkenberg
Untertuerkheim: Moenchsberg
Rotenberg: Schlossberg
Uhlbach: Goetzenberg
Obertuerkheim: Kirchberg
Hedelfingen: Lenzenberg
Rohracker: Lenzenberg
(all now suburbs of Stuttgart)

Grosslage: *Wartbuehl* (starting at Plochingen and from there into the Remstal)
Waiblingen: Steingrueble
Stetten: Pulvermaecher
Schnaiten: Lichtenberg
Struempfelbach: Gastenklinge

Grosslage: *Kopf*
Grossheppach: Wanne
Kleinheppach: Greiner
Korb: Hoernle
Waiblingen: Hoernle

BEREICH WÜRTTEMBERG UNTERLAND

Grosslage: *Wunnenstein*
Beilstein: Wartberg
Oberstenfeld: Lichtenberg
Grossbottwar: Harzberg
Kleinbottwar: Goetzenberg

Grosslage: *Salzberg*
Weinsberg: Hundsberg (the viticultural college is here)
Ellhofen: Ranzenberg
Lehrensteinfels: Steinacker
Grantschen: Wildenberg
Suelzbach: Altenberg
Wimmental: Altenberg
Willsbach: Diebelsberg
Affaltrach: Zeilberg
Eschenau: Paradies
Hoesslinsuelz: Zeilberg
Weiler: Schlierbach
Eichelberg: Hundsberg
Loewenstein: Wohlfahrtsberg

Grosslage: *Lindelberg* (Hohenlohe country)
Verrenberg: Verrenberg
Pfedelbach: Goldberg
Michelbach: Dachsteiger
Harsberg: Spielbuehl

BEREICH KOCHER-JAGST-TAUBER

Grosslage: *Kocherberg* (in the Kochertal)
Ingelfingen: Hoher Berg
Criesbach (now suburb of Ingelfingen): Sommerberg

Niedernhall: Engweg
Forchtenberg: Flatterberg

Grosslage: *Tauberberg* (the valley of the Jagst, Tauber and Kocher)
Bad Mergentheim-Markelsheim: Probstberg
Weikersheim: Karlsberg

LIST OF WÜRTTEMBERG ESTATES

Weingut und Schlosskellerei Freiherr von und zu Weiler
Staatliche Lehr- und Versuchsanstalt fuer Wein und Obstbau, Weinsberg
Estate Graf Adelmann, Kleinbottwar
Fuerstlich Hohenlohe Langenburg'sche Weingueter, Weikersheim
Schlosskellerei Graf v. Neipperg, Schwaigern
Wuertt. Hofkammer – Kellerei, Stuttgart.

ANBAUGEBIET BADEN

Weinbaugebiet: Oberrhein

The heading of this section shows the denomination 'Anbaugebiet Baden' for quality wine of a defined region and for Tafelweine 'Weinbaugebiet Oberrhein'. This again has two divisions:

1. for south Baden: Roemertor
2. for north Baden: Burgengau

Area 9,525 ha
78 per cent white wine 22 per cent red wine
Average crop 700,000 hl
26 per cent Müller-Thurgau 22 per cent Spätburgunder
13 per cent Ruländer 13 per cent Gutedel
7 per cent Silvaner 7 per cent Riesling
4 per cent Weissburgunder 2 per cent Traminer and Gewürztraminer 6 per cent Others (Freisamer, Nobling)

We must remember that this is the only area in German viticulture belonging to Zone B of the European Economic Community. As a result of this the minimum natural alcohol content of its Tafelweine and its quality wine is higher. This alone implies that the climatic conditions are such as to ensure a more rapid progress to ripeness in the case of all types of grape.

Tafelwein Minimum natural alcohol content 6° alcohol = 50° Oechsle
Minimum total (actual and potential) alcohol content 85°
Minimum total acidity 4·5 g/l

Quality wine and Quality wine with predicate:

Minimum natural alcohol content 7° = 56°

Minimum total alcohol content depends on the predicate and can be seen from this table

New varieties are constantly being tested on Baden's soils and the following have already passed the test:

Freisamer (Ruländer × Silvaner) and the
Nobling (Silvaner × Gutedel)

We must also refer to the Baden *Weissherbst*. Whereas in Württemberg *rosé* wine is produced by the pressing and fermentation of mixed red and white grapes, in Baden the blue Burgundy grape is treated like a white wine grape. The grapes are not fermented on the skins, but are treated as in white wines: very small particles of colour thus come into the wine, giving it just a touch of *rosé* colour. The Weissherbstwines are obligatory Quality wines and are produced in the full scale of predicates – the Beeren- and Trockenbeerenauslesen are delicious natural liqueurs.

Before a journey through the wine-producing *Bereiche* of Baden, here are a few hints:

The concentration, since the last war, of all its efforts into producing quality wines together with advertising have made Baden's name famous beyond its borders, and the wines occupy a prominent position in the minds of German consumers. Taking for granted the quality of the wine, the connoisseur's palate notes with delight the differences between the various wines. And there is much to remember. Ortenauer Riesling, Neuweierer Mauerwein, Kaiserstuehler Ruländer, Markgräfler or Seewein, they all evoke many happy memories; a stroll through the Baden wineland can give only an outline; the finer shades can only be detected by the expert's palate.

Baden actually consists of a number of areas, and one would have expected every one of them to have become a defined area of production. The clever and sensible Baden people knew that this would mean restriction to a large extent. Baden, as the only federal state in Zone B of the E.E.C. had to bear in mind that the sugar content of all its wines had to be relatively high. Well aware that quality wines must come from defined areas and blends of quality wines are only possible from one *Bereich*, Baden made itself a defined area and all 'subdistricts' became *Bereiche*, so that within their area blends of quality wines with predicate are possible.

The growers, local and federal authorities, science and research all have played their part; the vine grower may look forward with anticipation to the demands of a large European market. And the friend of

Authorized and recommended vines and their minimum must weights

WHITE WINE VARIETIES	Qualitätswein Alk.°/Oechsle	Kabinett Alk.°/Oechsle
Auxerrois	8·9°/69	10·3°/78
Freisamer	9·4°/72	10·8°/81
Gewürztraminer	9·4°/72	10·8°/81
Gutedel	8·4°/66	9·8°/75
Kerner	8·9°/69	10·3°/78
Morio-Muskat	8·4°/66	9·8°/75
Müller-Thurgau (Riesling × Silvaner)	8·4°/66	9·4°/72
Muskateller	8·4°/66	9·8°/75
Muskat-Ottonel	8·4°/66	9·8°/75
New crossings	9·4°/72	10·8°/81
Perle	8·4°/66	9·8°/75
Rieslaner	8·4°/66	9·8°/75
Riesling	8·0°/63	9·4°/72
Ruländer	9·4°/72	10·8°/81
Siegerrebe	8·4°/66	9·8°/75
Silvaner	8·4°/66	9·8°/75
Spätburgunder Weissherbst	8·9°/69	10·3°/78
Scheurebe	8·4°/66	9·8°/75
Traminer	9·4°/72	10·8°/81
Veltliner	8·4°/66	9·8°/75
Weisser Burgunder	8·9°/69	10·3°/78
Others	8·4°/66	9·8°/75

RED WINE VARIETIES		
Frühburgunder (early Burgundy)	8·9°/69	10·3°/78
Helfensteiner	8·9°/69	10·3°/78
Heroldsrebe	8·9°/69	10·3°/78
Limberger	8·9°/69	10·3°/78
Müllerrebe	8·9°/69	10·3°/78
New crossings	8·9°/69	10·3°/78
Portugieser	8·9°/69	10·3°/78
Saint Laurent	8·9°/69	10·3°/78
Spätburgunder	9·4°/72	10·8°/81
Trollinger	8·9°/69	10·3°/78
Others	8·9°/69	10·3°/78

Spätlese Alk.°/Oechsle	Auslese Alk.°/Oechsle	Beerenauslese Alk.°/Oechsle	Trockenbeerenauslese Alk.°/Oechsle
11·9°/88	13·9°/101		
12·4°/91	13·9°/101		
12·4°/91	13·9°/101		
11·4°/85	13·9°/101		
11·9°/88	13·9°/101		
11·9°/88	13·9°/101		
11·4°/85	13·4°/98		
11·9°/88	13·9°/101		
11·9°/88	13·9°/101		
11·9°/88	13·9°/101		
11·9°/88	13·9°/101		
11·9°/88	13·9°/101		
11·4°/85	13·4°/98		
12·4°/91	13·9°/101		
11·9°/88	13·9°/101		
11·9°/88	13·9°/101		
12·4°/91	13·9°/101		
11·9°/88	13·9°/101	17·5°/124	21·5°/150
12·4°/91	13·9°/101		
11·9°/88	13·9°/101		
11·9°/88	13·9°/101		
11·9°/88	13·9°/101		
12·4°/91	13·9°/101		
12·4°/91	13·9°/101		
12·4°/91	13·9°/101		
12·4°/91	13·9°/101		
12·4°/91	13·9°/101		
11·9°/88	13·9°/101		
12·4°/91	13·9°/101		
12·4°/91	13·9°/101		
12·4°/91	13·9°/101		
12·4°/91	13·9°/101		
12·4°/91	13·9°/101		

wine appreciates what is being done for him in this district. He knows that in a total area of 10,000 ha only first-class vines are planted, that those selected are suited to the soil conditions, and that an extensive post-war field clearance programme together with progressive cellar management have contributed to the success of the Baden wines.

Various vines have their favourite areas:

SPÄTBURGUNDER The blue Spätburgunder is the noblest of the red vines. The Weissherbst is its offspring, not a variety of its own. Its flavour is fresh and elegant and its quality based on the use only of the blue Spätburgunder variety.

GUTEDEL Grows mainly in the Markgrafschaft between Freiburg and Basel. It goes well with white meat.

RULÄNDER Grows mainly around the Kaiserstuhl, but also in different parts of Ortenau, Markgraeflerland and Kraichgau.

RIESLING Grows in the Bergstrasse and Kraichgau and Ortenau.

SILVANER, 7 per cent. Grows on the volcanic Kaiserstuhl.

WEISSBURGUNDER, 4 per cent. Grows on the Kaiserstuhl, Bergstrasse and Kraichgau.

TRAMINER AND GEWÜRZTRAMINER, 2 per cent. Dessert for a festival meal is its best description.

OTHER VARIETIES, 6 per cent.

Here then are the *Bereiche* and *Grosslagen*:

In the south along the Bereich Bodensee only a few vineyards remain of the once large viticultural area; the best ones among them are Meersburg, Konstanz, Ueberlingen and Hagnau. These produce a large quantity of the wines of Baden.

Grosslage	*Village*	*Vineyards*
Sonnenufer	Meersburg	Bengel, Fehrenberg, Chorherrenhalde, Lerchenberg, Jungfernstieg, Rieschen Saengerhalde, Burgstall

Between Basel and Freiburg is the Bereich Markgraeflerland, where the Gutadel vine introduced in 1780 now covers 90 per cent of the area and the wine is now known as 'Markgraefler'. It is a wine with a fine bouquet, gentleness and variety.

The Markgraeflerland counts among its more important wine-producing villages:

Grosslagen	*Villages*	*Vineyards*
Vogtei Roetteln	Weil a.R.	Schlipf, Stiege
	Loerrach	Sonnenbrunnen
	Efringen-Kirchen	Kirchberg, Sonnhole Oelberg, Steingaessle
	Haltingen	Stiege
Burg Neuenfels	Auggen	Paradies
	Britzingen	Altenberg, Rosenberg
	Sulzburg	Altenburg
	Muellheim	Pfaffenstueck, Sonnhalde Reggenhag
Lorettoberg	Ehrenstetten	Oelberg, Rosenberg
	Freiburg	Jesuitenschloss, Steinler
	Ebringen	Sommerberg
	Pfaffenweiler	Batzenberg Oberduerrenberg
	Schallstadt-Wolfenweiler	Batzenberg, Duerrenberg
	Schlatt	Maltesergarten Steingrueble

Not far away is the Bereich Kaiserstuhl-Tuniberg, the district of Germany with most sunshine. The soil is mostly of volcanic origin and the wine therefore is fiery and of strong character.

Grosslagen	*Villages*	*Vineyards*
Attilafelsen	Ober and Niederrimsingen	Franziskaner, Rotgrund
	Tiengen	Rebtal
Vulkanfelsen	Sasbach	Limburg, Rote Halde Scheibenbuck, Luetzelberg
	Jechtingen	Hochberg, Gestuehl, Enselberg, Eichert, Steingrube

Grosslage	*Villages*	*Vineyards*
Vulkanfelsen	Koenigsschaffhausen	Hasenberg, Steingrueble
	Burkheim	Feuerberg
	Bahlingen	Silberberg
	Bischoffingen	Enselberg
	Oberrotweil	Schlossberg, Kirchberg Kaesleberg, Eichberg Henkenberg
	Bickensohl	Herrenstueck, Steinfelsen
	Achkarren	Schlossberg, Castellberg
	Ihringen	Castellberg, Fohrenberg Kreuzhalde, Winklerberg
	Breisach	Augustinerberg Eckartsberg

Between Lahr and Baden-Baden lies the Bereich Ortenau, which as well as wine and fruits also produces tobacco. The expert would not necessarily call Offenberg the centre of Ortenau, he might just as easily call Durbach, Gengenbach, Zell, Weierbach or Oberkirch its centre. As the soil varies in this area, so does the wine in its qualities. Since the 1971 wine law came in there have been no more riddles about their names: a Riesling is a Riesling as anywhere else (not a Klingenberger), and the Traminer is called Traminer and not, as formerly, Clevner.

Grosslagen	*Villages*	*Vineyards*
Fuersteneck	Offenburg (Ortsteil Zell-Weierbach)	Abtsberg
	Ortsteil Fessenbach	Bergle, Franzensberger
	Durbach	Josephsberg, Kapellenberg, Kasselberg, Kochberg, Oelberg, Plauelrain, Steinberg, Schloss Staufenberg Schloss Grohl
Schloss Rodeck	Kappelrodeck	Hex vom Dasenstein (Red)
	Buehl	Burg Windeck, Wolfhag

Grosslage	*Villages*	*Vineyards*
Schloss Rodeck	Buehl	Sternenberg, Kastanienhalde
	Waldulm	Kreuzberg, Pfarrberg
	Altschweier	Sternenberg
	Neuweier	Altenberg, Mauerberg Heiligenstein, Gaensberg Schlossberg
	Steinbach	Stich den Buben Yburgberg
	Varnhalt	Klosterbergfelsen Steingrueble
	Baden-Baden	Eckberg, Saetzler
	Sasbachwalden	Alter Gott, Klostergut Fremersberger Feigenwaeldchen
	Sinzheim	Fruehmessler, Klostergut, Saetzler, Fremersberger Feigenwaeldchen Sonnenberg
	Lauf	Gut Alsenhof Schloss Neu-Windeck

Further south is the Bereich Breisgau, where apart from really great wines we also find little wines which are clean and beneficial thirst-quenchers like the Glottertaeler. From the Weissherbst to Muskateller they all enjoy a good reputation.

Grosslagen	*Villages*	*Vineyards*
Burg Zaehringen	Emmendingen	Halde
	Glottertal	Roter Burg
	Freiburg i.B.	Bergle, Schlossberg
Burg Lichteneck	Koendringen	Alte Burg
	Malterdingen	Bienenberg
	Kenzingen	Hummelberg, Roter Berg
Schutterlindenberg	Friesenheim	Huehnenbuehl

Baden-Baden is the gate to the Badische Weinstrasse (Baden Wine Road) which the tourist will discover is of unique beauty. As on a string of pearls, one famous vineyard follows another: Varnhalt,

Umweg, Steinbach, Neuweier, with its delicious Mauerwein in the *Bocksbeutel* bottle, Kappelrodeck with its Hex vom Dasenstein, Waldulm with its Spätburgunder red wine, also Eisental with Affenthaler red wine, in the monkey-embossed bottle. I name only a few of the many specialities of this district.

North of Karlsruhe and Wertheim is the Bereich Badische Bergstrasse/Kraichgau. Here grows a Riesling of delightful freshness. Many particularly enjoy the Silvaner. And there are experts who reckon that the Müller-Thurgau from Beckstein is the supreme example of this particular crossing.

The Bereich Badische Bergstrasse/Kraichgau has the following *Grosslagen*, villages and *Einzellagen*:

Grosslagen	*Villages*	*Vineyards*
Hohenberg	Dietlingen	Keulebuckel, Klepberg
	Ellmendingen	Keulebuckel
	Weingarten	Katzenberg, Petersberg
Mannaberg	Bruchsal	Burgwingert, Weinhecke Michaelsberg Klosterberg
	Oestringen	Hummelberg, Ulrichberg Rosenkranzweg
Stiftsberg	Sulzfeld	Burg Ravensburger Dicker Franz, Loechle Husarenkappe
	Heidelberg	Heiligenberg, Sonnenseite ob der Bruck
	Schriesheim	Schlossberg, Standenberg
	Sulzbach	Herrnwingert

In the midst of this South German wine-country stands Heidelberg with its castle.

Inside the castle – in the Koenigssaal (King's Hall) of the women's apartments – the guide points out to tourists an extremely practical apparatus, namely a pump used in earlier centuries to draw up wine out of the 'Great Cask' which stood underneath the hall. This famous cask was constructed by the Electoral Cellar-master Johann Jakob Engler the Younger in 1751 on the orders of the Elector Karl Theodor. It was capable of holding 220,000 litres (300,000 bottles). It was only filled three times, and has been leaking for a long time. The poet Scheffel made the thirsty Court Fool, the dwarf Perkeo, into a famous figure of fun. But nearly everybody in Heidelberg is both thirsty and inclined to make merry on good wine.

Wine formerly played its part even in the oral examination for a doctorate of Law. The first question to be answered by the candidate was 'Red or White?' while a jug of water was available for those candidates who preferred a cooling rather than an alcoholic beverage in such trying circumstances.

Once the examination was safely and successfully over, the reward was a fruit cup enjoyed in a boat on the Neckar by torchlight. Never have I tasted anything more delicious than the one prepared for me on just such an occasion by the friends to whom I had for years been teaching the secrets of making the perfect 'cup'.

The Bereich *Badisches Frankenland* around the river Tauber is the northernmost part of Baden. The word 'Madonnenländchen' is its best symbol. Where once it was the quantity of wines produced which astonished the student, it is now the quality of those wines, since only the very best positions in this area are reserved for viticulture.

Outstanding natural attributes, together with the well-organized efforts of the community towards the highest quality, have made these wines such a huge success.

Among the thirty villages of Baden in the Bereich Badisches Frankenland (Taubergrund and the Main valley) are the following:

Grosslage	*Villages*	*Vineyards*
Tauberklinge	Lauda	Altenberg, Frankenberg
	Reicholzheim	First, Kemelrain Satzenberg
	Koenigshofen	Kirchberg, Turmberg Walterstal
	Dertingen	Mandelberg, Sonnenberg
	Wertheim	Schlossberg

The Neckar flows through Baden to reach the Rhine at Mannheim, but practically the whole of its course is through the vineyards of Württemberg.

There is a nature trail near the Wunnensteins, 392 m (approx. 1,200 feet) above sea level. The vineyards around have been reorganized with this in view and the nature trail is 3 km long and designed to teach the wanderer everything about wine. The various kinds of grapes, the sites, the differences in soil, the different ways of planting and pruning are all explained. And along the nature trail the traveller has the opportunity to taste the local wines of a variety of grapes. One can also see an old press and can judge how difficult it was to make wine 200 years ago.

Baden is known by its wine markets at Offenburg and its wine fair in Freiburg. At the Offenburg market one may taste through the entire range of Baden's varieties, geographically and 'vinously'. At the 1973 market, no fewer than 567 wines were shown, 283 of the 1971 vintage, 258 of the 1972. The quantity involved was one million litres. Prices varied between DM 3·30 and DM 120 per bottle.

ESTATES IN NORTH BADEN

Fuerst Löwenstein-Wertheim-Rosenberg'sche Gutsverwaltung, Brombach, Krs. Tauberbischofsheim.

Staatl. Rebenveredlungsanstalt (Versuchs-und Lehrgut), Karlsruhe-Durlach, Karlsruhe.

Fuerst Löwenstein-Wertheim-Freudenberg'sches Weingut, Kreuzwertheim, Krs. Marktheidenfeld.

Staatl. Rebgut (Versuchs-und Lehrgut), Lauda, Krs. Tauberbischofsheim.

Weingut Freih. von Gemmingen, Schloss Guttenberg, Neckarmuehlbach (Krs. Mosbach).

Weingut Freih. von Gemmingen, Schloss Hornberg, Neckarzimmern, Krs. Mosbach.

Freiherr von Goeler'sche Weingutsverwaltung, Sulzfeld, Krs. Sinsheim.

Liegenschaftsamt der Stadtgemeinde Tauberbischofsheim, Tauberbischofsheim.

Graefl. Berkheim'sches Rentamt, Weinheim (Bergstrasse).

ESTATES IN SOUTH BADEN

A. Freih. Roeder von Diersburg, Diersburg.

Markgraefl. Bad. Weingut Schloss Staufenberg, Durbach, Salem.

Graf Wolff Metternich, Durbach.

Oberrrh. Weingutsbesitzer und Weingueter e.GmbH, Freiburg.

Versuchs-und Lehrgut fuer Weinbau Blakenhornsberg, Ihringen.

Staatl. Rebenveredlungsanstalt, Karlsruhe.

Stadtverwaltung, Lahr.

Freih. von Gleichenstein, Oberrotweil.

Freih. von und zu Franckenstein'sches Rentamt, Offenburg.

St. Andreas Hospital-Fond, Offenburg.

Weinbauversuchsgut Schloss Ortenberg des Landkreises Offenburg, Ortenberg.

The Baden State Domain at Meersburg is one of the oldest domains in Germany. It became the property of the state, when it was secularized. It cultivates 30 ha of Blue Spätburgunder, 14 per cent Müller-Thurgau, Ruländer, Traminer and others.

22

Bavaria

We turn now to the federal state of Bayern (Bavaria). Many readers may be astonished to find wine in a state well known for its beer production (the Octoberfest in Munich and so forth), but the largest part of the Franconian wine district belongs to Bayern. A very small part of it belongs to Baden (Bereich Badisches Frankenland).

ANBAUGEBIET FRANKEN

Weinbaugebiet for Tafelweine Main.
Area 3,059 ha
98 per cent white wine 2 per cent red wine
Average crop 120,000 hl
46 per cent Silvaner 41 per cent Müller-Thurgau
4 per cent Riesling

THE FRANCONIAN VITICULTURAL REGION The Franconian wine-growing region extends from Hanau in the west to Bamberg in the east, and from Bad Kissingen-Hammelburg in the north to the neighbourhood of Ansbach in the south. The total vineyard areas amount to 2,700 hectares (6,700 acres) and comprise 221 communities, shared by approximately 10,000 growers.

The Franconian vineyards are situated in maritime and continental-maritime zones, with the Spessart separating the two areas. To the west of the Spessart and the Lower Main the climate eastwards to the Spessart is continental-maritime. Consequently east of the Spessart summers are warm and winters cold. Spring is short, but autumn lasts longer and is very pleasant. The average annual temperature is 8 to 9°C (45 to 48°F); the average rainfall 550 mm (22 inches).

Due to the extraordinarily different kinds of soil and to the climate changing from west to east, a number of vine varieties are grown. Of course not every vine gives of its best in any soil; to give first-grade wines each vine needs the soil and climate for which it was developed, though modern cellar techniques may sometimes modify the characteristics of those wines which are dependent upon variety and soil.

The average annual yield is 40 to 50 hl (88–110 gallons) per ha. Nevertheless the small quantities of Franconian wines produced per ha have the fullest body and contain the highest extract of all the northern wine-growing areas.

People very often say Franconian wines are heavy; this is not due to their alcoholic content but to their extract. Therefore Franconian wines are used not only as table wines to increase the pleasure of a good meal, but also as a beverage for convalescents and elderly people.

Goethe preferred Franconian wines to all others. Quite apart from the great hospitality shown to guests in his home, Goethe's domestic wine consumption was anything but inconsiderable. Even when he was taking a cure in Carlsbad, he would order a whole barrel (about sixty litres) of Franconian table wine, which means that he expected to drink about two litres each day when undergoing his cure. His genuine last words (in the presence of the Director of Buildings, Coudray, on 22 March 1832) are said to have been: 'You haven't put any sugar in my wine?'

I have found that the proper occasions for drinking these so-called Stein wines are those where the textbooks suggest Chablis. Stein wines are finer and stronger, firm and nutty. It is always said that a Chablis can only be properly understood and enjoyed when drunk on its home ground, but that does not apply to Stein wines. The latter travel well and deserve to be more widely known.

The Silvaner vine, which is more intensively cultivated in Franconia than any other, produces wines with qualities varying according to the site. They may have an exquisite bouquet, or a juicy freshness, or again they may be racy and invigorating, or pleasantly full-bodied.

The late Dr. Kittel of Würzburg, who was fond of singing the praises of Franconian wines, stated that the scientific treatise written in the year 1179 by St. Hildegard, Abbess of Bingen, mentioned the healing properties of Franconian wine. An opportunity of testing these qualities arose in the seventeenth century when the Black Death was rampant in Franconia whither it had come from the Bohemian Forest in the east – bringing death and destruction in its train. A worthy canon of Würzburg, attacked by the plague and apparently dying, was anxious (so runs the tale) to have one last taste of his beloved Stein wine. He drank it – with miraculous effect. For two days and two nights he slept. Then he jumped out of bed – completely cured. The story of the miracle spread with incredible speed, and the whole of Franconia joyfully undertook the same cure as the canon. Those who were sick drank to get well, those who were well drank as a protective measure – apparently with excellent results.

Franconia is divided into three *Bereiche*:

1. Mainviereck (Main quadrangle)
2. Maindreieck (Main triangle)
3. Steigerwald

Many wine historians have pointed out that Franconia produces a large number of rare wines. There are very considerable differences, for instance, between the great first-grade products of Würzburg, Stein and Leisten.

And as to the other Franconian wines, there are:

the fine racy Steigerwaelder
the rich succulent Escherndorfer (Sites: Lump, Fürstenberg, Berg)
the elegant wines from the neighbourhood of Kitzingen (Grosslage Hofrat – other villages: Sulzfeld, Repperndorf)
the delicate Saale products
the aromatic Kallmuth
the pungent wine from the Tauber and Lower Main
the elegant Hoersteiner

and many others with varying characteristics. And of course each year the vintages differ, even from the same localities. It is a fact that the Climate and Soil Map of the Franconian viticultural districts by Dr. Weise and Dr. Wittman comprises no fewer than 633 maps (1:25,000). It is clear from this evidence that the one vine which produces the best under the local climatic conditions has yet to be found.

Franconian wines are traditionally bottled in a peculiar flask, known as a *Bocksbeutel*, the origin of which is obscure. Possibly a glass-blower may once have turned out a strange shape, either accidentally or intentionally, or maybe the Low German '*Bockesbeutel*' (a bag in which prayer books or other volumes were transported) had something to do with the original invention, and its name. It must be remembered, too, that there is a grape called 'Bocksbeutel', possibly a reference to its shape. Dr. Kittel ascribes the origin of the name directly to the bag-like shape (*Beutel*) of one of the internal organs of a goat's anatomy (*Bock*), which the characteristic Franconian flask resembles. This interpretation is far-fetched. If we remember that Rabelais in his novels *Gargantua* and *Pantagruel* speaks quite often of bottles called '*bréviaires*', in other words of bottles similar to a *Bocksbeutel*, we can accept the solution of the puzzle of '*Bocksbeutel*'.

It appears that the *Bocksbeutel* flagons have been in use for many centuries. The earliest documents relating to the plantation of vines in Franconia go back to the seventh century, and the first planters in this region were women, the nuns of the Benedictine convents of Ochsenfurt and Kitzingen. According to local legend they must have been very lively ladies – apparently when they went for walks they were followed by one of the servants of the convent carrying – not their prayer-books – but skins filled with wine!

Only quality wines of Franconia are allowed to be sold in the *Bocksbeutel* flagon; all the others have to be bottled either in the Rhine wine bottle, or any other bottle, but not the *Bocksbeutel*. The *Bocksbeutel* is almost exclusively reserved for Franconian wines, but is also used for certain high-grade Badenwines – the so-called Mauer wines. It is an old custom that these too should be sold in the *Bocksbeutel* flagon. By special agreement the Taubergrund and the Baden communities of Neuweier, Umweg and Varnhalt are allowed to bottle and sell in *Bocksbeutel*. They have combined to fight any other users of *Bocksbeutels* in Germany.

Franconian growers have a far harder task than those in other districts. Their vineyards are situated on slopes so steep that newcomers to the work can barely stand or walk on them.

The soil within the Franconian region is as varied as the qualities of the wine. In the eastern parts the vineyards are planted on red marl (a clayey soil); in the Main triangle, now Bereich Maindreieck, i.e., the part bounded by Schweinfurt, Ochsenfurt and Gemuenden, the wines are grown on efflorescent shell-lime soil; in the territory of the Lower Main on variegated sandstone, in the Alzenau lands in primitive rock. From Bamberg westwards towards Zell and to the south through the Steigerwald to the Aischgrund, vines are planted on loamy red marl, here frequently intercalated with gypsum (for example at Iphofen). It is this soil, usually heavy and water-laden – particularly in hot seasons – that produces good, mature wines, the reason being that its capacity for retaining moisture is very great and hardly ever fails, even in a very dry year.

As already mentioned, shell-lime soil is found in the country delimited by a line drawn south from Schweinfurt to Marktbreit and Ochsenfurt and then turning north towards Gemuenden, now Bereich Steigerwald. The same soil is met with in the side-valleys of the Werrn, the Saale and the Tauber; usually it is heavy and efflorescent. Whereever the steep slopes are well wooded, so that the trees supply moisture even in dry seasons, the vines are likely to flourish. But when there are no trees, the soil is liable to be sucked dry in hot years and consequently the vines suffer.

In the Bereich Mainviereck, north of Aschaffenburg, in the district of Alzenau, it is mainly the Riesling vine that flourishes on the primitive rock soil of Hoerstein, Wasserlos and Michelbach. The extremely well-ventilated soil is of volcanic origin and consists principally of weathered potash-mica slate. The wines are similar to those of the Rheingau.

Franconian viticulture is restricted to plots which are unsuitable for any other kind of plantation, i.e., to the warm southern, south-western, and western sites on the steep mountain slopes in the river valleys of the Main, the Franconian Saale, the Werrn, and the Tauber. Economic necessity drove the vine plantations from the valley and up into the steep hills.

Würzburg is the home *par excellence* of Franconian wines, and Würzburg's site, Stein, has given to Franconian wines the name by which they are known in other countries – Stein wines. Under the German wine law, the name 'Stein wine' is reserved for wines from the Würzburg sites 'Stein and Steinacker' and may not be used for Franconian wines as a whole. Any wine bottled in a *Bocksbeutel* with nothing on the label but the word 'Stein' (or 'Stein wine'), is assumed to be a Würzburg Stein and must meet this expectation.

In Würzburg we find the leading producers, viz. Bavarian Domain, Staatsweingut Hofkellerei, the Buergerspital (Citizen's Hospital), and the Juliusspital (Julius Hospital). Buergerspital, dedicated to the Holy Ghost, is a foundation endowed by the Würzburg citizen Johann von Steren in 1413 as a home for aged and impoverished Würzburg citizens. The foundation has always included some vineyards, and these in course of time have been gradually increased until they have become a large wine estate. The Buergerspital zum Heiligen Geist now owns about 100 hectares of vineyards which extend along the Main from Randersacker through Würzburg to Thuengersheim. Except for Rüdesheim on the Rhine, no German vineyards suffered quite so much from bomb damage as those in Würzburg.

The state wine estate in Lower Franconia originated in the vineyards owned by the former Prince-Bishop of Würzburg. Besides the vines grown on their own estate, these princes had enormous quantities of wine in their cellars which had been collected as tithes from the wine-growing population. When the rule of the Prince-Bishops came to an end, their large wine estate was made over to the Duchy of Würzburg, and in 1816 it was transferred to the Bavarian Crown as state property. With it went the one-time princely, later state, court cellars (Hofkellerei) in Würzburg, which from time immemorial had been linked to the estate. At present the state vineyards cover about 190 hectares, divided between the following estates:

Bereich Mainviereck

1. Hoerstein in Kahlgrund, between Aschaffenburg and Hanau
   Size: 17 ha
   Sites: Abtsberg (Grosslage Reuschberg)
   Types: Riesling, Rieslaner, Ortega, Müller-Thurgau, Osiris, Perle.

2. Grossheubach on the Main, opposite the romantic little town of Miltenberg
   Size: 5 ha
   Site: Bischofsberg (no *Grosslage*)
   Types: Spätburgunder, Frühburgunder, Müller-Thurgau.
3. Dorfprozelten on the Main
   Size: 22 ha
   Site: Predigtstuhl (no *Grosslage*)
   Types: Frühburgunder, Spätburgunder, Ortega.
4. Kreuzwertheim, opposite the town of Wertheim
   Size: 8 ha
   Site: Kaffelstein (no *Grosslage*)
   Types: Spätburgunder, Rieslaner, Perle.

Bereich Maindreieck

5. Hammelburg on the Franconian Saale not far from the world-renowned spa of Bad Kissingen
   Size: 15 ha
   Site: Trautlestal (Grosslage Burg)
   Types: Perle, Müller-Thurgau, Ortega.
6. Wuerzburger Stein
   Size: 39 ha
   Site: Stein (no *Grosslage*)
   Types: Riesling, Rieslaner, Mariensteiner, Silvaner, Fontanara, Albalonga, Traminer.
7. Wuerzburger Leiste–Marienberg
   Size: 14 ha
   Site: innere Leiste, Schlossberg (exclusive possession)
   Types: Riesling, Rieslaner, Silvaner, Ortega, Perle, Müller-Thurgau
8. Randersacker, 6 km south of Wuerzburg
   Size: 22 ha
   Sites: Pfuelben, Sonnenstuhl, Marsberg, Teufelskeller (Grosslage Leben)
   Types: Rieslaner, Riesling, Mariensteiner, Albalonga, Osiris, Müller-Thurgau, Silvaner.
9. Ippesheim, at the foot of the Franconian mountains
   Size: 4 ha
   Site: Herrschaftsberg
   Types: Perle, Ortega, Müller-Thurgau, Silvaner.
10. Lehrweingut Veitshöchheim
   Size: 32 ha
   Sites: Veitshöchheimer Woelflein, Thüngersheimer Scharlach (Grosslage Ravensburg)

Types: Silvaner, Riesling, Rulander, Weissburgunder, Rieslaner, Müller-Thurgau, Perle, Traminer and many new varieties.

Bereich Steigerwald

11. Abtswind on the west edge of the northern Steiger wood
    Size: 6 ha
    Site: Altenberg (Grosslage Schild)
    Types: Rieslaner, Scheurebe, Perle, Müller-Thurgau, Weissburgunder.
12. Handthal, 20 km from Bamberg
    Size: 6 ha
    Site: Stollberg (no *Grosslage*)
    Types: Müller-Thurgau, Ortega, Osiris, and other new varieties.

Here are the premier Franken wines to remember:

Würzburg Sites

1. '*Würzburger Stein*'
   (85 ha) includes the old sites 'Stein' and 'Lindleinberg'. Vines: Silvaner, Riesling, Rieslaner, Müller-Thurgau, Traminer, Ruländer and others.
2. '*Würzburger Pfaffenberg*'
   (50 ha) includes the old sites 'Pfaffenberg', 'Heinrichsleite', 'Würzburger Wand', 'Rossberg', 'Hoffleite' and 'Oehlberg'. Vines: Silvaner, Müller-Thurgau, Riesling, Kerner, Ruländer, Burgunder and a few more new crossings.
3. '*Würzburger Abtsleite*'
   (45 ha) includes 'Gutenthal', 'Neuberg', 'Abtsleite'. Vines: Silvaner, Riesling, Rieslaner, Müller-Thurgau, Traminer, Ruländer, Scheurebe and others.
4. '*Würzburger Innere Leiste*'
   (10 ha) known as such for many centuries. Vines: Riesling, Silvaner, Müller-Thurgau, Perle, Ortega and others.
5. '*Würzburger Kirchberg*'
   (35 ha) was formerly the vineyard of the village, but its wines have been marketed as Heidingsfelder 'Würzburger Kirchberg'. Vines: Silvaner and Müller-Thurgau.
6. '*Würzburger Schlossberg*'
   (5·5 ha) the old 'Schlossberg' and 'Felsenleiste'. Sole property of the State Domain. Vines: Müller-Thurgau, Perle, Ortega and other new crossings.

7. *'Würzburger Stein/Harfe'*
(7·8 ha) is the sole property of Bürgerspital; it is actually part of the 'Stein'; when applying for the registration of this site, the applicant stated: This name is part of history and tradition. In many poems and stories, this site is cited again and again. The wines are of great quality. Vines: Silvaner, Riesling, Traminer, Scheurebe and others.
Würzburg single sites are not part of any *Grosslage.*

Other vineyards of importance are:

Bereiche	*Grosslagen*	*Villages*	*Vineyards*
Maindreieck	Kirchberg	Escherndorf	Lump
			Fuerstenberg
	Ewig Leben	Randersacker	Maisberg
			Pfulben
			Sonnenstuhl
			Teufelskeller
	Burg	Saalecker	Schlossberg
	Ravensburg	Veitshoechheim	Woelflein
	*—	Randersacker	Dabug
Mainviereck	Reuschberg	Hoerstein	Abtsberg
Steigerwald	Burgweg	Iphofen	Julius-Echter-Berg
			Kronsberg
			Kalb
	Herrenberg	Castell	Schlossberg
	Schlossberg	Roedelsee	Kuechenmeister
Bayrischer Bodensee	—	Nonnhorn	Seehalde
			Sonnenbuechel

*—means no Grosslage

The state domains, which were for many years under the management of the most prominent viticulturist of Germany, Professor Dr. Breider, who has just retired and has been given a professorship at Würzburg University, have installed model plant and created admirable working arrangements both in their vineyards and in their cellarage systems and without any doubt produce the best of all Franconian wines.

The immense storage cellar in the 'Residenz' Palace at Würzburg – known as the most beautiful baroque palace in Germany – must have been planned by the original architect with an eye to the future development of a promising wine. It is fully adequate to all requirements.

A great variety of wines are grown on the state winelands:

Riesling, Silvaner, Müller-Thurgau, Scheurebe, Rieslaner (formerly Mainriesling) and Spätburgunder.

The Riesling is not notable for its production in any great quantity, but rather for the quality of its wines.

The Franconian Silvaner is rich and full, with a strong fruit flavour. The sunny slopes from which it originates have stamped it with an individual character.

The range of prices for Franconian wines (specially those grown where the climate is more 'continental') varies even more than in the Rhineland. In particular, Franconian crops are frequently damaged by early frosts. Hence the yield may be anything from one to eight hectolitres per hectare.

Further, certain Franconian wine specialities are only to be found in small amounts within large estates, in co-operatives, and especially among the small self-marketing wine growers.

Amongst the new varieties are those which have been developed by the Bavarian Institute of Viticulture in Würzburg over at least fifteen years.

We see a new district developing in the Franconian region in the valleys on the Saale where the new crossings are specially cultured and used for experiments.

I believe that vines like the Perle and Ortega which are planted here as experiments today, will in a few years' time cover the entire vineyard of the district, because these vines are successful in producing ripe grapes, when the Riesling and Silvaner cannot ripen. They not only come to full ripeness in indifferent years, but even Auslese and higher-class wines have been produced here in such vintages.

Bavaria has a foot in the Lake of Constance, at Lindau Bereich Bayerischer Bodensee (Bavarian Lake of Constance). The white wines made from these lake-side vineyards are known as Seeweine (lake wines) and are pleasant, refreshing wines.

The oldest wine cellar of Germany is in Franconia, at Kitzingen, which is considered to be the cradle of Franconian viticulture, under the convent of the Benedictine nuns. It is a two-floor cellar, built in A.D. 745 by the sister of King Pippin the Short, of the Franks, after she had been jilted by her lover. This cellar has survived the centuries. When at Whitsun in 1484 the convent was burnt down, the cellar survived. The convent was rebuilt, but was destroyed a second time in 1525. Once more rebuilt, it has served different purposes over the years.

In 1938 the building was acquired by the Bocksbeutel-Weinvertrieb Fränkischer Weingutsbesitzer (the Company of Franconian Growers and Distributors of *Bocksbeutel* wines). In 1945 two bombs penetrated the upper floor cellar, destroying 20,000 litres of wine in casks and 35,000 litres in *Bockbeutel* bottles; the building above ground was destroyed.

Everything has now been rebuilt in the old style. We find here the biggest wine cask in Franconia – it takes 30,000 litres – and this is the place where the Growers' Association stores its wines for maturation in cask and bottle.

IMPORTANT GROWERS IN FRANCONIA

Bayerische Landesanstalt fuer Weinbau und Gartenbau	87	Wuerzburg
Bocksbeutelweinvertrieb	8710	Kitzingen
Brennfleck, Josef	8711	Sulzfeld
Braun, Andreas	8712	Volkach
Buergerspital-Weingut z.Hl.Geist	87	Wuerzburg
Gebhardt, Ernst	8701	Sommerhausen
Geiger, Gebr.	8702	Thuengersheim
Fuerstl. Castell'sches Domaeneamt	8711	Castell
Fuerstl. Loewenstein-Wertheim-Rosenberg'sches Weingut	6983	Kreuzwertheim
Graf Schoenborn'sches Weingut		Schloss Hallburg
Juliusspital-Weingut	87	Wuerzburg
Leininger, Walter	8701	Eibelstadt
Maeuser, Alfred	8711	Sommerach
Meintzinger, P. O.	8711	Frickenhausen
Staedt. Weingut	8763	Klingenberg
Staedt. Weingut	8783	Hammelburg
Wirsching, Hans	8715	Iphofen

23

Red Hocks

These observations would not be complete without a reference to red hocks. In 1962, 83 per cent or 55,466 ha of the wine-producing area of Germany were producing white wine; 17 per cent or 11,671 ha red wine. In this connection I should like to quote Professor Saintsbury's expressed opinion in his *Notes on a Cellar-Book*. He writes:

> For the red hocks, however, I must put in a word, both in justice to them and in charity to my fellow-creatures. They – not merely Assmannshauser, which certainly is the best, but Walporzheimer, Ober-Inglheimer and others – are specifics for insomnia after a fashion which seems to be very little known, even among the faculty. Many years ago, when I was doing night-work for the press, and even after I had given that up, when I was rather unusually hard run at day-work, I found sleep on the off-nights as well as the others in the former case, and often in the latter, not easy to obtain. I was not such a fool as to take drugs, and I found hot grog or (what is not in itself inefficacious) strong beer, conducive to an uncomfortable mouth, etc., in the morning when taken only a few hours before. But a large claret glass or small tumbler of red hock did the trick admirably, and without deferred discomfort.

In good vintages the wines show a soft and delicate flavour, and though the red grapes ripen earlier than the white ones, under no circumstances can they be compared with the French growths. It is, therefore, easily understandable that there is practically no export of these wines; they are consumed within Germany, for foreign countries will in any case look for the fine red wines of Bordeaux or Burgundy, and not for Assmannshausen or any other German red wine.

The red-wine grape most favoured in Germany is the Blue Burgundy (Spätburgunder). Its wine is dark, strong and finely spiced. It flourishes on the Rhine, on the Ahr and above all in Baden. Next in flavour comes the Müller-vine (Black-Schwarz-Riesling) in Württemberg.

Lesser red wines are produced from the Blue Portuguese grape in the Palatinate (the Palatinate is the biggest red-wine region in Germany), in Rhinehessia and in Württemberg; and from the Limberger vine and the Trollinger (originating in the Tyrol) in Württemberg. The last-named produces a somewhat sour table wine. Then there is the Affentaler, which is produced near Buehl in Baden. This wine is getting quite popular since the Wine and Food Society in Liverpool included it in 1952 as a German speciality in their 'German Christmas Banquet', more I think on account of the 'make up' under which it is marketed than for its quality.

This village was originally called 'Ave Thal', i.e. 'Ave-Maria Tal' (*Tal* means valley) because of a monastery situated in the valley. In this part of the country 'V' is pronounced as 'F', so that people called the village 'Affental'; but *Affe* in German means a monkey. As a result of all this manipulation of the language, and in order to distinguish their wine from other districts, the growers used, and still use, a bottle on which a monkey is embossed.

The village Affental has disappeared from the map (the full name was Eisental-Affental). Now it forms the suburb Eisental of the town of Buehl. 'Affentaler' is now the name of a type of wine – similar to Liebfraumilch and Moselblümchen. Affentaler may be a Tafelwein, a quality wine or even a quality wine with predicate, it just depends upon the result of the official examination. Any quality can be offered in the Monkey-embossed bottle. An Affentaler Tafelwein must be from the Weinbaugebiet Oberrhein or Burgengau; an Affentaler Qualitätswein from the Anbaugebiet Baden with examination number; and an Affentaler Spätlese from the Anbaugebiet Baden, Bereich Ortenberg with examination number.

Red wines in Germany – like the French red wines from Bordeaux and Burgundy – are obtained by fermentation of the grape mash. Under the German wine law it is permissible, until 1979, to add to a German red wine a quantity of foreign red wine not exceeding 25 per cent of the total volume. This licence conveys a great commercial advantage to growers and wine merchants in Germany, as, with the exception of Baden and Württemberg, practically no region producing German red wines would otherwise be able to produce a wine suitable for ready sale.

ANBAUGEBIET AHR

Weinbaugebiet for Tafelweine Rhein.
Area 484 ha
57 per cent red grapes (31 per cent Portugieser 26 per cent Pinot Noir) 43 per cent white grapes

The German red-wine region *par excellence* is the Ahr valley, between 50° and 51° latitude. It is the smallest German region, 25 km along the lower Ahr, and is also the most northerly wine region in the world. The wine produced there is called Ahr-Burgundy. Grapes can ripen because volcanic soil and slate retain warmth and reflect it back on to the grapes during cool nights.

Though the Ahr district is the smallest German wine district, it is remarkable that there are still people willing to work these most difficult vineyards. 93 per cent of the vineyards on the Ahr are on very steep hills, 3 per cent on less steep hillsides and only 4 per cent are in the plain.

The growers on the Ahr are only to a very small extent wine growers alone; as a rule this only provides a small fraction of their income. Here one still finds vineyards in the old style with wooden stakes not far distant from each other. Reorganization and rationalization are necessary, but Nature has not forced the growers to do so because this small district is free from phylloxera and no replanting on root stock has been found necessary. Special experiments are going on with a new crossing of the two red-wine grapes which are grown in the Ahr district, namely Portugieser and late Burgundy grapes.

The growers try here to produce the 'Deckrotwein' in order to avoid using imported wine to give the Ahr wine colour, and have planted 1 per cent of all the vineyards with the special vine called 'Tiefrot' (dark red).

The Ahr wine growers are also trying to find new crossings. More than sixty crossings have been planted by the State Domain Marienthal and it is hoped that one of them, the 'Rotberger', will prove a success.

It is possible to taste a range of Ahr wines in the Rotweinprobierstube (Red-wine tasting room) in the Lennepark at Bad Neuenahr, which offers a warm welcome to all.

The whole specific region has

one *Bereich* – Walporzheim
one *Grosslage* – Klosterberg

and ten wine-growing villages

Altenahr	Walporzheim
Mayschoss	Ahrweiler
Rech	Bachem
Dernau	Bad Neuenahr
Marienthal	Heimersheim

Next on our list comes Assmannshausen, the city of Rhenish red wines, already partly dealt with under Rheingau.

Assmannshausen red wines are all derived from the Spätburgunder, the 'late Burgundy' vine. It is planted over an area of 28 hectares, mostly the property of the state domains. In this connection it may be noted that the entire viticultural region of the Rheingau (of which the Assmannshausen red-wine vineyards form a part) covers 2,500 hectares, one-sixtieth of the whole German viticultural area.

As the best red wine produced in Germany, the Assmannshauser has been praised in many publications. It is no Burgundy – despite the fact that it comes from a 'Burgundy' grape – but a Rhine wine with some of the qualities of a Burgundy. The difference is no doubt due to the difference in soil. The slate hills of the Rhine produce something less fine than the French Burgundy but, possibly for the same reason, rather stronger.

Here is a quotation from the Assmannshausen propaganda brochure:

> The fact that nothing but the Assmannshausen Burgundy grape can produce such full and noble 'quality' red wines has always aroused the envy of other German red-wine districts. Efforts were therefore made to transplant the Assmannshausen late Burgundy vines to Baden, to Württemberg, to the Main, to the Ahr, and elsewhere, and by these means to cultivate a wine of equal value. But the results were disappointing from the very first. It was clearly recognized on all sides that the failure could only have been avoided if the Assmannshausen soil had been transplanted together with the grape. Yes, indeed! Therein alone lies the secret. The nature of the soil is the deciding factor.
>
> The strong native vineyard soil consists of luminary efflorescent layers of Taunus phyllite slate, in colours ranging from bluish-red to violet. It is extremely favourable to the growth of the 'Late Burgundy' vine, which, brought from France, probably by Cistercian monks, has proved itself to be the best grape for the production of red wine. The Assmannshausen variety, which is a smooth noble red wine, has a slight characteristic flavour of almonds, a mild and velvety delicate pungency, and is fully and harmoniously rounded. Its colour varies – according to the maturity of the grapes – from fiery red to a dark garnet hue.

Unfortunately, what Assmannshausen has to say of its soil, the Burgundy growers can rightly say of their soil and climate. So the Assmannshauser is a red wine, but no Burgundy.

A wine from Assmannshausen sold pre-war in London at 660/– per dozen bottles (which then included only 12/– duty) was the most interesting wine I ever tasted. It was the 1934 Assmannshauser Hoellenberg Spätburgunder Rot-Weiss, Feinste Edelbeerenauslese, Estate Bottling Prussian Domain. This is a wine resulting from a very special kind of Beerenauslese of the late Burgundy grape. The grape gatherers of Assmannshausen, in good vintages, have a sickle-shaped enamel coated container hanging from their punnets; into these containers they put the selected sleepy berries, some of which have already shrunk and dried out to a raisin-like consistency. This is done because in these raisin-berries the beautiful blue dye in the grapeskin has been destroyed by the fungus (*Botrytis cinerea*) and the use of these otherwise valuable berries in the manufacture of the red wine would be detrimental to its natural ruby-red colour.

Now, whereas in preparing red wines the grape mash is allowed to ferment in order that the grape juice (colourless even in blue-skinned berries) may be enabled to absorb the blue dye from the skins the sleepy raisin-berries are pressed immediately. The juice gained by this process, coloured, rather sticky grape juice, is then fermented on the lines of the white wine process. If these raisin-berries were to be fermented with the rest in the mash, the must or wine would take on an unpleasant mouldy taste. As it is, they produce a white wine pressed from the noblest red-wine grapes; the juice having absorbed a certain amount of the skin dye, the wine has a yellowish, brownish or reddish tinge according to its quality.

The 1934 wines, as well as two later vintages, the 1938 and the 1950, are the most exceptional wines I have ever met.

I once gave this wine after lunch, instead of port. A wine shipper who was present considered it unorthodox to give hock as an after-dinner wine. For comparison therefore, a decanted bottle of 1908 vintage port was sent for. All present agreed that the Assmannshauser, with its low alcoholic strength, was to be preferred for after-lunch consumption.

This red-white wine must not be confused with a Schiller wine. Schiller wine is the name given to a wine pressed from a mixture of red and white grapes. The name has nothing to do with the poet Schiller, but was derived from the red-white (merging into pink) radiance or 'shimmer' of the wine. (The German verb for 'shimmer' is '*schillern*'.)

This species of wine was mainly developed during the worst crisis ever suffered by German viticulture – after the Thirty Years' War. During that period the many devastated vineyards were hastily replanted with any kind of vine likely to afford a good crop, whether it was a red-wine or a white-wine grape. Even nowadays the Swabians are very fond of their 'Schiller', but its production has been drastically reduced. In Württemberg as elsewhere there is a very strong tendency – wholly admirable from the viticultural point of view – to keep grape strains and vines pure by selective planting, selective harvesting and selective wine production. This tendency will no doubt lead to a still greater improvement in the quality of German wines.

In bad vintages such as 1954, when grapes cannot ripen and therefore do not produce colour substances, white wine is produced from the red grape which is used either locally or for the production of sparkling wine.

To recapitulate, the best-known German red wines are as follows:

Ahr	Walporzheimer
	Ahrweiler Daubhaus
	Neuenahrer Sonnenberg
Rhinehessia	Ingelheimer
Palatinate	Duerkheimer Fueuerberg
	Forster Neuberg

(According to a document in the Speyer Museum dated 1597, the 'Red Traminer' from Rhodt in the Oberhaardt was at that time considered to be the best wine 'growing on the long chain of hills from Bale to Cologne'.)

Rheingau:	Assmannshaeuser Hoellenberg
Württemberg:	Brackenheim
	Schwaigern
Baden:	Oberrotweiler Kirchberg
	Affentaler (type wine – the Baden red equivalent to the white Rhein Liebfraumilch and the Mosel Moselblümchen)
Franconia:	Klingenberg am Main

I cannot conclude this chapter without adding some further general remarks about German red wines. In my earlier book *Rhineland Wineland* I discussed them as they arose in the various areas of production.

My greatest objection is that German red wines are treated with *Süssreserve* and *Restsüsse* unlike the great wines of Bordeaux and Burgundy. To a large extent they carry the denomination 'Burgunder', but remind us more of Tarragona than Burgundy. The Germans like to drink red wine, but in the white-wine fashion. Franconia has restricted the *Restsüsse* to 1:5 even for quality wine with predicate, but they are still out of place in the range of red wines. Furthermore, the natural colour of German red wine even when fermented on the skins is very pale pink, *rosé* and not red.

In these circumstances one must welcome the fact that the Germans use their red grapes more and more for the production of Weissherbst and Schillerwein (i.e. *rosé* wines). The production of the Hessian Domain shows only Weissherbst amongst the 1970 wines.

Until a few years ago the red-white wines were Edelbeerenauslesen only (see above under Assmannshausen, p. 336), later Auslese was made and now the whole range. This includes Eiswein Auslesen 1969 and 1970, Auslese 1966, 1967 and 1969 and 1966 and 1967 Beerenauslesen. The 1969 were very sweet, i.e. liqueur wines, not good partners for food. So before choosing a German red wine for a dinner or banquet, make sure of the degree of sweetness.

Maps and Plans

1. Ihringen before and after the reorganization of the vineyards. Heavy lines indicate roads, thin lines are boundaries between different varieties of vine and shaded areas are uncultivated slopes.

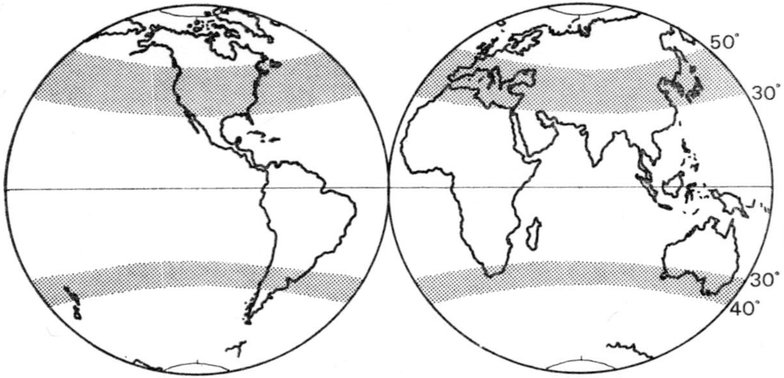

2. World wine distribution

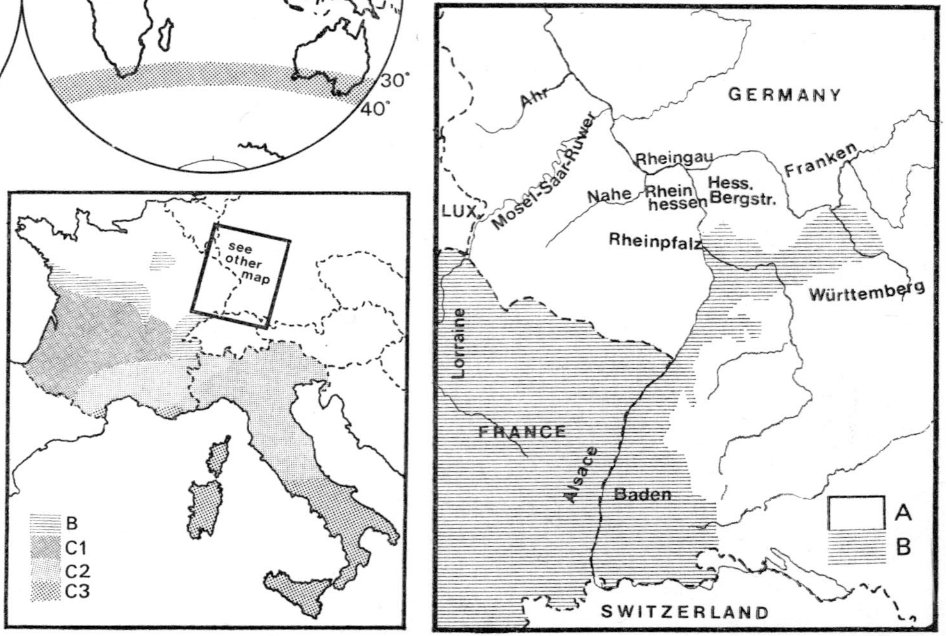

3a and b. The viticultural zones of the E.E.C.

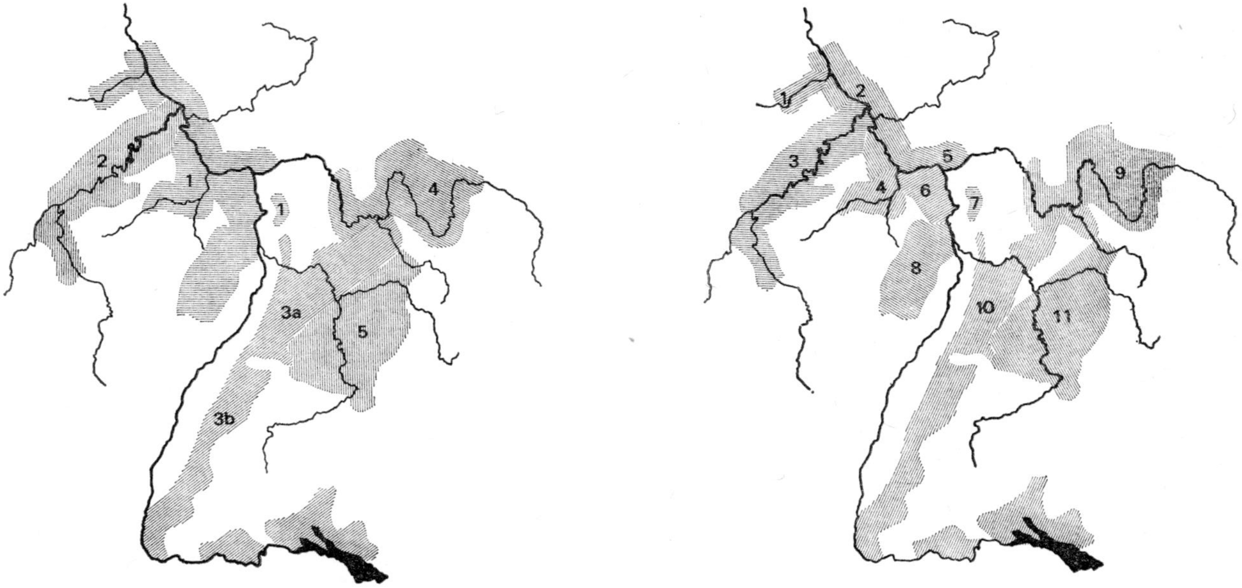

4. The German wine regions

a. The five table wine districts: 1 Rhein, 2 Mosel, 3 Oberrhein (3a Burgengau, 3b Römertor), 4 Main, 5 Neckar

b. The eleven designated regions for quality wine: 1 Ahr, 2 Mittelrhein, 3 Mosel-Saar-Ruwer, 4 Nahe, 5 Rheingau, 6 Rheinhessen, 7 Hessische Bergstrasse, 8 Rheinpfalz, 9 Franken, 10 Baden, 11 Württemberg

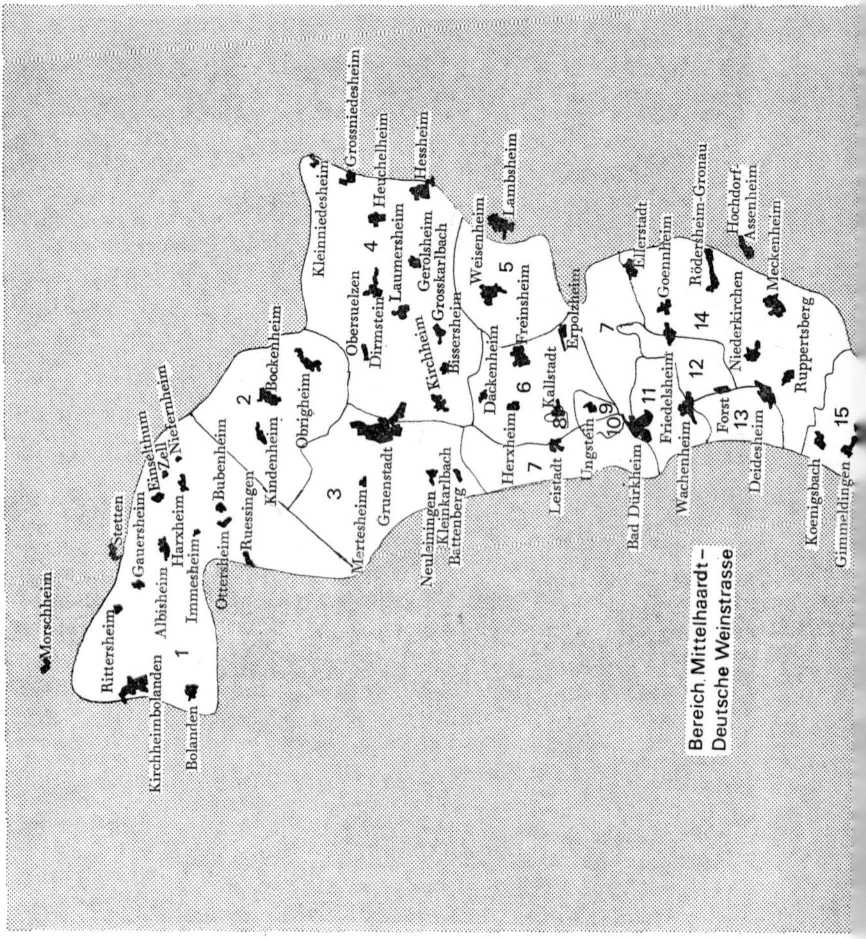
Bereich Mittelhaardt – Deutsche Weinstrasse
Morschheim
Kirchheimbolanden
Bolanden
Rittersheim
Albisheim
Immesheim
Gauersheim
Stetten
Harxheim
Ottersheim
Einselthum
Zell
Niefernheim
Bubenheim
Ruessingen
Kindenheim
Bockenheim
Obrigheim
Mertesheim
Gruenstadt
Neuleiningen
Kleinkarlbach
Battenberg
Kleinniedesheim
Grossniedesheim
Obersuelzen
Dirmstein
Heuchelheim
Laumersheim
Gerolsheim
Grosskarlbach
Hessheim
Kirchheim
Bissersheim
Weisenheim
Lambsheim
Freinsheim
Dackenheim
Herxheim
Kallstadt
Erpolzheim
Leistadt
Ungstein
Bad Dürkheim
Ellerstadt
Goennheim
Friedelsheim
Wachenheim
Forst
Deidesheim
Rödersheim-Gronau
Hochdorf-Assenheim
Niederkirchen
Meckenheim
Ruppertsberg
Koenigsbach
Gimmeldingen
1
2
3
4
5
6
7
8
9
10
11
12
13
14
15

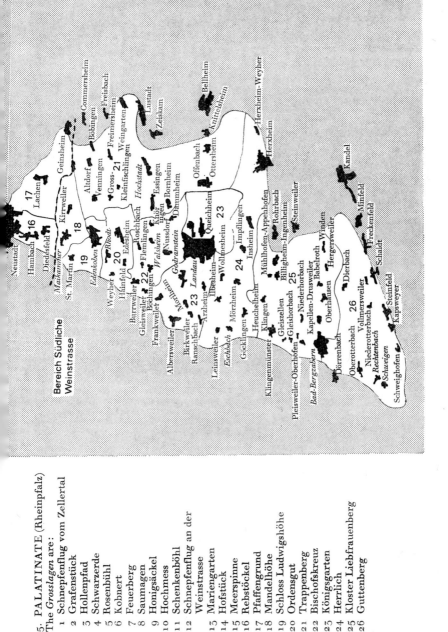

5. PALATINATE (Rheinpfalz)
The *Grosslagen* are:

1 Schnepfenflug vom Zellertal
2 Grafenstück
3 Hollenpfad
4 Schwarzerde
5 Rosenbühl
6 Kobnert
7 Feuerberg
8 Saumagen
9 Honigsäckel
10 Hochmess
11 Schenkenböhl
12 Schnepfenflug an der Weinstrasse
13 Mariengarten
14 Hofstück
15 Meerspinne
16 Rebstöckel
17 Pfaffengrund
18 Mandelhöhe
19 Schloss Ludwigshöhe
20 Ordensgut
21 Trappenberg
22 Bischofskreuz
23 Königsgarten
24 Herrlich
25 Kloster Liebfrauenberg
26 Guttenberg

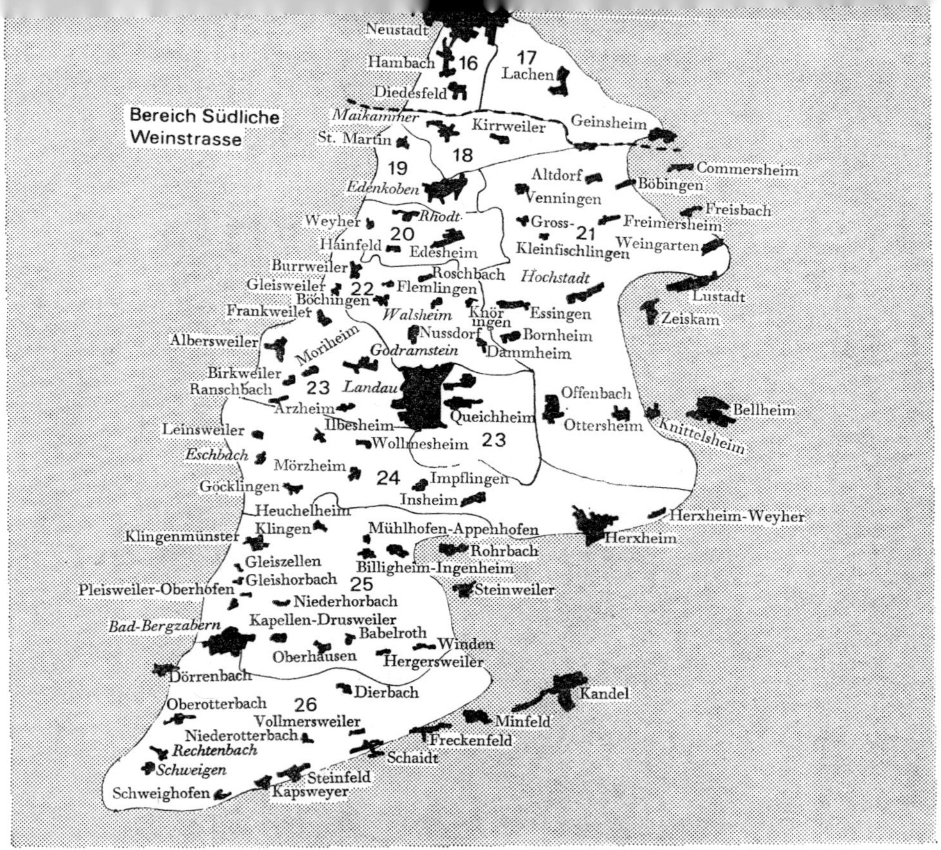

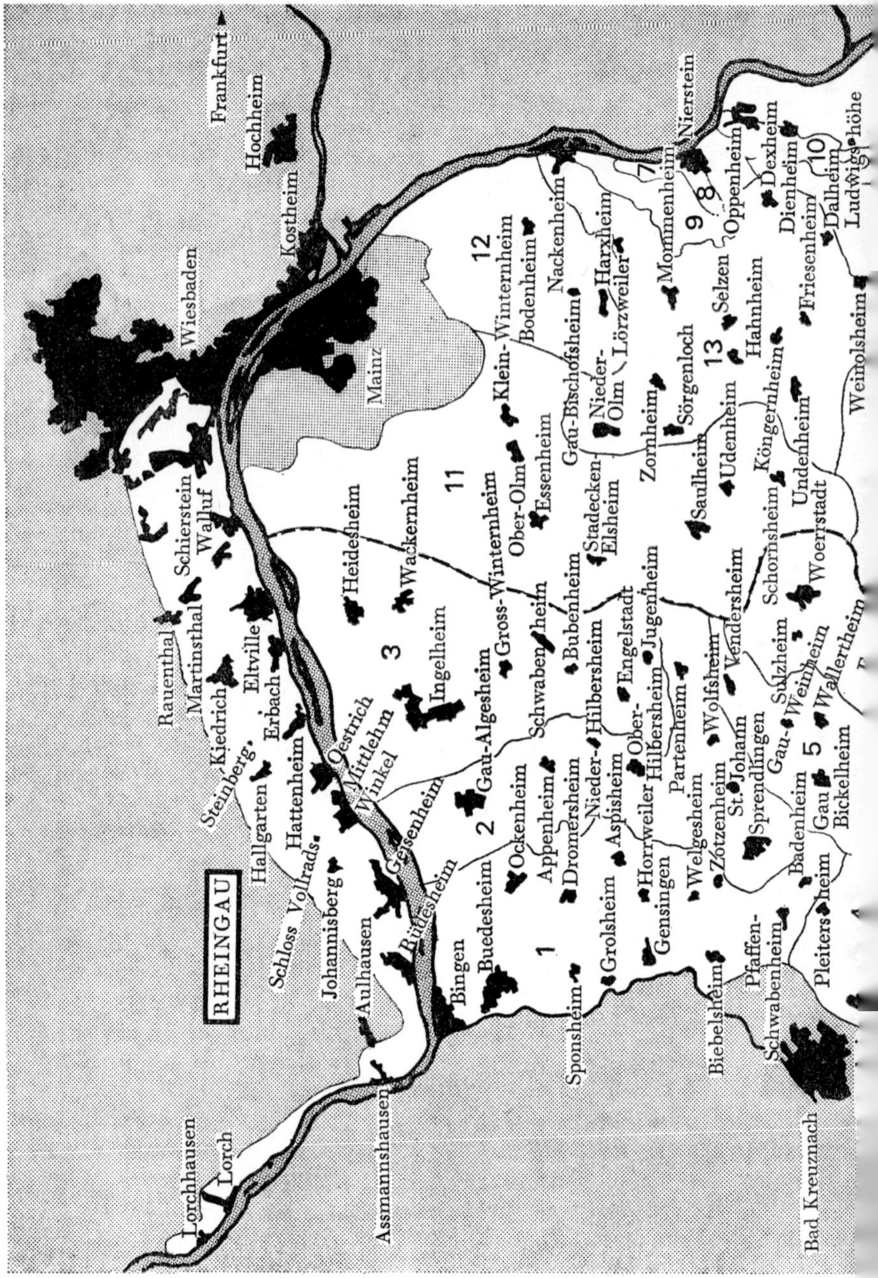
RHEINGAU
Frankfurt
Hochheim
Kostheim
Wiesbaden
Mainz
Schierstein
Walluf
Rauenthal
Martinsthal
Eltville
Kiedrich
Erbach
Steinberg
Hallgarten
Hattenheim
Oestrich
Mittlehm
Winkel
Schloss Vollrads
Johannisberg
Geisenheim
Aulhausen
Rüdesheim
Assmannshausen
Lorchhausen
Lorch
Bingen
Buedesheim
Heidesheim
Wackernheim
Ingelheim
Gau-Algesheim
Ockenheim
Appenheim
Dromersheim
Sponsheim
Grolsheim
Gensingen
Horrweiler
Aspisheim
Nieder-Hilbersheim
Ober-Hilbersheim
Schwabenheim
Gross-Winternheim
Bubenheim
Engelstadt
Jugenheim
Partenheim
Welgesheim
Zotzenheim
St. Johann
Sprendlingen
Wolfsheim
Vendersheim
Gau-Weinheim
Sulzheim
Wallertheim
Badenheim
Gau Bickelheim
Pfaffen-Schwabenheim
Pleitersheim
Biebelsheim
Bad Kreuznach
Ober-Olm
Essenheim
Klein-Winternheim
Stadecken-Elsheim
Gau-Bischofsheim
Bodenheim
Nackenheim
Nieder-Olm
Harxheim
Lörzweiler
Zornheim
Sörgenloch
Saulheim
Udenheim
Schornsheim
Undenheim
Köngernheim
Woerrstadt
Mommenheim
Selzen
Hahnheim
Nierstein
Oppenheim
Dexheim
Dienheim
Friesenheim
Dalheim
Weinolsheim
Ludwigshöhe
1
2
3
5
7
8
9
10
11
12
13

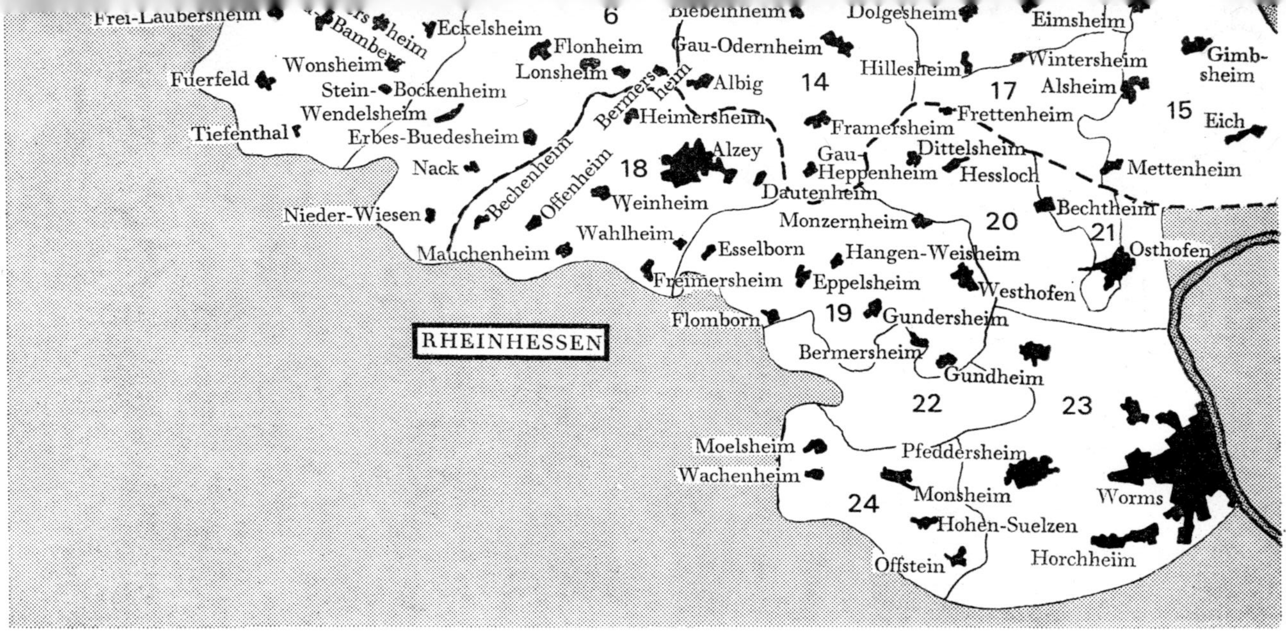

6. RHEINGAU and RHEINHESSEN

The Rheinhessen *Grosslagen* are:
Bereich Bingen: 1 St. Rochuskapelle, 2 Abtei, 3 Kaiserpfalz, 4 Rheingrafenstein, 5 Kurfürstenstück, 6 Adelberg
Bereich Nierstein: 7 Rehbach, 8 Auflangen, 9 Spiegelberg (see also Map 11), 10 Guldenmorgen, 11 Domherr, 12 Sankt Alban, 13 Gutes Domtal, 14 Petersberg, 15 Krötenbrunnen, 16 Vogelsgärten, 17 Rheinblick
Bereich Wonnegau: 18 Sybillenstein, 19 Bergkloster, 20 Pilgerpfad, 21 Gotteshilfe, 22 Burg Rodenstein, 23 Liebfrauenmorgen, 24 Domblick

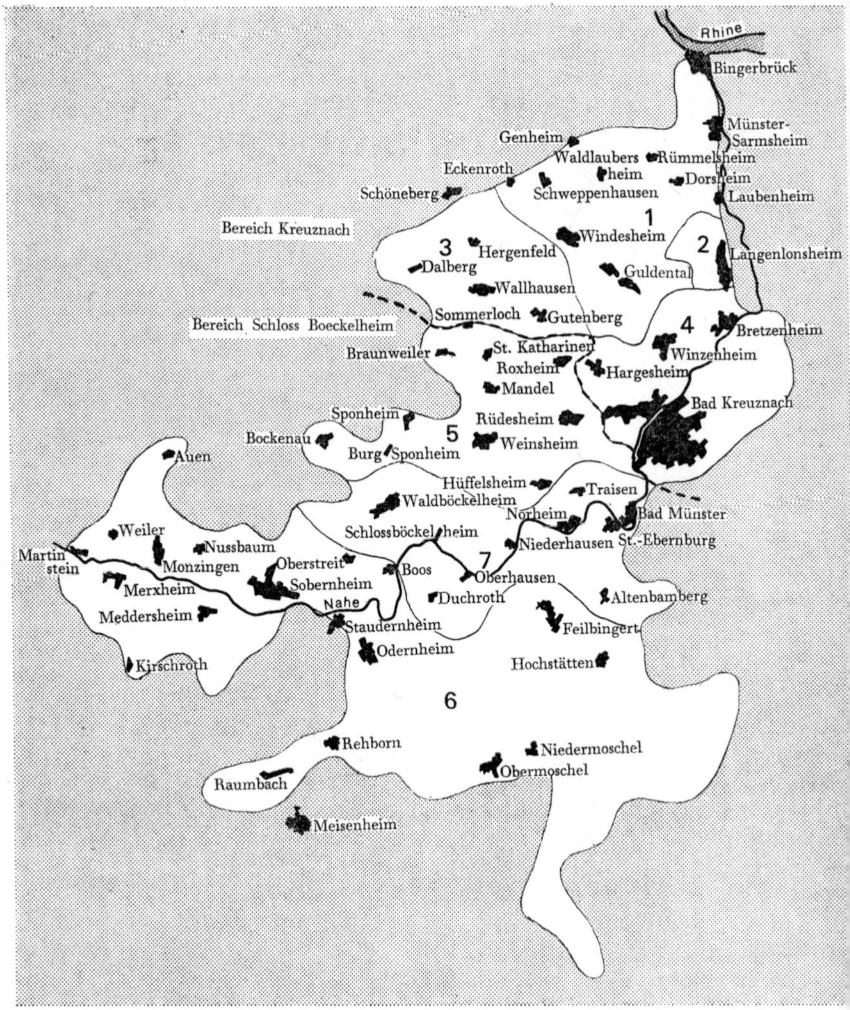

7. NAHE

The Nahe *Grosslagen* are:

1 Schlosskapelle
2 Sonnenborn
3 Pfarrgarten
4 Kronenberg
5 Rosengarten
6 Paradiesgarten
7 Burgweg

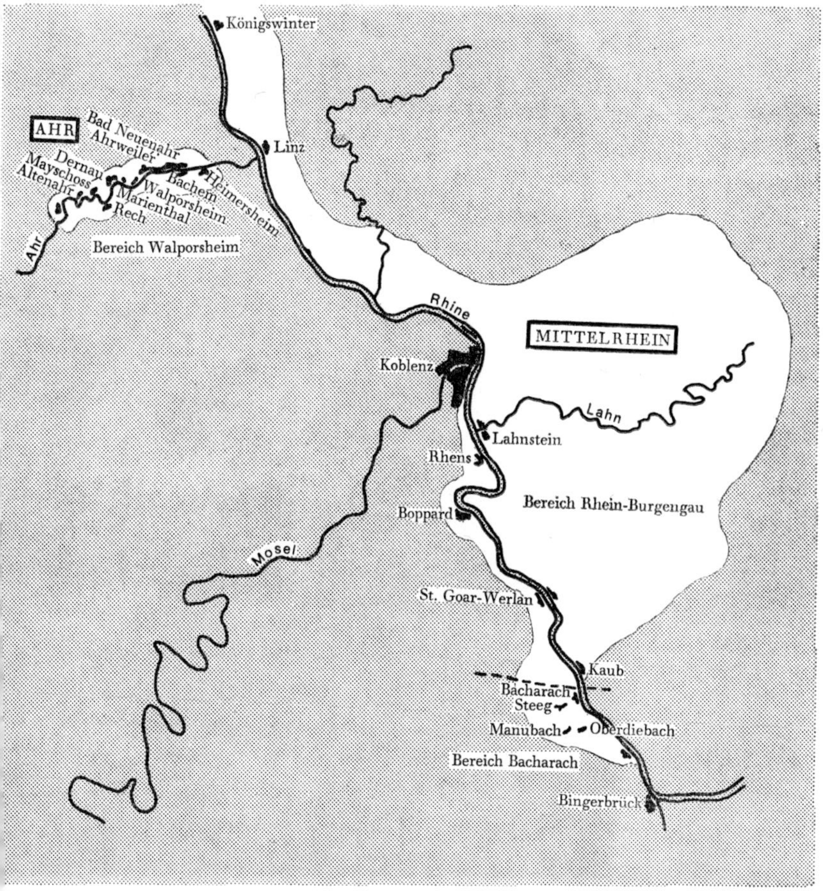

8. MITTELRHEIN and AHR

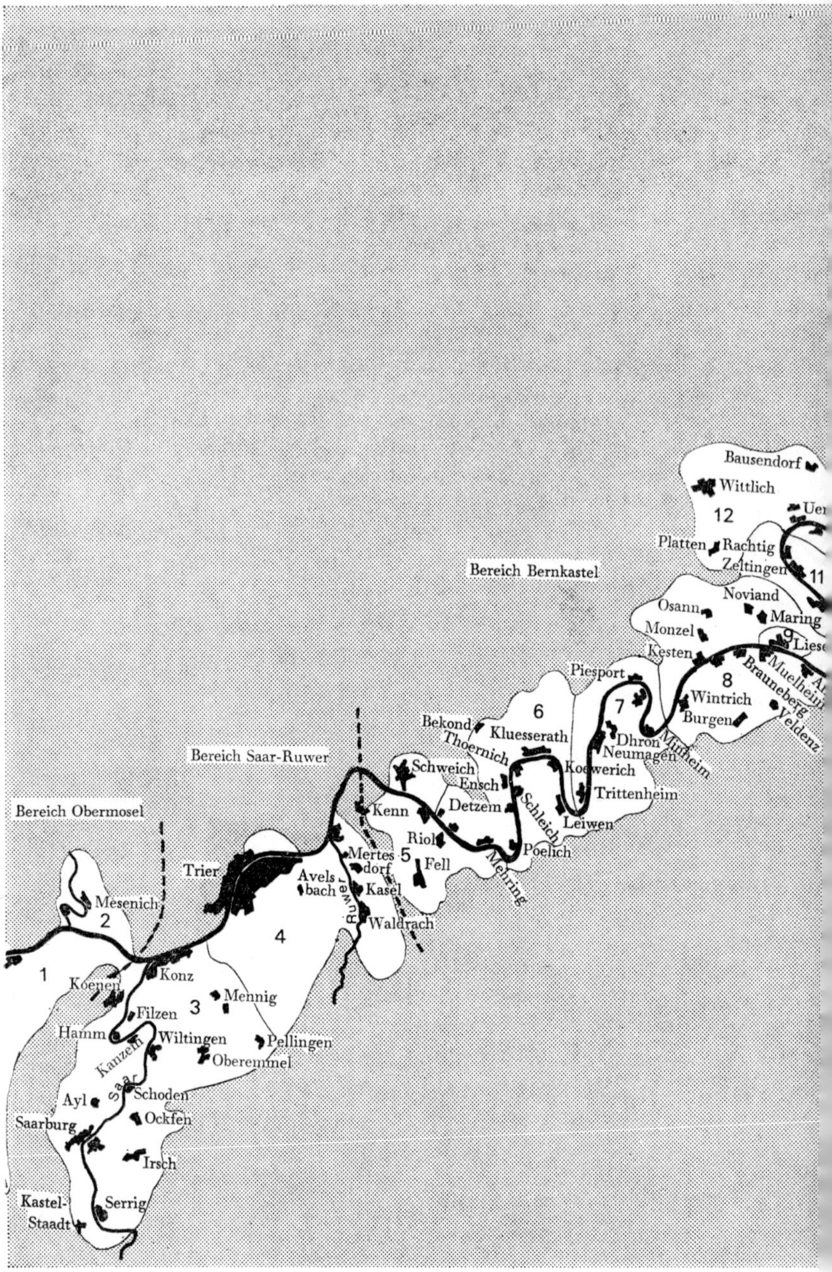
Bereich Obermosel
Bereich Saar-Ruwer
Bereich Bernkastel
Bausendorf
Wittlich
12
Platten
Rachtig
Zeltingen
11
Osann
Noviand
Maring
Monzel
9
Kesten
Piesport
8
Muelheim
Braunebeg
Wintrich
Burgen
Veldenz
7
6
Bekond
Klusserath
Thoernich
Dhron
Neumagen
Minheim
Schweich
Ensch
Koewerich
Trittenheim
Kenn
Detzem
Schleich
Leiwen
Riol
Poelich
Mertes dorf
5
Fell
Mehring
Trier
Avels bach
Kasel
Ruwer
Waldrach
Mesenich
2
4
1
Koenen
Konz
Mennig
Filzen
3
Hamm
Wiltingen
Pellingen
Kanzem
Oberemmel
Saar
Ayl
Schoden
Saarburg
Ockfen
Irsch
Kastel-Staadt
Serrig

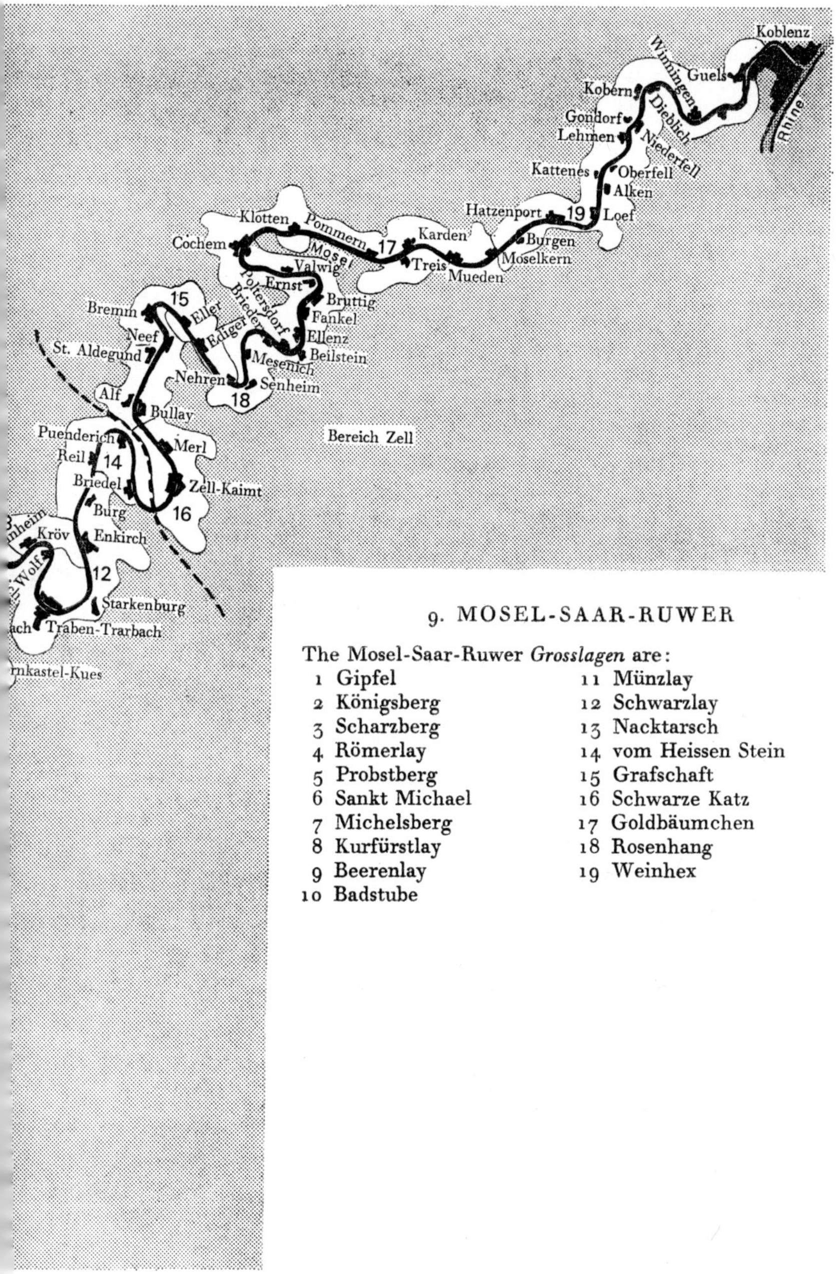

9. MOSEL-SAAR-RUWER

The Mosel-Saar-Ruwer *Grosslagen* are:

1 Gipfel
2 Königsberg
3 Scharzberg
4 Römerlay
5 Probstberg
6 Sankt Michael
7 Michelsberg
8 Kurfürstlay
9 Beerenlay
10 Badstube
11 Münzlay
12 Schwarzlay
13 Nacktarsch
14 vom Heissen Stein
15 Grafschaft
16 Schwarze Katz
17 Goldbäumchen
18 Rosenhang
19 Weinhex

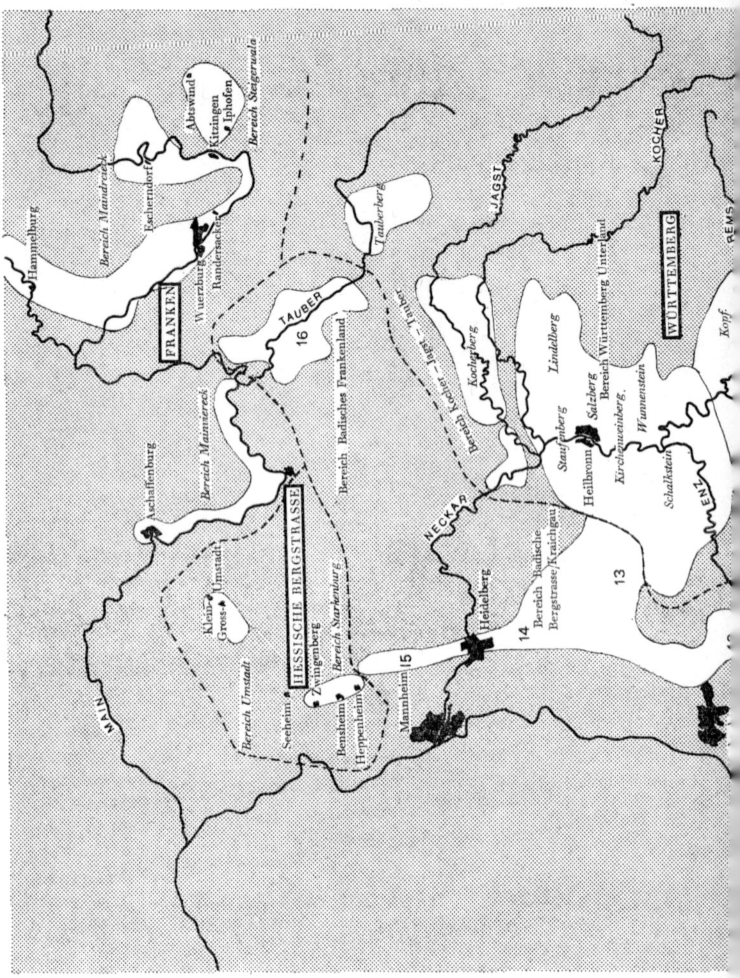
Hammelburg
Bereich Maindreieck
Escherndorf
Abtswind
Kitzingen
Iphofen
Bereich Steigerwald
FRANKEN
Wuerzburg
Randersacker
Tauberberg
JAGST
KOCHER
TAUBER
16
Bereich Badisches Frankenland
Bereich Kocher – Jagst – Tauber
Kocherberg
Lindelberg
Bereich Württemberg Unterland
WÜRTTEMBERG
REMS
Kopf
Aschaffenburg
Bereich Mainviereck
HESSISCHE BERGSTRASSE
Staufenberg
Salzberg
Heilbronn
Kirchenweinberg
Wunnenstein
Schalkstein
ENZ
NECKAR
Klein-
Gross-
Umstadt
Heidelberg
Bereich Badische Bergstrasse/Kraichgau
13
14
15
Zwingenberg
Bereich Starkenburg
Bereich Umstadt
Seeheim
Bensheim
Heppenheim
Mannheim
MAIN

M

10. BADEN, WÜRTTEMBERG, FRANCONIA and HESSISCHE BERGSTRASSE

The Baden *Grosslagen* are:

1 Sonnenufer
2 Vogtei Rötteln
3 Burg Neuenfels
4 Lorettoberg
5 Atillafelsen
6 Vulkanfelsen
7 Burg Zähringen
8 Burg Lichteneck
9 Schutterlindenberg
10 Fürsteneck
11 Schloss Rodeck
12 Hohenberg
13 Stiftsberg
14 Mannaberg
15 Rittersberg
16 Tauberklinge

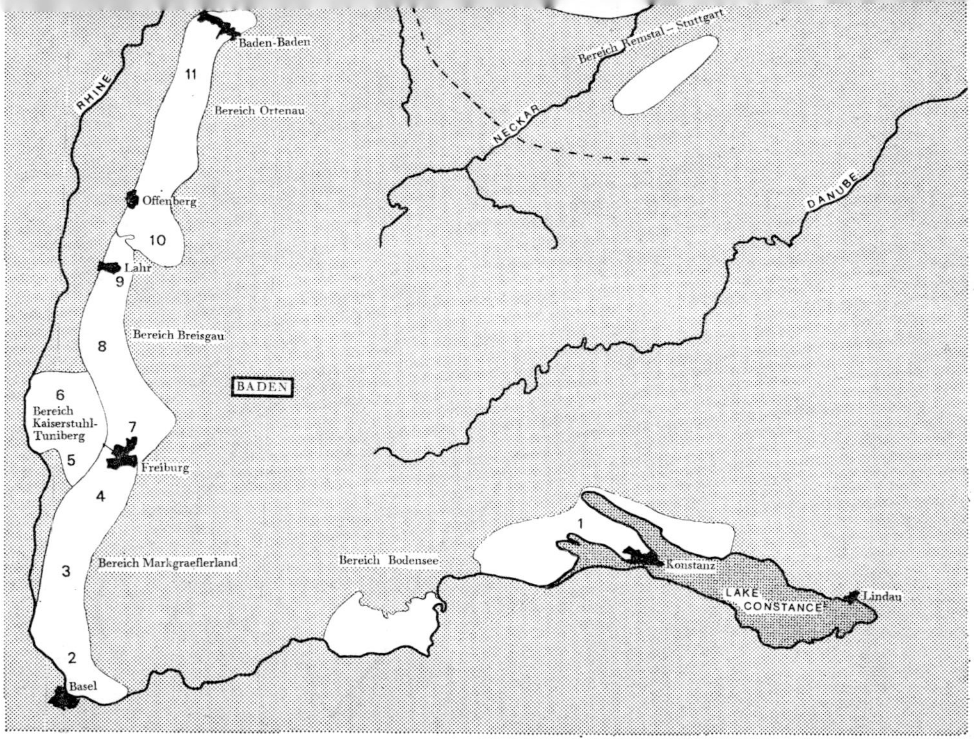

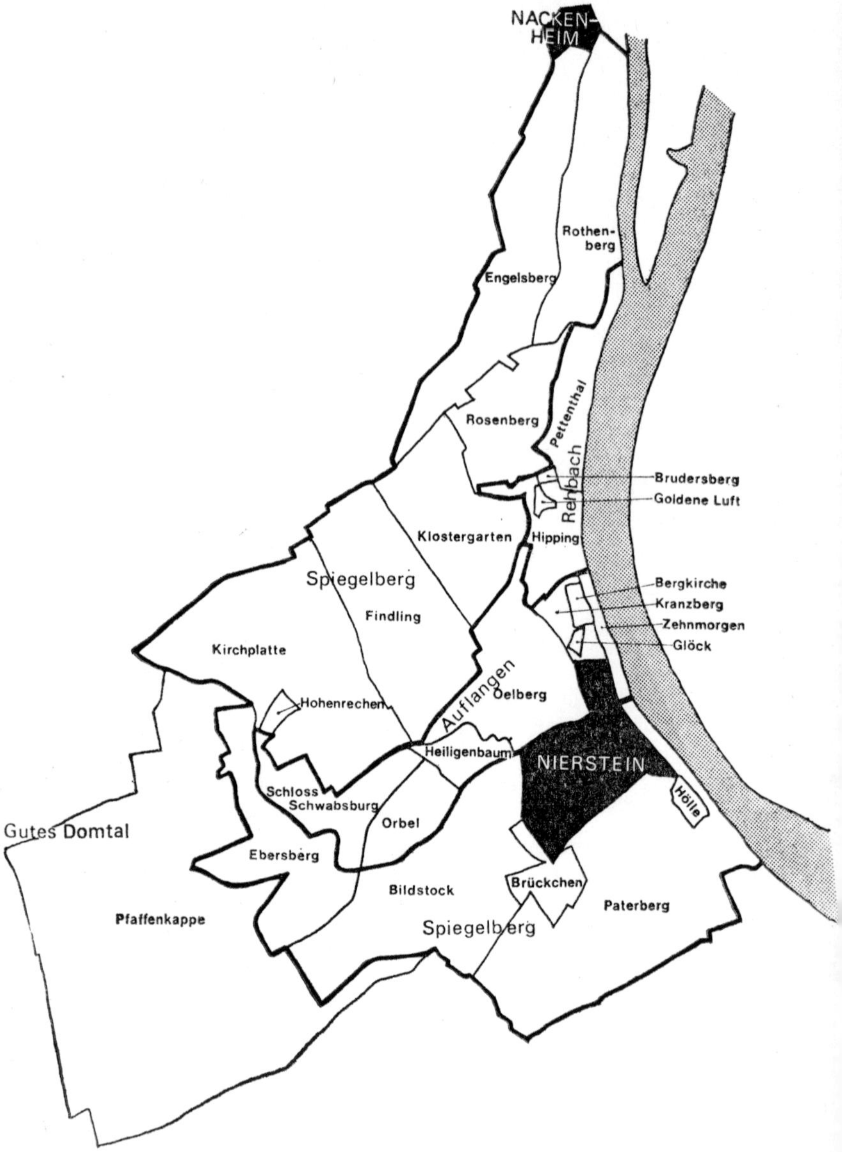

11. The Nierstein sites (see pp. 45–5 and 219ff.)

Glossary

Abfueller	bottler
Angegoren	fermenting
Ausgangsstoff	starting or raw material
Bereich	reach, department, sphere
Bereiten	to make, prepare
Bereitung	preparation, manufacture, making
Bereitungsverfahren	procedure in preparation (manufacture)
Bezeichnung	name
Deckwein	imported red wine to improve the colour of German red wine
Erzeuger	producer
Gemarkung	boundary, landmark
Gemeinde	village, community
Grosslage	grand site, greater site, enlarged or large site
Hersteller	manufacturer
Kenntlichmachung	marking
Kennzeichnung	any statement about the wine (some declarations are obligatory, some permitted)
Lage	site
Praedikat	predicate, title, mark
Trocken	dry, a wine containing less than 4 g per litre unfermented sugar
Umgebung	environment
Verbraucher	consumer
Verkaeufer	vendor
Weinbaugebiet	region, district for the production of Tafelwein (Rhein, Mosel, Main)
Weinbauuntergebiet	subregion (Roemertor, Burgengau, see p. 312)
Weinbereitung	preparation of the wine (vinification)
Zusammenschluss	association, society, cooperative

OFFICIAL DEFINITIONS OF SOME EXPRESSIONS

Abfuellen	to fill in a container with less than 5 litres potential contents and in the case of sparkling wine, not more than 3·2 litres and which is being actually closed (corked).

Ausland	*foreign* countries; all those regions which neither fall under this law nor belong to the regions where the official currency is the 'Deutsche Mark' (East Germany)!
Behandeln	to treat, addition of material and the use of some procedures.
Herstellen	to treat, blend, use finish, do anything which influences raw material, a final product.
Inverkehrbringen	is to offer, to have in stock in order to sell and to dispose otherwise 'feilhalten' (offer for sale and to hand to others).
Lagern	to store: is to be considered as production when a by-law based on the wine law considers storage as essential and if some goods are stored, storage influences the product or its raw material.
Verschneiden	blending is the mixing of various products if the action is not considered as 'adding of material or substances' according to by-laws issued, based on the wine law.
Verwerten	every alteration or addition of a raw material of a product to a food, which is neither Ausgangsstoff nor Erzeugnis.
Zusetzen	adding of material with the exception of blending.

APPENDICES

APPENDIX 1

Excerpt from European Communities Regulation (E.E.C.)
No. 816/70 of the Council

Article 16, No. 2
2. As from 1 September 1971 any new vine plantings, any replantings or any regrafting may only be done with recommended or authorised vine varieties.

Article 19
1. Increase of the natural alcoholometric strength referred to in Article 18 may only be obtained:
   (a) in respect of fresh grape must in fermentation or new wine still in the process of fermentation, by adding sucrose or concentrated grape must;
   (b) in respect of grape must, by adding sucrose or concentrated grape must or by partial concentration;
   (c) in respect of wine suitable for giving table wine and table wine, by partial concentration through cooling.

4. The addition of concentrated grape must may not have the effect of increasing the initial volume of fresh crushed grapes, grape must, grape must in fermentation or new wine still in the process of fermentation, by more than 11% in wine producing area A, by 8% in wine producing area B and by 6·5% in wine producing areas C.

When Article 18 (2) is applied, limits concerning increases of volume shall be increased to 15% in wine producing area A and to 11% in wine producing area B respectively.

5. Concentration may not lead to reduction of the initial volume by more than 20% and in no case to the increase by more than 2° of the natural alcoholometric strength of grape must, wine suitable for giving table wine or table wine which were the subject of that operation.

Article 20
1. Fresh grapes, grape must, grape must in fermentation and new wine still in fermentation may be the subject of:
- partial deacidification, in the wine producing areas A, B and C I;
- acidification and deacidification, in wine producing area C II, without prejudice to the provisions of paragraph 3;
- acidification, in wine producing area C III.

Acidification may only be carried out to the maximum limit of 1·50 g/l, expressed in tartaric acid.

Moreover, grape must intended for concentration purposes may be the subject of partial deacidification.

2. In years when climatic conditions have been exceptional, acidification of

the products referred to in paragraph 1 may be authorised in the wine producing area C I; under the same conditions, the maximum limit of 1·50 g/l, referred to in paragraph 1, may be brought to 2·50 g/l provided that the natural acidity of the products is not less than 3 g/l expressed in tartaric acid.

3. Acidification and enrichment, except by way of derogation to be decided case by case, as well as acidification and deacidification of the same product, are operations which exclude one another in turn.

Article 21

Sweetening of table wines shall be authorised,

(a) only with grape must which has at most the same total alcoholometric strength as the table wine in question when the fresh grapes, grape must, grape must in fermentation, new wine still in fermentation, wine suitable for giving table wine from which it is produced, or table wine itself were the subject of the operations referred to in Article 19 (1);

(b) only with concentrated grape must or grape must, provided that the entire alcoholometric strength of the table wine in question is not increased by more than 2°, when the products referred to under (a) have not been the subject of one of the operations referred to in Article 19 (1).

Article 24

1. Both over-pressing of grapes, whether or not crushed, and the pressing of wine lees are forbidden. The same shall apply to the fermentation of grape marc for purposes other than distillation.

ANNEX II

ALCOHOLOMETRIC STRENGTHS

1. *Actual alcoholometric strength*; the number of units of volume of alcohol contained in 100 units of volume of the product considered.

2. *Potential alcoholometric strength*; the number of units of volume of alcohol likely to be produced by the total fermentation of the sugar contained in 100 units of volume of the product considered.

3. *Total alcoholometric strength*; the sum of the actual and of the potential alcoholometric strengths.

4. *Natural alcoholometric strength*; the total alcoholometric strength of the product considered before any enrichment.

DEFINITIONS REFERRED TO IN ARTICLE 1 (4) (b)

1. *Fresh grapes*: the fruit of the grape vine used in vinification, ripe or even slightly withered, which may be crushed or pressed by normal wine cellar means and which may spontaneously produce alcoholic fermentation.

2. *Grape must*: the liquid product obtained naturally or by physical processes from fresh grapes.

3. *Grape must in fermentation*: grape must having an actual alcoholometric strength, less than three-fifths of its total alcoholometric strength.

4. *Concentrated grape must*: uncaramelised grape must.

- obtained by partial dehydration of grape must, carried out by any authorised method other than direct fire, in such a way that its density at 20°C is not less than 1·240:
- exclusively coming from the vine varieties referred to in Article 16:
- produced in the Community and
- obtained from grape must having at least the minimum natural alcoholo-

metric strength determined for the wine producing area where the grapes were harvested.

5. *Grape juice*: unfermented but fermentable grape must which has undergone the appropriate treatment for consumption in the unaltered state.

6. *Concentrated grape juice*: uncaramelized grape juice obtained by partial dehydration of grape juice, carried out by any authorised method other than direct fire, in such a way that its density at 20°C is not less than 1·240.

7. *Wine*: the product obtained exclusively from whole or partial alcoholic fermentation of fresh grapes whether or not crushed, or of fresh grape must obtained from such grapes.

8. *New wine still in fermentation*: wine in which alcoholic fermentation is not yet complete and wine which is not yet separated from its lees.

9. *Wine suitable for giving table wine*:
- coming exclusively from vine varieties referred to in Article 16:
- produced in the Community:
- having at least the minimum natural alcoholometric strength determined in respect of the wine producing area where it was produced.

10. *Table Wine*:
- coming exclusively from the vine varieties referred to in Article 16:
- produced in the Community:
- having, after any of the operations mentioned in Article 19, an actual alcoholometric strength not less than 8·5° and a total alcoholometric strength not exceeding 15°, that upper limit however, being brought to 17° in respect of wines produced in certain wine producing areas to be determined, obtained without any enrichment and no longer containing any residual sugar, and
- having, furthermore, a total acidity content not less than 4·50 g/l, expressed as tartaric acid.

12. *Sparkling wine*: with the exception of the derogations referred to in Article 27 (3), the product obtained by first or second alcoholic fermentation:
- of fresh grapes:
- of grape must:
- of wine suitable for giving table wine,
- table wine, or
- q.w.p.s.r.

characterised on opening the container by a release of carbon dioxide coming exclusively from the fermentation and which, kept at a temperature of 20°C in closed containers, has an excess high pressure of at least 3 atmospheres.

13. *Aerated sparkling wine*: the product:
- obtained, subject to the provisions of Article 27 (3), from table wine:
- obtained in the Community:
- characterised on opening the container by a release of carbon dioxide coming totally or partially from an addition of that gas, and
- having an excess pressure not less than 1 and not exceeding 2·5 atmospheres, when kept at a temperature of 20°C, in closed containers.

14. *Semi-sparkling wine*: – Perlweine – table wine:
- naturally containing carbon dioxide after first or second alcoholic fermentation, and
- having an excess pressure not less than 1 and not exceeding 2·5 atmospheres, when kept at 20°C in closed containers.

APPENDIX 2
Climatic Details

1. Comparison of Weather Conditions in 1967 and 60-year average (German wine lands taken as a whole)

Month	Average Temp-erature 1967 – °C	60-year average °C	Rainfall 1967 in mm	60–year average in mm	Hours of sunshine 1967	60-year average hours of sunshine
January	2·2	0·7	14·4	35·8	42·1	48·9
February	4·7	2·0	19·3	29·9	95·7	74·7
March	7·6	5·2	39·6	30·4	144·9	125·6
April	9·5	9·2	40·7	38·5	195·2	159·2
May	14·9	14·6	77·3	49·8	223·2	212·0
June	17·5	17·4	23·9	54·1	208·7	209·0
July	21·2	19·3	17·8	57·5	279·4	205·9
August	18·1	18·0	59·1	67·3	205·3	196·4
September	15·4	14·4	106·0	48·4	129·0	146·7
October	12·9	9·3	59·7	43·8	100·7	96·0

2. Temperatures and Rainfall for the Year 1967 compared with the average taken in Trier (Mosel)

Month	Temperature °C				Rainfall in mm	
	Monthly average	Long-term average	Maxi-mum	Mini-mum	Monthly Total	Long-term average
April	8·6	9·5	22·4	– 3·3	36·0	48
May	13·3	13·8	29·0	– 0·8	92·0	56
June	15·8	16·9	30·4	3·5	58·4	66
July	20·3	18·6	32·0	8·0	107·8	74
August	17·1	17·8	29·5	7·2	118·0	72
September	14·1	14·7	27·0	6·7	125·3	57
October	12·0	9·7	23·3	– 0·8	94·9	70

3. Start of Vegetation (day and month)

Vintage	1967	1966	1965	1964
Müller-Thurgau	27.4	26.4	5.5	29.4
Silvaner und Silvaner u. Riesl.	3.5	30.4	10.5	1.5

4. Start of Blossoming (day and month)

Vintage	1967	1966	1965	1964
Müller-Thurgau	22.6	11.6	25.6	9.6
Silvaner	21.6	9.6	30.6	8.6
Riesling	24.6	11.6	2.7	8.6

5. Start of Ripening (day and month)

Vintage	1967	1966	1965	1964
Müller-Thurgau	4.8	6.8	16.8	3.8
Silvaner	16.8	20.8	3.9	12.8
Riesling	17.8	26.8	12.9	15.8

6. Course of the Ripening Process of Riesling in the Kreuznacher Steinweg Site showing improvement in degrees Oechsle and Acidity per mille (5 vintages!).

	1953		1953		1964		1966		1967		Average	
Date	°Oe.	‰ A.	°Oe.	‰ A.	°Oe.	‰ A.	°Oe.	‰ A.	°Oe.	‰ A.	°Oe.	‰ Acid
19. 8.	28	27	34	b.30	32	b.30	20	b.30	25	b.30	—	—
30. 8.	52	24	60	21	50	22	32	b.30	40	b.30	33	27
10. 9.	72	17	83	15	60	15	50	24	59	26	43	—
20. 9.	76	15	84	11	68	13	59	16	69	21	60	—
30. 9.	86	12	86	11	78	11	70	14	71	18	68	17
10. 10.	—	—	94	9	80	10	75	11	78	16	73	14
At Harvest on the												
3. 10.	85	12										
19. 10.			97	8·5								
20. 10.					80	10						
7. 11.							76	7				
25. 10.									86	9		

7. Specific Gravity, °Oechsle, and Total Acidity (g/l) of Must (1967)

		September				October		
		1.	10.	20.	30.	10.	20.	30.
Müller-Thurgau	°Oechsle	62	68	70	71	70	71	71
	Acidity	14·6	10·9	8·8	8·6	8·2	7·5	6·5
Silvaner	°Oechsle	51	58	68	68	72	78	78
	Acidity	21·7	13·7	11·8	11·3	9·2	9·0	8·0
Riesling	°Oechsle	47	59	69	72	79	81	81
	Acidity	28·8	19·5	16·3	13·5	11·8	11·3	9·0

8.

Grape Variety	Spec. Gravity of Must from	°Oechsle to	Total Acidity g/l from	to
Müller-Thurgau	60	100	5·0	10·2
Morio-Muskat	60	75	8·5	13·5
Portugieser	62	75	7·0	10·5
Spätburgunder	75	88	9·0	11·0
Ruländer	85	110	7·0	10·5
Gewürztraminer	88	94	3·2	7·6
Silvaner	60	105	5·0	12·5
Riesling	65	105	5·5	13·0
Scheurebe	75	104	7·0	13·2

The approximate percentage in the different ranges of the white-wine musts was as follows:–

under 64° Oechsle	—
60—69° Oechsle	25%
70—79° Oechsle	40%
80—89° Oechsle	25%
90° Oechsle and more	10%

9. The Quality (1967)

	Specific gravity of must		Acidity	
Kind of grape	Beg. of Harvest	End of Harvest	Beg. of Harvest	End of Harvest
Riesling	55–70	70–83	16–19	10–13
Müller-Thurgau	60–70	70–80	12	10–11
Elbling	50–55	60–62	15–18	14–15

10. Ripening Comparisons by means of Grape Analyses

	1960				1965			
	26. 8.		9. 9.		3. 9.		14. 9.	
Kind of grape	°Oe.	Acid	°Oe.	Acid	°Oe.	Acid	°Oe.	Acid
Siegerrebe	62	6·1	—	—	55	11·0	62	7·2
Malinger	64	6·9	—	—	48	11·0	60	9·5
Müller-Thurgau	46	13·8	60	13·2	40	23·0	56	14·9
Silvaner	56	13·7	62	11·8	28	34·0	36	28·7
Weissburgunder	—	—	60	15·4	33	31·5	50	26·5
Traminer	—	—	72	13·5	38	35·0	51	24·0
Ruländer	70	13·5	76	12·5	38	36·0	49	25·6
S 88	—	—	66	13·2	—	—	42	30·5
Riesling	45	25·6	62	20·7	28	35·0	40	30·0
Portugieser	43	16·0	50	10·6	31	33·0	39	29·0

	1966				1967			
	25. 8.		12. 9.		28. 8.		11. 9.	
Kind of grape	°Oe.	Acid	°Oe.	Acid	°Oe.	Acid	°Oe.	Acid
Siegerrebe	74	4·7	—	—	80	6·2	87	5·1
Malinger	80	5·6	—	—	75	9·4	—	—
Müller-Thurgau	53	12·2	75	9·5	60	12·3	67	8·5
Silvaner	49	18·2	65	10·1	47	21·2	59	13·8
Weissburgunder	60	17·3	66	9·4	54	19·1	65	11·5
Traminer	60	13·6	66	7·4	51	21·0	75	12·2
Ruländer	64	15·0	81	10·5	52	20·0	74	13·0
S 88	32	26·0	57	13·7	45	21·7	54	16·1
Riesling	30	27·5	55	17·0	46	25·9	65	20·6
Portugieser	45	17·0	56	9·5	50	12·8	71	7·5

11. Average Final Specific Gravity of Must at Time of Harvesting

	1959		1960		1964	
	Oechsle	Acid	Oechsle	Acid	Oechsle	Acid
Siegerrebe	90	5·0	65–70	4·5	82	5·3
Malinger	85	6·1	70–72	6·2– 7·5	70	5·7
Müller-Thurgau	82– 96	3·8–6·3	71–83	6·2– 9·4	65– 77	6·8–7·0
Silvaner	94–105	5·6–6·3	70- 75	9·5–10·3	70– 82	6·8–7·8
Weissburgunder	-	-	70	11·5	78	7·2
Traminer	104–108	6·4	76–80	9·5–11·5	87– 96	5·7–6·2
Ruländer	107–111	6·2–6·7	88	11·3	94–100	6·3–6·7
S 88	-	-	73	11·0	86	7·2
Riesling	95–102	6·1–7·1	68–76	10·5–13·8	79– 84	6·8–7·6
Portugieser	70– 82	5·2–5·8	55	9·5	60– 68	5·2–5·6

	1965		1966	
	Oechsle	Acid	Oechsle	Acid
Siegerrebe	73	6·8	84	4·5
Malinger	71/72	8·0– 8·8	85	5·4
Müller-Thurgau	59–67·5	8·0–10·2	68–87/92	6·1–7·2
Silvaner	56–59	11·2–18·1	80	6·8
Wiessburgunder	65–72	9·7–11·8	93– 95	6·2
Traminer	77	10·5	91	6·1
Ruländer	74	11·8	100–104	7·0
S 88	72	12·6	88– 91	6·9
Riesling	64–76	13·0–13·6	83– 92	6·7–8·1
Portugieser	49–52	12·7–13·3	61– 72	3·8–6·4

12. *Yield of Harvest* (*Estimates*)

Riesling	80 to 90 hl/ha
Müller-Thurgau	120 to 130 hl/ha
Elbling	70 to 75 hl/ha

13. *Development of Riesling during Vegetation in Site of Medium Quality*

	1967	1966	1965	1964	1963	1962
Vegetation	6. 5.	1. 5.	15. 5.	3. 5.	12. 5.	9. 5.
Start of Blossom	23. 6.	12. 6.	30. 6.	10. 6.	26. 6.	27. 6.
End of Blossoming	2. 7.	20. 6.	14. 7.	18. 6.	5. 7.	11. 7.
Start of Ripeness	30. 8.	7. 9.	2. 10.	22. 8.	23. 9.	19. 9.

	1961	1960	1959	1958	1957
Vegetation	18. 4.	25. 4.	6. 5.	7. 5.	27. 4.
Start of Blossom	23. 6.	12. 6.	16. 6.	28. 6.	17. 6.
End of Blossoming	30. 6.	24. 6.	22. 6.	4. 7.	23. 6.
Start of Ripeness	13. 9.	6. 9.	22. 8.	8. 9.	5. 9.

14.

	Temperature °C				Rainfall in mm	
Month	Monthly average	Long-term average	Maximum	Minimum	Monthly total	Long-term average
April	8·6	9·5	22·4	−3·3	36·0	48
May	13·3	13·8	29·0	0·8	92·0	56
June	15·8	16·9	30·4	3·5	58·4	66
July	20·3	18·6	32·0	8·0	107·8	74
August	17·1	17·8	29·5	7·2	118·0	72
September	14·1	14·7	27·0	6·7	125·3	57
October	12·0	9·7	23·3	−0·8	94·9	70

APPENDIX 3

Production 1970

Federal State	Total Must hl/ha	Total Must hl	White Must hl/ha	White Must hl	Red Must hl/ha	Red Must hl
Nordrhein-Westfalen	44·7	805	45·3	770	34·7	35
Hessen	102·2	347,971	105·7	343,557	76·1	4,414
Rheinland-Pfalz	139·3	7,229,457	137·3	6,498,186	160·9	731,271
Baden-Württemberg	132·6	2,092,510	122·0	1,189,086	149·7	903,424
Bayern	77·0	202,458	76·8	199,044	92·3	3,414
Saarland	199·7	15,818	199·8	15,800	130·0	18
Western Germany	134·2	9,889,019	130·8	8,246,443	153·9	1,642,576
1969	83·4	5,947,354	84·7	5,149,202	75·7	798,152
1968	86·1	6,047,598	83·8	4,954,766	98·7	1,092,832
1967	87·4	6,069,362	87·8	5,120,717	85·3	948,645
1966	69·5	4,809,358	70·1	4,060,845	67·5	608,580
1965	73·2	5,035,473	72·3	4,160,536	84·2	739,467
1964	104·7	7,185,349	105·3	6,006,052	110·0	945,973
1963	88·3	6,034,147	89·3	5,069,559	86·6	742,809
1962	58·5	3,927,919	58·7	3,253,506	63·8	552,147
1961	53·9	3,574,479	54·2	2,958,128	58·0	501,428
1960	115·8	7,433,246	116·0	6,120,632	127·1	1,044,369
1959	70·5	4,302,661	72·0	3,562,671	73·3	549,600
1958	81·1	4,799,854	81·4	3,878,922	88·8	640,921
1957	38·5	2,264,128	39·3	1,849,371	41·0	292,050
1956	15·6	930,228	17·9	842,945	6·2	47,167
1955	40·1	2,408,102	40·7	1,918,590	46·5	359,883
1954	52·6	3,100,083	54·0	2,488,225	58·9	445,174
1953	45·1	2,455,865	48·2	2,024,074	48·8	337,623
1952	50·8	2,712,601	53·1	2,160,291	53·9	364,579
1951	59·3	3,112,439	60·4	2,398,127	70·5	471,211
1950	65·6	3,244,399	66·4	2,482,064	74·7	465,642

APPENDIX 4

The Wine Grower's Year

Work in Vineyard	*n Cellar*
JANUARY Pruning; Moving manure and fertilizers to vineyard; Clearing the vineyard of all surplus material; Cutting of vines for planting later in the year; Clearing the land, hoeing with grubbing axe or trench plough, producing deep furrows for planting of new vineyards. Digging 20–50 cm deep to bring fertile subsoil to surface.	1st racking
FEBRUARY Pruning; Manuring; Preparing new replantings of vineyards; Ploughing.	2nd racking; filtration
MARCH Pruning; Removing vine cuttings; Bending and binding of the vines; Planting new vineyards.	Starting of bottling
APRIL Manuring; Toil of soil; Planting new vineyards.	Bottling
MAY Fighting against frost and other enemies of the vines and fungi; Cutting of non-bearing branches; Planting new vineyards.	Treatment of the wine; observation of development
JUNE Fighting against pests; Cutting of leaves and branches; Hoeing the soil; Special work after thunderstorms. (One still remembers the dreadful storm and hail which destroyed a great part of the 1973 crop of Rüdesheim (Rhine) in July 1973.)	
JULY Fighting against pests; Treatment of soil; Cutting of branches and leaves; Hoeing of the soil.	
AUGUST Last fight against pests; Hoeing.	

SEPTEMBBR Preparing for harvest; Fighting against birds; Preparing all tools; Hiring the grape pickers.	
OCTOBER Start of grape picking (early ripening grapes).	Preparing casks and material for harvest
NOVEMBER Harvesting; Pressing of grapes.	Vinification
DECEMBER Start of pruning; Clearing the vineyard of all surplus material; Cutting of vines for planting later in the year; Clearing the land, hoeing with grubbing axe or trench plough, producing deep furrows for planting of new vineyards; Digging 20–50 cm deep to bring fertile subsoil to surface.	Start of racking

APPENDIX 5

Time and cost of vineyard work

	Rheinhessen		Pfalz		Mosel	
	Std/ha	%	Std/ha	%	Std/ha	%
1. Pruning including work connected with it	161	18·2	111	13·8	307	13·0
2. arranging the vine and binding	58	6·6	58	7·2	197	8·3
3. work with the leaves	165	18·7	132	16·4	586	24·8
4. other work	18	2·0	24	3·0	39	1·7
5. all work regarding the vine itself	402	45·5	325	40·4	1,129	47·8
6. manual work with the soil	37	4·2	32	4·0	228	9·6
7. mechanical work with the soil	50	5·7	47	5·9	128	5·4
8. total work with the soil	87	9·9	79	9·9	356	15·0
9. fertilizing	12	1·3	11	1·4	39	1·7
10. manuring	13	1·5	14	1·7	50	2·1
11. total	25	2·8	25	3·1	89	3·8
12. fighting pests and diseases	42	4·7	45	5·6	193	8·2
13. crop picking	310	35·1	317	39·4	524	22·1
14. some other additional work	18	2·0	13	1·6	75	3·2
15. working hours total	884	100	804	100	2,366	100
16. working hours excluding crop picking	574	64·9	487	60·6	1,842	77·6

(With acknowledgements to Professor Kalinke and Ing. grad. Willner.)

APPENDIX 6

Sugar and Alcohol

To calculate from the known content of sugar to the potential alcohol content, or exactly how much alcohol would be produced if the fermentation goes on and all sugar is turned into alcohol, one reckons that generally 46·5 to 47 per cent is obtained as a result of fermentation, but remembering that 1 gram per litre of sugar is unfermentable. Thus, if the sugar content is 100 grams per litre, the fermentable content is 99 grams per litre; the potential alcohol would be 99 × 0·465 or 99 × 0·47.

This is a calculation of grams of sugar into grams of alcohol per litre. If one wants to calculate the volume per cent of alcohol, the formula is different: the fermentable sugar has to be divided by 17, the result making the potential alcohol content. Here is the conversion table Oechsle degrees into % volume alcohol.

°Oe	°Alcohol	°Oe	°Alcohol	°Oe	°Alcohol
40	4·4	77	10·2	114	15·9
41	4·5	78	10·3	115	16·1
42	4·7	79	10·5	116	16·3
43	4·8	80	10·6	117	16·4
44	5·0	81	10·8	118	16·6
45	5·2	82	10·9	119	16·7
46	5·3	83	11·1	120	16·9
47	5·5	84	11·3	121	17·0
48	5·6	85	11·4	122	17·2
49	5·8	86	11·6	123	17·3
50	5·9	87	11·7	124	17·5
51	6·1	88	11·9	125	17·7
52	6·3	89	12·0	126	17·8
53	6·4	90	12·2	127	18·0
54	6·6	91	12·4	128	18·1
55	6·7	92	12·5	129	18·3
56	6·9	93	12·7	130	18·4
57	7·0	94	12·8	131	18·6
58	7·2	95	13·0	132	18·8
59	7·3	96	13·1	133	18·9
60	7·5	97	13·3	134	19·1
61	7·7	98	13·4	135	19·2
62	7·8	99	13·6	136	19·4
63	8·0	100	13·8	137	19·5

°Oe	°Alcohol	°Oe	°Alcohol	°Oe	°Alcohol
64	8·1	101	13·9	138	19·7
65	8·3	102	14·1	139	19·8
66	8·4	103	14·2	140	20·0
67	8·6	104	14·4	141	20·2
68	8·8	105	14·5	142	20·3
69	8·9	106	14·7	143	20·5
70	9·1	107	14·8	144	20·6
71	9·2	108	15·0	145	20·8
72	9·4	109	15·2	146	20·9
73	9·5	110	15·3	147	21·1
74	9·7	111	15·5	148	21·3
75	9·8	112	15·6	149	21·4
76	10·0	113	15·8	150	21·5

40 Oechsle degrees 4·4 degrees of Alcohol, 67 Oechsle degrees 8·6 degrees of alcohol.

APPENDIX 7

Scale showing the difference between alcohol by weight and by volume:

Alcohol g/l	Alcohol Vol/%
70·0	8·82
74·0	9·33
78·0	9·83
80·0	10·08
84·0	10·59
88·0	11·09
90·0	11·34
94·0	11·85
98·0	12·35
100·0	12·60
104·0	13·11
108·0	13·61
110·0	13·86
114·0	14·37

APPENDIX 8

Wine Zones in the E.E.C.

Table Wines

Zone	Natural alcohol contents		Alcohol Enrichment Rule	Alcohol Enrichment Exception	Total alcohol contents after enrichment		Actual alcohol contents	
	Minimum Volume %	(Degree Oechsle)	Maximum Volume % (Alcohol g/l)	Maximum Volume % (Alcohol g/l)	Maximum Volume	(Alcohol g/l)	Minimum Volume	Alcohol g/l
A White Wine			3·5 (28)	4·5 (36)	11·5	(91)		
A Red Wine	5	(44)	4* (33)	5* (40)	12	(95)		
B White Wine	6	(50)	2·5 (20)	3·5 (28)	12	(95)		
B Red Wine					12·5	(99)	8·5	(67)
C I	7	(57)		—	12·5	(99)		
C II	8	(63)	2 (15)	—	12·5	(103)		
C III	8·5	(66)		—	13·5	(107)		

* These figures are in force up to 31.1.1980 for red wines of the Portugieser grape in the provinces of Darmstadt, Rheinhessen-Pfalz, Koblenz and Unterfranken. From 1.2. onwards the same figures as for white wine are applicable.

*Quality Wines of Specific Regions**

Zone	Natural alcohol contents E.E.C. law: Minimum Volume %	Natural alcohol contents National law: Strength at sale (degree Oechsle)	Alcohol enrichment Rule / Exception: Maximum Volume % (Alcohol g/1)	Total alcohol contents after enrichment: Maximum Volume % (Alcohol g/1)	Total alcohol contents: Minimum Volume % (Alcohol g/1)
A	6 (50)		As with table wine	Not fixed by E.E.C. law National law applicable**	9 (71)
B	7 (57)				
C I	8 (63)				
C II	9 (69)				
C III	9·5 (73)				

* In the new German wine law parliament has placed on the federal states the obligation to fix final figures based on climate, soil and grape.

** In the new German wine law the maximum total alcohol contents after enrichment has been fixed as follows: in Zone A for red wine 12·5°; in Zone B for red wine 13°; for all others 12·5°.

APPENDIX 9

Quality Wines Permitted Restsuesse in Rheinland-Pfalz

	1 *Riesling*	2 *Elbling*	3 *All others, including red, Rosé and Rotling*
Ahr	2 : 1		3 : 1
Mittelrhein	2 : 1		3 : 1
Mosel-Saar-Ruwer*	2 : 1	2 : 1	3 : 1
Nahe, without Bereich Sued	2 : 1		3 : 1
Rheinpfalz	2·5 : 1		3 : 1
Rheinhessen	2·5 : 1		3 : 1
Nahe, Bereich Sued	2·5 : 1		3 : 1

	Tafelwein
Rhein	3 : 1
Mosel	3 : 1

Examples: If the Tafelwein originates from a *Weinbaugebiet* or *Untergebiet* (region or subregion) and the label does not give a smaller geographical unit, then the permitted proportion of Restsuesse : alcohol is 3 : 1. If, however, a Tafel wine label from the region 'Mosel' gives a geographical origin the name of a *Bereich* or village, the same proportions are applicable as for a quality wine Mosel-Saar-Ruwer, as stated above.*

Mosel: Riesling 3 : 1
Mosel: Bereich Bernkastel Riesling 2 : 1
Mosel: Bereich Bernkastel Müller-Thurgau (or any other vine but Riesling) 3 : 1

APPENDIX 10

Bavaria Residual sugar – alcohol proportion

Residual sugar – alcohol proportion.

For Tafelwein

1. Wine-growing district Main	
a. White and rosé wines	1 : 3
b. Red wine and Rotling	1 : 5
2. Bereich Lindau	
all varieties of wine	1 : 3

For quality wine

1. Area Franken	
a. White and rosé wines	1 : 3·5
b. Red wine and Rotling	1 : 5
2. Bereich Lindau (Lake Constance)	
all wines	1 : 3

For quality wines with predicate

1. District Franken	
a. White and rosé wines	1 : 3
Quality wine with predicate Kabinett	1 : 3
Quality wine with predicate Spätlese	1 : 3
b. Red wine and Rotling	
Quality wines with predicate Kabinett and Spätlese	1 : 5
2. Bereich Lindau	
all wines	1 : 3

APPENDIX 11

Points Valuation for the Testing of Wines by Sight, Taste and Smell as used in Official Examination

1. *Colour:*

White wine	Red Wine	Rosé	Rotling	Points
pale	bright red	bright	bright	0
rich colour	browny red	red	browny red	0
bright	red	reddish	dark red	1
typical	typical	typical	typical	2

Possible score: 0–2
Minimum points: 2

2. *Clarity:*

	Points
cloudy	0
bright	1
star bright	2

Possible score: 0–2
Minimum points: 1

3. *Bouquet:*

faulty	0
without character	1
harmonious	2
fine bouquet	3
flowery	4

Possible score: 0–4
Minimum points: 2

4. *Taste:*

faulty	0
needs enrichment	1–3
little wine, can stand on its own	4–6
harmonious	7–9
ripe and noble	10–12

Possible score: 0–12
Minimum points: 6

APPENDIX 11

Evaluation Summary of the Individual Marks

Minimum Points	
(a) for quality wine	11
(b) for quality wine with predicate Kabinett	13
(c) for quality wine with predicate Spätlese	14
(d) for quality wine with predicate Auslese	15
(e) for quality wine with predicate Beerenauslese	16
(f) for quality wine with predicate Trockenbeerenauslese	17

APPENDIX 12

Points Valuation for the Testing of Sparkling Wines by Sight, Taste and Smell

		Minimum Points	
	Points	Quality and Sparkling Wine	Predicate Sparkling Wine
1. Sparkle:			
large pearls (bubbles) of short duration	0		
small pearls (bubbles) of long duration	1	1	1
2. Clarity:			
cloudy	0		
clear	1	1	1
star-bright	2		
3. Colour:			
more or less than normal	1		
typical	2	2	2
4. Bouquet:			
faulty or without character	0 to 1		
vinous, clean	2	2	
typical for the origin or the vine	3 to 4		3
5. Taste:			
faulty, without character or plump	0 to 2		
small but fresh, pleasing	3 to 5	5	
racy, elegant or steely	6 to 7		7
ripe, noble	8 to 9		
6. Balance of Acidity – Sweetness – Alcohol:			
not harmonious	0		
harmonious	1	1	1
excellent	2		
Total	20	12	15

Bibliography

Allen, H. Warner, *The Romance of Wine*, London 1931.
Arbeitsgemenischaft Bad., (Herwig E.) *Weinland Baden Württemberg*, Mannheim 1959.
Basserman-Jordan, F.v., *Die Geschichte des Weinbaus*, Frankfurt 1923.
Das Weinmuseum etc. zu Speyer am Rhein, Speyer 1947.
Der Weinbau der Pfalz im Altertum, Speyer 1947
Becker, Theo, *In der Rebe das Leben*, Neustadt 1970.
Berger, *Die Rheinreise*, Bonn 1954.
Berlet, J., *Pfalz und Wein*, Neustadt 1928.
Bewerunge, W., *Deutscher Wein an Donau und Rhein.*
Binding, R. G., *Moselfahrt aus Liebeskummer*, Potsdam 1941.
Boehle, *Gastlichkeit am Oberrhein*, Heidelberg 1961.
Christoffel, K., *Rebe und Wein in Goethes Weltbild*, Heidelberg 1948
Trost und Weisheit des Weines, Heidelberg 1949.
Claus, *Der Riesling und seine Weine*, Geisenheim, 1967.
Deichmann, Dr. and Wolf, *Weinchronik*, Berlin 1950.
Deutsche Weinzeitung (periodical Mainz), 'Von der Traube bis zu Flaschenfullung', Mainz 1950.
Engel, *Die Weinbehandlung*, Vienna 1950.
Foreign Office, *Vine Culture and Wine Trade of Germany*, London 1907.
Gareis, Karl, *Die Staatlichen Domänenweingüter im Rheingau*, Eltville 1929.
Goldschmidt, Fritz, *Weingesetz*, Mainz 1933.
Deutschlands Weinbauorte und Weinbergslagen, Mainz 1951.
Hallgarten, S. F., *Rhineland Wineland*, London 1967.
Harpers, *Wine Gazette* (Periodical).
Hennig, *Chemische Untersuchungsmethoden fuer Weinbereiter*, Stuttgart 1950.
Herwig, Eugen, *Weinfahrten in Schwaben*, Mannheim 1971.
Fahrten durch das Badenland, Mannheim 1971.
Heuss, Theo, *Weinbau und Weingaertnerstand in Heilbronn*, Neustadt 1950.
Hieronimi, H., *Weingesetz*, Munich 1958.

Hofbauer, O., *Handbuch der praktischen Kellerwirtschaft*, Bobzano 1920.
Hoffman, Gayer, *Das schwäbische Weinland*, Stuttgart 1965.
Hölscher, Georg, *Das Buch vom Rhein*, Cologne 1925
Holthoefer-Neuse, *Das Weingesetz*, Berlin 1952.
Jeffs, J., *The Wines of Europe*, London 1971.
Johnson, Hugh, *World Atlas of Wine*, London 1972.
Jung, H., *Wenn man beim Weinesitzt*, Duisburg 1949.
Kayser, E., *Weinbau und Winzer im Rheingau*, Wiesbaden 1906.
Klenk, E., *Die Weinbeurteilung*, Stuttgart, 1960.
Klinger, *Fuehrer durch das Weinbaugebiet der Rheinpfalz*.
Kloster Eberbach, *Deutscher Kunstverlag*, Berlin 1947.
Lebensfreude aus Rheinhessen (Omnibus edition by Winegrowers' Association), Mainz 1954.
Koch, H. J., *Weinwirtschaftsgesetz*, Neustadt 1963, 1965.
Weingesetz 1969, Neustadt *1961*.
Weingesetz 1971, Frankfurt *1971/1974*.
Linck, Otto, *Das Weinland am Neckar*, 1964.
Loeb, O. W., and Prittie, T., *Moselle*, London 1972.
Mangold, *Schwäbische Weinstrasse*, Stuttgart.
Matuschka, R.v., *Neuzeitlicher Weinbau*, Frankfurt, 1927.
Meissner, *Praktische Behandlung kranker Weine*, Stuttgart 1924.
Meyer, Felix, *Rhein-Mosel-Pfalz*, Wiesbaden 1926/7.
Weinbau und Weinhandel an Mosel, Saar und Ruwer, Coblenz 1926.
Mueller, K., 'Geschichte des badischen', *Weinbaus*, Lahr 1953.
Nessler, *Die Bereitung Pflege u. Untersuchung des Weines* (9), Stuttgart 1930.
Popp, F., *Das Moselland und sein Wein*, Berncastel 1948.
Puls, *Die Weinkostprobe*, Punderich 1940.
Reben, *Beschreibende Sortenliste*, Bundessortenant (Office for registration of vines), Hanover 1971.
Redding, *History and Description of Modern Wines*, London 1851.
Renz, Neumann, *Das neue Weinrecht 1970*, Stuttgart, 1969.
Rheinlands Weine, Cologne 1928.
Rheinweine Hessens, Mainz 1927.
Rouel, *La Vigne et les Vins Allemands*, Coblenz 1950.
Rudd, H. R., *Hocks and Moselles*, London 1935.
Rupp, *Staatliche Weinbaudomäne Mainz*, Mainz 1951.
Ruthe, Wilhelm, *Flaschenweinmuseum im Kurhaus Wiesbaden*, Austria 1948.
Saintsbury, George, *Notes on a Cellar-Book*, London 1921.
Schätzlein, C. H., *Die Gewinnung des Weines*, (6), Neustadt 1949
Der Ausbau der Weine, Neustadt, 1946.

Tätigkeitsbericht der Landesanstalt fuer Wein-, Obst-, und Gartenbau, Neustadt a.d. Haardt 1950.
Scheu, G., *Mein Winzerbuch*, Neustadt 1950.
Schmidt di Simoni, E., *Die edlen Weine der Pfalz*, Stuttgart 1968.
Schoenberger, F., *Geschichte von Zeltingen und Rachtig an der Mosel*, Neustadt 1939.
Schoonmaker, F., *Encyclopedia of Wine*, London 1967.
Simon, A., and Arntz, H., *Champagne und Sekt*, Berlin 1962.
Simon, A., and Hallgarten, S. F., *The Great Wines of Germany*, New York 1963.
Sneets, *Die Abtei Eberbach*, 1943.
Spang, F. S., *Vom Weinbau in Gau-Bickelheim*, Gau-Algesheim 1947.
Sprater, *Rheinischer Wein und Weinbau*, Heidelberg 1948.
Stein, G., *Reise durch deu deutschen Weingarten*, Munich 1966.
Steinberg, *Die Lehr- und Forschungsanstalt Geisenheim*, Wiesbaden 1949.
Third International Oenological Symposium, Stellenbosch 1972.
Tovey, C., *Wine and Wine Countries*, London 1877.
Troost, G., *Die Technologie des Weines*, Stuttgart 1953.
Zipfel, W., *Weinrecht Kommentar*, Munich 1972.

Periodicals:

Rebe und Weine, Weinsberg.
Der Deutsche Weinbau, Wiesbaden.
Weinberg und Keller, Bernkastel.
Die Weinwirtschaft, Neustadt.

Index

Abtswind, 329
Abtweiler, 240
Achkarren, 318
Acids:
ascorbic, 120
carbonic, 120, 130
citric, 180
metatartaric, 121
silicic, 120
sorbic, 131
sulphurous, 180
tannic, 120
tartaric, crystals, 140
Acidity, 94, 132
Acids, 91, 99
Active carbon, 120
Affaltrach, 311
Affenthal, Affenthaler, 320, 333, 338
Ageing of wines, 81, 132, 166
Ahr, 334
Ahrweiler, 194, 335
Albalonga, 74, 75
Alben, 72
Albersweiler, 199
Albig, 217, 218, 219
Albisheim, 207
Albumen, 84, 91
Alcohol, 128; *see also* Appendices
Alf, 279
Alken, 282
Allen, H. Warner, 61, 213
Alsenz, 193, 231, 238
Alsheim, 217, 222, 223
Altdorf, 200
Altenahr, 335
Altenbamberg, 193, 238, 241
Altitude of vineyards, 44
Altschweier, 319
Alzey, 210, 215, 216, 217
American vine, 28
America roots, 27
Amides, 91
Ammonium, 91
Andel, 268, 269
Annaberg Estate, 206, 209
Annweiler, 199
Anreicherung, 113
Ansbach, 323
Appenheim, 227
Arabinose, 125
Armsheim, 228
Arzheim, 199
Aschaffenburg, 327
Aspisheim, 224
Assmannshausen, 287, 300, 335, 338
Auen, 239
Auerbach, 301
Auggen, 317
Augusta Luise grape, 74
Aulhausen, 300
Auslese, 104, 105
Ausonius, 23, 252, 265
Austria, 111
Auxerrois grape, 71
Avelsbach, Domain, 193, 260, 261
Ayl, 256

Babelroth, 199
Bacchus vine, 73
Bacharach, 195, 242
Bachem, 335
Bad = Spa, *see under* individual names of towns
Baden, 303, 312
Baden-Baden, 318, 319
Badenheim, 217, 224
Bahlingen, 318
Bamberg, 323
Basserman-Jordan von, 166, 202, 209
Battenberg, 206
Bausendorf, 276
Bechenheim, 216
Bechtheim, 215
Bechtolsheim, 217, 218

Beckstein, 320
Beerenauslese, 106
Beilstein, 311
Bekond, 267
Bellheim, 200
Bengel, 276
Bensheim, 287, 301, 302
Bentonite, 84, 120
Bereich, 50
Bergstrasse, Badische, 316, 320
Bergstrasse, Hessische, 301
Bergzabern, Bad, 198, 199
Bermersheim, 215, 228
Berncasteler Doctor, 58, 125, 269
Bernkastel, 260, 263, 264, 269
Besigheim, 310
Beuren, 279
Bible, 19, 20
Bickensohl, 318
Biebelnheim, 217, 218
Biebelsheim, 223, 224
Billigheim-Ingenheim, 199
Bingen, 193, 223, 224, 225, 232
Bingerbrueck, 232, 239
Birkenfeld, 231
Birkweiler, 199
Bischoffingen, 318
Bismarck, 298
Bisserheim, 208
Black Forest, 195
Blauer (Blue) Spaetburgunder, 72
Blauer (Blue) Trollinger, 72
Blending, 38, 40, 123
Blends, E.E.C., 157
  naming of, 158
Blossoming, statistics, 363
Board of Examination, 135
Bobenheim, 204
Bockenau, 235, 239
Bockenheim, 197, 207
Bocksbeutel, 191, 320, 325
Bodenheim, 193, 216, 218
Bodensee, *see* Constance, Lake of
Boebingen, 200
Boechingen, 200
Boeddiger, 43, 286
Bolanden, 57, 207
Boos, 240
Boppard, 243
Bornheim, 200, 228
Bosenheim, 223, 241
Botrytis gris, 98
Bottle sickness, 132
Bottling, 130
Bouquet, 96, 140
Brackenheim, 338
Brands, 160
Brauneberg, 264, 267, 268
Braunweiler, 235, 239
Breider, Prof. Dr. Hans, 69, 70, 74, 330
Breisach, 318
Breisgau (Bereich), 319
Bremer Ratskeller, 141
Bremm, 279
Brentano, Freiherr v., 302
Bretzenheim, 233, 240
Briedel, 277
Briedern, 280
Britzingen, 317
Bruchsal, 320
Bruttig-Fankel, 280
Bubenheim, 207, 228
Buedesheim, 223, 232
Buehl, 318, 319
Buerklin-Wolf, Dr., 209
Buhl, v., 209
Bullay, 280
Burg, 275, 276
Burg Layen, 239
Burgen, 147, 268, 282
Burgsponsheim, 235, 239
Burgundy, white, 71
Burrweiler, 198, 200

Cabinet, *see* Kabinett
Caesar, 21, 22
Callbach, 241
Cannstatt, Bad, 310
Carbonic acid, 99, 130
Casel, *see* Kasel
Casks, giant, 24, 332
  sizes of, 162
Castell, 330
Caub, *see* Kaub
Certificate of quality, 101
Chaptalization, 113
Charlemagne, 23, 36, 220
Chasselas grape, 72
Château Yquem, 110
Chlorophyll, 92
Cicero, 22
Citric acid, 94
Cleansing of must, 112
Clevner grape, 303, 318
Climate, 43
Climatic details, 362
Coblenz, *see* Koblenz

Cochem, *see* Kochem
Colleges, viticultural, 84
Cologne (Koeln), 191
Colour, 139
Commersheim, 200
Constance, Lake of (Bodensee), 303, 316, 331
Control Board, 135
Control number, 135
Corkiness, 140
Corks, 132, 168
Corkscrews, 143
Courtillier musque, 71
Criesbach, 311
Crossings, 74
Crystals, tartaric acid, 140
Cues, *see* Kues
Customs Union, 25

Dackenheim, 205
Dagobert, King, 274
Dalberg, 240
Dalheim, 217, 221
Dammheim, 200
Daubach, 239
Dautenheim, 216
De-acidification of must, 96, 128
Deckrotwein, 75, 159
Deidesheim, 166, 202, 204, 208
Dernau, 335
Dertingen, 321
Detzem, 267
Deutschherrenberg, 273
Devrient, Ludwig, 179
Dexheim, 217, 264
Dextrose, 91
Dhron, 264, 265
Diabetics, wine for, 71
Dieblich, 282
Dieburg, 302
Dienheim, 217, 222, 223
Dierbach, 198
Dietersheim, 223, 232
Dietlingen, 320
Dietzenbach, 302
Diodor, 21
Dirmstein, 208
Diseases, 79
Disraeli, 298
Dittelsheim, 215
Doctor, *see under* Bernkastel
Doerrenbach, 198
Doktor, 264
Dolgesheim, 217, 222
Domains, State:
  Ahr, 335
  Baden, 322
  Franconia, 327
  Hessen, 162, 286, 287
  Mosel, 260
  Nahe, 235
Domitian, Emperor, 22
Dorfprozelten, 328
Dorn-Duerkheim, 217, 223
Dorsheim, 240
Dotzheim, 286
Drakon, 20
Dromersheim, 224
Duchroth, 238, 240
Duerkheim, Bad, 196, 201, 204, 209, 337
Duesseldorf, 191
Durbach, 66, 318
Dusemond, 268

East Germany, 30
Eberbach, Kloster, 243
Ebernburg, 237
Ebersheim (Mainz), 217
Ebringen, 317
Eckelsheim, 229
Eckenroth, 240
Edenkoben, 198, 200
Edesheim, 200
Ediger-Eller, 279
Edward III, King, 37
Edward VII, King, 263
E.E.C. Blends, 157
Efringen-Kirchen, 317
Ehrenfelser, 71
Ehrenstetten, 317
Eibingen, 299
Eich, 217, 222
Eichelberg, 311
Einselthum, 207
Einsheim, 217, 222
Einzellage (single site), 50
Eisental, 320, 334
Eiswein, 86, 107, 132, 167, 177
Eitelsbach, 258, 262
Elbling grape, 61, 71, 247, 254, 303
Ellenz-Poltersdorf, 280
Ellerstadt, 202, 204
Ellhofen, 311
Ellmendingen, 320
Eltville, 287, 289
Emmendingen, 319
Engelstadt, 228

Enkirch, 264, 275
Enrichment, 94, 113
Ensch, 267
Ensheim, 228
Entschleimen (cleansing), 112
Eppelsheim, 215
Erbach (Bergstrasse), 301
Erbach (Rheingau), 287, 291
Erbes-Briedesheim, 228
Erden, 264, 274, 275
Ernst, 280
Erpolzheim, 205, 206
Erzeugerabfuellung, 153, 155
Eschbach, 199
Eschenau, 311
Escherndorf, 325, 330
Esselborn, 215
Essenheim, 217
Essingen, 200
Esslingen, 310
Examination, 102
  number, 135
  points, 378, 380
Export, 128
Extract, 105

Faber grape, 71
Faerbertraube, 75
Fancy names, 160
Feilbingert, 241
Fell, 265
Fellbach, 310
Felsberg, 43, 286
Fendant, 72
Fermentation, 98, 99
Fessenbach, 318
Filters, 131
Filzen, 256
Findling, 75
Flein, 310
Fleischmann, Dr., 209
Flemlingen, 200
Floersheim, 286
Flomborn, 215
Flonheim, 228
Flurbereinigung, 28, 33
Flussbach, 276
Fog, 44
Foil covering, 86
Fontanara, 74
Forchtenberg, 312
Forst, 196, 203, 204, 208, 337
Framersheim, 217, 218
France, 39
Franconia, 70
Franconian wines, 323
Frankfurt am Main, 286, 287
Frankweiler, 199
Franzenheim, 258
Frauenstein, 286
Freckenfeld, 198
Frei-Laubersheim, 223, 229, 230
Freiburg, 316, 319–22
Freimersheim, 200, 216
Freinsheim, 205, 206
Freisamer vine, 71, 313
Freisbach, 200
French Revolution, 24
Frettenheim, 215
Friedelsheim, 202, 204
Friesenheim (Baden), 319
Friesenheim (Rheinhessen), 217, 221
Frost, 31
Fructose, 91
Fruehburgunder vine, 72
Fruit sugar, 91
Fuder, 162
Fuellwein, 159
Fuerfeld, 223, 230

Gabsheim, 217
Gallia (Gaul), 21
Gau-Algesheim, 226, 227
Gau-Bickelheim, 229
Gau-Bischofsheim, 216, 218
Gau-Heppenheim, 217, 218
Gau-Odernheim, 217, 218
Gau-Weinheim, 229
Gauersheim, 207
Geisenheim, 33, 56, 297, 298
  Viticultural College, 84
Gemmrigheim, 310
Geneva, Lake of, 72
Genheim, 239
Gensingen, 223, 224, 232
Gewuerztraminer, 65
Gimbsheim, 217, 222
Gimmeldingen, 201, 209
Glan, 239
Gleishorbach, 198
Gleisweiler-Oberhofen, 198
Gleiszellen, 198
Glottertal, 319
Glucose, 91
Godramstein, 199
Goecklingen, 199
Goedecke, Director, 236
Goennheim, 204

Goethe, J. W. von, 220, 226, 324
Gormheim, 202
Graach, 271, 272
Graefenhausen, 200
Graft, 27
Grafted vines, 80
Grantschen, 311
Grape crushing, 98
Grape sugar, 91
Gravity, specific of must, 93
Greeks, 21
Grober, 72
Grobriesling, 72
Grolsheim, 208, 223, 224, 232
Gross-Umstadt, 302
Gross-Winternheim, 228
Grossbottwar, 311
Grossfischlingen, 200
Grossheppach, 311
Grossheubach, 328
Grosskarlbach, 208
Grosslage, 50, 53
Grossniedesheim, 208
Gruenstadt, 206
Guels, 282
Guldental, 233, 239
Gumbsheim, 229
Gundelsheim, 310
Gundersheim, 215
Gundheim, 215
Guntersblum, 217, 222, 223
Gutedel grape, 61, 71, 72, 316
Gutenberg, 239

Haardt, 194, 209
Hackenheim, 223, 229
Hagnau, 316
Hahnheim, 217, 221
Hainfeld, 200
Hallgarten (Nahe), 241
Hallgarten (Rheingau), 27, 294
Haltingen, 317
Hambach, 198, 201
Hamburg, 191
Hamm (Boppard), 243
Hamm (Saar), 256
Hammelburg, 328
Hanau, 323, 327
Handthal, 329
Hangen-Weisheim, 215
Hargesheim, 233, 240
Harsberg, 311
Harvesting:
  start, 87
  time, 88
  yield, 366
Harxheim (Rheinhessen), 216
Harxheim (Palatinate), 196, 207
Hattenheim, 287–91, 292
Hatzenport, 282
Haustrunk, 107
Heating of wine, 121
Hechtsheim (Mainz), 218
Heddesheim, 233
Hedelfingen, 310
Heidelberg, 24, 195, 320
Heidesheim, 227
Heilbronn, 306, 310
Heimersheim (Ahr), 335
Heine, 243
Helfensteiner, 72
Henderson, 252
Hennig, Professor, 85
Henry VI, Emperor, 199
Heppenheim, 301
Hergenfeld, 240
Hergersweiler, 199
Heroldrebe, 72
Herxheim, 147, 205, 199
Hessen, 285
Hessen-Nassau, 287
Hessheim, 208
Hessloch, 215
Heuchelheim, 199
Hillebrand, Walter, 105
Hillesheim, 217, 222
Hochdorf-Assenheim, 202
Hochheim, 286, 287, 288, 289
Hochstadt, 200
Hochstaetten, 241
Hockweiler, 258
Hoerstein, 325, 326, 327, 330
Hoesslinsuelz, 311
Hofstueck (Grosslage), 202
Hohen-Suelzen, 216
Hohenstauffen, 199
Horrweiler, 224
Hueffelsheim, 234, 240
Humidity, 44
'Huntsche Wein', 71
Hupperath, 276
Huxelrebe, 71
Hybrids, 38

Ice wine, 167, *see also* Eiswein
Ihringen, 264, 318
Ilbesheim, 199
Immersheim, 208

Impflingen, 199
Impregnation method, 180
Improved wines, 108
Ingelfingen, 311
Ingelheim, 23, 227, 228, 337
Insheim, 199
Iphofen, 326, 330
Ippesheim, 223, 241, 328
Irsch, 257

Jagst valley, 308
Jechstingen, 317
Jefferson, Thomas, 291
Jemsched, 20
Johannisberg, 23, 56, 297; *see also under* Schloss Johannisberg
Johnson, Hugh, 200, 294
Josephshof, 272
Jugenheim, 228

Kabinett, 102
Kaisertuhl, 313, 316
Kallmuth, 325
Kallstadt, 196, 204, 205, 206, 209
Kaltenes, 282
Kandel, 198
Kanzem, 256
Kanzler vine, 71
Kapellen-Drusweiler, 199
Kappelrodeck, 318
Kapsweyer, 198
Karl Friedrich von Baden, 37
Karlinke, Prof. Dr. H., 85
Karthaeuserhofberg, 258, 259, 262
Kasel, 262
Kassel, 286
Kastel-Staadt, 257
Kaub (Caub), 242
Kellerabfuellung, 156
Kellerman, Marshal, 297
Kenn, 264
Kenzingen, 319
Kerner vine, 71, 73
Kerzenheim, 57, 208
Kesten, 268
Kiedrich, 287, 289, 290
Kimich, 209
Kindenheim, 207
Kinheim, 276
Kirchberg, 310
Kirchheim-Bolanden, 207, 208
Kirrweiler, 200
Kirschroth, 240
Kissingen, Bad, 323, 328
Kittel, Dr., 324
Kitzingen, 325, 331
Klein-Umstadt, 302
Klein-Winterheim, 216, 217
Kleinberger grape, 72
Kleinbottwar, 311
Kleinelbling, 72
Kleinfischlingen, 200
Kleinheppach, 311
Kleinkarlbach, 206
Kleinniedesheim, 208
Kleinpereich, 72
Klevner (Clevner), 150
Klingelberger, 150, 303
Klingen, 199
Klingenberg (Franconia), 338
Klingenmuenster, 198
Kloster Marienthal, 193
Klotten, 281
Kluesserath, 267
Knittelsheim, 200
Knoeringen, 200
Kobern-Gondorf, 282
Koblenz (Coblenz), 243, 244, 282
Kochem, 281
Kocher valley, 306, 308
Koendringen, 319
Koenen, 256
Koengernheim, 217, 221
Koenigsbach, 201, 208
Koenigschaffhausen, 318
Koenigshofen, 321
Koewerich, 267
Kokhi, 20
Konstanz (Constance), 316
Konz, 254, 256
Korb, 311
Korlingen, 258
Kraichgau, 303, 316, 320
Kreuznach, Bad, 223, 232, 240, 241
Kreuzwertheim, 328
Kroev, 264, 276
Kues (Cues), 264, 269
Kurpfalz, 195

Label, 154
Lagen, general, 50
names of, 51
Lahn, river, 243
Lahr, 318
Lambsheim, 206
Landau, 199
Landeck, castle of, 199
Langenlonsheim, 233, 240

Laubenheim (Mainz), 217
Laubenheim (Nahe), 232, 240
Lauda, 321
Lauf, 319
Lauffen, 306, 310
Laumersheim, 208
Lehmann-Hilgard, 209
Lehmen, 282
Lehrensteinfels, 311
Leinsweiler, 199
Leistadt, 196, 205
Leiwen, 267
Lesegut, aus dem, 153, 155
Levulose, 91
Lex Salica, 20
Liebfrauenstift, 211
Liebfraumilch, 152, 159, 211, 212
Lieser, 264, 268, 269
Limes, 22
Limberger vine, 72, 77
Linz, 243
Loef, 282
Loerrach, 317
Loerzweiler, 216, 217, 218, 220
Loesenich, 276
Loewenstein, 311
Longfellow, 298
Longuich, 264
Lonsheim, 228
Lorch, 300
Lorchhausen, 300
Lorelei rock, 242
Louis the German, 23
Ludwigshoehe, 217, 222, 223
Lustadt, 200
Luxembourg, 39, 48, 68, 244

Madeleine Angevine grape, 71, 74
Madenburg, 199
Madonnenlaendchen, 321
Maikammer, 198, 200
Main, river, 325
Mainriesling, 68, 69
Mainz, 193, 210, 216, 217
Mainz-Kostheim, 286, 289
Malic acid, 91
Malolactic fermentation, 95, 99
Malterdingen, 319
Mandel, 234, 239
Mannheim, 195
Manubach, 242
Marbach, 310
Marcobrunn, 149, 291
Marienburg, 190
Mariengarten, Grosslage, 203
Mariensteiner grape, 74
Marienthal (Ahr), 335
Marienthal, Kloster Rheingau, 194
Maring-Noviand, 267
Markgraefler wine, 313, 317
Markgrafschaft, 316
Marseilles, 21
Martinstein, 239
Martinsthal, 289, 290
Matuschka-Greiffenclau, Graf, 141, 296
Mauchenheim, 216
Mauerwein, 313, 320
Maximin-Gruenhaeuser, 262
Mayschoss, 335
Meckenheim, 202
Meddersheim, 240
Meersburg, 191, 316, 322
Meerspinne, 202
Mehring, 265
Meisenheim, 240
Mennig, 256
Mergentheim, Bad, 312
Mertesdorf, 262
Mertesheim, 207
Merxheim, 239
Méthode Champenoise, 180
Mettenheim, 217, 222
Metternich, Fuerst v., 297
Michelbach (Franconia), 326
Michelbach (Wuerttemberg), 311
Micro-climate, 46
Mildew, 80
Miltenberg, 328
Minfeld, 198
Minheim, 266
Mittelheim, 50, 294, 295
Moelsheim, 216
Moerzheim, 199
Mommenheim, 217, 221
Monasteries, influence of, 23
Monsheim (including Kriegsheim), 216
Montagna grape, 74
Monzernheim, 215
Monzingen, 238, 239
Morio-Muskat, 70, 73
Morscheid, 258, 263
Morschheim, 207
Mosel Valley, 245
Moselbluemchen, 283
Moselkern, 281
Moselsuersch, 282

Mostgewicht, 93
Mueden, 281
Muelheim, 264, 268
Muelhofen-Appenhofen, 199
Mueller-Rebe, 72
Mueller-Thurgau Rebe, 64, 68, 73, 247
Muellheim, 317
Muenster-Sarmsheim, 232
Muenster am Stein, Bad, 237, 240
Munich (Muenchen), 191
Muscatona, 74
Muskat-Ottonel, 71
Muskateller, 319
Mussbach, 201, 209
Must, 59
  acidity of, 94
  chemical analysis, 93
  cleansing of, 112
  de-acidification, 96
  evaluation of, 92

Nack, 228
Nackenheim, 210, 217–19
Nahe, river, 230
Nassau, Duke of, 287
'Natur', 150
Natural wine, 38
Nature trail (Baden), 321
Neckar, river, 321
Neckarsulm, 310
Neckarweihingen, 310
Neef, 279
Nehren, 278
Nervi, 22
Neu-Bamberg, 223, 229
Neudorf, 290
Neuenahr, Bad, 335
Neuleiningen, 206
Neumagen, 264, 265
Neustadt, 201, 209
Neuweier, 313, 319, 326
Nieder-Hilbersheim, 227
Nieder-Olm, 217, 221
Nieder-Wiesen, 228
Niederemmel, 266
Niederfell, 282
Niederhausen, 193, 235, 236, 237, 240
Niederhorbach, 198
Niederkirchen, 202, 209
Niedernhall, 312
Niederotterbach, 198
Niederrimsingen, 317
Niefernheim, 196, 207
Nierstein, 52, 57, 193, 210–17, 219
Nitrates, 91
Nitrogen, 121
Noah, 19
Nobling vine, 75, 313
Nonnenhorn, 330
Norheim, 237, 240
Nussbaum, 240
Nussdorf, 200, 201

Ober-Hilbersheim, 227
Ober-Olm, 216, 217
Oberdiebach, 242
Oberemmel, 255, 256
Oberfell, 282
Oberhaardt (Upper Haardt), 197
Oberhausen (Nahe), 238, 240
Oberhausen (Palatinate), 200, 239
Oberkirch, 318
Obermosel (Bereich), 253
Oberotterbach, 198
Oberrinsingen, 317
Oberrotweil, 318, 338
Oberstenfeld, 311
Oberstreit, 240
Obersuelzen, 208
Obertuerkheim, 310
Obrigheim, 207
Ockenheim, 224
Ockfen, 255, 260, 261
Odenwald, 195
Odernheim, 239, 240
Oechsle:
  acidity, statistics, 364
  standard, 93
  tables (alcohol), 371
Oehringen, 308
Oesterreicher, 67, 197
Oestrich, 56, 294, 295
Oestringen, 320
Offenbach (Palatinate), 200, 239
Offenburg, 318, 322
Offstein, 216
Oidium, 80
Olewig, 258
Oppenheim, 193, 210, 216, 217, 222
Optima grape, 75
Ordish, 82
Originalabfuellung, 142, 156
Originalabzug, 149
Ortenau, 313, 316, 318
Ortsteil, 56, 156
Osann-Monzel, 268

Osiris, 20
Osiris grape, 74
Osthofen, 215
Ottersheim, 200, 208
Otto II, Emperor, 287
Oxidation, 99

Palatinate, 194
Partenheim, 227
Pellingen, 256
Peptones, 91
Perkeo, 320
Perle, Wuerzburger, 70, 331
Perlwein, 59, 126, 180
Peronospera, 44
Pests, 79
Pfaffen-Schwabenheim, 223, 224
Pfaffengrund, 202
Pfaffenweiler, 317
Pfalz (Palatinate), 194
Pfalzgraf, 194
Pfeddersheim, 211
Pfedelbach, 311
Phylloxera (Reblaus), 26, 82, 259, 306, 335
Piesport, 264, 266
Pinot, Chardonnay, 71
  Gris, 69
  Noir, 72
Pitchstone, 196
Planig, 223, 241
Plantings, new, 30
Platten, 276
Pleitersheim, 224, 229
Pliny, 36
Pluwig, 258
Poelich, 267
Polyvinyl Polypyorolidone, 121
Pommern, 281
Portugieser, blauer (Portuguese blue grape), 72, 73
Posidanius, 21
Potassium bitartrate, 91
  ferrocyanide, 120
Praedikatssekt, 179, 182
Probus, Roman Emperor, 22
Production, statistics, 367
Puenderich, 277

Qualitaetsschaumwein, 181
Quality certificate, 101
Quality wine (Qualitätswein), 107
Quarts de Chaume, 110
Queichhambach, 200
Queichheim, 199

Rabelais, 325
Rachtig, 273
Racking, 123
Raeuschling vine, 115, 303
Rainfall, 44
  statistics, 362, 366
Randersacker, 328, 330
Ranschbach, 199
Rationalization, 33
Rauenthal, 287, 289, 290
Raumbach, 240
Reblaus (phylloxera), 26
Reblausgesetz (phylloxera law), 26
Rech, 335
Refrigeration of wine, 122
Rehborn, 240
Reicholzheim, 321
Reil, 277
Rems valley, 306, 308
Reorganization of vineyards, 33
Reppendorf, 325
Residual sugar, 377
Restsuesse (Restzucker), 113
Revolution, French, 24
Rheingau, 285, 287
Rhine front (Rheinfront), 210
Rhinehessia (Rheinhessen), 209
Rhodt, 200, 338
Richard Lionheart, King, 199
Rieslaner, 64, 68, 69, 74
Riesling grape, 61, 247, 316
Riol, 265
Ripening, statistics, 363, 364, 365
Rittersheim, 57, 207
Rivaner, 68
Rivenich, 266
Riveris, 258, 263
Rochusberg, 225
Roedelsee, 330
Roedersheim-Gronau, 202
Roemerglass, 191
Rohracker, 310
Rohrbach, 199
Romans, 21, 36, 190
Root-vines, 27
Roschbach, 200
Roseewein, 124
Rossdorf, 302
Rot-Weiss, 336
Rotberger, 75
Rotenberg, 310
Rotling, 101

Roxheim, 235, 240
Rudd, Hugh R., 294
Ruedesheim (Nahe), 146, 234, 240
Ruedesheim (Rheingau), 146, 167, 190, 287, 299
Ruemmelsheim, 240
Ruessingen, 57, 207
Rulaender vine, 69, 73, 316
Ruppertsberg, 202, 208
Ruwer, 261

Saale, river, 325
Saarburg, 254, 257
Saemling, *see* Scheurebe
St. Aldegund, 279
St. Barbarawein, 104, 149
St. Hildegard, 324
St. Johann, 227
St. Katharinen, 235, 239
St. Kilian, 23
St. Laurent grape, 77
St. Martin, 198, 200
St. Nikolauswein, 104, 149
Saintsbury, Prof., 333
Salic emperors, 199
Salica, *Lex*, 20
Sasbach, 317
Sasbachwalden, 319
Saulheim, 217
Sausage market, 204
Schaidt, 198
Schallstadt-Wolfenweiler, 317
Scharlachberg (Bingen), 232
Scharlachkopf, 231
Scharzberg, 255
Scharzhofberg, 156
Schaumwein, 179, 380
Scheurebe, 64, 70, 73
Schierstein, 286, 289
Schiller wine, 101, 337, 338
Schlatt, 317
Schleich, 267
Schloss Boeckelheim (Bereich), 232–235
Schloss Johannisberg, 82, 149, 150, 151, 156, 162, 297
Schloss Vollrads, 141, 149, 151, 156, 296
Schlossboeckelheim (village), 193, 232, 235, 240
Schnaiten, 311
Schoden, 255
Schoenberg, 301, 302
Schoeneberg, 240
Schornsheim, 217
Schriesheim, 320
Schubring, Dr., 193
Schwabenheim, 228
Schwabsburg, 219
Schwaigern, 338
Schwegenheim, 200
Schweich, 265
Schweigen-Rechtenbach, 197, 198
Schweighofen, 198
Seeheim, 302
Seewein, 313, 331
Sehlem, 266
Sekt, 179, 181, 380
Selzen, 217, 221
Senheim, 280
Septimer, 75
Serrig, 193, 255, 257, 260, 261
Sickingen, Franz von, 237
Siebeldingen, 200
Siebengebirge, 241
Siefersheim, 229
Siegerrebe, 71
Silesia, 23
Silvaner, 67, 316
Silver chloride, 121
Simon, André L., 15
Sinzheim, 319
Sisi vine, 74
Site, *see* Lagen
Site names, 51
Slate, 246
Sleepy fruit, 91
Sobernheim, 240
Soergenloch, 217, 221
Soil, 42, 196
Solon, 20
Sommerau, 258
Sommerloch, 239
Spaetburgunder, 73, 316
Spaetlese, 104
Spessart hills, 323
Speyer, 190
Spiesheim, 217, 218
Spindler, Wilhelm, 209
Sponheim (Nahe), 235
Sponsheim (Rheinhessen), 224, 232, 239
Sprendlingen, 227
Spritzig, 99, 130
Stabilizationsfonds, 31
Stadecken-Elsheim, 217
State Domain, *see* Domains
Statistics, general, 29

Staudernheim, 240
Steeg, 242
Steigerwald, 325
Stein wines, 324
Steinbach, 319
Steinberg, 23, 149, 156, 163, 164, 287, 293
Stein-Bockenheim, 229
Steinfeld, 198
Steinhardt, 241
Steinweiler, 199
Stetten, 207, 311
Storage of wine, 140
Stromberg, 233
Struempfelbach, 311
Stueck, 162
Stuttgart, 307, 310
Suebs, 22
Suessreserve, 113, 126, 160, 338
Suessung, *see* Sweetening
Suelzbach (Wuertt), 311
Sugars, kinds of, 91
Sulphur, 118
Sulphurous acid, 37
Sulzbach, 320
Sulzberg, 317
Sulzfeld (Baden), 320
Sulzfeld (Franconia), 325
Sulzheim, 228
Sunshine hours, 45 and Appendix 2
Sweetening, 94, 108
Switzerland, 39, 68
Sylvaner, *see* Silvaner
Sylvesterwein, 104, 149

Tacitus, 22
Tafelwein, 157
Talheim, 310
Tank fermentation, 183
Tannic acid, 91
Tartaric acid, 91, 140
Tasting, 135
Tauber valley, 308, 321, 325
Temmels, 260
Temperature, 43
  statistics, 362, 366
Tiefenthal, 224, 229
Tiefrot grape, 335
Tiengen, 317
Traben-Trarbach, 260, 264, 273, 274
Traisen, 237, 240
Traminer vine, 61, 65, 303, 316
Transvasion method, 180
Traubenmaische, 59
Traubenmost, 59
Treatments, chemical, 118
Treis-Karden, 281
Trier, 190, 193, 257, 258, 260, 262
Trifels, castle of, 199
Trittenheim, 264, 265
Trockenbeerenauslese, 106
Trogus Pompeius, 21
Trollinger vine, 71, 72, 304
Troost, G., 90
Twelfth Night wine, 105

Udenheim, 217
Ueberlingen, 316
Uelversheim, 217, 222
Uerzig, 264, 274
Uhlbach, 310
Undenheim, 217, 221
Ungstein, 196, 204, 205, 209
Untertuerkheim, 310

Valentinian, Roman Emperor, 220
Varnhalt, 319, 326
Vegetation, statistics, 363, 366
Veithoechsheim, 328, 330
Veldenz, 268
Vendersheim, 229
Venningen, 200, 264
Verrenberg, 311
Versailles, treaty of, 179, 182
Victoria, Queen, 289
Vines:
  classification, 60
  list of, 62
Vineyards:
  age, 83
  register, 41, 49, 150
  reorganization, 33
  replanting, 28, 30
  work, time and cost, 370
Vintages, 169
Vitis silvestris, 21
Volksmundlagen, 56
Vollmersweiler, 198
Volxheim, 224, 229
Vosges mountains, 194, 195

Wachenheim (Palatinate), 203, 204, 208
Wachenheim (Rheinhessen), 216
Wachstum, 149
Wackernheim, 227
Wahlheim, 216
Waiblingen, 311

Waldboeckelheim, 238, 240
Waldhilbersheim, 233
Waldlaubersheim, 239
Waldrach, 262, 263, 264
Waldulm, 319, 320
Wallertheim, 229
Wallhausen, 239
Walporzheim, 335
Walsheim, 200
Wasserlos, 326
Weber, K. J., 220
Wehlen, 260, 264, 271, 272
Weikersheim, 312
Weil a.R., 317
Weiler (Nahe), 238, 242
Weiler (Wuerttemberg), 311
Weinbergrolle, 52, 150
Weinbergsordnung, 41
Weingarten (Baden), 320
Weingarten (Palatinate), 200
Weinheim, 216
Weinlehrpfad, 189
Weinolsheim, 217, 221
Weinsberg, 306, 311
  Institute, 307
Weinsheim, 234, 240
Weinstrassen:
  Baden, 319
  Nahe, 232, 239
  Palatinate, 197
  Rheingau, 288
  Wuerttemberg, 310
Weintor, 197
Weisenheim (Palatinate), 204, 206
Weissburgunder, 71, 316
Weissherbst, 101, 313, 316, 319, 338
Welgesheim, 224
Welschrisling, 65
Wendelsheim, 228
Wenzel, Emperor, 242
Wertheim, 321
Westhofen, 214
Weyher, 198, 199, 200
Wicker, 286
Wiesbaden, 166, 286, 289
Wies-Oppenheim, 211
Willner, Ing.grad. S., 85
Willsbach, 311
Wiltingen, 255
Wimmental, 311
Wind, 46
Winden, 199
Windesheim, 232
Wine:
  area (German), 25
  collections of, 166
  definition of, 59
  distillate, 129
  falsifications, 36
  German, details of, 40
  grower's year, 368
  law of the E.E.C., 38
  law, history of, 35
  laying down of, 141
  library, 190
  museums, 189, 190, 259
  old, 166
  press, 88
  roads (*see* Weinstrassen), 189
  red, 100
  rosé (Rosee), 101
  Rotling, 101
  seminars, 261
  storage of, 140
  white, 100
  zones in the E.E.C., 375
Winkel, 56, 295
Winningen, 282
Wintersheim, 217, 222
Wintrich, 268
Winzenheim, 233, 241
Winzingen, 209
Wittlich, 260, 276
Woellstein, 229
Woerstadt, 228
Wolf, 273, 274
Wolfsheim, 227
Wollmesheim, 199
Wonsheim, 229
Worms, 210, 211, 212
Wuerttemberg, 303
Wuerzburg, 190, 325, 327, 328, 329
Wuerzburger Perle, 70
Wunnenstein, 321
Wyoming, U.S.A., 84

Yeast, 98

Zabergau, 308
Zehntwein, 24
Zeiskam, 200
Zell (Franconia), 146
Zell (im Hamm), 57, 146, 277
Zell (Mosel), 146, 264, 276
Zell (Palatinate), 146, 196
Zell-Weierbach (Baden), 146, 318

Zeller Schwarzer Herrgott, 66, 207
Zellerthal, 57
Zeltingen, 264, 272
Zones, viticultural, 48
Zornheim, 217, 221
Zotzenheim, 224
Zuerich, 37
Zwingenberg, 301